"*Separate but Equal* is at once eminently erudite and commendably readable. James France's authoritative volume will be of immense value not only for students of the Cistercian Order but for anyone interested in medieval religious culture."

— Mette Birkedal Bruun
University of Copenhagen

"With this book, we finally have a comprehensive history of the medieval Cistercian lay brothers. James France skillfully employs a wide range of sources to illuminate the lay brothers' social origins, their economic functions, and their religious ideals, and he carefully assesses both the lay brothers' contributions to the Order and their eventual decline. He convincingly argues that the medieval Cistercians never resolved the tensions created when they formed the lay brotherhood as an institution separate from the monks but never equal to them. France explores the ramifications of these tensions with great sensitivity, and he argues that it was this fundamental inequality between monks and lay brothers that ultimately led to the lay brothers' demise."

— Martha Newman
University of Texas at Austin
Author of *The Boundaries of Charity:*
*Cistercian Culture and Ecclesiastical Reform,*
*1098–1180*

CISTERCIAN STUDIES SERIES: NUMBER TWO HUNDRED FORTY-SIX

# Separate but Equal

## Cistercian Lay Brothers 1120–1350

by

*James France*

α

Cistercian Publications
www.cistercianpublications.org

LITURGICAL PRESS
Collegeville, Minnesota
www.litpress.org

A Cistercian Publications title published by Liturgical Press

**Cistercian Publications**
Editorial Offices
Abbey of Gethsemani
3642 Monks Road
Trappist, Kentucky 40051
www.cistercianpublications.org

1    2    3    4    5    6    7    8    9

**Library of Congress Cataloging-in-Publication Data**

France, James.
    Separate but equal : Cistercian lay brothers, 1120-1350 / by James France.
        p.    cm. — (Cistercian studies series ; no. 246)
    Includes bibliographical references (p.        ) and index.
    ISBN 978-0-87907-246-9 — ISBN 978-0-87907-747-1 (e-book)
    1. Cistercians.    2. Lay brothers.    3. Brothers (Religious)    I. Title.

BX3451.F73    2012
271'.12—dc23                                                    2012027736

I dedicate this book to three friends without whose help and support it would not have been possible for me to write it: Hilary Costello, OCSO, E. Rozanne Elder, and Brian Patrick McGuire, coupled with grateful thanks to my editor, Mark A. Scott, OCSO.

# Contents

List of Illustrations    ix

List of Abbreviations    xi

Introduction    xiii

*Chapter 1*    Who Were the Lay Brothers?    1

*Chapter 2*    Manual Labor of Monks before the Lay Brothers    36

*Chapter 3*    *Illiterati*    57

*Chapter 4*    *Barbati*    76

*Chapter 5*    Two Monasteries within the Precincts
of the Monastery    88

*Chapter 6*    "Assigned to Plows and Mattocks"    113

*Chapter 7*    Separate but Equal    151

*Chapter 8*    *Vitae* of Lay Brothers and Lay Brothers in *Vitae*    172

*Chapter 9*    Virtues and Vices    199

*Chapter 10*    The Onslaught of Demons    231

*Chapter 11*    Visions of the Other World    249

*Chapter 12*    Not *Conversi* but *Perversi*    269

*Chapter 13*    Decline and Near Extinction    300

*Appendix 1*    Lay Brothers in Miracle Stories    323

*Appendix 2*    Principal Citations of Lay Brothers in *Exempla*    325

*Appendix 3*    Cistercian Lay Brother *Usages*    333

Bibliography    345

Index    359

# Illustrations

Fig. 1. Engraving of effigy of lay brother Konrad Zeuffel and his mother, dated 1348. — p. 12

Fig. 2. Corbel in cloister at Pforta in Thuringia—lay brother and hired worker. Photo by Rainer Oefelein; used by permission of Cornelia Oefelein. — p. 29

Fig. 3. Carving of lay brother's head on a capital in the cloister of Flaran in Gascony. Photo by James France. — p. 52

Fig. 4. Carving of four heads—two lay brothers and two masons—on chapter house boss at Suléjow in Poland. Photo from Dr. Krystyna Bialoskorska; permission pending. — p. 54

Fig. 5. Pen-and-ink drawing of twenty lay brothers building abbey of Schönau. Used by permission of Germanisches Nationalmuseum. — p. 55

Fig. 6. Miniature in Hugh of Fouilloy's *Aviary* with monk and lay brother surmounted by a dove and a hawk. Used by permission of Bibliothèque Royale de Belgique. — p. 63

Fig. 7. Caricature of Henry, lay brother scribe from Ter Doest in Flanders. — p. 67

Fig. 8. Lay brothers on the tomb of Saint Stephen of Obazine in Limousin. Photo by James France. — p. 78

Fig. 9. Boss of lay brother master builder in abbey church at Salem. Photo courtesy of Regierungspräsidium Tübingen. — p. 80

Fig. 10. Plans of *domus conversorum* at Byland, Yorkshire, and Beaulieu, Hampshire. Used by permission of Paul Clark. — p. 89

Fig. 11. Property Register of Tennenbach with initial containing the seated cellarer Johannes Meiger facing a lay brother and a hired hand. Photo courtesy of Generallandesarchiv Karlsruhe. — p. 91

Fig. 12. The lay brothers' "lane" with thirty-five seats at Byland, Yorkshire. Photo by Terryl N. Kinder; used by permission. — p. 93

Fig. 13. Lay brothers' range at Fountains, Yorkshire, consisting   p. 98
of twenty-two bays. Photo by Terryl N. Kinder; used by
permission.

Fig. 14. Brother J, keeper of the wool-store and wardrobe at   p. 110
Beaulieu, Hampshire. © The British Library Board. Add 489
78 f 41v.

Fig. 15. Grange barn at Great Coxwell belonging to Beaulieu,   p.117
Hampshire. Photo by Tessa France. Used by permission.

Fig. 16. Interior of the grange barn at Beaumont belonging   p. 131
to Clairvaux. Photo by James France.

Fig. 17. Chapel at the St. Leonard's grange belonging to   p. 136
Beaulieu, Hampshire. Photo by Tessa France. Used by
permission.

Fig. 18. Our Lady of Mercy with four monks on left and   p. 152
four lay brothers on right. Image f. 145r from manuscript
I F 413; used by permission of The University Library in
Wroclaw.

Fig. 19. Lay brothers on the reverse of the tomb of Saint   p. 191
Stephen of Obazine. Photo by James France.

Fig. 20. Stained glass from cloister of Altenberg depicting   p. 202
Saint Bernard at the deathbed of a lay brother. Photo by
James France.

Fig. 21. Choir stall carving at Doberan in Mecklenburg   p. 237
showing lay brother with the devil. Photo by Harry Harden-
berg; used by permission.

Fig. 22. Caesarius of Heisterbach in a miniature from   p. 246
Altenberg; a detail in the upper flourish shows a monster
with its legs perched on a lay brother's head. RBA 124 87
(Düsseldorf—Universität—und Landesbibliothek MS C 27,
fol. 1r); © Rheinisches Bildarchiv Köln.

Fig. 23. Stained glass from the cloister of Wettingen, Switzer-   p. 257
land, of lay brother kneeling before the Virgin and Child.
Photo by Peter Hoegger; used by permission.

Fig. 24. Pen-and-ink drawing of lay brothers at Schönau   p. 286
disobeying their abbot. Used by permission of Germanisches
Nationalmuseum.

# Abbreviations

| | |
|---|---|
| *AC/ASOC* | *Analecta Cisterciensia/Analecta Sacri Ordinis Cisterciensis* |
| *AS* | *Acta Sanctorum* |
| BC | "Beaupré" Compilation |
| *BMS* | The Clairvaux *Breve et memoriale scriptum,* in Waddell |
| Canivez | *Statuta capitulorum generalium ordinis cisterciensis* |
| *CC* | *Collectaneum exemplorum et visionum clarevallense* |
| CF | Cistercian Fathers Series |
| *Cîteaux* | *Cîteaux Commentarii Cistercienses* |
| CS/CSQ | *Cistercian Studies/Cistercian Studies Quarterly* |
| CSS | Cistercian Studies Series |
| CWS | Classics of Western Spirituality |
| CCCM | Corpus Christianorum, Continuatio Mediaevalis |
| *DM* | Caesarius of Heisterbach's *Dialogus miraculorum* |
| *DM* Hilka | Caesarius of Heisterbach's *Libri VIII miraculorum* |
| EC | Ebrach Compilation |
| *EM* | Conrad of Eberbach's *Exordium magnum,* in Griesser |
| *EO* | *Ecclesiastica officia* |
| Ep | Letter |
| Ep M | *Letter to Maurice* |
| *EP* | *Exordium parvum* |

| FC | Fürstenfeld Collection |
| GF | Goswin's *Fragmenta* |
| Griesser | Conrad of Eberbach's *Exordium magnum* |
| LM | Herbert of Clairvaux's *Liber miraculorum* |
| LP | Peter of Cornwall's *Liber revelationum* |
| LR | Richalm von Schöntal's *Liber revelationum* |
| PL | Patrologia Latina |
| RB | Rule of Saint Benedict |
| SBOp | *Sancti Bernardi Opera* |
| SC | Bernard of Clairvaux's *Sermones semper Cantica Canticorum* |
| SM | Salem *Liber miraculorum* |
| Spec Car | *Speculum Caritatis* by Aelred |
| Statuta | *Statuta capitulorum generalium ordinis cisterciensis*, in Canivez |
| UC | *Usus conversorum*, in Waddell |
| VA | Life of Arnulf of Villers |
| Vita A | Life of Aelred |
| VP | *Vita prima Bernardi* |
| VW | Life of Wulfric of Haselbury |
| Waddell | *Usus conversorum* |

# Introduction

A strict interpretation of the Rule of Saint Benedict was one of the main planks in the Cistercian reform. All the early Cistercian texts and many comments by outside observers remark on this. According to the *Exordium parvum* the monks, while still at Molesme, "often spoke to each other, lamented, and were saddened by the transgression of the Rule of Saint Benedict."[1]

William of Malmesbury in his Chronicle also mentions their distress that they were not able to follow "the purity of the Rule," and he stressed the importance the Cistercians attached to this by saying, "So intent are they on their Rule, that they think not a jot or tittle of it should be disregarded."[2] Writing in about 1135, the Norman monk Orderic Vitalis described the reforming community as endeavoring "to carry out a literal observance of the Rule of Saint Benedict,"[3] and he quotes Robert as saying to his monks:

> We have made our profession, my dear brothers, according to the Rule of our holy father Benedict, but it seems to me that we have not observed it in every point. We have many customs which are not laid down there, and we carelessly overlook a number of its precepts. . . . I propose therefore that we should observe the Rule of Saint Benedict in everything, taking care not to turn aside either to the left or to the right.[4]

[1] *EP* 3, in Waddell 1999, 421: *inter se, Dei gratia aspirati, de transgressione Regulae beati Benedicti patris monachorum loquebantur, conquerebantur, contristabantur.*

[2] William of Malmesbury 1968, 349.

[3] Orderic Vitalis 1969–80, 3: 338–39.

[4] Orderic Vitalis 1969–80, 4: 312–13: *Nos fratres karissimi secundum normam sancti Benedicti professionem fecimus sed ut mihi videtur non eam ex integro tenemus.*

Writing in the 1140s, the Premonstratensian abbot Philip of Harvengt claimed that with the foundation of Cîteaux the "monastic order, formerly dead, was revived: there the old ashes were poked . . . and the Rule of Benedict recovered in our times the truth of the letter."[5]

A return to the Rule, either the spirit or the letter, was mentioned over and over again and yet, paradoxically, there are two important ways in which the Cistercians chose to deviate from the Rule, one of them by omission and the other by addition.

The omission from the Rule consisted of doing away with the *oblati* (youngsters offered to the monastery by their parents, also known as *nutriti*, those given board in the monastery).[6] The deviation by addition was the introduction of the institution of lay brothers or *conversi*, a very recent form of religious life within an increasingly clericalized monasticism. The contribution to the Cistercians in the twelfth and thirteenth centuries was immense, both materially and spiritually, and forms the subject of this book. From the foundation of the New Monastery, as Cîteaux was originally called, both monks and lay brothers were allowed to join only as adults. From then on, entering either branch of the Cistercian family became a matter of free choice, what today would be defined as a "vocation," at least in theory, for in fact an alternative was not always available. The minimum age for the reception of a novice, whether choir monk or lay brother, had originally been fifteen years, but sometime around the middle of the twelfth century it was raised to eighteen.[7] The Cistercians were not the first to introduce lay brothers. They were a distinctive feature of the monastic reform of the late eleventh century and had already been introduced at a number of other places, but the Cistercians developed the insti-

---

*Multa quae ibi non precipiuntur observamus, et de mandatis eiusdem plura neglegentes intermittimus. . . . Laudo igitur ut omnino regulam sancti Benedicti teneamus canentes ne ad dexteram vel ad sinistram ab ea deviemus.*

  [5] Philip of Harvengt, *De institutione clericorum*, 4:125, PL 203: 836–37, trans. Constable (1985), 43.

  [6] See chapter 1, p. 30.

  [7] Waddell 2002, 225.

tution to so full an extent as to become a model for subsequent Orders. The best concise definition is that of a twentieth-century lay brother, Conrad Greenia: "A laybrother is a religious brother under vows, dedicated to a life of toil, and occupying an auxiliary position in his community."[8]

## Earlier Lay Brother Studies

The first modern work on lay brothers was published over a hundred years ago (1905) by the Cistercian monk Eberhard Hoffmann. Hoffmann introduces his book by saying that "the lay brother institution undoubtedly belongs to the least explored aspect of the internal development of the Cistercian Order, both as regards its origin, its position in the Order, its tasks, and its importance."[9] Almost the same could be said today. While there have been a number of critical editions of early texts as well as important articles, most of them concentrating on a particular aspect of the subject, there has not been a multifaceted study that draws on all available sources and looks at lay brothers from every angle and across disciplines. Notable exceptions include two further monographs, one in English by James S. Donnelly[10] and a second in German by Michael Toepfer,[11] and a seminal article by Kassius Hallinger[12] outlining the pre-Cistercian origin of the institution, its development, and its adaptation by a number of monastic bodies, a topic also discussed by Giles Constable.[13]

The contribution of the *conversi* (lay brothers) to the phenomenal material success of the Cistercians in the twelfth century is generally acknowledged and is well documented.[14] They played a

---

[8] Greenia 1981, 39.

[9] Hoffmann 1905, 3: "Zu den bis jetzt am wenigsten aufgeklärten Punkten in der inneren Entwicklung des Cisterzienserordens gehört unstreitbar das Konverseninstitut, seine Entstehung, seine Stelle, seine Aufgabe, seine Bedeutung."

[10] Donnelly 1949.

[11] Toepfer 1983.

[12] Hallinger 1956.

[13] Constable 1973.

[14] See, for example, Lekai 1977, 282, and Southern 1970, 257.

key part in the establishment and growth of granges, the quintessential feature of the Cistercian agrarian economy. The growth both of the membership of the communities and of their estates made it necessary for the Cistercians to send out colonies to establish new monasteries, and the lay brothers deserve a fair share of the credit for having made the rapid expansion possible. By 1124, around the time of the introduction of *conversi* and the formation of the earliest granges, only twenty-six abbeys had been founded, but by 1151—when the expansion's zenith was reached—over three hundred had been established in places as disparate as Norway, Sicily, Ireland, and Poland.[15] The topic of the Cistercian agrarian economy is covered by a number of important regional studies, notably by R. A. Donkin for Britain, Werner Rösener for Germany, and Charles Higounet for France. Colin Platt has written about granges in Britain generally, and T. A. M. Bishop about the granges in Yorkshire.[16] There are articles by Coburn V. Graves and Richard Roehl dealing with the later development of the Cistercian economy from direct exploitation to leasing, and for statistical data referring to British conditions James S. Donnelly's article, "Changes in the Grange Economy of English and Welsh Cistercian Abbeys," is particularly useful, as is Toepfer's monograph for German abbeys. With data from southern France, Constance Berman has demonstrated the agricultural superiority of the Cistercians over other farmers on the basis of a large and largely fit young workforce of lay brothers whose board and lodging was their only material reward and who were not encumbered by dependents. As a result of their efforts, unit costs were low and the yield consequently increased.[17]

A detailed account of the lay brothers' daily life, their horarium, their devotions, their diet, their clothing, their profession, and the many crafts they practiced appears in the *Usus conversorum*, to which

[15] Williams 1998, 14.

[16] There are three fine monographs on granges: Beaumont belonging to Clairvaux (Wissenberg 2007), Vaulerent belonging to Chaalis in northern France (Higounet 1965), and the granges belonging to the English abbey of Beaulieu, Great Coxwell, and St. Leonard's (Horn and Born 1965).

[17] Berman 1986, 79.

additional regulations, known as *Breve et memoriale scriptum*, were later added for the use of Clairvaux. We now have a new critical edition of both documents, with a translation and superb detailed notes, by Fr. Chrysogonus Waddell, OCSO, to supplement the classic study by Fr. Othon Ducourneau.[18] I have been able to use translations from the new English edition of the *Exordium magnum*,[19] as well as Fr. Martinus Cawley's translation of the *Life of Arnulf of Villers*[20] and Pauline Matarasso's of the *Life of Wulfric of Haselbury* by John of Forde.[21]

Statutes of the General Chapter, especially those of a judicial nature, are an indispensable source for our knowledge of lay brothers. We have the classic edition by Fr. Joseph-Marie Canivez and now also the new critical edition by Fr. Chrysogonus Waddell, who examined statutes up to 1201. Waddell has mainly been used for statutes to that date, while later statutes quoted have been taken from Canivez. Statutes tell us a good deal about the extent to which lay brothers adhered to the *Usus conversorum* regulations, but until now they have been most extensively studied for the light they throw on violations of discipline. As a result of Donnelly's study, *The Decline of the Cistercian Laybrotherhood*, which is based largely on statutes, a consensus in Cistercian historiography has arisen whereby violations of discipline have been viewed as the overwhelming cause of the decline and near extinction of the Order. Donnelly's list of one hundred twenty-three revolts paints a picture of unmitigated disaster, a view challenged by Megan Cassidy-Welch, who presents her own list. In another study, *Monastic Spaces and their Meaning*, based on eight Yorkshire abbeys, she examines the ambiguous space lay brothers occupied within the Cistercian

---

[18] Waddell 2000; Ducourneau 1929.

[19] Conrad of Eberbach, *The Great Beginning of Cîteaux*, trans. Benedicta Ward and Paul Savage, ed. E. Rozanne Elder, CS 72 (Collegeville, MN: Cistercian Publications, 2012). I am grateful to Dr. Elder for having supplied me prior to publication with translations of chapters in which lay brothers are featured.

[20] Cawley 2003.

[21] John of Forde (CF 79). I am grateful to Pauline Matarasso for having supplied me, prior to publication, with chapters in the *Life of Wulfric of Haselbury* in which lay brothers are featured (John of Forde [CF 79]).

world, in both its economy and its spirituality.[22] Fr. Edmond Mikkers, OCSO, has drawn attention to the limitations of considering the institution only from an economic perspective.[23] Ernst Werner maintains that the lay brothers perpetuated the class divisions of feudalism, claiming that "monks stood with both legs inside feudal society."[24] Jean Leclercq refers to the lay brothers' state of humility as being matched by that of humiliation.[25] Martha G. Newman points to the fact that when monks described the multiplicity of roles in the monastery, lay brothers were ignored altogether.[26] Kassius Hallinger sees the decline as the inevitable consequence of a lessening of religious fervor,[27] as does Louis Lekai, who also points to the attraction of the new mendicant orders.[28] In a recent article Brian Noell, noting the considerable power exercised by many lay brothers in their communities, suggests that they did not rebel because they were unscrupulous or because they were oppressed, but because they were not properly rewarded by their superiors for their successful management of the monastic economy.[29] Generally speaking, the incidents of violence traced by Donnelly have been seen as an inherent symptom of the lay brothers' inequality. I shall argue that the disciplinary problem was no greater among lay brothers than among monks and that the increase in the number of incidents in the course of the late twelfth and early thirteenth century points to a general crisis in the Order rather than to lay brother resentment and that therefore the decline is attributable to other causes, chiefly social and economic factors outside the control of the Cistercians.

[22] Cassidy-Welch 2001, 167–93.

[23] Mikkers 1962, 113–29.

[24] Werner 1958, 354–55: *Die Mönche standen mit beiden Beinen innerhalb der feudalen Gesellschaft.*

[25] Leclercq 1965, 241.

[26] Newman 1996, 102–3.

[27] Hallinger 1956.

[28] Lekai 1977, 341. The historiography of Cistercian lay brothers is discussed in Lescher 1988.

[29] Noell 2006.

## Lay Brothers in the *Exemplum* Literature

Any study of the Cistercian lay brothers needs to emphasize that because they were illiterate everything that was written about them was the work of monks. In the words of Christopher Holdsworth, "what we know of lay brothers comes through a monkish filter."[30] Most typical are the moralizing stories of visions and revelations that constituted the *exemplum* literature and the *Lives*, but chronicles, charters, and General Chapter statutes also tell a great deal about the daily life and mentality of lay brothers. The many miracle stories may, in the words of Martha Newman, "have reflected the monks' ideals for the lay brothers rather than the lay brothers' actual behavior."[31] We owe a great deal of our knowledge of the *exemplum* literature to the pioneering work of Brian McGuire in a series of articles published in the 1180s, most of them reproduced in the collected studies *Friendship and Faith*,[32] and to the more recent work of Stefano Mula.[33]

Like hagiography, *exempla* have to be used carefully because their main purpose was didactic, to edify and encourage imitation or avoidance, to foster the bonds of community, and to engender in the novices a strong sense of Cistercian identity. Not only were they not an expression of the lay brothers' own perspective, they were also not intended to record objective data for future reference. They belong to the archetypal "mirror for the diligent, a spur to the indolent," the phrase William of Malmesbury used when he described the Cistercians as a model for all monks.[34] Like all good teaching aids they could also be more effective by being humorous, and the long afterlife of many of the stories confirms this. Yet Adriaan Bredero in his study of Saint Bernard's *Life*, the *Vita prima*, suggests that, in spite of all the limitations of hagiography, on "close reading" the authors managed to convey a picture not just of a

[30] Holdsworth 1973, 67.
[31] Newman 1996, 28.
[32] McGuire 2002.
[33] Mula 2002, 2010, and 2011.
[34] William of Malmesbury 1968, 351.

conventional saint but also of a real human being.[35] I believe that in the same way the *exemplum* literature tells us a great deal about the way of life of lay brothers, their social background, their work, and their living conditions. In addition, on "close reading" we also gain an insight into their aspirations and spiritual lives and this I contend amounts to catching a glimpse into their spirituality. The *exemplum* literature has in the past been either ignored or dismissed as of dubious validity or on the whole only cursorily acknowledged in lay brother studies, and I make no apology for quoting from this, our most important source, extensively.

A closer look at the earliest known literary account of a named lay brother reveals a heartfelt admiration of the monk-author for his subject. Although written in the second half of the twelfth century, it refers to an episode that took place around 1140:

> During the first years of my conversion, a lay brother named Yves, who was very devout, lay dying at the monastery of Clairvaux. To a brother who was visiting him, one who is still alive today and can bear witness today, he said: "An angel of the Lord appeared to me, showing me his beautiful and joyful countenance as I lay here in my weakness. And he said, 'You humans do well to desire the sight and presence of the Lord. If you knew how much he loves you, how much he wants you, with what longing he waits for you, you would hurry to him with far more fervent affection.'" These were his last words, to which his serene summons, which immediately followed, bore sufficiently trustworthy testimony.[36]

[35] Bredero 1996, 16.

[36] Geofredo di Auxerre 1970, 79–80; *Sermo* 3 (CF42, 40): *In primis annis conversionis nostrae, laicus quidam frater Ivanus nomine, admosum religiosus, in coenobio Claraevallis ad extrema devenit. Interea visitanti sese fratri qui hodieque superstes, hodieque testis existit: "Angelus, inquit, Domini gratissimum mihi et gratulabundum exhibens vultum, impraesentiarum humilitati meas apparuit, dicens: 'Merito desideratis vos homines praesentiam Domini et conspectum; si cui tamen innotuisset quantum ipse vos diligat, quantum cupiat, quam desideranter expectet, longe ferventiori ad eum properaret affectu.'" Haec illius verba novissima, quibus testimonium satis credibile praebuit placidissima eius vocatio sine dilatione secuta.*

In these words from his *On the Apocalypse* Geoffrey of Auxerre recounts an episode from the time he first entered Clairvaux in 1140. Within a few years this Paris scholar, who described his conversion as going from "empty studies to the cultivation of true wisdom,"[37] became Saint Bernard's secretary, travel companion, and friend. He conceived the idea of writing Bernard's *Life*, took notes, and himself wrote the last three books of the *Vita*. He became abbot of Igny in 1156 and of Clairvaux in 1162, but three years later he was forced to resign as part of the settlement of the Thomas Becket controversy between the Cistercians and Henry II of England. Geoffrey must have been rehabilitated, for in 1170 he became abbot of Fossanova and in 1176 of Hautecombe, where he remained until his death in about 1188.[38]

The same story is found in the so-called Beaupré collection. Here the Clairvaux *conversus* recounted to the visiting brother what the angel had told him:

> You men rightly long to see the presence of the Lord. If nevertheless he makes known to anyone how much he loves you and how much he longs for those who desire him, he hastens to him with a much more fervent love. After these words he died.[39]

Geoffrey's account in his sermon is once again repeated, this time almost verbatim, in an unedited *exemplum* collection, Paris manuscript BNF Lat. 14657, the only difference being that the more personal detail that the event occurred shortly after his conversion is omitted and that the lay brother is called Vivian and not Yves as in the sermon.[40] Although composed at the abbey of Saint

---

[37] *VP* 4:2.10 (PL 185:327): *Ab inanibus studiis ad verae sapientiae cultum.*

[38] Debuisson 1992, 70–72. See also Bredero 1996, 49; Newman 1995, 213 and 217.

[39] BC f 106r: *Merito desideratis vos homines praesentiam domini et conspectum. Si cui tamen innotuisset quantum ipse vos diligat quam cupiat quam desiderantur expectet longe ferventiori ad eum properaret affectu. Post haec verba protinus expiravit.*

[40] I am grateful to Stefano Mula for drawing my attention to this collection, an edition of which he is currently preparing. See also Mula 2010, 910, n. 6.

Victor in Paris, the collection contains a number of Cistercian *exempla* and, because of the inclusion of the lay brother story, Stefano Mula suggests that Geoffrey may himself be the author of at least part of the collection.[41] Mula further asserts that the first extensive Clairvaux collection, edited by Olivier Legendre as *Collectaneum exemplorum et visionum Clarevallense* and previously ascribed to Prior John, was probably begun during Geoffrey's abbacy and possibly even owes its origin to his initiative.[42] Seven of its chapters contain stories referring to lay brothers.[43]

Shortly afterwards (ca. 1178) Herbert, having resigned as abbot of Mores, returned to Clairvaux, where he was responsible for compiling the *Liber visionum et miraculorum Clarevallense* before becoming archbishop of Torres in Sardinia in about 1181.[44] Here lay brothers are more prominently featured, being mentioned in seventeen chapters. At the same time Conrad, while a monk at Clairvaux between 1177 and 1193 before becoming abbot of Eberbach,[45] started yet another collection, the *Exordium magnum Cisterciense sive narratio de initio cisterciensis ordinis*. Approximately half of his stories are repeated from Herbert, either verbatim or somewhat elaborated; of the twenty-five chapters in the *Exordium magnum* referring to lay brothers, eleven were drawn from Herbert.

Much the most prolific and most famous collection from the Clairvaux family was Caesarius of Heisterbach's *Dialogus miraculorum*, begun in the second decade of the thirteenth century and based in part on material from an earlier collection from Himmerod. Lay brothers make an appearance in 83 chapters out of a total of 746, a large number of which feature stories from outside the monastery. Other collections from the Clairvaux filiation in

---

[41] Stefano Mula e-mail to me, 16 December 2010.

[42] Mula refers to Geoffrey as "one possible candidate for the push behind the creation of this literature" (Mula 2010, 905).

[43] For references to lay brothers in miracle stories, see Appendix 1.

[44] PL 185: 1271–1384; although no modern edition exists, one by Giancarlo Zichi, Graziano Fois, and Stefano Mula is in preparation (Mula 2010, 910). For Herbert's life see Morlot 2002, 42–43; I am grateful to Stefano Mula for this reference.

[45] Mula 2010, 905.

which lay brothers are featured include Goswin's *Liber miraculorum* and compilations from Salem, Ebrach, and one of indeterminate origin formerly thought to have come from the abbey of Beaupré in northern France.[46] A few such collections were found in monasteries of the Morimond filiation. Among them was one from Fürstenfeld in Bavaria, which was merely a shorter version of Herbert's *Liber miraculorum*, and Richalm of Schöntal's *Liber revelationum*. From the other proto-abbeys, Pontigny and La Ferté, or their filiations, we know of none. Because their dispersal was almost entirely limited to the Clairvaux filiation, and only to those houses east of Clairvaux, Stefano Mula cautions against attributing the themes they convey to the whole Cistercian order.[47] Nevertheless, the collections, based on oral accounts of events mostly transmitted by abbots gathered at Cîteaux for the annual General Chapter, contain stories of lay brothers from almost every part of Europe, including France, Germany, Britain, Denmark, Lithuania, Poland, and Spain.

The evident esteem of Geoffrey of Auxerre for the lay brother he had known was frequently repeated by later authors who held up lay brothers as exemplars of humility, the monastic virtue *par excellence*. Similar testimonials by modern Cistercians to the saintly lives of lay brothers they have known are quite common. In his edition of the *Usus conversorum*, Chrysogonus Waddell acknowledges his debt to lay brothers for his "being drawn" by their example "to a deeper life of humble service and fraternal love." In his words: "to be in the presence of old Br. Albert or Br. Paul for any length of time was to be schooled in the craft of prayer. You had only to look at our Br. Ferdinand, or to exchange a few words with him, to understand what Cistercian simplicity is all about."[48]

---

[46] Although the origin of the *exemplum* collection in BNF MS Lat. 15912 is not known, I have chosen to refer to it throughout as the "Beaupré" compilation.

[47] For the geographical diffusion of the collections see Mula 2011. Seventeen manuscripts of Herbert's *Liber miraculorum* and twenty of Conrad's *Exordium magnum* are listed.

[48] Waddell 2000, 8.

When Cistercian authors committed tales they had heard to writing in the last two decades of the twelfth century and the first two of the thirteenth in the form of *exempla*, they had good reason to include stories of exceptional lay brothers they had known or heard about. The security the Cistercians had originally enjoyed was a thing of the past: their tithe-privilege and privilege of epis-copal exemption had brought them into conflict with bishops. The reputation for avarice they had gained in amassing large tracts of land led to attacks by clerics like Gerald of Wales and Walter Map.[49] Conrad of Eberbach felt obliged to caution the Cistercians to flee *negligentia* and *oblivio*,[50] and he and other *exemplum* compilers would have drawn comfort from extolling the humblest members of the Cistercian family. As these compilers represented the third genera-tion of monks, they sensed that the earlier, more heroic age had come to an end. They displayed a degree of anxiety and they felt the need to create a myth in the dictionary sense of a story about superhuman beings, here represented by the lay brothers. The need for vigilance had already been anticipated by Saint Bernard, who originally opposed the idea of building a larger monastery on the grounds that "worldly folk can rightly think ill of us for our levity and changeability, and blame us for letting our excessive wealth drive us to insanity, as if, indeed, we had such wealth!"[51] Only the pragmatic reason that they desperately needed more space for an exploding population made him change his mind. Bernard had already voiced his objection to "the vertiginous height of churches, their extravagant length, their inordinate width and costly furnish-ings" in his *Apologia ad Guillelmum*.[52]

---

[49] For this see the chapter on "The Critics of the Monks" in Knowles 1940, 662–78.

[50] *EM* 1.9 (Griesser 60).

[51] *VP* 2: 5.29 (PL 185: 285): *Poterunt homines saeculi male de nobis sentire, quod aut leves sumus et mutabiles; aut nimiae, quas tamen non habemus, divitiae nos faciunt insanire.*

[52] *Apologia ad Guillelmum abbatem* 12: 28 (*SBOp* 3: 104); trans Matarasso 1993, 55: *Oratoriorum immensas altitudines, immoderatas longitudinis, supervacuas latitudines, sumptuosas depolitiones, curiosas depictiones.*

## Changing Times

The second half of the thirteenth century was a time when many Cistercian churches were being enlarged and others rebuilt. Some, like Royaumont in northern France and Altenberg in the Rhineland, were built in the high Gothic style of French cathedral architecture. It is therefore not surprising that some of the stories circulating about simple lay brothers should have been chosen by the *exemplum* compilers as a reminder of the frugality of former times. The need for larger churches with multiple chapels had arisen as the proportion of choir monks in priestly orders had increased and provision for an increasing number of private masses had to be made. Although Conrad of Eberbach attributes the safe escape of a lay brother from demons to the fact that "at every single altar stood priests with their ministers celebrating,"[53] the hidden purpose of generally eulogizing the simple lay brothers may have been the compilers' way of showing disapproval of the increasing clericalization. From the time of the desert and in the days of Saint Benedict monks had been laymen, and it was only natural that lay brothers should be seen as more authentic representatives of the cenobitic life.

With the arrival of the thirteenth century the rustic simplicity that had thus far characterized Cistercian life was no longer seen as adequate to meet the challenges presented by the broader and intellectually more sophisticated appeal of the new mendicant Orders. In the polemic between those monks who were opposed to intellectual pursuits and those who saw a need for a greater emphasis on studies, lay brothers may have been held up as exemplars of the primitive Cistercian ideal. Many monks probably continued to be opposed to secular learning, as is evidenced by the dream of the saintly lay brother Christian of Aumône, who is said to have seen demons chanting *sic et non* in a parody of a scholastic debate.[54] There was probably still support for the earlier General Chapter statute prohibitions against the study of canon law, against

---

[53] *EM* 2.2 (Griesser 99–100): *Ad singula altaria sacerdotes cum ministris stabant salutaris hostiae immolationem summa cum devotione celebrantes.*

[54] Leclercq 1953, 25.

Hebrew studies, and against the writing of verse.[55] But under the leadership of Stephen of Lexington those who saw a need for a greater emphasis on studies won and, shortly after his election as abbot of Clairvaux in 1243, *studia* were established first in Paris and some years later in Montpellier, Toulouse, and Oxford. The trend toward higher learning was irresistible and stories about the simple unlettered lay brothers were no longer productive for maintaining the status quo or reversing the tide.

## Lay Brothers and Nuns

While not forming part of this study, there were also lay brothers in Cistercian women's houses (*conversi monialium*) as well as lay sisters (*conversae*), both taking their vows from the abbess. As a result of the importance attached to strict adherence to enclosure, nuns were inevitably, to a large degree, dependent on male support for their material as well as spiritual needs. This was perhaps the greatest distinguishing feature between the two branches of the Order. The obligation to defer to men imposed a restriction on the nuns that circumscribed their ability to retain what may be called a fully Cistercian character.

While monks were responsible for the spiritual direction of the nuns—the *cura monialium*—saying Mass, hearing confessions, and preaching on certain days, the nuns' own *conversi* were responsible for discharging their business with the outside world as well as taking care of a multitude of menial tasks and manual labor outside the enclosure. One of their roles was to limit the nuns' accessibility. An example of this is found in the twelfth-century *Life* of Saint Stephen of Obazine.[56] Here the ingenious arrangement whereby the Cistercian nuns of nearby Coyroux received what they needed

---

[55] *Statuta* 1188: 7 (Waddell 2002, 149); *Statuta* 1198: 25 (Waddell 2002, 411); *Statuta* 1199: 1 (Waddell 2002, 420).

[56] *Étienne d'Obazine* 1970, 100: *Quomodo autem in corporeis necessitatibus ministrentur, ita ut nec ipse foras exeant, nec alii intus accedant, breviter intimandum est. In exitu claustri duo sunt ostia, unum contra alium, interque brevis et modica porticus continetur. Et interioris quidem ostii clavem priorissa custodit, exterioris vero frater maturus atque probatus qui ipsius loci procurator est constitutus. . . . Porro hic frater quem procuratorum vel*

without having contact with the outside world is described in detail. At the exit of the cloister there was a corridor with a door at each end. The key to the outer door was kept by an aged and trusted lay brother porter. He placed the nuns' provisions, bread, wine, herbs, and wood in the corridor, locked the outer door, and knocked on the door with a stick to notify the prioress, who would then open the inner door to remove the provisions. The restriction imposed by strict enclosure also meant that the role of *conversae* was very different from that of lay brothers in men's houses. While the majority of these were employed on the outlying granges, lay sisters only had a small amount of agricultural and horticultural work, confined within the precinct, and they were largely employed as domestic servants. As a result the proportion of *conversae* to nuns was considerably lower than that of *conversi* to monks in men's houses.

The limitations imposed on women by society inevitably resulted in the lives of Cistercian nuns being very different from those of their male counterparts. They were altogether less homogenous: although their monasteries were generally smaller, there were a few notable exceptions; some were full members of the Order while others merely followed Cistercian usages, and there was a greater variety in customs, dress, and architecture. In the same way, the number and role of their *conversae* and *conversi* varied enormously and the subject belongs to another and different treatment. The lay members of the male and female houses of the Order were too dissimilar to warrant inclusion of *conversi monialium* and *conversae* in this study.

In their extensive coverage of the contribution of lay brothers to the Cistercian agrarian economy, a number of important studies have done justice to their role in the phenomenal growth of the Order in the twelfth and thirteenth century. Violations of discipline undoubtedly played a part in the decline of the institution, but a closer look reveals that monks and even abbots were equally guilty and that the General Chapter data refer as much to a general decline as pointing to a degenerate lay brotherhood.

---

*portarium diximus, utpote laicus, exteriorum curam habet commissam, cuncta necessaria a monasterio deferens, nihil a secularibus petens nisi quod ipsi sponte dederint sive transmiserint.*

Further evidence of breaches of discipline is found in the extensive *exemplum* literature, but equally important is the testimony to the saintly lives of many lay brothers and the way they were held up by the monk-authors as exemplars representing the simplicity of an earlier heroic age.

In the end it was the fundamental inequality between monks and lay brothers that was responsible for the inevitable demise of the lay brother institution, a phenomenon that has been replicated throughout history when attempts have been made to segregate groups of people. The title of this book—*Separate but Equal*—denotes the dichotomy between the two Cistercian groups, which in the long term was not sustainable and which, in recent times, has found potent expression in tensions among individuals, groups, and entire societies based on such factors as race, gender, and religion.

# Chapter 1

# Who Were the Lay Brothers?

It was then that they decided, with the bishop's permission, to take in bearded lay brothers, whom they would treat as themselves in life and death—the status of monk apart—and also hired men, because without such backing they did not see how they could fully observe, day and night, the precepts of the Rule.[1]

These few lines in chapter 15 of the *Exordium parvum* announce the institution of lay brothers by the Cistercians. Their introduction may be seen as the founding fathers' recognition that, in spite of the importance they attached to manual labor, the proper celebration of the Divine Office could not be achieved without additional help. If manual labor was subordinate to the *Opus Dei* for monks, for lay brothers the toil of their hands had preference over their simpler devotions. The lay brothers, described by R. W. Southern as "second-class monks,"[2] formed a lower class of religious whose spiritual needs had not been adequately met in the early medieval church. They were, according to Othon Ducourneau, generally recruited from "the inferior and illiterate classes, peasants and workmen, sons of serfs, of smallholders and poor artisans."[3]

The contrast with the military, noble, and scholarly class to which the first Cistercian monks belonged could not have been

---

[1] *EP* 15 (Waddell 1999, 435; Matarasso 1997, 7): *Tuncque definierunt se conversos laicos barbatos licentia episcopi sui suscepturos, eosque in vita et morte, excepto monachatu, ut semetipsos tractaturos, et homines etiam mercenaries; quia sine adminiculo istorum non intelligebant se plenarie die sive nocte praecepta Regule posse servare.*

[2] Southern 1970, 257.

[3] Ducourneau 1929, 2: 161.

greater and has been well documented. According to Orderic Vitalis, "noble warriors and learned scholars have flocked to them on account of the novelty of their practices."[4] Saint Bernard, whose family was "distinguished in worldly terms" (*claris secundum dignitatem saeculi*) may be counted among them. His father was "a military man of long-standing loyalties" (*vir antiquae et legitimate militiae fuit*).[5] Bernard's brother Andrew, from being "a recruit for the world, became a knight for Christ" (*de tirone saeculi factus est miles Christi*) and another brother, Gerard, is described as "a knight skillful in the use of arms" (*miles in armis strenuus*).[6] The *Vita prima* has a story of a group of young knights on a visit to Clairvaux whom Bernard greeted and asked to put down their arms, as it was Lent. They refused, but drank the beer Bernard had blessed and then offered them. They left, but after a while they returned and asked to be received into the novitiate, thus "offering their hand for the knighthood of the Spirit" (*spirituali militiae dextras dederunt*), and, the *Vita prima* goes on, "some of them are militant in God's service to this day" (*quorum quidam adhuc militant Deo*).[7] More than a century later James of Voragine has the same story, but instead of the visitors being knights they are students, the other group from which so many of the early monks were recruited, and instead of being asked to put down their arms they are requested to refrain from "their usual frivolities and debauchery," a needless request as they, like the knights, also returned and gave up their lives to God.[8]

These upper-class monks have inevitably been contrasted with the lay brothers, who are generally described as belonging to the lower classes. The Count of Champagne, Theobald, friend of Saint Bernard, was one of those who granted their servants permission to join Cistercian houses as lay brothers after freeing them from serfdom. Elphège Vacandard calls them "religious of inferior status"

---

[4] Orderic Vitalis 4.326: *multi nobiles athletae et profundi sophistae ad illos pro novitiate singularitatis concurrent.*

[5] *VP* 4:1.1 (PL 185:227).

[6] *VP* 4:310.11 (PL 185:232, 233).

[7] *VP* 1:11.55 (PL 185:257).

[8] James of Voragine 1998, 220.

who owed their inferiority to their humble extraction.[9] The ideal lay brother has been described as "servile, humble, simple-minded, deferential, and dutiful."[10] In much of the literature *conversus* in time came to mean laborer. Michael Toepfer calls them "workmen in monastic clothing" and Richard Roehl "villeins in monastic dress."[11] R. W. Southern observed that "virtually for the first time in the history of medieval western Christendom, they [the Cistercians] offered a full assurance of salvation to illiterate men"[12]

The inferior position of *conversi* in the social structure of the twelfth-century monastery reflects the division of functions between *conversi* and monks, as expressed in the brief descriptions in a number of *exempla* and *vitae*: Herbert of Clairvaux refers to *conversi* as "honest and religious," "religious and full of good works," and "good and trustworthy"; Conrad of Eberbach describes them as "religious and God-fearing," "pure and of great simplicity," and "religious and of great gentleness"; Caesarius of Heisterbach uses the descriptions "a very humble and gentle person," "an upright man and well disciplined," "a plain good man enfeebled by age," "child-like, simple and pure," and "a simple good man"; in the *Life* of Stephen of Obazine there is "a simple and innocent" lay brother, while in Jocelin's *Life of Waldef* we find one who is "a very simple man, unintelligent, and slow of speech" (*valde simplex, hebes, et impeditae linguae*).[13] The picture conjured up by these portrayals reminds one of the lay brother to whom Saint Bernard said that until coming to the monastery "you had neither stockings nor shoes, you walked half naked, you were tortured by cold and hunger."[14]

---

[9] Vacandard 1927, 1:450–51.

[10] Noell 2006, 260.

[11] Toepfer 1983, 39; Roehl 1972, 87.

[12] Southern 1970, 257.

[13] *LM* 1.32; 1.14; 1.27 (PL 185:1304, 1291, 1300); *EM* 4.13; 4.18; 4.20 (Griesser 238, 243, 246); *DM* 4.4; 8.43; 10.5; 7.52 (Strange 1:175; 2:114; 2:221; 2:73; Scott and Bland 1:197; 2:42; 2:175; 1:538); *Étienne d'Obazine* 1970, 218; *Jocelin of Furness* 1952, 328.

[14] *LM* 1.29 (PL 185:1302): *quondam forte sine caligis et calceis, vel etiam seminudus incedere solibas; et cum esses forsitan fame et frigore afflictus.*

Although the great majority of lay brothers were undoubtedly recruited from the lowest classes of society, the idea that there was a gulf between the highborn monks and the common lower-class *conversi* is misleading. Much has been made of the fact that the lay brothers were distinguished by belonging to the class of the *illiterati*,[15] but at a time when schooling was rudimentary and there was no literature in the vernacular almost everyone fell into that category, including those who joined the Cistercians as monks and were only introduced to "letters" (Latin) as part of their monastic formation.[16] The lay brothers may have been illiterate, but, as we shall see, they played a vital part in the administration of the monastic estates, especially in their role as grange masters.

## Similarity in Social Background of Monks and *Conversi*

There is also plenty of evidence that the social background of monks and lay brothers was at times the same. One of the stories about the saintly lay brother Simon of Aulne and his gift of prophecy tells of a lay brother from Villers, Evirgeld, whose blood brother, Ulrich, was a monk in the same house.[17] Another lay brother at Villers, Henry, who was responsible for the monastery's *hospitium* for the poor, was the son of a cleric, Christian, who had become a monk at Himmerod and whose other son, John, also became a monk there.[18] At Løgum (*Locus Dei*) in Denmark the *cantor*, a monk, together with his blood brother, a *conversus*, was accused of conspiring against their father-abbot of Herrevad.[19] In his *Life of Wulfric of Haselbury*, John, abbot of Forde, refers to a priest by the name of Segar who is said to have had three sons who were monks at Forde and a fourth who became a lay brother in the same

[15] Noell 2006, 257.

[16] *Instituta* 77; Waddell 2002, 559.

[17] *DM* 3.33 (Strange 1:150–55; Scott and Bland 1:171–72). For the story see p. 179.

[18] *DM* 4.31; 7.16 (Strange 1:202; 2:17–23; Scott and Bland 1:229, 477; Martene and Durand 1717, 3:1371).

[19] *Statuta* 1191.41; Waddell 2002, 229–30.

house.[20] Citing this example, Henry Mayr-Harting concludes that the distinction between monks and lay brothers does not seem to have been purely social and that only those who had the capacity for learning could become choir monks.[21]

## Service Outside the Enclosure

Because of the importance attached to the statute "That a monk ought not to live outside the cloister,"[22] which quotes the Rule as its authority,[23] contact with the outside world fell largely on the lay brothers. Although they were ultimately answerable to the cellarer, a monk, they were largely responsible for the monastery's business: the sale of surplus produce, and the purchase of a large variety of necessities. These activities took place at markets in neighboring towns and were facilitated by many abbeys establishing town houses or "courts."[24] In 1189 the General Chapter decreed that these courts were to be manned only by lay brothers and not by monks.[25]

Frequent travel, which involved both temptations and dangers not experienced at the monastery, was an essential part of the job. Conrad of Eberbach tells of an extremely gentle and humble lay brother from Clairvaux who "once had to travel through a wooded pass when he was away on business for the monastery. He fell into the hands of robbers who stripped him and took his horse and his luggage, leaving him with nothing but his charity."[26] He fell on his

---

[20] *Vita Beati Wulfrici* 1.20: *presbyterum Segarium nomine qui tres filios in monasterio de Forda monachos habuit et quartum in eadem domo fratrum conversum* (John, Abbot of Ford 1947, 38).

[21] Mayr-Harting 2011, 151.

[22] *Instituta* 6; Waddell 1999, 459: *Quod non debeat monachus extra claustrum habitare.*

[23] *RB* 66 (McCann 1976, 74).

[24] For Cistercian trade see Williams 1998, 385–97.

[25] *Statuta* 1189.11 (Canivez 1:112).

[26] *EM* 4.20 (Griesser 246): *quadam vice pro negotiis ecclesiae suae in via directus necesse habuit per fauces cuiusdam memoris solus transire. Contigit autem eum ibidem in manus incidere latronum, qui etiam despoliantes eum iumentum quoque, quo vehebatur, cum sarcinulis rapuerunt et nihil ei penitus praeter solam caritatem reliquerunt.* The story had already appeared in the *Liber miraculorum; LM* 1.7 (PL 185:459–61).

knees begging God to forgive the robbers. When they returned and saw him still on his knees they were moved to repent and returned all they had stolen from him.

Most extreme was probably the case of Lawrence, whose travels were recorded in Herbert's *Liber miraculorum* and repeated by Conrad of Eberbach.[27] It is said that after Bernard's death he was sent by the prior of Clairvaux, Philip, to King Roger of Sicily to negotiate for the monastery. However,

> When he was about to enter Rome, learning that the king had very recently died, he was troubled in soul and did not know what to do. Turning therefore to prayer, groaning and weeping he invoked Blessed Bernard and said: "My father, the chariot of Israel and its rider, why have you abandoned me? Woe is me, holy father, what shall I do, the poor and miserable soul that I am and altogether destitute of consolation?"[28]

Lawrence was worried that now that Bernard and Roger were both dead the personal tie had been broken and no one would receive him and offer him a helping hand. Previously, when he had brought greetings and letters from Bernard, kings and governors had been happy to bask in Bernard's celebrity "as if they received a blessing from heaven" (*tamquam coelitus missam benedictionem suscipiebant*). Concerned about the failure of his mission, he turned to Bernard, who appeared to him and told him to continue, confident of success. When he reached Sicily the new king gave him a considerable sum of gold with which "to build the new church at Clairvaux" (*ad aedificationem novae basilicae Clarevallensis*). On his way back Lawrence received still further gifts that enabled him to purchase a herd of ten buffalos, draft animals two or three times larger than usual cattle, and in spite of considerable hazards he drove

---

[27] *LM* 2.30 (PL 185:1340–42); *EM* 4.34 (Griesser 268–70).

[28] *LM* 2.30 (PL 185:1340): *Qui cum Romam fuisset ingressus, comperto quod idem rex nuperrime mortuus esset, consternatus animo est, et quid facere deberet prorsus ignorabat. Conversus ergo ad orationem cum gemitu et lacrymis beatum Bernardum invocabat, dicens: "Pater mi, currus Israel et auriga ejus, ut quid dereliquisti nos? Heu me! Pater sancte, quid dicam, vel quid faciam ego pauperculus et misellus, et ego omni solatio destitutus?"*

them successfully across the Alps all the way to Clairvaux, where they were established as a new breed (*novi generis bestias intulit*).[29]

A number of instances of danger are recorded. In 1246 a *conversus* from Furness in Cumbria fell off his horse and drowned while on the business of his house.[30] At Øm (*Cara insula*) in Denmark the abbot, Ture (1263–1268), "enjoined the monk Bjørn and the lay brothers Herman and Henrik to travel to the land of the Wends in northeastern Germany with horses and other goods in order to buy corn," of which there was a shortage in Denmark at the time, but before they were able to embark they were attacked and deprived of their horses. While resisting, Henrik was brutally kicked and he died a few days later. Herman was robbed and left almost naked. When news reached the abbey "the sorrow was so great that it is not possible to put it into words."[31] In 1251 the abbot of La Ferté was ordered to investigate the charge against a lay brother from the daughter house of Mazières who was said to have severely beaten a lay brother from Morimond on his way to General Chapter so that blood had been drawn.[32]

Traveling on business inevitably exposed lay brothers to temptations of the flesh as well as danger. When a lay brother who had been responsible for transporting his abbey's wine on a barge to Flanders stopped for the night, his host's maidservant prepared his bed and placed her own bed at the foot of it:

> When the lay brother had said Compline he went to bed; and as soon as the light was out, she undressed silently, and lay down in the bed she had prepared, touching the feet of the lay brother with her bare feet, and coughing to let him know that she was there. But the lay brother never perceived the wiles of this adder, thinking that the bed had been prepared for some other man. She bit the heels of the horse, that is of the lay brother, but its rider, that is, the spirit of the man, did not fall backwards by any consent; for as soon as he heard

---

[29] *LM* 2.30 (PL 185:1342).
[30] Williams 1998, 86.
[31] *Scriptores Minores* 1917–1922, 2: 238–39.
[32] *Statuta* 1251.72 (Canivez 2: 374).

a woman's voice he got up forthwith, dressed himself, went
to the window of the room, and there, occupied in prayer,
awaited the morning.[33]

A number of *conversi* from three abbeys in Denmark, probably
accompanying their abbots to General Chapter at Cîteaux, were less
successful in resisting the temptations offered outside the cloister.
In 1240 the abbess of Roermond in the Low Countries lodged
a complaint against the visiting lay brothers from Herrevad, Tvis,
and Øm. Two German abbots were ordered to acquaint themselves
with the facts of the case, and in the following year the abbot of
the Danish abbey of Esrum was ordered to notify the culprits of
their punishment. The nature of the offense is described: they had
gone out after dinner and had visited a tavern, staying until late
at night, and by their behavior they had harmed the reputation of
the Order.[34]

Abbots were usually accompanied by lay brothers on their
travels. According to Jocelin of Furness, Waldef, the saintly abbot of
Melrose, "when riding used to take with him one monk and a lay
brother and only three servants, and he would go only when necessity urged or compelled,"[35] thus complying with a General Chapter
statute from 1195 prohibiting unnecessary travel outside the monastery.[36] Abbots going to Cîteaux for the General Chapter were
not to bring a monk "but let him be content with one lay brother
or one servant" (*sed contentus sit uno converso vel uno serviente*),[37] and

---

[33] *DM* 4.100 (Strange 1: 271; Scott and Bland 1: 308–9): *Conversus cum dicto
completorio isset cubitum, essetque lucerna extincta, illa silenter vestes exuit, in lectum
praeparatam se reclinavit, nudis pedibus conversi plantas pulsans, et quia ipsa foret, tusci-
endo se prodens. Non has cerastis insidias conversus observaverat, aestimans alicui virorum
eundum lectum fuisse praeparatum. Mordebat illa ungulas equi, id est, conversi, sed as-
sessor eius, scilicet spiritus, per consensum non cecidit retro, quia mox ut vocem muliebrem
audivit, illico surrexit, vestes induit, et ad fenestras solarii vadens, orationes suas dicendo,
mane illic expectavit.*

[34] *Statuta* 1240.69 (Canivez 2: 229), and 1241.26 (Canivez 2: 235).

[35] Jocelin of Furness 1952, 127: *In equitando monachum et conversum cum tribus
tantum servulis coitinerantes habere consuevit, quo tamen necessitas invitavit aut compulit.*

[36] *Statuta* 1195.16; Waddell 2002, 316–17.

[37] *Instituta* 44; Waddell 1999, 475–76.

in fact the statutes record a number of instances of lay brothers traveling with their abbots to Cîteaux. Lay brothers who accompanied abbots on their travels, either to the General Chapter or in visiting daughter houses, did so largely in their capacity as grooms, but at times they would also have been valued companions. The lay brother Adolph is mentioned as a companion of the abbot of Val-Dieu (*Vallis Dei*) on his way to visit his motherhouse of Eberbach.[38] The sixth abbot of Clairvaux, Gerard (1170–1175), who "traveled into parts of Germany to make visitations at monasteries which Clairvaux had founded in those regions" was accompanied by a lay brother. When they reached Trier Gerard wished to return to the shrine of the saints at Saint Matthias and so, one day on the way "before he went to bed, he spoke to his lay brother privately and ordered him to have two horses ready before dawn, and go alone with him to Saint Matthias."[39] Unnecessary travel, however, was curtailed by the General Chapter: in 1190 three abbots were punished for illegally allowing the mission of a group of lay brothers to Jerusalem in connection with the Third Crusade (1184–1192).[40]

The value attached to the services of lay brothers outside the cloister is acknowledged in Innocent II's Bull of 1132, addressed to Stephen Harding at Cîteaux. The Pope wrote: "From now on, no archbishop, bishop, or abbot may receive or retain, without your permission, any of the *conversi*, who are not monks, but who have made profession in your monastery." The ruling was paraphrased in another Bull to Saint Bernard and repeated to Abbot Guichard of Pontigny in 1142.[41] An exception was made in the case of bishops of the Order who were each assigned up to two monks and three

---

[38] *DM* 5.29 (Strange 1:312–15; Scott and Bland 1:357).

[39] *EM* 2.27 (Griesser 131): *priusquam cubitum iret, conversum suum secretius alloquitur et, ut duos equos sibi ante lucem sternat, imperat, ipseque solus cum eo ad sanctam Mathiam vadat.*

[40] *Statuta* 1190.35, 36 (Waddell 2002, 204).

[41] *Cîteaux, Chartes* 1961.93: *Porro conversos vestros, qui monachi non sunt, post factam in vestris coenobiis professionem nullus archiepiscoporum, episcoporum, vel abbatum, sine vestra grata licentia suscipere, aut susceptum retinere praesumat* (*Clairvaux, Receuil des Chartes*, 6; Quantin 1854, 1:360).

*conversi.*[42] In spite of the prohibition, many prelates as well as kings and nobles continued to recruit lay brothers as messengers, companions, and almoners. In 1200 the abbot of Silvanès was punished by the General Chapter for lending a lay brother to a bishop.[43] Reinhold, archbishop of Cologne, is said to have been advised to seek out from houses in his diocese "faithful and far-sighted lay brothers to look after the episcopal farms and restore the annual income by their industry," and *conversi* were recruited from Kamp and Altenberg.[44] Their reputation as farmers was so high that when Obazine in the Limousin joined the Cistercian Order in 1147 lay brothers were among those who were sent to instruct them in Cistercian ways: two of them were monks and "two were lay brothers, no less devout and highly skilled in their trade" (*non minus religiosi et in sua quique arte decenter instructi*). A third lay brother, said to be "expert at dealing with cattle and whose hard work contributed much to the prosperity of the house" (*in nutriendis animalibus solers ac peritissimus fuit, cuius labore et industria domus nostra in temporalibus multum excrevit*), stayed behind and remained there for the rest of his life.[45]

Royal and noble demands for the services of lay brothers continued, as the number of prohibitions by the General Chapter and penalties imposed for violations indicates,[46] but the pressure from powerful benefactors was sometimes such that concessions had to be made. In 1220 the General Chapter was forced to allow monks as well as lay brothers to work for archbishops, bishops, and kings.[47] Richard I of England had a lay brother as an almoner, and a monk and two lay brothers accompanied King Andrew II of Hungary on a pilgrimage to the Holy Land.[48]

[42] *Statuta* 1185.1 (Waddell 2002, 120).

[43] *Statuta* 1200.35 (Waddell 2002, 466).

[44] *DM* 4.62 (Strange 1:230; Scott and Bland 1:262): *conversos fideles atque providos accommodaret, qui et curtibus praeessent, et annos redditus sua industria reformarent.*

[45] *Étienne d'Obazine* 1970, 114.

[46] *Statuta* 1157.47 (Waddell 2002, 597); 1175.33 (Canivez 1:84); 1193.57 (Canivez 1:169); 1213.53 (Canivez 1:414); 1218.31 (Canivez 1:490); 1219.30 (Canivez 1:509).

[47] *Statuta* 1220.3 (Canivez 1:516–17).

[48] *Statuta* 1197.30 (Waddell 2002, 391); 1212.66 (Canivez 1:404).

**Knights and Clerics Who Became Lay Brothers**

Although lay brothers were drawn mostly from the rural poor, the traditional image of them as *rudes, simplices, idiotae,* or *illiterati* does not always fit and there were a number, as Brian Noell has pointed out, who were distinguished either by their lineage or by their attainment. The number of those who do not fit the frequently depicted stereotypes was, it must be stressed, infinitesimal in relation to the total.[49] Among the exceptions were one of Saint Bernard's uncles, Milo, lord of Montbard, who became a lay brother at Cîteaux; Alexander, prince of Scotland (d. 1229), who entered the French abbey of Foigny as a lay brother; and Salamon, prince of Austria, who entered Heiligenkreuz.[50] Another was Pons, a knight and the hermit founder of Silvanès in the south of France who, having handed his monastery to the Cistercians, secured the election of one of his community as abbot while he, according to his biographer, "remained a lay brother out of humility" for the rest of his life.[51] Another notable exception at a later date was Konrad Zeuffel, who became a lay brother at Ebrach in Franconia, where he was buried near the entrance to the new sacristy endowed by his kinsmen, the two brothers Zeuffel, who belonged to a patrician family from Würzburg. His grave monument, only known from an eighteenth-century engraving, shows him recumbent, his hands folded in prayer, with his head, with a long beard and the usual fringe, resting on a cushion (fig. 1).[52] He is wearing the cloak (*cappa*) and hood covering only his shoulders and chest (*caputium scapulas et pectus tantummodo cooperiens*) as laid down in the *Usus conversorum*.[53] Next to him lies his mother, Matilda, referred to as *maxima benefactor*.

Among those who distinguished themselves by their achievement was Simon of Aulne, who, as we shall see, had proved his powers of prophecy to the satisfaction of his fellow-brother, Evirgeld.[54]

---

[49] Noell 2006, 262–65.

[50] Ducourneau 1929, 2:161–63.

[51] Kienzle 1995, 219–43.

[52] Ebrach 1739, 21–22; Wiener 1985, 272, 290.

[53] *UC* 16 (Waddell 73, 189).

[54] See chap. 8, p. 179.

*Fig. 1* Engraving of effigy of lay brother Konrad Zeuffel and his mother, dated 1348.

Caesarius met him at Heisterbach and devoted one of his longest chapters to him. It was written during Simon's lifetime between 1219 and 1221, some years before his *Vita*, which appeared shortly after his death in 1229.[55] Descended from the counts of Gueldre, Simon entered Aulne as a lay brother at sixteen and became master of the grange of Colomies. His reputation spread so widely that a cleric from the Curia came from Rome to consult him. Upon the cleric's return to Rome news of Simon's powers reached the pope, Innocent III, who summoned him to the Lateran Council in 1215 and offered to ordain him, but he refused on account of his humility. Caesarius then recounts the story of Conrad, who was later to become abbot of Villers, then of Clairvaux, then promoted to Cîteaux, and finally made a cardinal by the pope. One day, when Conrad was still a novice at Villers, Simon was at Mass with Abbot Walter of Villers and a number of other monks and lay brothers of Aulne when he

> saw the spirit of Conrad, though his body was then far away, standing near him and wearing a golden crown upon his head; he could read also the thoughts of his heart, and the prayers in which he was then engaged at Villers. After the Mass, he drew Walter aside and said: "When you see Brother Conrad, the novice at Villers, tell him to be on his guard, for he will suffer certain temptations in the coming year; such and such were his meditations, and such and such his prayers during today's Mass; and you may be sure that one day he will be a great personage in our Order."[56]

---

[55] *DM* 3.33 (Strange 1:150–55; Scott and Bland 1:169–73); Roisin 1947, 47–49; Noell 2006, 263.

[56] *DM* 3.33 (Strange 1:152; Scott and Bland 1:170–71): *videt item Simon spiritum iam dicti Conradi, corpore satis a se remoti, coram se stare, et coronam aureum in capite gestare. Vidit et cogitationes cordis eius, atque orationes, in quibus tunc versebatur in Vilario. Finita missa, secrete locutus est Waltero, dicens: Cum videritis nonnum Conradum novicium Vilariensem, dicite ei, ut caveat sibi, quia huiusmodi tentationes patietur hoc anno. Tales enim cogitationes, talesque orationes iam habuit in missa, et sciatis quia magna persona erit in ordine.*

When Abbot Walter questioned Simon about Conrad's thoughts and prayers he was astounded to find that they corresponded exactly with what Simon had told him.

In the same way, when a Yorkshire knight, Ralph Haget, a member of a well-known landed family, became dissatisfied with the life he was leading he turned for advice not to an abbot or a monk but to a humble lay brother, Sunnulph of Fountains,

> who shone with singular grace and purity; he was simple and illiterate, but the Lord had taught him. For a book he had his conscience, for teacher the Holy Spirit, and reading the book of experience he grew daily in the knowledge of holy things, and he also had the spirit of prophecy.[57]

Hugh of Kirkstall, Ralph Haget's biographer, records how he, having heard the voice of Christ asking him from the Cross why he had not responded to the call, fell to his knees and relented. When he told Sunnulph what had occurred and that he would follow his advice, Sunnulph replied: "At Fountains you shall take the religious habit, and there, when your race is run, you will end your life."[58] Ralph Haget, like so many of the early Cistercians, "was a soldier of this world but did not loosen his belt, but changed it for a better, joining the camp of the Hebrews, later to be the first among the people of God,"[59] that is, abbot of Kirkstall 1182–1190/1 and of Fountains 1190/1–1203.

Alan of Lille, a noted Paris master known as *doctor universalis* and famous for his theological treatises and poetic works, retired to Cîteaux, where he spent his remaining days in obscurity as a

[57] *Fountains, Memorials* 1863.118: *singularis gratiae et puritatis enituit, Sunnulphus nominee; homo simplex et illiteratus, sed Dominus erudierat eum. Habebat, pro codice, conscientiam; spiritum sanctum pro eruditore; et legens in libro experientiae, crescebat cotidie in scientia sanctorum; habens etiam spiritum revelationis.* For Sunnulph, see Knowles 1940, 357; Baker 1972, 104; Cassidy-Welch 2001, 191.

[58] *Fountains, Memorials* 1863.120: *In monasterio Fontanensi habitum religionis assumes, et consummato cursu, diem inibi claudes extremum.*

[59] *Fountains, Memorials* 1863.117: *Miles quondam in saeculo, militiae cingulum non solvit, sed mutavit, in melius; adjungens se castris Ebreorum, princeps postmodum futurus in populo Dei.*

lay brother looking after sheep.[60] He died in 1203 and was buried in a place of honor in the cloister near the door to the church, across from the tombs of the founding abbots, Alberic and Stephen Harding. A monument marking the site was sculpted in 1482 on the orders of Abbot Jean de Cirey. Known only from a poor engraving, it portrayed Alan with sheep at his feet representing his life as a simple brother, and books above his head referring to his past career in Paris.

Caesarius of Heisterbach records a problem that arose when tonsured clerks concealed their identity and entered as lay brothers:

> So great is the virtue of humility that often for the love of it, clerks who come to the Order conceal the fact that they are not laymen, preferring the herding of cattle to the reading of books, and holding it better to serve God in humility than to be set over others because of their holy orders or literary learning.[61]

Caesarius declared that it was desirable to prevent this in future, but that the General Chapter had four years previously laid down that those who had taken vows as *conversi* should remain as lay brothers. He was referring to a statute of 1213.[62] The same year a deacon who pretended to be a layman was admitted as a lay brother. When the abbot learned of this he took the matter to the Chapter in the following year and the decision was reversed. As a result a statute in 1214 decreed that "clerks in holy orders who, wearing lay clothes, have been received as lay brothers are to be expelled."[63] Some years earlier (1202) a subdeacon entered

---

[60] Mantour 1736, 193–232, and Plate 12.

[61] *DM* 1.39 (Strange 1:46–47; Scott and Bland 1:50–51): *Tanta est virtus humilitatis, ut eius amore saepe ad ordinem venientes clerici, laicos se simulaverint, malentes pecora pascere, quam libros legere, satius ducentes Deo in humilitate servire, quam propter sacros ordines vel literaturam ceteris praeesse.*

[62] *Statuta* 1213.1 (Canivez 1:404): *Item monasticam simplicitatem servare et imitari cupientes, statuimus ut qui in tonsura et habitu saeculari ad Ordinem accedunt, et habitum conversi accipiunt, in eodem habitu perseverent.*

[63] *Statuta* 1214.59 (Canivez 1:429): *clerici sub habitu saeculari et in sacris ordinibus constituti, qui in conversos recipiuntur, cum hoc abbati constiterit, eiiciantur.*

Grandselve in southern France as a lay brother, concealing the fact that he was a subdeacon. He left his monastery and entered another as a subdeacon; there he was promoted to deacon. When it was discovered that he had previously been a lay brother he was expelled from the Order never to return.[64]

A study of the names of monks and *conversi* in the *Necrologium Lundense* and the *Libri Datici Lundense* shows that at a time when the Cistercian houses in Denmark were mostly ruled by foreign abbots and when approximately half the monks were foreign born, practically all lay brothers bore Danish names.[65] The remarkable lay brother Thorkil from Øm in Denmark, who later became not just a monk but an abbot,[66] was in one respect probably like many twelfth-century lay brothers for, in the words of the abbey's chronicle, he had "from childhood been brought up with and among the monks, for he was born near the monastery."[67] One of the lay brothers on the grange of Leeheim belonging to the German abbey of Eberbach is said to have been brought up on the grange.[68] In Wales, even at the English-speaking Anglo-Norman abbey of Margam many of the names of lay brothers in the thirteenth century were Welsh, among them Anian, Cnaithur, Caradog, Kethereth, Richard Cnicht, and Rhiryd, while at nearby Tintern, not far away in the Wye valley on the English border, the names of lay brothers known in 1261 are all typically English—John of Ailburton, William of the Marsh, Roger of Kingswood, Will Penreche, and Richard the Parmenter—clearly indicating that, as in Denmark, lay brothers were on the whole locally recruited.[69]

Examples abound of knights who chose to become lay brothers in preference to joining the Cistercians as monks, as would have seemed more normal. John of Forde refers to one in his *Life of*

---

[64] *Statuta* 1202.14 (Canivez 1:277).

[65] France 1990, 148.

[66] For Thorkil, see chap. 7, p. 162.

[67] *Scriptores Minores* 1917–1922. 2: 193: *qui cum monachis et inter monachos in puero nutritus, utpote iuxta claustrum natus.*

[68] Mossig 1978, 431.

[69] Williams 1976, 118.

*Wulfric of Haselbury* and applauds his motivation for having chosen to become a lay brother: among Wulfric's

> friends and closest of all to the holy man was Brother William, the lay brother hospitaller of Forde. A man of the highest general repute, but in our opinion highest of all in that, having spurned in the very flower of his youth the pomp of the king's court, he reigns prosperously to this day in the poverty of Christ.[70]

The perfect example from Clairvaux is the young nobleman who "was not wise in high subjects, but submissive to humble duties, and being sent to a grange, became a shepherd of sheep."[71] One day in the field he had a vision of his cousin who had died young. He asked for three Masses to be said for him. With the permission of his grange master, the lay brother hastened to the abbey and arranged for the Masses to be said. He subsequently heard from his cousin that as a result of these prayers he had been freed from his punishment.

A similar lay brother recruit was Liffard at Himmerod in the Rhineland: "a man of good birth and therefore his humility the more meritorious, he did not scorn to feed the pigs of the monastery, and even begged to have that office."[72] One day while feeding his pigs he came across a tree he considered perfect for making troughs for his pigs: "at once the tree fell as if it had been hewn down by an axe," and his prayer was answered.[73] Caesarius of Heisterbach has another story about Liffard. Toward the end of his life, after he

---

[70] *VW* 1.14 (John, Abbot of Ford 1933, 28; CF 79:114): *Horum unus et inter ipsos beato viro familiarissimus fuit frater Willelmus conversus hospitalis de Forda, vir clarissimae omnino opinionis; sed clarior ut credimus opinione sua qui in ipso adolescentaie sue flore regalis curie pompam aspernatus, in Christi paupertate felicius usque hodie regnat.*

[71] *DM* 12.33 (Strange 2:342–43; Scott and Bland 2:321–22): *qui non alta sapiens, sed humilibus consentiens, ad quondam grangiam missus, factus est ibi opilio ovium.*

[72] *DM* 10.54 (Strange 2:254; Scott and Bland 2:215–16): *Hic cum esset homo bene natus, ut per humilitatem amplius mereretur, porcos monasterii pascere non despexit, imo precibus idem officium obtinuit.*

[73] *DM* 10.54 (Strange 2:254; Scott and Bland 2:216).

had looked after pigs for many years, he was tempted by the spirit of pride, saying, "What is it that I am doing? I am well-born, and yet I am despised by all my friends because of this menial office."[74] He decided to leave, but then in a vision he was taken through the lay brothers' choir and the cloister, through doors normally kept locked at night, and into the cemetery where the graves were opened. He was terrified, the temptation passed, and he decided to stay among the pigs.

Among other lay brothers of good birth were the "former distinguished knights" (*quondam milites praeclari*) Henry de Weiss, John de Salinth, John de Roist, Walter de Riklam, Francis de Lachem, and James de Glym, all of whom joined Villers as lay brothers.[75] Among the noblemen and knights who joined at Himmerod were *Dominus* Arnold von Bramshorn (entered 1234/50), Count Hermann III von Virneburg (ca. 1238), the knight Paynus von Gilsdorf (before 1263), Gerlach von Rheimbachweiler (ca. 1265), and Heinrich von Dudenhofen, all of whom entered with property including houses and vineyards.[76] Caesarius of Heisterbach has a story of the knight Walewan who at first was a novice monk at Himmerod but later, in his humility, decided to become a lay brother. He had come

> to Himmerod arrayed in all his armor and riding upon his charger, and thus armed entered the convent; and, as our elders who were present have told me, he went under the guidance of the porter down the middle of the choir to the altar of the Blessed Virgin and there, with all the convent looking on, he laid down his arms and took up the habit of religion. It seemed to him fitting and proper that he should lay down the warlike trappings of the world there where he proposed to assume the garments of a soldier of Christ.[77]

---

[74] *DM* 4.4 (Strange 1:175: Scott and Bland 1:197–99): *Quod est quod ago? Homo sum bene natus, sed propter hoc vile officium omnibus amicis meis despectus.*

[75] Ducourneau 1929, 2: 161

[76] Toepfer 1983, 98.

[77] *DM* 1.37 (Strange 1:45–46; Scott and Bland 1:49): *cum dextrario et armis suis militaribus Hemmenrode venit, armatus claustrum intravit, et sicut mihi retulerunt seniores nostri, qui tunc praesentes erant, portario illum ducente, per medium chorum vadens, conventu inspiciente, et novam conversionis formam mirante, super altare Virginis se obtulit,*

Other noblemen chose to become lay brothers at the German abbeys of Salem, at Haina, where they are found among the twenty-four named lay brothers, and at Marienstatt.[78] In the south of France a knight was admitted at Grandselve (Haute-Garonne),[79] and Bernard Sicard, a member of the knightly class entered Valmagne (Hérault) as a *conversus* in 1193.[80]

Some did not adjust easily to their new reduced state. A knight named Odacar joined the monastery of Kamp in the Rhineland as a lay brother, taking the name Gerard. Like many of his background he found it hard to adjust to his new life:

> Somewhat inopportune thoughts of riches and social status used to come to him especially at the time of prayer. The flies in the mind extinguished the sweetness of ointment, that is, devotion in prayer, as scripture says: "One dead fly can spoil the scent-maker's oil" [Eccl. 10:1]. He was frequently disciplined and implored the prayers of various saints hoping by their help to be freed, but to no avail.

The story forms part of the *Vita* of the saintly Archbishop Engelbert of Cologne and it ends with Gerard seeking the saint's intercession. As a result of Engelbert's prayers he was freed and never had those feelings again.[81]

The kind of problem experienced by Gerard at Kamp and by Liffard at Himmerod may in part explain the General Chapter decision in 1188 whereby noblemen were in future obliged to enter as monks and not as lay brothers. Another statute stipulates that not

---

*armisque depositis, in eadem domo religionis habitum suscepit. Visum est ei congruum, ibi militiam deponere saecularem, ubi assumere proponebat militiam spiritualem.*

[78] Toepfer 1983, 84, 106–18.

[79] Williams 1998, 81.

[80] Berman 2000, 166–67.

[81] *Vita et miracula Engelberti, DM* Hilka 1937, 3:302: *Huic cogitationes divitiarum ac dignitatum secularium tam importune fuerunt, maxime orationis tempore, ut quasi musce menti eius involantes suavitatem unguenti, id est devotionem orationis, illic extinguerunt, ut dicit auctoritas: "Musce morientes perdunt suavitatem unguenti." Qui cum frequenter disciplinas corporales reciperet et diversorum suffragia sanctorum imploraret, illorum auxilio sperans liberari, nec proficeret.*

only nobles but any others potentially more useful as monks should not be allowed to enter as lay brothers. Yet another version states that "nobles who are better suited to the office of monks than to the labors of *conversi* should become monks rather than *conversi*."[82] Chrysogonus Waddell points out that the reason given was admittedly utilitarian: such candidates would be of greater use as monks. Jacques Dubois speculates that the influx of lay brothers had been so great that the General Chapter found there was a greater need for nobles as monks.[83] Ducourneau argues that many of the upper-class recruits owed their vocation to a momentary enthusiasm they were later to regret and that their consequent suffering would also lead to the suffering of others.[84] Another reason may be that by 1188 the former great influx of recruits of choir monks was beginning to dry up. Throughout history the chasm between the cultural and social backgrounds of divergent groups has invariably been the cause of tension and conflict. It is therefore likely that, at a time when incidents of the violation of monastic discipline were on the increase,[85] the General Chapter chose to act in reaction to disputes between the two groups that had already begun to take place, or in recognition of what the chapter members perceived as an impending conflict between them. As some of the examples quoted above show, not least stories in the thirteenth-century *Dialogus miraculorum*, a number of knights continued to enter as lay brothers after 1188 and, as in so many other respects, the General Chapter failed to enforce its prohibition. One story in the *Dialogus miraculorum*, however, tells us that it had not always and everywhere been completely forgotten. Caesarius of Heisterbach records how

---

[82] *Statuta* 1188.10 (Waddell 2002, 151). The three versions are:

1. *Nobiles laici venientes ad monasterium non fiant conversi sed monachi.*

2. *Provideant abbates ne personas generosas et quae in officio monachorum possunt utiliores esse quam conversorum inter converses recipient, sed magis inter monachos.*

3. *Generosae personae qui magis idonei sunt ad officium monachorum quam conversorum laboribus, fiant monachi potius quam conversi.*

[83] Dubois 1972, 212.

[84] Ducourneau 1929, 2:162–63.

[85] For this see chapter 12.

a certain soldier renounced the world and entered the Cistercian Order. Because he was illiterate and was noble they gave him a master and, instructed to some extent in letters, he continued as a monk and not a lay brother. Although under this master for a long time he was not able to learn anything except the two words "Ave Maria" which he eagerly retained and devotedly remembered so that wherever he went he constantly repeated them.[86]

## Motivation: Necessity Rather than Fear of God

In spite of the abundant testimony to the quality of life of *conversi* and the stories of the humility displayed by upper-class recruits, the motives of a great many men for becoming *conversi* seem to have been mixed and indeed often divorced from any sense of religious vocation, very often through no particular fault of their own. Among the recruits were the victims of the early Cistercian policy of depopulating the villages they acquired and converting the land into granges. Many smallholders who lost their land as a result of this policy had little alternative and joined the lay brotherhood.[87] Property acquired at the end of the twelfth century to form the Eberbach grange of Hadamar included the lands of twenty-two *homines suos proprios* who, in obtaining their freedom, probably remained as *mercenarii* or may have entered as lay brothers.[88] In the south of France depopulation of villages appears to have been the main source of recruits. Donations were made by many peasants on condition that the donor or his sons be admitted as *conversi*. Examples are found in the charters of, for example, Boulbonne, Gimont, and Berdoues, all in southern France.[89] Lands donated by peasants who subsequently entered Silvanès contributed to the formation of the grange of Promillac.[90] At Sorø in Denmark a number of peasants became *conversi* when

---

[86] *DM* Hilka 1937, 3:206.
[87] For the policy of depopulation, see chap. 6, pp. 121–27.
[88] Mossig 1978, 360–61.
[89] Berman 1986, 55.
[90] Berman 1986, 49.

their land was acquired by the monks.[91] In this category too was a lay brother, Oluf Kviter, from another Danish abbey, Øm, who is mentioned in that abbey's Chronicle. He had donated two *curiae* to the abbey "with their woods, lands, houses, and animals" he himself had bought; as a result of his gift a yearly pittance of extra food was provided for the community. Like many who joined as lay brothers in similar circumstances, he subsequently became a grange master.[92] Sometimes donations were made by another member of their family for the reception of young men either as monks or as lay brothers. Thus at Fountains Michael de Dishforth donated a bovate of land with toft, croft, and turbary for the health of his soul and those of his ancestors and particularly for his brother, Gilbert, who had been received as a lay brother.[93] At Margam in Wales Gille of Seis became a lay brother in about 1200 upon the transfer of twenty-four acres of land to the abbey.[94] Three named *conversi*—Wolfram, Siegfried, and Ortwin—donated property upon their entry at the Eberbach grange of Gehaborn.[95] The *Historia Fundationis* of the Yorkshire abbeys of Byland and Jervaulx records how at the customary annual visitation the abbot of Byland had found the daughter house of Jervaulx greatly demoralized. To relieve the distress he gave them five baskets of grain and ten of malt and, "in addition with the approval of our convent he gave them ten bovates of land in Ellington which brother Serlo, our *conversus*, gave us when he entered our house, with ten oxen and ten cows, and six mares with their foals in the same pasture."[96] The charter that follows refers to Serlo as the cook.

---

[91] France 1990, 147.

[92] *Scriptores Minores* 1917–1922, 2:201–2: *cum omnibus dictis curiis attinentibus, silvis, terris, domibus et pecoribus.*

[93] Wardrop 1987, 252.

[94] Williams 1984, 1:156.

[95] Mossig 1978, 231.

[96] Burton 2006, 49–50: *Insuper dedit eis per assensum conventus nostri decem bovatas terre in Ellington quas frater Serlo conversus noster dedit nobis ad suum ingressum in domum nostrum cum decem bobus et decem vaccis ibidem et sex equabus cum pullis earum in eadem pastura.*

The plight of many is graphically revealed in a story told by the Dominican Humbert of Romans (d. 1277) in a sermon to Cistercian lay brothers:

> Cistercian lay brothers frequently come from a condition of poverty to this condition in order to find what they need to sustain them. Thus it happened that a man who at home was used to eating black bread succeeded in being received as a lay brother in order that he might be given white bread. On the day he was admitted he prostrated before the abbot who asked him, "What do you ask for," to which he replied, "White bread, and often!" Thus many in this Order seek white bread. They must first and foremost be taught to seek the kingdom of God, then not to divert any property belonging to the house without permission either to their friends or to anyone else.[97]

The poor lay brother's answer is of course a parody of the standard response in the profession ceremony: "The mercy of God and your mercy."[98]

According to Conrad of Eberbach, Saint Bernard is said to have rebuked a lay brother for overconfidence, saying:

> Were you not just a poor miserable sort of fellow who, having nothing or almost nothing in the world, fled to us more out of necessity than out of the fear of God, begging for admission with many prayers? For the sake of God we took you in destitute and gave you food and clothing and the common goods, just the same as those men among us who are well educated and nobly born, and made you as one of them.[99]

---

[97] Humbert de Romans 1677, 470: *Conversi Cisterciensium frequenter veniunt de statu paupertatis ad hunc statum ut habeant sustentationem vitae. Unde accedit, quod eum cuidam, qui erat de familia eorum, et comedebat cum alia familia panem nigrum, concessum fuisset, ut reciperetur in conversum comedebat panem album, et instructus fuisset, quod veniret coram Abbate in die receptionis, et ipso prostrate quaereret Abbas quid quaereret: respondit: Panem album, et hoc frequenter. Et sic sine dubio multi in illo ordine quaerunt panem bonum, et instruendi sunt, ut primo quaerant in illo ordine regnum Dei, ei iustitiam eius.*

[98] EO 102.3 (Griesser 1956, 263): *Misericordiam Dei et vestram.*

[99] EM 4.19 (Griesser 244–45): *Enimvero tu non es ille pauperculus et miserabilis homo, qui cum nihil aut prope nihil haberes in saeculo, necessitate forsitan magis quam*

A man named Gerung had come to Himmerod, where he lived for some time in secular dress but, when he became seriously ill, "put on the habit more through dread of hell than love of the Order and was carried to the infirmary of the lay brothers."[100] Toward the end of his life one of the other *conversi*, Ludo, had a vision of vultures flying around his fellow brother and horrid misshapen creatures gathering round him. Realizing that they were devils there to snatch the brother's soul, he shouted out, begging them to leave. As they did not obey, he shouted again: "I command you in the name of the Lord," at which they flew away. Caesarius ends with the moral of the story: "How the prayers of brothers present help monks in their death agony, will be shown by that vision."[101]

Caesarius of Heisterbach expresses his view of many *conversi* in much the same terms as did Hildegard of Bingen, who referred to them as "false prophets" (*pseudo-prophetes*).[102] Of the motivation of many who joined as lay brothers he says that "a vast number are driven to enter by the furnace of poverty. . . . I have known some who, when their fathers or brothers were taking the vows, refused to follow their example then, but when they had consumed all their property, they concealed their need with a mantle of piety and made of necessity a virtue."[103]

---

*timore Dei cogente ad nos confugisti multis precibus tandem aditum impetrando? Nos vero causa Dei collegimus inopem et parem te fecimus in victu atque vestitu ceterisque communitatibus his, qui nobiscum sunt, sapientibus atque nobilibus viris, et factus es quasi unus ex illis.* This is one of the many stories Conrad of Eberbach has taken from Herbert of Clairvaux's *Liber miraculorum*, in this case almost word for word. It is also found in the Fürstenfeld Collection; Kompatcher Gubler 2005, 244–46. See also p. 160.

[100] *DM* 11.15 (Strange 2:283; Scott and Bland 2:251): *magis timore gehennae quam amore patriae habitum induens, in infirmitorium conversorum deportatus est.*

[101] *DM* 11.15 (Strange 2:283–84; Scott and Bland 2:251): *Ego vobis praecipio in nomine Domini ut exeatis . . . . Quantum vero agonizantibus fratrum praesentium oratio prosit, eadem visione declarabitur.*

[102] PL 197:264. For Hildegard of Bingen's view of the lay brothers, see chap. 12, pp. 283–84.

[103] *DM* 1.28 (Strange 1:34; Scott and Bland 1:36–37): *ita plurimos intrare compellit camimus paupertatis. . . . Novi quosdam, qui, patribus sive fratribus convertentibus,*

Economic necessity was among the motives of many recruits, but the Cistercians were also able to offer employment to a surplus of workers created by an increase in population and to provide living conditions superior to those that could be offered by most lay masters. But, above all, by becoming lay brothers weaker members of rural society experienced a security and continuity of employment not found elsewhere while at the same time enjoying the benefits of belonging to a prestigious Order, and a place in society totally outside their reach in any other occupation.

On rare occasions criminals or even murderers found their way into the ranks of the lay brothers in an attempt to disguise their past, much in the same way that men in modern times have joined the French Foreign Legion, or as a sanctuary in which to escape justice. In 1240 a young man (*adolescens*) who was a shoemaker entered Waverley, almost certainly as a lay brother, and because of his trade was put to work in the cobblers' workshop.[104] After a while a knight arrived with his retinue and charged him with homicide. He may or may not have been guilty, but in spite of the protests of the abbot and other monks who were responsible for his well-being he was seized and carried off. After much trouble the abbot appealed to the king and eventually won the brother back. All Cistercian houses and granges were by papal decree declared exempt from civil action and the brother shoemaker returned to the abbey.

Some owed their conversion to exceptional circumstances. Among these was a boy whose story is told in John the Hermit's *Vita quarta* of Saint Bernard. While he was sailing on the river Loire his boat struck a bridge with some force, as a result of which he fell into the river and drowned. When Bernard heard of this he ordered the boy to be brought to him and, after the saint had prayed over him, the boy rose immediately. The story ends: "From that day the boy loved the holy man with great affection and he came to Clairvaux where he became a lay brother by the name

---

*converti renuerunt, et cum consumsissent omnia dimissa, tunc primum venerunt, necessitatem pallio devotionis palliantes, vel potius de ipsa necessitate virtutem facientes.*

[104] Waverleia, Annales de, 325–27: *adveniens quidam adolescens sutoriae artis, in sutrino nostro susceptus est.*

of Tescelin Smack (Nascardus) because he was taken up from the water and fished out like a fish."[105]

The backgrounds and achievements of *conversi*, then, were multifarious. Among them were noblemen, military knights, peasants who had been evicted when their lands were swallowed up to form granges, brothers noted for their prophetic powers and extreme asceticism, negotiators, businessmen, efficient administrators, smallholders who chose the lay brothers' lot in preference to their independent but precarious existence, and many who had no other choice.

Although the social position of most would have been greatly improved by their joining the ranks of the lay brothers, according to Roehl "nonmaterial considerations and motivations could play a large part, perhaps even the largest part, in the decision of a peasant to become a *conversus* in the Cistercian order."[106] The *conversi* represented a new form of religious life. In the words of David Knowles, "in the early twelfth century the appeal made by this vocation to the illiterate, who had for many centuries been neglected by monasticism, was immediate and widespread."[107]

As we have seen, although there are many examples of lay brothers who on account of their privileged background or their achievement did not conform to the traditional image, the vast majority of *conversi* were of humble extraction and limited aspiration, and it must be stressed that religious motivation was and remained a determining factor for a multitude of those who chose to enter as lay brothers. Among the large numbers of "simple and upright" men, as they are so often described, was a lay brother from Clairvaux whose reward for a life of toil and devotion was recorded by Herbert of Clairvaux and is found again in the Beaupré Collection of *exempla* and repeated by Conrad of Eberbach:

---

[105] *Vita quarta* 11 (PL 185:546): *Tunc a die illa et deinceps Hominem Dei, ut patrem filius affectuosissime diligens, postea profectus in Claram-Vallem, ibi conversus factus est, dictus Tescelinus Nascardus, quia de aqua fuerat sublatus, et piscatus sicut piscis.* "Nascardus" comes from Naca, meaning a fishing boat or smack. I am grateful to Fr. Hilary Costello for unraveling the meaning.

[106] Roehl 1972, 88.

[107] Knowles 1940, 215.

When he came to his last moment he opened his eyes and he saw holy angels present there to assist him on his death-bed. He said at once to the brothers standing around: "Don't you see the angels of God who have come here? Strike the tablets[108] very quickly for it will announce my death." When he had said these things his soul immediately departed. There is no doubt that the holy angels, whom he had the privilege of seeing, received him.[109]

## The Origin of the Cistercian Lay Brotherhood

The citation from the *Exordium Parvum* given above announcing the institution of lay brothers was probably written as an introduction to the new customary, some time before but close to 1147. The author was Raynard de Bar, former monk of Clairvaux and disciple of Saint Bernard who, after the short unsuccessful abbacy of Guy at Cîteaux, succeeded Stephen Harding to that office in 1134/1135. They contain, as in a nutshell, the principal attributes that define the Cistercian lay brotherhood.

"It was then that they decided" (*tuncque definierunt*) tells us that, contrary to what has often been asserted, lay brothers or *conversi*, as they were known, were not there from the very beginning. That it was necessary to obtain "the bishop's permission" (*licentia episcopi*) indicates their lay status, on account of which the bishop had the *cura animarum* in their regard. Their lay status is reinforced by their description as *laici*, and their non-clerical status is again emphasized by adding *barbati*, their beards defining them as laymen, who at the time were generally bearded, in contrast to the clean-shaven monks

---

[108] *EO* 94 (Griesser 1956, 257): *percussa crebris ictibus tabula in claustro ante infirmitorium.*

[109] *LM* 1.14 (PL 185:1291): *Conversus quidam de supradicto coenobio, homo religiosus et bonae operationis, cum jam ad extrema devenisset, apertis oculis vidit angelos sanctos praesentes assistere lectulo suo. Qui statim circumstantibus fratribus ait: "Nunquid non aspicitis angelos Dei qui modo advenerunt? Pulsate quantocius tabulam, quoniam ipsum praestolantur exitum meum." Et cum ista dixisset, protinus egressa est anima. Nec dubium quin eam susceperint angeli sancti, quos praevidisse mercuerat.* The same story is found in the Fürstenfeld Compilation (Kompatscher-Gufler 2005, 237), and in the *Exordium magnum*, but at greater length: *EM* 4.23 (Griesser 250).

who were distinguished by their tonsure. They made the same vows as the monks and were therefore religious and, as full members of the community, the monks would treat them "as themselves in life and death"; in other words, they had the same rights, both material and spiritual. Although they were religious, they were not bound by the Rule because they did not follow the detailed provisions for celebrating the hours as laid down by Saint Benedict. The qualification "the status of monk apart" (*excepto monachatu*), however, was all-important, for they were precluded from ever becoming monks or from holding any of the important offices and they did not have a vote in abbatial elections.

The reference to "hired men" (*homines mercenarii*) is worthy of emphasis, for the hirelings' contribution to the economic success of the Cistercians has received scant attention. A General Chapter statute from 1198 testifies to the important part they played at the granges. There the lay brothers followed the calendar of the neighboring parish churches so that their workdays coincided with those of their hired laborers.[110] Visual evidence of their cooperation with the *conversi* is provided by a corbel from the cloister at Pforta in Thuringia (fig. 2). The corbel has two heads, one with long curly hair and a beard, clearly a layman, and the other a typical lay brother with a neat beard and fringed hair. The services performed by hired laborers assisting the lay brothers made it possible for the monks to observe the Rule in its entirety "day and night" (*die sive nocte*), in other words, celebrating the canonical hours, seven in the daytime and one at night, the Work of God—the *Opus Dei*—which may be said to constitute the very *raison d'être* of monasticism. The choice of the word *amniculus* to denote the role of the lay brothers as "backing" or "assistance" or "aid" to the monks is particularly graphic for, according to Dubois,[111] in its general meaning it referred to a vine prop as used in a wine-growing region, an apt description and perfectly fitting for Cîteaux, located in Burgundy, which had received the famous vineyard of Meursault only months after its

---

[110] *Statuta* 1198.12 (Waddell 2002, 406): *Solemnitates transpositas Conversi in Grangiis agant in grangiis die sua, quando et seculares observant.*

[111] Dubois 1972, 165.

*Fig. 2* Corbel in cloister at Pforta in Thuringia—lay brother and hired worker.

foundation.[112] Figuratively we see Cîteaux as the mystical vine now supported by its props, the lay brothers and their hired hands. The lay and yet religious status of the *conversi*, their relationship with the monks, their support and that of the hired laborers, which enabled the monks to minimize their contact with the outside world and fully observe the Rule, will be explored later.[113] But as the institution of lay brothers was such a distinctive feature of the Cistercian Order, we will first examine whether there were any antecedents, and then, as we have seen that they were not there from the beginning, when the Cistercians first introduced them.

### The "Old Style" and the "New Style" of *Conversi*

A number of conflicting views have been argued on the origin of lay brothers. The question is both complex and controversial, not least owing to the name "*conversus*" itself, the meaning of which

[112] Marilier 1961, 38.
[113] See chapter 2.

was constantly changing.[114] The "converted one" was anyone who, "turning round," entered religious life. In chapter 58 of the Rule, "On the Reception of Brethren," Saint Benedict refers to one who "newly comes to be a monk" (*noviter veniens quis ad conversionem*), and one of the vows monks and lay brothers made at profession was that of *conversio morum*, conversion of life or way of living.[115]

Although the Cistercians developed the institution of the lay brotherhood on an unprecedented scale and to its fullest extent, it was not original to them but had been a distinctive feature of the monastic reform associated with the eremitical movement a century earlier. Several centuries before, however, the word *conversus* had been widely used to mean those adults who had themselves chosen the monastic life as distinct from the child-oblates, *oblati*—those offered to the monastery by their parents, described in the Rule as "the offering of the sons of the rich and of the poor"[116]—and *nutriti*, those given board in the monastery. By the twelfth century a confusion of terminology had developed when *conversi* came to mean either Benedictine monks who had entered as adults or Cistercian lay brothers. To distinguish between the two, the earlier monk *conversi* have been termed the "old type" and the Cistercian lay brothers, and those belonging to the other newer orders, the "new type."[117] The greater literacy and acquaintance with the liturgy of the child-oblates or *oblati* who had been educated in monastic traditions and had been in the monastery since childhood resulted in the other group, the *conversi*, being sometimes referred to as *monachi illiterati*. Little by little *conversus* became synonymous with *illiteratus*.[118] As the two titles were equally interchangeable when referring to lay brothers, it is hardly surprising that the distinctions have been blurred and that the "old style" has sometimes been confused with the "new

[114] For the origin of lay brothers and the emergence of the two types, see Hoffmann 1905, 9–15; Hallinger 1956, 1–104; Donnelly 1949, 4–14; Lekai 1977, 334–35.

[115] *RB* 58.1, 17 (McCann 1976, 62, 63).

[116] *RB* 59 (McCann 1976, 65).

[117] Dom Jean Leclercq referred to this as the "nouvelle manière" or "new way" (Leclercq 1965, 240).

[118] Ducourneau 1929, 147–49.

style." The confusion is perhaps greatest as regards Cluny, where the "new style" lay brothers were introduced in the last decade of the eleventh century but where the "old style" are known to have coexisted with the new for a long time. Therefore, when around 1146 Abbot Peter the Venerable referred to *conversi barbati* at Cluny it is not clear whether he had the old or the new in mind.[119]

Groups of laymen who performed practical tasks on behalf of the monks and at the same time sometimes acted as go-betweens with the local secular community had from an early date been attached to monasteries. Known as the *familia*, they have been described as "a half-way stage between the professed *conversi* and the hired paid workers and servants."[120] Kassius Hallinger asserts that the lay brotherhood owed its origin to the closer integration into the monastic community of some of these laymen who wanted to identify more closely with the ideals of the monks without becoming monks and whose status was, bit by bit, defined and regularized.[121] Just as the distinction between the "old" and the "new" type of *conversus* is blurred, the transition from the *familia* into what we recognize as the lay brother community is unclear. The "new" type is thought to have begun with the eleventh-century eremitical movement in Italy. In about 1012 Romuald of Camaldoli formed a group of lay servants into an organized body next to his hermitage. It became an indispensable aid to the hermit-monks that enabled them to live out their vocation of solitude. Its members were described as lay servants who "lived like monks and were employed in the external work of the monastery" (*qui monastico more vivebant, curamque exercebant rerum exteriorum monasterii*).[122] His example was followed by John Gualbert at Vallombrosa in 1039–1059, by Peter Damian at Fonte Avellana in 1143–1158, and was introduced independently of the earlier Italian examples by the Swabian reform congregation of Hirsau before 1079; from there it spread to a number of other important

[119] Hallinger 1956, 20; Constable 1973, 326.
[120] Williams 1998, 88.
[121] Hallinger 1956, 59.
[122] Leclercq 1965, 239.

German abbeys: Ottobeuren in 1102, Admont in 1104, Lorsch in 1105, and Michelsberg in Bamberg in 1112. Cluny, as we saw, introduced lay brothers in the last decade of the eleventh century, a few years later than the Carthusians, who provided for lay brothers from the time of their foundation in 1084.[123] The regulations governing the lay brothers in these disparate communities across many parts of Europe naturally varied according to the variety of functions expected of them. The question here is: when were they introduced by the Cistercians?

## When Were Lay Brothers Introduced?

The paragraph in the *Exordium Parvum* announcing the decision to introduce "bearded laybrothers . . . and also hired hands" (*conversos laicos barbatos . . . et homines etiam mercenarios*) follows the Cîteaux monks' discussion of "by what planning, by what device, by what management, they would support themselves in this life"[124] and inevitably elicits the question "when?"

A number of conflicting answers to this have been offered. The suggestion by Eberhard Hoffmann, repeated by Ducourneau and then again by James Donnelly, that Cistercian *conversi* may have been introduced in 1100 or 1101, cannot be substantiated,[125] for the situation the monks foresaw of not being able to "fully observe, day and night, the precepts of the Rule"[126] without assistance would not arise until they had acquired lands sufficiently far removed from Cîteaux to prevent them from cultivating these without neglecting their all-important choir duties. When Robert and his companions settled at Cîteaux in 1098 the demesne was sufficient in size to support them, and no outside help would have

---

[123] Hallinger 1956, 12–32.

[124] *EP* 15 (Waddell 1999, 254): *quo ingenio, quove artificio, seu quo exercitio in hac vita . . . sustentarent.*

[125] Hoffmann 1905, 28; Ducourneau 1929, 140; Donnelly 1949, 12. According to Werner Rösener (2009, 83) "the lay brother institution was one of the peculiarities of the Cistercian constitution from the beginning."

[126] *EP* 15 (Waddell 1999, 254): *non intelligebant se plenarie die sive nocte precepta regule posse servare.*

been required. A year later he returned to Molesme and those monks who wanted to were given permission to follow him.[127] At Cîteaux the years that followed were difficult and, as the situation remained unchanged, it is unlikely, as tentatively suggested by Terryl Kinder, that lay brothers were introduced during the abbacy of Robert's successor, Alberic—in other words, before 1108.[128] According to Megan Cassidy-Welsh "lay brothers were a constituent part of the Cistercian Order almost from its legislative inception"; in other words, they were not introduced until the beginning of Stephen Harding's abbacy in 1108.[129] The statement in the *Exordium Parvum* that "only rarely did anyone come there in those days to imitate them"[130] may be seen, according to Adriaan Bredero,[131] as an exaggeration to highlight the arrival of thirty recruits under Saint Bernard's leadership and to make Bernard look as if he were the savior of the Cistercian experiment. In fact, preparations for a new foundation appear to have been in progress before the arrival of Bernard and his companions in 1113, but by this time the situation had already begun to change and the need for assistance would soon arise. The New Monastery, as Cîteaux was known at the time, "in a short time made no little progress—God working withal—in its holy way of life; it shone in popular esteem, it grew in necessary resources."[132] The foundation document of the first daughter of Cîteaux, La Ferté, states that fifteen years after its founding in 1113 "the number of brethren at Cîteaux was such that neither the existing estates were sufficient to support them, nor could the place where they lived conveniently accommodate them."[133] Although the pressure was relieved by the four new foundations in four years, La Ferté, Pontigny, Clairvaux, and Morimond, the problem of how to deal with the changed situation following

---

[127] *EP* 7 (Waddell 1999, 424).

[128] Kinder 1997, 307.

[129] Cassidy-Welsh 2001, 169.

[130] *EP* 16 (Waddell 1999, 256): *quod raro quis illis diebus illuc ad eos imitandos venerit.*

[131] Bredero 1996, 201–02.

[132] *EC* 2 (Waddell 1999, 401): *in brevi non mediocriter, Deo cooperante, in sancta conversatione profecit, opinione claruit, rebus necessaris crevit.*

[133] *Cîteaux* 1961, 66–67.

the acquisition of land not in the immediate vicinity of the abbey needed to be addressed. As with much of early Cistercian legislation, the introduction of *conversi* was the pragmatic response. This is likely to have taken place shortly after the first four foundations at a date Dubois has estimated to before 1115 and Hallinger as between 1115 and 1119.[134]

These suggested dates are corroborated by evidence from the manuscript illuminations produced in the Cîteaux scriptorium in 1109 and 1111.[135] The image of a monk in a white cowl in Stephen Harding's Bible, completed in 1109, is the earliest known portrayal of a Cistercian monk. The manuscript of Gregory the Great's *Moralia in Job*, completed two years later, has altogether five illuminated initials with genre scenes of monks at work and one of a monk in a scene of a violent struggle.[136] One of the work scenes has a monk in a threadbare habit attacking the trunk of a tree with an axe while a well-dressed young man is perched at the top of the tree lopping branches. He is too well dressed to be one of the hired laborers the Cistercians employed and is undoubtedly a young nobleman belonging to the class to which a large number of the early Cistercian recruits belonged, and can therefore be assumed to be one of the earliest novices, whose distinctive habit was not introduced until the thirteenth century. Three further initials depict either other novices or hired hands. The total absence of portrayals of lay brothers in the early Cîteaux manuscripts may be interpreted as an indication that they were not introduced until after 1111.[137]

The period between 1111 and 1119 seems the likeliest for the introduction of *conversi*. By 1115 Cîteaux had four daughter houses and Stephen Harding, anxious to ensure unity of observance, would have wanted to address himself to the composition of a customary for his monks, the *Ecclesiastica officia*. This he followed by usages

[134] Dubois 1972, 168; Hallinger 1956, 10.

[135] For these see Zaluska 1989.

[136] Some of these are illustrated in France 1998, color plate 24 and illustrations 37, 45, and 134.

[137] As suggested by Auberger 1986, 141–42.

for the lay brothers; Waddell suggests a date in the early 1120s.[138] The *Ecclesiastica officia*, like the *Usus conversorum*, was written by Stephen Harding himself[139] and also contains a number of regulations affecting lay brothers. They were, for example, required to clean the church, the cloister, and the chapter house on Good Friday.[140] This and other detailed requirements in both usages indicate that by the early 1120s the lay-brother institution was well established, but the earliest explicit mention of lay brothers occurs in the letter of confirmation of the *Carta caritatis prior* by Pope Callistus II on 23 December 1119, in which they are referred to as *conversi laici*.[141]

---

[138] Waddell 2000, 20.

[139] Waddell 2000, 21.

[140] *EO* 22 (Griesser 1956, 201): *laici fratres refectionis hora vel aliis quibus poterunt horis claustrum et capitulum mundent.*

[141] Waddell 1999, 452.

# Chapter 2

# Manual Labor of Monks before the Lay Brothers

## "The Purity of the Rule"

The reason for the departure of Robert and his twenty-one companions from Molesme, as given in the *Exordium Cistercii*, the account of Cistercian origins, is as follows:

> So it was that the lovers of the virtues soon enough began thinking upon poverty, fruitful mother of a virile stock, at the same time perceiving that, though one could live there in a holy and respectable manner, this still fell short of their desire and purpose to observe the Rule they had professed.[1]

The desire of the early Cistercians for a stricter interpretation of the Rule of Saint Benedict is well known and, as previously mentioned, is referred to in all early Cistercian texts as well as being commented upon by a number of outside observers.

For the Benedictine Orderic Vitalis, writing in about 1135, the internal debate that had gone on between the two factions at Molesme had revolved around their attitude to manual labor. He comments approvingly on monastic founders who in the past had "introduced numerous dependents to carry out all the external

---

[1] *EC* 1 (Waddell 1999, 400): *Unde et mox virtutum amatores et paupertate faecunda virorum cogitare coeperunt. Simulque advertentes ibidem, etsi sancta honesteque viveretur, minus tamen pro sui desiderio atque proposito, ipsam quam professi fuerant Regulam observari.*

duties and established monks to devote their time to sacred reading, devout prayers for their benefactors, and the divine office."[2] He adds that it is "for peasants to perform work in the fields," while "monks who have voluntarily renounced the vanities of this world for the service of the King of Kings live peacefully in their enclosed cloisters."[3] The final straw for Orderic, as for the opponents of the reforming party at Molesme, was that

> peasants, whose true lot is continual toil, might grow use-
> less through idleness and should lounge lasciviously, wasting
> their time in coarse laughter and idle sport; or that noble
> knights and gifted philosophers and learned scholars who
> have renounced the world should be compelled to spend
> their time in servile and unbecoming labors and occupations
> like lowborn servants in order to earn their bread.[4]

Disapproval of the devotion of the Cistercians to manual labor was also voiced by Peter the Venerable, the great abbot of Cluny, when he said: "We have shown that it is not possible for a people fed on a poor vegetable diet to cope with the hard work that tough rural folk can undertake. Being undernourished they do not have the strength for such a hard life, for sometimes they have to bear the strong heat of the day, sometimes the hazards of rain storms, sometimes bitter cold and frosts."[5]

---

[2] Orderic Vitalis 1969–80, 4:318-20: *multitudinemque clientum ad exteriora ministeria pleniter explenda subegerunt, monachosque lectionibus et sacris orationibus pro cunctis benefactoribus suis et coelestibus ministeriis intentos esse constituerunt.*

[3] Orderic Vitalis 1969–80, 4:320–21: *ut rustici ruralia sicut decet peragant opera . . . monachi autem qui sponte relictis huius mundi vanitatibus regi regum militant claustralibus septis.*

[4] Orderic Vitalis 1969–80, 4:320–21: *Absit ut rustici torpescant ocio, saturique lascivientes cachinnis et inani vacent ludicro, quorum genuine sors labori dedita est assiduo egregii vero milites et arguti philosophi ac dicaces scholastici si renunciant seculo, cogantur servilibus et incongruis more vilium mancipiorum studiis seu laboribus occupari pro victu proprio.*

[5] Peter the Venerable, Letter 28 (PL 189:144): *Et ut primo impossibile demon-stremus quomodo fieri potest, ut gens languida, oleribus et leguminibus fere nullas vires corporandibus, imo ipsam vitam vix sustentantibus enutrita, et idcirco non parum debilitata, asperrmum ipsis quoque rusticis et bubulcis agriculturae laborem ferat, et tam duram ruris*

The argument between the Benedictines and the reformers continued, but Robert "withdrew with twelve men of like mind" (*recessit ab eis cum XII sibi assentientibus*)[6] and settled at Cîteaux. Writing in the 1140s, Philip of Harvengt claimed that with the move from Molesme to Cîteaux the "monastic order, formerly dead, was revived: there the old ashes were poked . . . and the Rule of Benedict recovered in our times the truth of the letter."[7]

The lesson of Molesme was remembered in the later move of a reforming party from the English Benedictine abbey of Saint Mary's, York, which led to the foundation of Fountains in Yorkshire as a Cistercian abbey. The aim of the monks there was the same as that of the founding fathers of Cîteaux: "to follow Christ in voluntary poverty and bear His cross; to be allowed to observe fully the Gospel and the Rule of the blessed father Benedict."[8]

## The Cistercian Work Ethic

The restoration of manual labor to its rightful place in the monastic horarium was one of the main planks of the Cistercian reform. The Benedictine ideal of a balance between the three main elements of monastic life—liturgical prayer, reading, and manual labor (*Opus Dei, lectio divina, and labor manuum*)—had over the years given way to one in which the proliferation of offices and extra liturgical ceremonies had taken over virtually the whole day, leaving little or no time for other activities. The demarcation among the three was not fixed: spiritual reading was a form of worship, and it was possible to pray while working. In the dialogue between a Cluniac and a Cistercian the Cistercian asserts that "while at work, those who love and fear God not only sing the whole Psalter . . .

---

*eversionem et surversionem, aliquando aestus ardore, aliquando imbrium, nivium et frigoris importunitate societa patiatur?*

[6] Orderic Vitalis 1969–80, 4:322–23.

[7] Philip of Harvengt, *De institutione clericorum*, 4:125 (PL 203:836–37), trans. Constable 1985, 43.

[8] *Fountains* 1863, 23–24: *Quatinus pauperem Christum in voluntaria paupertate sequerentur, et Christi crucem in corpore suo portare, idemque Evangelicam pacem regulamque plene beati patris Benedicti observare non impedirentur.*

but suffer heartfelt remorse and frequently shed tears."[9] Manual labor was both essential, as a means of subsistence following the Cistercian rejection of the traditional monastic income from rents, tithes, and the possession of churches, and intrinsic to a life of poverty and a way to salvation. It formed an essential part of monastic life as defined by Saint Benedict in chapter 48 of the Rule: "Idleness is the enemy of the soul. The brethren, therefore, must be occupied at stated hours in manual labor," and only if this is observed are they truly monks "when they live by the labor of their hands, like our father and the apostles."[10] A manuscript of statutes from Vauclair (Aisne) gives a long list of occupations: scribes, book repairers and book binders, Mass host bakers, glass blowers, locksmiths, and wood turners,[11] crafts to be practiced within the enclosure in accordance with the Rule in order to facilitate attendance at Office.[12]

The early Cistercian work ethic was absolutely central to the eleventh-century reform and it therefore comes as a surprise that the introduction of lay brothers has led a number of scholars, in their enthusiasm for the new institution, either to underrate or altogether to ignore the contribution of the monks themselves to the Order's tremendous economic growth. Although not dismissing the input of the monks altogether, James Donnelly asserts that the *conversi* "would save the choir monks from the distractions of temporal business and too frequent contact with the secular world,"[13] and in another work devoted entirely to the Cistercian lay brothers Michael Toepfer says that their care of the abbeys' material provision allowed the monks to devote themselves predominantly to the *Opus*

---

[9] *Dialogus duorum monachorum* 2:54 (Idung of Prüfening 1990, 149; CF 33:94): *In ipso quoque labore per misericordiam dei non solum integri psalterii decantationes, sed etiam cordis compunctiones et lacrimarum effusiones frequenter fiunt a timentibus et amantibus deum.*

[10] *RB* 48 (McCann 1976, 53).

[11] Waddell 2002, 585: *Monachi non scribant, nec aliquam artem exerceant, nec libros emendent vel ligent, vel hostias faciant, aut vitreos aut clavos aut tornaturum extra terminos, nisi cementarii et carpentarii, et qui hostias faciunt.*

[12] *RB* 66 (McCann 1976, 74).

[13] Donnelly 1949, 17.

*Dei* and *lectio divina*.[14] In his study of Cistercian granges in Lower Saxony, Hans Wiswe asserts that the concept of "the Benedictine *ora et labora* was as it were rationalized and thereby intensified by splitting the two component parts" between the two groups, monks and lay brothers.[15] According to Megan Cassidy-Welch the *conversi*'s main task was manual work, "leaving the choir monks free to concentrate on prayer." Marcel Aubert says that "the exploitation of the estate rested almost entirely on the lay brothers."[16] A more negative view is expressed by Ludo Milis:

> The lay brethren who actually did the work in the fields, as the translation of the ideal of manual labor into reality, were a double substitute: on the one hand for the monks to whom (and to whom only) the Rule of Saint Benedict applied, and whose fast did not physically allow more than a ritualized participation in agricultural work, on the other hand as a substitute for the labor done by the tenants.[17]

Dom Jacques Winandy comments tersely: "the abandonment of manual labor led to the institution of lay brothers."[18]

Although a number of scholars have either altogether ignored the contribution of the monks to the Cistercian economy in the twelfth century or at least underestimated it, it is generally agreed that the spectacular material success of the Order could not have

[14] Toepfer 1983, 29: "Indem die Gruppe der Konversen gerade in diesem Betrieb [materielle Versorgung] tätig wurde, habe sie es den Mönchen erlaubt, sich im vorgeschriebenen Masse dem Chorgebiet, Gottesdienst und Studium zu widmen." See Cassidy-Welch 2001, 169; Aubert 1947, 1:55: "L'exploitation du domaine reposait presque entièrement sur les convers."

[15] Wiswe 1953, 92: "Das benediktinische 'ora et labora' wurde gleichsam durch Zerlegung in seine beiden Bestandteile rationalisiert und damit intensifiziert."

[16] Cassidy-Welch 2001, 169; Aubert 1947, 1:55: "L'exploitation du domaine reposait presque entièrement sur les convers."

[17] Milis 1992, 33.

[18] Jacques Winandy, *La Vie Contemplative* (1950), 139, quoted in Hallinger 1956, 43: "L'abandon du travail manuel a eu pour consequence l'institution des frères convers."

been achieved without the lay brothers.[19] At the same time it is inconceivable that the monks, whose reform was to a large measure based on restoring manual labor to the monastic horarium, would in the twelfth century have deviated from the ideal defined in the *Instituta*. After all, one of the reasons for the reform was, according to the prologue of the *Exordium parvum*, that the monks "may sweat and toil even to the last gasp in the strait and narrow way which the Rule points out; till at last, having laid aside the burden of flesh, they happily repose in everlasting rest."[20] On occasion the eagerness of the monks for farm work seems to have gone too far. John of Forde, writing in the second half of the twelfth century, refers to monks so absorbed in fieldwork that they forgot about the spiritual welfare of their brethren and of themselves: "They labor with such great sweatings of their brow to bring forth from the earth bread that will perish, that they have no energy left for the bread which does not perish but endures to life everlasting."[21]

The *Instituta* decreed that "Monks of our Order should derive their means of subsistence from the work of their hands, from farming, and from animal husbandry."[22] That monks were not exempt from manual labor is clear from the chapters in the *Ecclesiastica officia* (the early Cistercian customary written during the abbacy of Stephen Harding) on "Work" (*De labore*), in which detailed regulations are laid down on "The Seasons of Mowing and Harvest" (*De tempore secationis et messionis*), in which the additional work required at harvest time is specified.[23] The monks' presence at the granges

---

[19] For example, Lekai 1977, 282: "The monks' often spectacular success can be adequately explained on the grounds of three basic factors: the accumulation of extensive tracts of land; the employment of lay brothers in large numbers; consistent planning and efficient administration."

[20] *EP* Prologue (Waddell 1999, 233): *in arta et angusta via quam regula demonstrat usque ad exhalationem spiritus desudent, quatenus deposita carnis sarcina, in requie sempiterna feliciter pausent.*

[21] John of Ford, Sermon 89 (Beckett 1977–1984, 6:78).

[22] *Instituta Generalis Capituli* (Waddell 1999, 459): *Monachis nostri Ordinis debet provenire victus de labore manuum, de cultu terrarum, de nutrimento pecorum.*

[23] *EO* 75 and 84 (Griesser 1956, 241–42; 248–49).

during the harvest is suggested by statutes dated 1180 and 1194.[24] Evidence of their part in the material success of the order as well as admiration for the sacrifice this entailed for the large number of noblemen and scholars who joined their ranks is plentiful. In a letter to a friend, Peter de Roya, one of Saint Bernard's novices, wrote of the monks of Clairvaux:

> It is impossible to describe the impression produced on the mind by the sight of these men when engaged at work, or when on the way to or from the scene of their labors. Everywhere it can be seen that they are led, not by their own spirit, but by the spirit of God. For they accomplish every action with such tranquility of mind, such unalterable serenity of expression, such beautiful and edifying order that, although they work extremely hard, somehow they always seem at rest and never show signs of fatigue, no matter how heavy their toil.[25]

The best-known story of monks at work is one that tells of the Virgin, accompanied by Mary Magdalene and Elizabeth the mother of John the Baptist, coming down from the hills above Clairvaux at harvest time to wipe the sweat from the brows of the hardworking monks. The importance attached to the story was such that it is found in five different versions.[26] The *Collectaneum Clarevallense* has a chapter entitled "How the Blessed Mother of God visited the monks of Clairvaux at harvest time" and protected them against the temptations they might be exposed to away from the monastic enclosure.[27] In Herbert's *Liber miraculorum* the purpose is said to be a visitation of the harvesting monks: *ad visitandos messores suos venit.*[28] In the *Exordium magnum* the monk who witnesses the vision is named as Rainald and the reapers include lay brothers as well as monks.[29] The story is repeated by Caesarius of Heisterbach, who substituted Mary's mother Anne for Elizabeth. Here the three

---

[24] *Statuta* 1180.10 (Waddell 2002, 90); 1194.61 (Waddell 2002, 304–5).
[25] Quoted in Luddy 1950, 349–50.
[26] For this, see McGuire 1983, 39–40.
[27] *CC* 4.16 (Legendre 2005, 289).
[28] *LM* 1.1 (PL 185:1274).
[29] *EM* 3.13 (Griesser 176–77).

saints are not inspecting the monks but giving them comfort from the heat of the sun by fanning them with the flaps of their sleeves. Caesarius records that the impact of the story on him was so great that it was responsible for his conversion.[30] He refers to the story later and reverts to the original visitors, Mary, Mary Magdalene, and Elizabeth. A monk is said to have repeatedly asked the saintly lay brother Henry, master of the Himmerod grange of Hart, to intercede for him: "One day after saying Compline in the chapel of the grange of which he was head, he was praying for him, when as he prayed, there appeared to him three matrons of wonderful beauty."[31] The three were named as Mary, Mary Magdalene, and Elizabeth. After they disappeared he knew that his prayer had been answered when he saw a dove descend upon the head of the monk.

The same admiration for the industry of the monks of Øm in Denmark was shown by their bishop, Sven of Århus (1166–1191). According to the Øm Chronicle, "if he met the community going out to work or returning home, he retreated, saying that he was un-worthy to meet those for whom the angels of God stood watch and among whom they dwelt," and if he was on horseback he and those who accompanied him would dismount until the monks had passed.[32]

Abbots were not exempt from work in the fields. Even the head of a large house like Saint Aelred of Rievaulx, though weak in body, "did not spare the soft skin of his hands, but manfully wielded with his slender fingers the rough tools of his fieldtasks to the admiration of all."[33] Even Saint Bernard was not spared. Like so many of the early recruits of noble birth he did not find work easy. According to the *Vita prima*, at harvest time he had neither the strength nor the skill (*impotens et nescius*) to join the monks in

---

[30] *DM* 1.17 (Strange 1:24–25; Scott and Bland 1:25–26). For the way the vision changed the life of Caesarius of Heisterbach, see Mula 2010, 904.

[31] *DM* 7.15 (Strange 2:17; Scott and Bland 1:472–73): *Quod cum promisisset, et die quadam dicto completario in oratorio grangiae, cuius magister erat, pro ipso preces funderet, apparuerunt oranti tres matronae mirae pulchritudinis.*

[32] *Scriptores Minores* 1917–1922, 2:188.

[33] Daniel, Vita A 12; Powicke 1950, 22; CF 57:105–06: *Nec pepercit pelli manuum suarum tenerrime, quin pocius digitos graciles grossa utensilia rusticorum operum viriliter complectens, admirabiles conatus expressit coram omnibus.*

harvesting. Bernard was ordered to rest, but saddened at this, "he took refuge in prayer and with abundant tears begged God to be given the grace for harvesting" (*ad orationem confugit, cum magnis lacrymis postulans a Deo donari sibi gratiam metendi*). His prayer was answered, and as the reward, harvesting became the work he liked best.[34] Speaking of one of Bernard's successors at Clairvaux, Henry de Marcy (1176–1179), Conrad of Eberbach suggests that abbots did not always participate at harvest time, but he says that Henry "even worked with his hands, sweating it out sometimes with the rest of the brothers." Conrad recounts how "one day, at harvest time, this venerable abbot was energetically working with his brethren in harvesting the hay from the meadows at the grange on the other side of the river Aube near the monastery of Clairvaux."[35] Henry was in fact so keen to give an example to his monks that when he was asked to anoint a lay brother who was near death he sent a substitute, a decision for which he was castigated and one he was to regret even after he had been made a cardinal.

## The Founding Ideals in *Exempla* and Manuscript Illumination

Evidence from the thirteenth century tells us that a century later the founding ideals relating to monastic work were still alive. Caesarius of Heisterbach, in his *Dialogue on Miracles,* tells of a lay brother from Himmerod, Mengoz, who had injured himself while working in the kitchen and was ordered by his abbot not to die while the abbot was away at General Chapter at Cîteaux. When the abbot returned he heard the board being struck and the bells ringing, thus telling him that the brother had died.[36] The abbot woke him up and asked him where he was, to which he replied:

---

[34] *VP* 1.24 (PL 185:240–41).

[35] *EM* 2.30 (Griesser 137): *etiam labori manuum aliquoties pro tempore cum ceteris fratribus insudabat. . . . Accidit enim quadam vice, ut isdem venerabilis abbas tempore secationis colligendo foeno instans in pratis grangiae, quae trans flumen Albam sita proxima est monasterio Claraevallis, cum fratribus suis impigre laboraret.* This was the grange of Outre Aube.

[36] According to the *Ecclesiastica officia*, when a monk dies a wooden gong is beaten and the church bell is rung four times over (*EO* 94; Griesser 1956, 257).

"In paradise. A golden seat was set for me at the feet of our Lord and when you called me back Dom Isenbard, our sacristan, came and dragged me from that seat," whereupon he ordered Mendoz to return to the abbot. Mendoz then went on: "I saw Isenbard in great glory, but on his foot appeared a spot, because when he was with us, he went out to work unwillingly." Caesarius's novice enquired why "a spot should appear on the glory of an inhabitant of heaven," to which Caesarius's monk answered that it was "for the sake of the living, that the glory might be a comfort to a monk of good life and the spot a warning to those who are careless."[37] Although Isenbard had been punctilious in his attendance in choir, his reluctance to play his part in the manual work of his community had left a permanent mark.

The dedication of the early monks to manual labor before the introduction of lay brothers is well documented in the form of manuscript illumination. An example is found in the commentary of Saint Gregory the Great on the book of Job made in the Cîteaux scriptorium around 1111, commissioned by Stephen Harding and perhaps even the work of the abbot himself.[38] One of the scenes represents the archetypal agricultural activity of harvesting grain. On the right the curved figure of a tonsured monk in a tattered brown tunic and scapular is in the process of cutting some of the grain with a sickle, forming, together with some of the grain still standing, an easily recognizable initial *Q(ui)*.[39] That three of the monastic work scenes show monks cutting down trees, one of them aided by a novice,[40] is no coincidence, for Cîteaux and many other

---

[37] *DM* 11.11 (Strange 2:278; Scott and Bland 2:245–46): "*In paradiso. Posita mihi erat sedes aurea secus pedes Dominae nostrae; et cum me revocares advenit dominus Ysenbardus sacrista noster, trahensque me de sede eadem. . . . Vidi eundem Ysenbardum in multa Gloria, in cuius pede apparuit macula, eo quod nobiscum existens, invitus iret.*" . . . "*Propter viventes visio eadem ostensa erat, ut Gloria monachis bene viventibus esset ad consolationem, macula vero negligentibus ad corruptionem.*"

[38] Dijon, Bibliothèque municipale MSS 168, 169, 170, 173. The attribution is tentatively given in Zaluska 1989, 77. Illustrated in France 1998, illus. 134.

[39] Dijon, Bibl. mun. MS 170, fol. 75v.

[40] Dijon, Bibl. mun. MS 170, fol. 59r; MS 173, fol. 167r, and MS 173, fol. 41r, illustrated in France 1998, color plate 24; Rudolph 1997, illus. 35 and 23.

monasteries were in forest areas, as Orderic Vitalis attests when he says that "they built monasteries with their own hands in lonely, wooded places." The need for clearing is amply revealed by these images.

Another vital part of daily life, domestic work, the kind of activity that would have taken place in the southern cloister range, is represented by a picture of two monks folding linen, which ingeniously forms the initial *M* at the beginning of book 12.[41] There are three more work scenes, two of them referring to the agrarian economy of the Cistercians. One of them has a youth threshing, his contorted figure and the flail he yields forming the initial *S*, while two youths picking grapes, evidence of the importance of winemaking in the economy of Cîteaux, are depicted within the initial *E*. A third initial depicts three men, two of them folding some cloth while the third sits on the ground with something on his lap that resembles a bundle of wool.[42] The figures in the last three images are well-dressed, have neat hair and elegant pointed shoes, and are most likely young noblemen and therefore the earliest representations of Cistercian novices who, as already mentioned,[43] did not at first have their own habit, although it is also possible that they may be among the hired laborers used by the Cistercians. As has been noted, the fact that no lay brothers feature in the *Moralia in Job* illuminations suggests that they may not have been introduced by the time these were produced in 1111.[44]

After the Cistercians introduced lay brothers, around 1120, the two groups worked alongside each other aided by hired laborers. As L. M. Sullivan has pointed out, the distinction between the tasks they performed was not one of varying occupations as much as of locations.[45] Both performed domestic tasks, worked in the various

[41] Dijon, Bibl. mun. MS 170, fol. 20r, illustrated in Rudolph 1997, illus. 16.

[42] Dijon, Bibl. mun. MS 173, fol. 148r; MS 170, fol. 32r; and MS 173, fol. 92v, illustrated in Rudolph 1997, illus. 33, 17, and 28.

[43] See chap. 1, p 34.

[44] The Cîteaux workers have sometimes mistakenly been described as lay brothers (e.g., in Coppack 1993, color plate 3), although, being tonsured, they are clearly monks.

[45] Sullivan 1989, 179.

workshops, and participated in the agricultural and horticultural work on the home farm; work on the granges, however, was the preserve of lay brothers alone. As the Cistercian in the dialogue with the Cluniac monk puts it: "We put great effort into farming which God created and instituted. We all work in common, we [choir monks], our lay brothers and our hired hands, each according to his capability, and we all make our living in common by our labor."[46]

From charter evidence we know that monks were still working in the fields alongside lay brothers in southern France at abbeys like Valmagne in the 1160s and even later.[47] Pictorial evidence of the two groups working together in felling trees is provided by a unique miniature that covers the full width of a folio in an English manuscript of the *Commentary on the Apocalypse* by the Franciscan friar Alexander, dated to the third quarter of the thirteenth century.[48] A note in the margin on the left reads: "Here is the monastery of Cîteaux whose brothers are engaged in manual labor and whose abbot of the same place sent four abbots with a group of brothers to different places. One of these was blessed Bernard who was sent to Clairvaux."[49] The figure on the far left is Stephen Harding, before whom a group of monks, the abbots of the first four daughter houses, are kneeling. An explanatory note in the right margin tells us that the four figures on the far right, each holding a book and depicted within niches of different design and color, represent the founding abbots of the four "elder daughters" referred to in the text. In the middle, dominating the scene and indicative of the centrality of *labor manuum*, are the six large figures, each wearing a similar habit consisting of a tunic and a scapular with hood attached and each wielding an axe. Three of them are tonsured and therefore represent monks, while the other three—the one on the

---

[46] Idung of Prüfening 1717, cols. 1623-24: *Rusticationi quam Deus creavit, et instituit, operam damus, et omnes in commune laboramus, nos et fratres nostri, et mercenarii nostri, unusquisque secundam suam possibilitatem, et omnes communiter de labore nostro vivimus.* Trans. Idung of Prüfening 1977, 94.

[47] Berman 2000, 167 and 211.

[48] Illustrated in France 1998, color plate 6.

[49] Cambridge, University Library, MS Mm. 5, 31, fol. 1135.

extreme left, the one on the extreme right, and the one in the
middle holding on to the tree—have the distinctive fringe that
identifies them as *conversi* and, although it is less clear, they are also
bearded. We have here a unique example of a depiction of the two
groups engaged side by side in the same occupation.

## Monks and Lay Brothers as Builders

The critic of the Cistercians, Walter Map, marveled at the way
the monks lived "like the apostles by the work of their own hands,"
although he claimed that it was not to be so for long.[50] By the time
he and Orderic were writing, lay brothers had been introduced
and it is possible that they and other early commentators were
including them as well as monks when praising their achievement
in the direct exploitation of their lands, even though they were
not specifically mentioned. In the same way, when Orderic said
that "they have built monasteries with their own hands in lonely,
wooded places" he may have had both groups in mind, and yet the
earliest wooden buildings at Cîteaux must have been the work of
the monks on their own, aided by hired laborers, as they predated
the arrival of lay brothers by more than a decade. According to the
*Exordium Cistercii* "they found a desert place and began building it
into an abbey" (*inventam heremum in abbatiam construere coeperunt*),[51]
and, in the words of the *Exordium parvum* the duke of Burgundy,
Odo, "completed from his own resources the wooden monastery
they had begun" (*monasterium ligneum quod inceperunt de suis totum
consummavit*).[52] Soon afterwards, and again before the lay brothers
were introduced, the wooden buildings were replaced by the chapel
built in stone, which was consecrated in 1106.[53]

Even after the introduction of lay brothers, monks remained active as builders, often aided by hired laborers. According to the *Vita
Prima*, when new buildings were constructed at Clairvaux in 1135,

[50] Walter Map 1983, 77.
[51] *EC* 2 (Waddell 1999, 401).
[52] *EP* 3 (Waddell 1999, 421).
[53] Aubert 1947, 1:152; Ferguson 1983, 74–75.

"with this abundance of funds, workmen were speedily hired. The brethren too engaged themselves on the job in every way. Some hewed timber; some shaped stone; some laid walls."[54] Although it is not clear who these brethren were, the absence of distinction suggests that they consisted of monks as well as lay brothers. The monks who left Saint Mary's Abbey in York originally lived under a giant elm tree, for "there were no shaped timbers, no dressed stones, but only a poor hut and, as it were, a dwelling covered in humble thatch for the shepherds."[55] In 1133 Saint Bernard sent Geoffrey d'Ainai, a monk, to help in the building of Fountains. Before this he already "had set in order and established many monasteries, especially those whose members by the counsel of the holy man [Bernard] changed the habit for greater perfection of their life and submitted themselves to the monastery of Clairvaux."[56] Other monks trained by him were involved in the construction of some of the daughter houses: Adam set out Kirkstead (1139), Woburn (1145), and Vaudey (1147), while Robert, the founding abbot, set out the buildings of Newminster (1138) and Alexander, the first abbot of Kirkstall (1147–1182) was responsible for setting out the final site.[57]

The earliest Cistercian buildings were almost always constructed of wood, which was both cheaper and easier to erect than stone.[58] According to the Cistercian constitution "a new abbot is not to be sent to a new place . . . without there having first been constructed these places: oratory, refectory, dormitory, guest quarters, and gatehouse—so that they may straightaway serve God there and live there in keeping with the Rule."[59]

---

[54] *VP* 2:5.31 (PL 185:285): *Abundantibus sumptibus, conductis festinanter operariis, ipsi fratres per omnia incumbebant operibus. Alii caedebant ligna, alii lapides conquadrabant, alii muros struebant.*

[55] *Memorials of Fountains* 1863, 34: *Nulla ibi ligna dolata, nulla saxa complanata, sed pauper tugurium et pastorum quasi tabernaculum, humili desuper cespite contectum.*

[56] *Memorials of Fountains* 1863, 46–47.

[57] Ferguson 1983, 80–86; Robinson 2006, 51; 307, n. 67.

[58] For this see Ferguson 1983, 74–86.

[59] *EC* 9 (Waddell 1999, 408): *Non mittendum esse abbatem novum in locum novellum . . . nisi prius extructis hiis officinis: oratorio, refectorio, dormitorio, cella hospitum, et portarii, quatenus ibi statim et Deo servire et regulariter vivere possint.*

The lay patron was usually responsible for providing these rudimentary buildings and, as the quotation implies, they were built for the monks and not by them. In some cases, however, the monks and lay brothers may themselves have been involved. The chronicle of the Danish abbey, Øm, records how, after four years at an unsuitable site, they moved in 1172 to their "new home having first erected houses, or rather huts" (*erectis in novo loco tuguriis potius quam domibus*).[60] And at Rievaulx in Yorkshire the monks coming from Clairvaux "set up their huts near Helmsley . . . by a powerful stream called the Rie" in 1132.[61] The monks sent by Saint Bernard as an advance party "to investigate the situation carefully and report back to me faithfully" (as Bernard said in a letter)[62] may have played some part in the erection of the "huts."

Prior to the settlement of an abbot with twelve monks and ten lay brothers at Barnoldswick in Yorkshire, given to the monks of Fountains by Henry de Lacy in 1147, and five years before their final move to Kirkstall, the abbot of Fountains sent an advance party of "brothers to build humble buildings according to the custom of the Order and called the place Mount Saint Mary" (*missis fratribus officinas humiles erexit secundum formam ordinis novum nomen loco imponans montem sancta Maria*),[63] the "brothers" probably consisting of both monks and lay brothers. At Meaux the founder Count William

> had a certain great house built with common mud and wattle, where the mill is now established, in which the arriving lay brothers would dwell until better arrangements were made for them. He also built a certain chapel next to the aforementioned house, which now is the cellarer's chamber, where all the monks used the lower floor as dormitory and the upper to perform the divine office devoutly.[64]

---

[60] *Scriptores Minores* 1917–1922, 2:177.

[61] Ailred 1950, 12.

[62] Ep. 92 (*SBOp* 7:241; James 1953, 142).

[63] Kirkstall 1895, 174.

[64] *Melsa, Chronica* 1866–1868, 1:82; Ferguson 1983, 79: *Fecit ergo aedificari quondam magnam domum, licet ex vili cemate, ubi nunc stabilitur pistrinum, in qua conventus adventurus, donec providentius pro eis ordinaretur, habitaret. Fecit etiam quondam*

At Byland in Yorkshire the *domus conversorum* was finished in about 1165 and is the earliest surviving building to have been completed, an indication that the lay brothers occupied the site in advance of the monks to construct the remaining buildings, most of which were completed by the time the monks moved from their former site at Stocking in 1177, with the exception of the church, which was not finished until the 1190s.[65]

A number of General Chapter statutes refer to monks and lay brothers engaged in building work. Two from 1157 remind monks that such involvement did not excuse them from attending offices in choir, and restrict monks and lay brothers to work only for their own abbeys or other monasteries of the Order, and not for outsiders.[66] There is also evidence of the expertise of lay brothers as surveyors. Alan, a *conversus* from Buildwas, was sent to Ireland by his abbot to look at land the abbey had been given there by Hervé de Montmorency. Following his report, plans for a new foundation were dropped, for he found that "the desolation of the place, the sterility of the lands and the wilderness and ferocity of the barbarous inhabitants" made the site unsuitable. The decision was probably colored by the hostility of the local population, for the site was later acquired by St Mary's, Dublin, and the foundation of Dunbrody was made, eventually becoming one of the most prosperous houses in Ireland.[67]

In 1224 a lay brother from the Frisian abbey of Aduard was sent to Clairvaux by his abbot to study the architecture of the buildings there as a model for the building of Aduard.[68] As a reward for the success of his mission he was buried in the church, an honor not even accorded to abbots, and an effigy, known only from a literary source, was erected near the west end of the nave, where he had started the building that was only completed in 1263. The bricks

---

*capellam juxta domum praedictam, quae modo dicitur camera cellerarii, ubi monachi omnes in inferiori solario postea decubabant, et in superiori divina officia devotius persolvebant.*

[65] Harrison 1999, 27–28.
[66] *Statuta* 1157.29, 47 (Waddell 2002, 585, 597).
[67] Stalley 1987, 35–37.
[68] Aubert 1947, 1:97–98.

*Fig. 3* Carving of lay brother's head on a capital in the cloister of Flaran in Gascony.

used for this were transported from the abbey's own kiln to the building site by a human chain of lay brothers.

Evidence in the form of surviving architectural sculpture underlines the contribution of lay brothers as builders. As none of the examples are earlier than the fourteenth century, however, by which time the number of lay brothers had declined sharply, their involvement would by then have been largely in a supervisory capacity, hired masons and carpenters carrying out most of the physical work.

A boss dated to about 1320 in the church at Salem in southern Germany depicts a bearded figure thought to have been of a lay brother master builder.[69] Another lay brother from Salem is known to have been responsible for the building of the tower at Bebenhausen in the fifteenth century.[70] A carving of a bearded head, partly covered by a hood but with the characteristic fringe showing, is found on a fourteenth-century capital at Flaran in Gascony (fig. 3). Similar to the Salem boss, it probably also represents a lay brother.

The church at Maulbronn was rebuilt in the Gothic style shortly after 1420. The master builder is known to have been the lay brother Berthold, whose contribution is commemorated by a carved figure on a corbel in the north transept of the church.[71] He is bearded with his head partly covered by his hood and is shown in a crouching position, his left hand on his knee, and in the right hand he holds a stonemason's hammer, the symbol of his craft.

Two remarkable iconographic examples bear witness and pay tribute to the cooperative achievement of lay brothers and professional masons. One of them is provided by a corbel from Pforta in Thuringia.[72] The other is a circular boss in the chapter house of Sulejów in Poland that shows four primitively carved bearded heads (fig. 4). Two of them have the very pronounced fringed hair characteristic of lay brothers while the others do not, and they may represent two lay brothers and two professional masons. One of

[69] See figure 9.
[70] Toepfer 1983, 86.
[71] Illustrated in France 1998, 201.
[72] See figure 2.

*Fig. 4* Carving of four heads—two lay brothers and two masons—on chapter house boss at Suléjow in Poland.

them may portray Simon, a lay brother from Tuscany, whose portrait in the form of a carved corbel of a bearded head with straight-cut hair is found in the refectory of another Polish abbey, Wachock, and whose signature is also there (the inscription F. SIMON appears on the façade of the church) and at still another Polish abbey. He headed a group of Italian craftsmen associated with the construction of the Italian abbeys of Fossanova, Casamari, and San Galgano who were active in Poland between 1217 and 1239 and were responsible for building four monasteries, Wachock, Koprzywnica, Sulejów, and Jedrzejów.[73]

The only pictures showing the building of Cistercian abbeys in the twelfth century are late or post-medieval. Two out of ten pen and ink drawings from around 1600 show scenes of the building of Schönau in southern Germany, founded in 1144/45. Three of them depict the lay brother revolt under Abbot Gottfried.[74] All

[73] See Białoskórska 1966, 14–22, where it is also illustrated (illus. 3).
[74] One of these is illustrated in France 1998, 132.

CONSTRVXERE DOMVM CONVERSI SCHONAVIENSEM
QVOS PIVS INDVXIT RELIGIONIS AMOR.

*Fig. 5* Pen-and-ink drawing of twenty lay brothers building abbey of Schönau.

ten were probably copied from the glass that had been installed in the Schönau refectory in the late twelfth century. One of the two building scenes shows the construction operation in great detail and is highly imaginative (fig. 5). At the same time it is historically questionable in that it portrays a large workforce consisting exclusively of lay brothers, with no monks or lay workers participating. The only comparable example survives from Walkenried, where twenty-one lay brother masons and blacksmiths are said to have been responsible for building the church in 1223–1231.[75] The drawing shows twenty bearded lay brothers at work, their hoods over their heads. In the distance stones are being extracted from the quarry and dressed; a wagon with a team of four oxen is carting the stones down to the site while another is returning empty for another load. Two brothers on a ladder are carrying mortar to the roof where others are receiving a large stone brought up by hoist. In the foreground two brothers are moving a stone, three are mixing mortar, two others are dressing stones, while yet another is having a rest and drinking from a bottle. At his feet is a flagon he has tied to a pole so as to cool it in the stream. Another brother is crossing the stream carrying a long rule and a square. Another square and template hang on the wall. In the second drawing of the Schönau building scene the church has been completed and work is in progress on the east range adjoining the north transept of the church.[76] The spirit of revival that prevailed in the late Middle Ages is here expressed in the interest shown in the pioneering days of the Order. In looking back with pride to the days when hard physical work was the norm they hoped to be able to regain some of the primitive spirit that had eroded with the passage of time.

---

[75] Wiswe 1953, 97.
[76] Illustrated in *Zisterzienser* 1981, 431.

# Chapter 3

# *Illiterati*

The Prologue to the *Usages*, the lay brothers' book of regulations, describes lay brothers as being "simple and unlettered" (*simpliciores et sine litteris*).[1] According to this "no one is to have a book or learn anything except the *Pater noster*, the *Credo in Deum*, the *Miserere mei, Deus* and this not from a written text, but only by heart" (*non littera sed cordetenus*).[2] There is no mention in the *Usages* that books were also prohibited in the granges, but an early description of Clairvaux which refers to the two granges in the vicinity of the abbey makes it clear that books were not kept there: "You would take these granges not as the living quarters of lay-brothers but for monastic cloisters were it not that ox-yokes, ploughs and other farm implements betray the inhabitants' status and that no books are opened there."[3]

Lay brothers are sometimes referred to as "ignorant of letters" (*litterarum rudis*)[4] and frequently as *illiterati*, which meant lacking in knowledge of Latin. They are sometimes also known as *rudes, simplices*, or *idiotae*.[5] Writing to Hildegard of Bingen around 1169, the prior of Eberbach, Meffried, referred to "the secular and unlearned people

---

[1] *UC* Prologue (Waddell 2000, 56).

[2] *UC* 9 (Waddell 2000, 68).

[3] PL 185:572; translation from Matarasso 1993, 290: *Grangias has non conversorum esse habitacula, sed claustra monachorum crederes, nisi vel juga boum, vel aratra, vel instrumenta alia rusticanis apta laboribus, habitantes suos proderent, et nisi quod in eis libri non explicantur.*

[4] *LM* 1.16 (PL 185:1292)

[5] Leclercq 1965, 241.

[*secularibus et idiotis*] who have taken up the spiritual way of life, those that we call *conversi*."[6] It is important to bear in mind that there was no derogatory connotation attached to the idea of illiteracy in the Middle Ages as there is today: all books were in Latin, almost all of them of interest only to clerics, and there was no need for people to acquire the skill. In this respect Cistercian lay brothers were no different from the vast majority of the population in the twelfth century.

The *illiterati* even included some of those who entered Cistercian houses as monks. The *Ecclesiastica officia*, the usages for monks, refers to *monachi illiterati*, that is, monks who, although part of the monastic community, do not understand letters and who, at the anointing of the sick, are allowed to confess in the Romance language in the same way as lay brothers.[7] Such monks were also known as *monachi laici*. Conrad of Eberbach has a story of one, presumably an unschooled nobleman, who complied with the General Chapter decree of 1188 requiring that "uneducated noblemen coming to the monastery shall become monks, not lay brothers."[8] Describing him and the lay monks generally, Conrad says:

> They may have attained minimally the substance of human learning through which one climbs to the heights of perfection, nevertheless they had the illuminating grace and the life-giving Spirit who taught them a knowledge incomparably more effective than that of the world. One of these was a lay monk, learned not in the letter but in the spirit.[9]

[6] Hildegard of Bingen, *Epistolae* (PL 197:260), trans. Hildegard of Bingen 1994, 182: *de saecularibus et idiotis ad spiritualem conversationem conversis, quos nos conversos dicimus.*

[7] *EO* 93.33-35 (Choisselet & Vernet, 268): *Si conversus est vel monachus qui non intelligat litteras. Idem illi romane exponat sacerdos. Et conversus romane confiteatur. Se pecasse. cogitatione. locutione. et opera. Similiter monachus romane confiteatur. Si suum nescit CONFITEOR.*

[8] *Statuta* 1188.10 (Waddell 2002, 151): *Nobiles laici venientes ad monasterium non fiant conversi sed monachi.*

[9] *EM* 4.12 (Griesser 236): *Qui etsi humanae scientiae fabricam, per quam ad perfectionis culmen niterentur, minime consecuti sunt, habebant tamen gratiam illuminantem et Spiritum vivificantem. Qui de omnibus, quae oportebat, saeculari scientia incomparabiliter efficacius eos docebat. Talium quidam monachus laicus non littera doctus, sed spiritu.*

Generally, however, *illiterati* and *conversi* were synonymous, as were *literati* and *clerici*,[10] and there was no need for lay brothers to acquire the knowledge required of the monks for the monastic liturgy and offices. Among them was the remarkable lay brother Sunnulph, who lived at Fountains in the second half of the twelfth century and was described in very much the same terms as those Conrad used in the story of the lay monk. Although only "a simple and illiterate man," he was nevertheless "instructed by the Lord; instead of books, he held on to his conscience; he had the Holy Spirit for a teacher; reading the book of experience, he grew daily in the knowledge of holy things and possessed even the spirit of revelations."[11] Some clerics even chose out of humility to become lay brothers and concealed the fact that they were not laymen, "preferring the herding of cattle to the reading of books."[12]

Lay brothers were not bound by the Rule and did not take part in two of the three key monastic activities—the full monastic *Opus Dei* and *lectio divina*.[13] Any possible intellectual development was severely discouraged by a *horarium* that did not allow them free time for recreation as well as by the restriction imposed by the strict rule of silence.[14] Their main intellectual stimulation was provided by the abbot's sermon on a number of feast days when the lay brothers attended the monks' chapter, standing in the cloister gallery listening through the openings into the chapter house, or when the abbot, or a monk deputed by him, usually the *magister*

[10] Mahn 1951, 53: "Cependant 'convers' et 'illittré' tendent a devenir synonymes."

[11] *Fountains* 1863, 118: *homo simplex et illiteratus, sed Dominus erudierat eum. Habebat, pro codice, conscientiam; spiritum sanctum pro eruditore; et legens in libro experientiae, crescebat cotidie in scientia sanctorum; habens etiam spiritum revelationis.*

[12] *DM* 1.39 (Strange 1:46; Scott and Bland 1:50): *Tanta est virtus humilitatis, ut eius amore saepe ad ordinem venientes clerici, laicos se simulaverint, malentes pecora pascere, quam libros legere, satius ducentes Deo in humilitate servire quam propter sacros ordines vel literaturum ceteris praeesse.*

[13] In the ceremony of profession the lay brother promises obedience to the abbot, but there is no mention of the Rule of Saint Benedict (Waddell 2000, 71). Furthermore, according to the Rule (*RB* 4 and 66) monks are obliged to remain within the enclosure.

[14] Waddell 2000, 59–61; 64–66.

*conversorum*, would address them on all remaining Sundays in their own chapter room.[15]

An instance of these occasions is recorded in an *exemplum* from the abbey of Salem in southern Germany where chapter "took place on a solemn day in the monks' chapter house and the lay brothers were present. One of the lay brothers who had reached an advanced age listened to the sermon leaning on a staff taking his place at the entrance of the chapter house."[16] He noticed that some of the brothers were asleep, and promptly fell asleep himself. While asleep he had a vision of a young well-dressed man carrying silver dishes with food and drink that he offered to everybody. With the exception of two monks and five lay brothers, everyone refused. He then "brought along a young lady who was very beautiful, slender and good-looking, and offered her to them. They all rejected her and did not even look at her except for those who had helped themselves from his food. Having received the girl freely, they kissed and fondled her."[17]

The lay brother told the abbot, who at first refused to believe him, thinking him to be mad. He asked the others, who confessed that they had also fallen asleep and had dreamed what the old man had seen and reported. The account ends with the lesson to be drawn: "Hence we must apply ourselves with great vigilance of soul and body to the sermons when they are preached."[18]

---

[15] Waddell 2000, 183–85. Smaller abbeys would not have had their own chapter room and chapter was probably held in the refectory.

[16] Liebers 1993, 81: *Contigit in quadam congregatione cisterciensi dum abbas quadam die sollempni sermonem in capitulo monachorum faceret et conversi praesentes adessent. Ut unus conversorum qui iam ad etatem fere decrepitam pervenerat baculo sustenante ad sermonem audiendum convenerit.*

[17] Liebers 1993, 81: *autem iuvenis predictus puellam nimis teneram et delicatam et egregie forme introduxit coram eis singulis eam offerens et voluntati eorum tradens. Quam omnes respuerunt nec ad illam intenderunt exceptis illis qui prius iuvenis servitium acceptaverant et de cibariis eius contigerant. Nam isti oblatam puellam libenter accipientes inter amplexus deosculabantur et lascivis contactibus insistebant.*

[18] Liebers 1993, 81: *Hinc cogitandum est cum quanta animi et corporis vigilantia divinis debeamus intendere sermonibus dum coram nobis predicantur.* For instances of somnolence in choir see p. 96.

After a hard week's work it is understandable that the benefit derived from the chapter sermons was sometimes minimal. Caesarius of
Heisterbach records an occasion at which he was present. The abbot
was preaching in the chapter house when "several of the brethren,
chiefly lay brothers, went to sleep, and some even began to snore."
The abbot discovered the remedy by beginning a tale with the words
"there was once a king named Arthur," realizing to his chagrin that
a secular story would have a greater impact on tired brethren than
his usual sermonizing, which had a the soporific effect.[19] That the
lay brothers were more prone to fall asleep is hardly surprising, given
that the abbot's talk was in Latin, although, as Michael Casey has
pointed out, Bernard probably spoke a kind of pidgin, a Latin with
enough French words to make him more comprehensible, a practice
that was probably adopted by other abbots. Bernard's sermons were
subsequently reworked for publication for a wider readership.[20]

### Hugh of Fouilloy's *Aviary*

Hugh of Fouilloy's Book of Birds, *Aviarium* or *Aviary*, is an
allegorical and moralized treatise on birds in the same way that a
bestiary treats of animals in general, and it belongs to the literature
of *exempla*.[21] Focusing on monastic virtues, it was an important
teaching text directed to lay brothers and to the masters who
were charged with their formation and pastoral care. Apart from
the weekly sermon given by the abbot or his delegate,[22] the aviary
provided them with their main means of mental stimulation and
it therefore gives us a rare insight into monastic attitudes toward
lay brothers and the formation of their spirituality. It has been described as a "contemplative *ruminatio*"[23] and firmly belongs to the
tradition of monastic theology.

---

[19] *DM* 4.36 (Strange 1:205; Scott and Bland 1:233): *plures, maxime de conversos,
dormitare, nonnullos etiam stertere conspiceret, exclamavit: Audite, fratres, audite, rem vobis
novam et magnam proponam. Rex quidem fuit, qui Artus vocabatur.*

[20] Casey 2011, 87.

[21] For a critical edition and translation see Clark 1992. See also Abeele 2003.

[22] *UC* 11 (Waddell 69–70; 183–85).

[23] Abeele 2003, 270.

Hugh of Fouilloy, an Augustinian prior, wrote the *Aviary* some-time between 1130 and 1140 at the request of the lay brother Rain-ier, and it is therefore also known as "The Little Book for Rainier the Lay Brother called the Kindhearted" (*Libellus quidam ad Rairerum conversum cognomine Corde Benignum*). Consisting mostly of scriptural exegesis, it is divided into two parts; the first has a number of chapters on the dove, the hawk, the sparrow, and the turtledove, while the second comprises twenty-three chapters, each devoted to a different bird. At least 125 manuscripts of the *Aviary* from all across Europe survive, the great majority illustrated. Although Hugh and Rainier were both Augustinians and not Cistercians, the *Aviary* soon achieved considerable popularity at Cistercian abbeys, especially those with large numbers of lay brothers. Twenty-nine copies survive from li-braries of the white monks, suggesting that they became the most frequent owners, surpassing the Benedictines, with eighteen copies, and even the Augustinians. Some of the earliest surviving illustrated copies belonged to the abbeys Ter Duinen, Aulne, Heiligenkreuz, and Zwettl. Some abbeys even had more than one copy: Clairmarais had two and Clairvaux three, evidence of the work's extensive use.

In the Prologue to Book One Hugh likens himself to a dove and Rainier, who like so many of the early lay brothers was a for-mer knight,[24] to a hawk. He remarks:

> See how the hawk and the dove sit on the same perch. I
> am from the clergy and you from the military. We come to
> conversion so that we may sit within the life of the Rule, as
> though on a perch; and so that you who were accustomed to
> seizing domestic fowl now with the hand of good deeds may
> bring to conversion the wild ones, that is, laymen.[25]

The contrast between the two is conveyed graphically at the opening of the treatise in a large number of the manuscripts. A

---

[24] See p. 11.

[25] Clark 1992, 118: *Ecce in eadem pertica sedent accipiter et columba. Ego enim de clero, tu de militia. Ad conversionem venimus ut in regulari vita quasi in pertica sedeamus; et qui rapere consueveras domesticas aves, nunc bonae operationis manu silvestres ad con-versionem trahas, id est saeculares.*

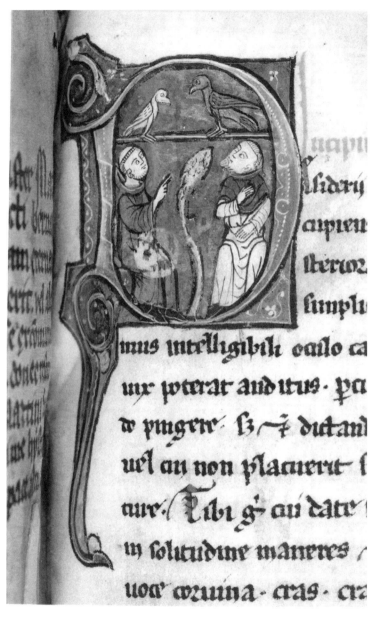

*Fig. 6* Miniature in Hugh of Fouilloy's *Aviary* with monk and lay brother surmounted by a dove and a hawk.

miniature in a mid-thirteenth-century manuscript shows the initial "D" at the opening of the Prologue to Book One[26] (fig. 6):

> Desiring to fulfill your wishes, dearest friend, I decided to paint the dove whose wings are *silvered and the hinderparts of the back in pale gold* [Ps 67:14], and by a picture to instruct the minds of simple folk, so that what the intellect of the simple folk could scarcely comprehend with the mind's eye, it might at least discern with the physical eye, and what their hearing could scarcely perceive, their sight might do so.[27]

The illustration shows a tonsured monk in a grey cowl on the left and a bearded lay brother with fringed hair and wearing a white tunic and brown detachable hood on the right.[28] The monk, who is facing the lay brother and has his right hand raised in a teaching mode, probably represents the *magister conversorum*. The lay brother before him is listening attentively, his right hand placed on his chest. Above the monk is a white dove, above the lay brother a grey hawk, the two sitting on the same perch. Although the provenance of the manuscript is not known, the way the two are portrayed suggests that it most likely belonged to a Cistercian house.

Another copy of the *Aviary*, an early thirteenth-century example from the Austrian abbey of Heiligenkreuz, has a full-page miniature in red, black, and brown ink. It shows a seated monk on the left, but Rainier, on the right, is depicted not as a lay brother but as the knight he was before his conversion to spiritual warfare.[29] The words *clericus* and *miles* appear above the two figures. While the monk reads from a book, a mounted Rainier holds a falcon in one hand and has one hound with him on the horse and another on the ground. Above them, as in the other image, are the dove and the hawk and the words "Behold, the hawk and the dove sit on the same perch,"

[26] Brussels, Bibliothèque Royale, MS 8536-43, fol. 73.

[27] Clark 1992, 116: *Desiderii tui, carissime, petitionibus satisfacere cupiens, columbam cuius pennae sunt deargentatae et posteriora dorsi eius in pallore auri pingere et per picturam simplicium mentes aedificare decrevi, ut quod simplicium animus intelligibili oculo capere vix poterat, saltem carnali discernat; et quod vix poterat auditus percipiat visus.*

[28] For the lay brother's hair and clothing see chapter 4.

[29] Heiligenkreuz, Austria, MS 226, fol. 129v; illustrated in France 1998, 94.

repeating the words of the text. They are portrayed within a frame, the sides of which are referred to as "a wall of holy thoughts" and "a wall of good deeds." Below the figures are the words *contemplativa vita* and *vita activa*; the juxtaposition of the two is reminiscent of the use made of the Mary and Martha theme by Nicholas of Clairvaux and of *interiora* and *exteriora* used by Burchard of Balerne in his *Apologia de barbis* in defining the difference between the two groups.[30]

Hugh of Fouilloy justified his claim that he uttered "simple things about subtle matters" (*de subtilibus simplicia dicam*) by asserting that he was writing for the unlettered. In the Prologue to Book Two he reiterated Saint Gregory the Great's celebrated pronouncement in his two letters to Severus approving the value of art as an educational aid for the illiterate[31] by saying that images would help those who could not cope with the text: "For what Scripture means to the teachers, the picture means to simple folk. For just as the learned man delights in the subtlety of the written word, so the intellect of simple folk is engaged by the simplicity of a picture."[32]

Paradoxically, in spite of Saint Bernard's objection to claustral art (*Apologia ad Guillelmum Abbatem* 28 and 29) because it became a distraction to the monk who ought to be concentrating on reading books and not looking at images, he would have had no problem with the use of the *Aviary* as a teaching aid for lay brothers. Although he had only seculars in mind when he said he would tolerate art "on the grounds that they [the images] harm only the foolish and the grasping and not the simple-hearted and devout,"[33] it was the illiteracy of those outside the cloister that excluded them from the monastic injunction against art, and as the *conversi* were both lay and illiterate, the relaxation Bernard granted seculars would have applied equally to them. Bernard made the

---

[30] For Mary and Martha see chap. 7, pp. 166–70; for Burchard of Balerne see p. 83.

[31] PL 77:1128–30.

[32] Clark 1992, 118: *Quod enim doctoribus innuit Scriptura, hoc simplicibus pictura. Sicut enim sapiens delectatur subtilitate scripturae, sic simplicium animus detinetur simplicitate picturae.*

[33] *Apologia* 28 (*SBOp* 3:106; Matarasso 1993, 57): *Patiamur et haec fieri in ecclesia, quia etsi noxia sunt vanis et avaris, non tamen simplicibus et devotis.*

same distinction between what was suitable for a lay as opposed to a monastic audience in the opening sentence of Sermon One on the Song of Songs: "The instructions that I address to you, my brothers, will differ from those I should deliver to people in the world, at least the manner will be different."[34] He would have had this equally in mind when addressing the lay brothers and would, like Hugh, have chosen to say "simple things about subtle matters."

Martha Newman has identified the main difference between the spirituality of monks and lay brothers as literacy.[35] The spirituality of monks was informed to a large extent by nuptial imagery in which feminine virtues were highlighted, in contrast to the more masculine spirituality of the lay brothers, a spirituality based on the mortification of the flesh in imitation of the suffering Christ. The distinction between the two may also be seen in the visual impact of the *Aviary* with its meditation on monastic virtues and the way this helped to form a distinctive lay brother spirituality.

## Literate Lay Brothers

The stipulation that lay brothers were not to possess books tells us that among the lay brothers there were some who were literate, but whereas reading and writing were a necessity for clerics, for lay brothers, who were to remain lay,[36] the skill was superfluous.

Some lay brothers had no doubt learned to read and write before entering the monastery. Among them may be counted the scribe at Løgum (*Locus Dei*) in Denmark, the lay brother Tue. His copy of Peter of Riga's *Aurora*, a versified version of the Bible, has—in transgression of a statute of 1199 prohibiting the writing of verse[37]—the following inscription at the end of the manuscript: *hos Tuuo conversus depinxit metrice versus.*[38]

---

[34] *Super Cantica Canticorum* 1 (*SBOp* 1:3): *Vobis, fratres, alia quam aliis se saeculo, aut certe aliter dicenda sunt.*

[35] Newman 2003, esp. 182–88.

[36] *Capitula* 22, in Waddell 1999, 190.

[37] *Statuta* 1199.1 (Waddell 2002, 420).

[38] McGuire 1982, 31. The manuscript is in the Royal Library, Copenhagen, MS Gl. Kgl. S. 54.

*Fig.* 7 Caricature of Henry, lay brother scribe from Ter Doest in Flanders.

Perhaps the most exceptional example of a literate lay brother was the accomplished scribe and experienced calligrapher Henry, under whose leadership an important scriptorium was established at the Flemish abbey of Ter Doest in the second half of the thirteenth century.[39] He is thought to have learned his craft before joining the Order at an advanced age, and he may have done so in the workshop of the counts of Flanders in Bruges. Among his known works are a large Bible in four volumes and a manuscript of Saint Augustine. An inscription identifies him as the scribe, a rare example of the writing of a lay brother and unique in its inclusion of an amusing self-portrait in the opening initial: "Brother Henry, lay brother of Ter Doest, wrote this book" (*Hunc librum scripsit frater Henricus conversus beate Marie professus in thosan*) (Fig. 7).[40]

Other lay brothers who had acquired the skill after entering the monastery are featured in a number of stories in *vitae* and *exempla* written by monks. Some of these tales were probably meant as a disincentive to lay brothers who might be tempted to encroach on what was considered a monastic preserve, a warning against the dangers inherent in disobeying the rule forbidding literacy. Other writers, however, expressed a profound admiration for the extraordinary gifts with which some exceptional *conversi* were endowed. Among these was Herbert of Clairvaux's account of the Clairvaux lay brother who, although he had three times left the monastery and

[39] Lieftinck 1953, 46–48.
[40] Bruges, Openbare Bibliotheek, MS 13, fol. 180v.

three times been received back, eventually amended his ways after a severe illness. Rejoicing at his good fortune, he began to sing the sweetest melodies and the brethren came together to witness what was described as a miracle, for the lay brothers' devotions consisted of the recitation of prayers by heart as distinct from the monks' singing of the Office. Saint Bernard is said to have "preached a most devout sermon in the chapter house, commending in him the fruit of penitence and extolled his marvelous patience to all as an example."[41] A more graphic description of the lay brother's affliction and subsequent spiritual recovery is given in the *Exordium magnum*. First,

> decay entered into the bones of the aforesaid brother and his leg became hideously ulcerated and with a cancerous abscess and the anguish of this illness increased every day until the flesh on either side of the ulcer was eaten away to the bare bone and the wound was teeming with worms.[42]

In due course he tasted the sweetness of his patience when

> he shouted his joy in songs of heavenly praise as if intoxicated on the new wine of heaven and, with his countenance aglow, this unlettered man who had never learned to sing or read was singing the sweetest hymns and melodies of the songs of Zion [Ps 136:3]. *At hearing his voice a multitude* of brothers *came together* [Acts 2:6] to see what great miracle had happened to this man, weighed down by such great miseries and calamities, at the very moment of death singing and rising triumphant over death, saying, "*O death where is your victory?* [1 Cor 15:55]. Look, I am a great sinner, a very poor sort of man."[43]

---

[41] *LM* 1.17 (PL 185:1292–93): *Unde etiam sermonem devotissimum in capitulo faciens, commendavit in eo poenitentiae fructum, et mirabilem patientiam eius omnibus proposuit in exemplum.* The same story later found its way verbatim into the Fürstenfeld Collection (Kompatscher-Gufler 2005, 240–41).

[42] *EM* 4.16 (Griesser 241–42): *Ingressa est putredo in ossibus praedicti fratris et percussus est circa femora ulcere pessimo, apostemate canceroso, et crescente in dies angustia languoris totus distabuit, ita ut carnibus circa locum ulceris undique corrosis ossa nudata patescerunt et vulnera vermibus scaturirent.*

[43] *EM* 4.16 (Griesser 241–42): *Qua gustata tamquam musto caelesti inebriatus protinus erupit in iubilum praeconii caelestis et serenata facie coepit idiota et qui numquam*

Conrad of Eberbach has the same ending, namely that Bernard "greatly rejoiced and preached a very stirring sermon about him to the brothers in chapter."[44]

Admiration for the extraordinary intellectual talents of a lay brother is found in the *Vita quarta* of Saint Bernard. A monk, a friend of the saint, used to go for walks with a lay brother, Humbert, for whose edification he translated "a book of miracles of the holy Father" (*librum miraculorum sancti Patris*). In a vision Humbert was presented with two books. At first he is said to have been frightened, thus indicating that he was aware of the ruling in the *Usages* banning books, but when he was told that God would come to his help, he relented.[45] Although he "did not know the alphabet, God enlightened him" (*nec etiam alphabetum noverat. Deo tamen illuminante*), and he made great strides. In a short time "he was not only able to read but even began to sing sweetly" (*non solum legere, verum etiam cantare satis decenter et convenienter sciret*),[46] an unusual observation because singing was also not a skill required by lay brothers for the recitation of their simple prayers. Humbert is said to have written of "miracles which were either unknown to writers or had been overlooked by writers. He wrote elegantly and carefully in a literary form so that almost immediately we were lifted up in admiration."[47] The writer ascribes Humbert's talent in the first place to God and then to the merits of Bernard, but also "to the faith and obedience of the brother" (*assignamus denique fidei et obedientiae fratris*).[48]

---

cantare aut legere didicerat, cum suavissima melodia quosdam novos multumque delectabiles hymnos ac modulos cantare de canticis Sion. Facta autem hac voce convenit multutudo fratrum videre cum grandi miraculo hominem tantis miseriis et calamitatibus oppressum in ipso mortis accessu cantando et tripudiando morti insultantem et quodammado dicentem: Ubi est mors, victoria tua? Ecce ego magnus peccator et pauperculus homuncio.

[44] *EM* 4.16 (Griesser 242): *multum exhilaratus sermonem devotissimum ad fratres in capitulo fecit.*

[45] *Vita quarta* 2 (PL 185:531).

[46] *Vita quarta* 3 (PL 185:533).

[47] *Vita quarta* 3 (PL 185:533): *Nonnulla miraculorum ipsius, quae vel scriptoribus ignota, vel per negligentiam fuerant praetermissa, tam decenter, tam bene, tamque eleganter litteris commendavit, ut subinde rapti in admirationem.*

[48] *Vita quarta* 3 (PL 185:533).

In his *Liber miraculorum* Herbert of Clairvaux has a story about "an honest and religious man but nevertheless only an illiterate layman" (*homo erat honestus et religiosus, laicus tamen, atque illiteratus*), and therefore probably a lay brother, the keeper of the wardrobe at Clairvaux, named Walter.[49] He was ordered by a girl in a dream to celebrate Mass. In the story as repeated by Conrad of Eberbach in an elaborated form, Walter is referred to as a "lay monk" (*monachus laicus*) who "had no less faith and devotion than did the lettered and the learned" (*doctis et litteratis fide et devotione non inferior*): "not a little astonished at such a novel command, he hesitated out of modesty, thinking of the humbleness of his own person, but out of respect, constrained by authority, he did not dare to resist and hastened to obey."[50] When he awoke he knew all the words of the Mass by heart, although he had previously known none of them as he was unable to read and "for many years he retained it in his memory" (*per plurimos annos in memoria tenuit*). Although lay brothers could not aspire to join the ranks of the monks, it was obviously quite possible for them on occasion to visualize themselves as performing monastic and priestly tasks.

In a curious story in the *Life* of Saint Hedwig, duchess of Silesia, who died in 1243, Hedwig's chaplain tries to pass off a lay brother as a priest who could say Mass for her. On one occasion the saint was not satisfied with attending only one Mass, and she therefore ordered her chaplain to fetch another priest. Anxious to comply with her wishes but unable to find a priest, he tricked her by presenting her with a Cistercian lay brother, probably from the neighboring abbey of Lubiaz (Leubus). The story is illustrated in the picture cycle of her *Life* commissioned by one of her descendants in 1353. It shows the bearded and balding lay brother in a long cloak being presented to Hedwig by her tonsured chaplain. The caption reads, "Here her chaplain named Martin tricks her by

---

[49] *LM* 1.32 (PL 185:1304); the story is repeated in the Fürstenfeld Collection (Kompatscher-Gufler 2005, 247).

[50] *EM* 4.15 (Griesser 240): *Ille vero super novitiate praecepti huius non parum attonitus, simul etiam personae suae humilitatem considerans nutabat quidem prae verecundia, sed praecipientis auctoritate pressus nec resistere ausus velociter paruit imperanti.*

presenting a lay brother to her as if he were a priest who would read Mass for her."[51]

In his *Life of Waldef*, Jocelin of Furness refers to a lay brother called Walter from Melrose in Scotland as "very simple, ignorant, and slow of speech" (*valde simplex, hebes, & impeditae linguae*),[52] almost a stereotypical description of a Cistercian lay brother. He had come under the spell of the devil, who had prevailed upon this illiterate man "to study until he learned by rote the ceremonies and prophesies of the Old Law and succeeded little by little in darkening his mind's eye with regard to the practice of the Christian religion and the keeping of regular life, until he had almost lost the light of reason and preferred the Jewish sect to a belief in Catholic truth."[53] In a dream Walter had a vivid vision of heaven, then of purgatory, and finally he reached hell where "he heard a great weeping and wailing, and no one could see for the blackness of the shadows."[54] Later Saint Waldef appeared and ordered him to be "diligent and persevere in observing the holy regimen of the order in which you have been called,"[55] and, according to the story, after the vision Walter became "clever and eloquent" and then "during the rest of his life he adhered strictly to the rules."[56] That may be so, and yet we are told that now he was able to "compose impromptu rhythmic verse that had style and beauty, as easily as we talk the common speech of every day. Using this gift, he afterwards wrote noble verses in the English tongue: Gospel paraphrases and

---

[51] Gottschalk 1967, 118; the picture is reproduced in France 1998, 135.

[52] Jocelin of Furness 1952, 176

[53] Jocelin of Furness 1952, 170: *hominem illiteratum veteris Legis caerimoniis & prophetis ad litteram discendis insudare faciebat; coepit ergo paulatim mentis oculis circa cultum Christianae religionis & vitae regularis custodiam caligare, donec lumen rationis pene perderet, & Judaicam sectam veritati Catholicae credendo praeferret.*

[54] Jocelin of Furness, 172–73: *Ibi ploratum tantum et ululatum audivit, et neminem pre tenebris densissimis videre potuit.* See also pp. 260–63.

[55] Jocelin of Furness, 175: *diligenter & persevezanter observa Ordinis.*

[56] Jocelin of Furness, 176: *subtilis effectus & eloquens . . . . Ipse in reliquum vitam suam in magna religione composuit.*

narratives and expositions drawn from them, sayings of the church fathers, and his own as well as others' visions."[57]

Ironically, it seems to have been forgotten that he had acquired his skill at the instigation of the devil and that he had vowed to adhere in future to the rules, for "his hearers, even the abbots and other important personages, used to be overcome with admiration and he would often bring tears to their eyes" (*audientes etiam abbates et alias excellentes personas in admirationem & multoties in lachrymas resolvit*).[58] Like Humbert's, this lay brother's literary talent was so great that the irregularity of his position was overlooked by the writer.

Herbert of Clairvaux has a similar story in which the same disregard for Cistercian lay brother regulations and the same admiration by monks for the literary skills of a lay brother are revealed. Admittedly, in the story the literary lay brother confessed his sins before dying, but he was not castigated for "discoursing on the scriptures in eloquent Latin" (*Latino eloquio de Scripturis sanctis disseruit*):

> The brothers in the infirmary at Clairvaux came together in joy and admiration, conferring about the lay brother who had a worthy life and who, when he was near to death, began to speak in eloquent Latin. He had not learned to read Latin and yet he discoursed on sacred Scripture with a brilliant sermon. He only taught what agreed with sound doctrine. He had a charming way of speaking so that those who saw him witnessed this miracle of speech and were thunderstruck. Having done this for some time he made a good confession and in his last moments he was carried away with the joy of heavenly light.[59]

---

[57] Jocelin of Furness, 176: *ita ut in promptu haberet rhythmos componere rhetorice & venuste, sicut nos consuevimus loqui quotidiano ac plano sermone: unde & postea Evangelia plura & expositiones eorum rhythmice dictavit.*

[58] Jocelin of Furness, 176.

[59] *LM* 1.16 (PL 185:1292): *Solent frequenter fratres infirmarii Clarevallenses cum gaudio atque admiratione referre, de quodam honestae vitae converso, qui cum devenisset ad mortem, coepit loqui Latino eloquio. Et, cum nunquam Latinas litteras didicisset, mira quaedam de Scripturis sacris lucilento sermone disserebat; nihil penitus proferens, nisi quod*

This short and straightforward story was one of the many that found their way into Conrad of Eberbach's *Exordium magnum*, approximately half the stories in which were based on Herbert's *Liber miraculorum*.[60] Here, as elsewhere, Conrad amplifies the narrative. He notes the intervention of the Holy Spirit as a result of which "this rustic fellow who had never learned letters" (*homo rusticanus, qui numquam litteras didicerat*) became articulate, and he adds:

> The lay brothers [*fratres laici*] who did not know Latin were amazed at the novelty of this, and fetched some of the monks to hear him, and in a dazzling discourse the sick brother also expounded the mysteries of the Scriptures to them. What is more, he sang sweet canticles about the mysteries of holy Church with such a well-modulated voice, which they had never before heard, that all who heard it were astonished at the unheard of miracle and touched by the exquisite chant.[61]

Unlike Herbert, Conrad then goes on to explain the meaning of the story. True to monastic tradition, he asserts that the fear of God is the beginning of wisdom and is to be preferred to the learning of the schools. He amplifies the Pauline dictum that there is no distinction between "Greek and Jew, slave or free, male and female" (Gal 3:28; cf. Col 3:11) by adding "lettered and unlettered" (*litteratus seu illiteratus*), and he describes the lay brother as "this new theologian" (*novus iste theologus*).

---

sanae doctrinae congruebat. *Praeterea quasdam suaves cantilenas, quae nusquam audiri consueverant, modulatis vocibus depromebat, ita ut videntes miraculi novitiate obstupefaceret, et cantuum suavitate mulceret. Qui dum haec aliquandiu faceret, tandem in bona confessione animam reddidit, et extrema lucis illius gaudium occupavit.* The story is repeated verbatim in the Fürstenfeld Collection (Kompatscher-Gufler 2005, 239).

[60] *EM* 4.17 (Griesser, 242–43). For Conrad's use of Herbert's *Liber Miraculorum*, see McGuire 1979a, 42–49. See also Casey 1990, 37–64, at 45.

[61] *EM* 4.17 (Griesser, 242); CF 72:351: *Mirabantur fratres laici, qui litteras nesciebant, quaenam esset haec rei novitas, et accitis quantocius monachis in audientia nihilominus eorum isdem infirmus scripturarum mysteria luculento sermone pandebat. Praeterea suaves quasdam cantilenas de mysteriis sanctae ecclesiae modulatis vocibus decantabat, quae nusquam audiri consueverant, ita ut audientes miraculi novitate attonitos redderet et cantus suavitate mulceret.*

In all these stories admiration of the monk-writers for the literary skills of some exceptional lay brothers eclipsed the transgression of the ruling against the possession of books and pursuit of intellectual activities, of which they must have been aware. But erring lay brothers did not always get off so lightly. A lay brother at Kamp in the Rhineland had learned to read from the monks. He caused books to be written for him and began to take pleasure in the vice of private ownership. His appetite for learning grew to such an extent that he finally apostasized. He returned, but twice more the lure of the secular schools was so great that he left again. In a vision the devil promised him that if he went on learning he would be rewarded by becoming bishop of Halberstadt. When he heard that the bishop had died he stole a fine horse so that he might come to his see with dignity, but he was discovered, arrested, and found guilty, and he "ascended, not the throne of a bishop, but the gallows as a convicted thief." Caesarius of Heisterbach adds: "You see to what kind of end the devil's promises lead!"[62]

An English lay brother was obliged to learn letters following a vision of Christ. He was a simple and devout man and would hardly ever say anything other than "Ave, Maria," one of the few prayers lay brothers were allowed to learn, but Christ ordered him to go to his abbot and confess according to the custom of the Church, saying:

> When you have made your confession you may say to him that you will recite the whole Psalter each day for three days. But to do this, since you have never learned letters, you will be taught from then on and become adept and the best man of learning. Having done this, on the third day you may return to me without delay. And so it came about.[63]

---

[62] *DM* 5.16 (Strange 1:294; Scott and Bland 1:336–37): *Vides ad quem finem promissio diaboli tendat?*

[63] BC fol. 85r–85v: *Quibus confessis dices ei ut tibi per tres dies singulis singula indicat psalteria. Ad quod cum numquam litteras didiceris, ita doctus eris ilico et disertus quasi fueris optime litteratus. Hoc peracto ad me die tertia sine dubio reverteris. Et factum est ita.* I am grateful to Brian McGuire for providing me with the text and to Fr. Hilary Costello for its transcription and translation. See also p. 253.

As these stories make clear, literate lay brothers were very much the exception and there is no doubt that the vast majority were and remained *illiterati*. In this respect they were no different from almost all outside the monastery who, like them, as members of an agrarian society tilled the soil and hewed wood and had no need, or opportunity, to acquire the skill of reading.

# Chapter 4

# *Barbati*

The institution of lay brothers by the Cistercians is first mentioned in a paragraph of the *Exordium parvum* in which they are referred to as "bearded laybrothers" (*conversos laicos barbatos*).[1] Having entered the religious life as adults, they were *conversi*, but because they remained lay they kept the beard that was the fashion for laymen in the twelfth century, thus distinguishing themselves from unlettered monks who had also entered as adults, the *monachi laici*.[2] To avoid any confusion and to conform to the custom of the time, the early fathers of Cîteaux called them *conversi laici barbati*, and sometimes just *barbati*. The fuller title defined them as religious—that is, bound by their vows—and at the same time as laymen.

The lay brothers' beards not only marked their separation from the *monachi laici* (the illiterate monks); the beard also distinguished them physically from the choir monks, just as—as we shall see—their clothing and their places in the church and in the claustral buildings did. The beard physically and visually set *conversi* apart from monks who, being clerics, were clean-shaven and tonsured, a point made by the Cistercian in the *Dialogue Between a Cluniac and a Cistercian*: "all tonsured monks are clerics."[3] The monastic tonsure was also known as the monastic crown or *corona*. It represented

---

[1] *EP* 15 (Waddell, 435).
[2] Ducourneau 1929, 2: 140.
[3] *Dialogue* 3: 41; Idung of Prüfening 1990, 179; CF 33:132–33: *omnes coronati monachi clerici sunt.*

Christ's crown of thorns and his royal priesthood. The *corona* was a sign that the cleric-monk had put off worldly things and now belonged to the service of God. It consisted of a narrow horizontal circular band of hair, approximately one inch wide, forming a circle around the head above the ears, with the rest of the head shaven.[4] This is how it is seen in medieval art and it provides us with the clearest and safest way of identifying cleric monks as against both laymen and lay brothers.

The beard as an essential distinguishing feature of lay brothers carried great significance, as may be seen from an anecdote in the well-known story of the lay brother conspiracy at Schönau under Abbot Godfrey (1182–1192).[5] The leader of the conspiracy, described as *minister satanae*, is said to have "shaved his beard with a razor, the wretched man thereby intending to stir up a scandal."[6]

Surprisingly, there is no reference to lay brothers' beards in the *Usages*, but two local collections of General Chapter statutes from the northern French abbeys of Signy and Vauclair, both datable to around 1159, prescribe that the beard of the *conversi* should not exceed the width of two fingers beneath the chin.[7] Such a modest beard would have required fairly frequent trimming. A ruling in the *Usus conversorum* indicates the importance attached to the avoidance of physical contact: it was decreed that one lay brother was not to wash the head of another; this probably referred to the periodic shaving of the head and trimming of the beard.[8] A statute from the Vauclair collection stipulates that the trimming was to be done by the lay brother himself.[9] In early years shaving took place seven times a year, but in 1257, when it was increased to twelve times for the monks, it remained seven times for lay brothers. The following year this was changed so as to bring the lay brothers'

---

[4] For the monastic tonsure see France 1998, 83.

[5] For this see pp. 281–89.

[6] *EM* 5.10 (Griesser, 294): *quia barbam suam novacula penitus abrasisset, quod quidem miser ille intentione commovendi scandali fecerat.*

[7] Waddell 2002, 635, 660: *Barbe conversorum non excedant duos digitos sub mento.*

[8] *UC* 21 (Waddell 2000, 193).

[9] Waddell 2002, 660: *Barbe conversorum sine aliorum manibus ab ipsis preparentur.*

*Fig. 8* Lay brothers on the tomb of Saint Stephen of Obazine in Limousin.

practice into line with the monks', with shaving and trimming also taking place twelve times a year.[10]

There are no pictorial representations of lay brothers from the twelfth century, but the neat and modest beards envisaged by the early statutes may be seen in the magnificent sculptured monument to Saint Stephen of Obazine dated to about 1280, the earliest known portrayal of lay brothers. Stephen's effigy in high relief is surmounted by a slanting roof consisting of six trifoliate arcades each containing a group of figures: on the left the Virgin and Child are enthroned, then, kneeling before them, is Stephen, accompanied by the abbots of the daughter houses who were received into the Cistercian Order together with Obazine in the Limousin in 1147. Four more arcades contain representatives of the different elements of which the Obazine community was composed: monks, lay brothers, nuns from the nearby Coyroux, and lay workers shown with their sheep. Here four lay brothers with neat, short beards trimmed according to the statute prescription are portrayed as members of the wider Cistercian family (fig. 8).[11]

Other examples of neat, pointed beards can be seen in the drawing in brown ink of "Brother J keeper of the wool store" at the abbey of Beaulieu close to the English Channel, a choir stall carving from the abbey of Doberan in northern Germany and, although somewhat longer but still pointed, the beard of the caricaturist scribe Henry from the Flemish abbey of Ter Doest, all dated to the second half of the thirteenth century.[12] Although the prescription regarding the length of beards and frequency of trimming remained in force, in later portrayals lay brothers are sometimes depicted with flowing beards of considerable length.[13] A later change to a longer style with full moustache is suggested by a statute of 1303, which decrees that any lay brother who shaves his moustache or shortens his beard "against the approved custom

[10] *Statuta* 1257.4 (Canivez 2:426); *Statuta* 1258.12 (Canivez 2:440).
[11] The six arcades are illustrated in France 1998, 47.
[12] See figs. 14, 21, and 7.
[13] For example, fig. 1.

*Fig. 9* Boss of lay brother master builder in abbey church at Salem.

of the Order" (*contra consuetudinem approbatam*) is to have his beard pulled out by tongs (*forcipibus*).[14]

While there was a great variety in the length and shape of the lay brothers' beards, their style of hair was invariably the same. As with beards, there were no directions in the *Usages* for lay brothers to follow, but a statute required them to "shave the beard below the chin and above in keeping with secular hairstyles."[15] Although it is not clear what this entails, it may point to the way their necks and temples were normally shaven, leaving them with the distinctive fringe in a pudding-bowl style that may be seen in the examples mentioned and in all other representations of lay brothers. An example is found in the carving of a bust that forms a round boss in the north transept of the abbey church of Salem in southern Germany. It shows a bearded figure with straight-cut hair, the hood drawn up behind his head. It is thought to be a representation of a lay brother master builder in about 1320 (fig. 9). The same distinctive fringe may be clearly seen on a lay brother in the Tennenbach property register.[16] Despite the silence of the *Usages* or any reference to it in any narrative or legislative documents, the distinctive fringe is as much a distinguishing feature of lay brothers in medieval art as the beard.

In light of the inclusion of the title "bearded" in the very first reference to lay brothers, it is surprising that they were not subsequently referred to as *barbati* more often. In the *Usus conversorum* the word *conversus* is used thirty-one times, *frater* thirty-three times, and *laicus* three times, and the terms are often combined as *frater conversus* or *frater laicus,* but *barbatus* never occurs.[17] Similarly, lay brothers are always referred to as *conversus* or *frater laicus* in the *Ecclesiastica officia* and never as *barbatus*.[18] Moreover, no lay brothers are referred to

---

[14] *Statuta* 1303.5 (Canivez 3:310).

[15] Waddell 2002, 673: *Si conversus barbam suam sub mento raserit et supra secundum modum secularium, vel radere fecerit, tam rasus quam rasor ultimi sit per annum, et non communicabunt nisi ad nutum abbatis.*

[16] See fig. 10.

[17] Waddell 2002, 88–89, 98, 106.

[18] Griesser 1956.

as *barbati* in any of the early *exemplum* collections like Herbert's *Liber miraculorum* or Conrad of Eberbach's *Exordium Magnum*. The only time the term is used by Caesarius of Heisterbach is to refer to an avaricious lay brother whose provost spoke of him as "my good fellow with a beard," and in this case the lay brother was not a Cistercian but a Premonstratensian.[19]

The most frequent reference to the lay brothers' beard seems to come from satirists who took great delight in ridiculing it. In a fable in which Odo of Crediton refers to the Cistercians and the Premonstratensians as white sheep and the Benedictines and canons regular as black sheep, a bearded goat signifies Grandmontine and Cistercian *conversi* "whose flowing beards they won't let anyone shave. They argue about which order is better. . . . They can wear any type of beard imaginable, but they shall never enter into glory unless they have grace in their heart and live lives transparently good to both God and men. So goes the verse:

> If being bearded could make anybody blessèd
> In the whole world there is nothing holier than the goat.
> A saint's not made by a robe, white or black,
> Nor can asinine crosses produce the justice men lack.[20]

In a sermon criticizing the greed of the Cistercians, the poet Gautier de Coincy (1177–1236) refers to the lay brothers' beards as being "so long that one could make large wreaths out of them."[21] On the other hand, this general lack of reference to the lay brothers' beards is offset by an exhaustive treatise devoted entirely to the subject, which is also the only known medieval work devoted to beards.

---

[19] *DM* 4.62 (Strange 1:229; Scott and Bland 1:261).

[20] Jacobs 1985, 127–28: *per hyrcum barbatum, Grandi montenses et conversi Cistercienses qui barbas habent prolixas et radi nob permittunt. Isti quandoque inter se contendunt quis ordo melior [sit]. . . . Similiter barbati, qualemcumque barbam habeant, nunquam intrabunt in gloriam, nisi in corde habeant gratiam et coram Deo et hominibus bonam vitam. Versus: Si quem barbatum faciat sua barba beatum, / in mundi circo non esset sanctior hyrco. / Sanctum nulla facit nigra, candidi vestis ovina(rum), / Nec quemquam iustum facit unquam crux asinina.*

[21] Batany 1969, 256.

## Apologia de Barbis

Around the year 1160 Burchard, abbot of Bellevaux in eastern France, wrote a curious but often humorous treatise addressed to the lay brothers of his daughter house of Rosières entitled *An Apology Concerning Beards*.[22] It is a *tour de force*, pushing biblical texts to the limit and extracting every possible ounce of word play from the words *barba* and *barbarus*, which appear in more than a dozen varieties, beginning with the opening sentence: "I may be called *barbilogus* [beard-speaker] because I am giving a *barbisonant* [beard-resounding] talk on *beards*."[23] This has been called a medieval masterpiece of *plaisanterie*.[24] Burchard wrote it to make amends for having criticized the lay brothers for their disorderly behavior and unchaste lives. He discusses different kinds of beards, and the question whether to have beards or not. He describes the beards of the apostles and of holy men and the distinctive beards of the Jews, and he distinguishes the cut of the beards of lay brothers from the "military or urban style" (*militaris aut urbana figuratio*). According to him beards are a sign of fortitude, wisdom, maturity, and spiritual strength. The length of the lay brothers' beards, he writes, should accord with what was required by the General Chapter, namely, the width of two fingers.[25]

Addressing the lay brothers, Burchard writes: "You people have the beard without the crown, we clerics the crown without the beard."[26] The contrast could scarcely be greater or the difference in status more clearly stated. Great significance was obviously attached

---

[22] Burchardus de Bellevaux 1985, 151–224. The text is analyzed and discussed by Giles Constable in the introduction to the critical edition (pp. 47–150). Burchard had been a monk of Clairvaux, a disciple of Saint Bernard, and abbot of Balerne (Jura)—and therefore is more commonly known as Burchard of Balerne. On Burchard, see also Chauvin 1989.

[23] Burchardus de Bellevaux 1985, 151: *Barbilogus fortisan dicar, quia de barbis facio sermonem barbisonantem.*

[24] Mikkers 1962, 119.

[25] Burchardus de Bellevaux 1985, 162: *longitude barbae ultra duos digitos sub mento non descendat.*

[26] Burchardus de Bellevaux 1985, 165: *Vos populus cum barba sine corona, nos clerus cum corona sine barba.*

to the difference in hairstyle.[27] The lay brothers "cultivate carnal works" (*carnalia exercetis opera*) to sustain the "old man" (*veterem hominem*); monks "cultivate spiritual pursuits" (*spiritualia exercemus studia*) to strengthen the "new man" (*novum hominem*) "so as to cut off superfluous things which are indicated in the shaving of hair and beard" (*ut abscidamus a nobis superflua, quod in rasione capitis et barbae figuratur*). Lay brothers have beards so they may prepare "exterior things" (*exteriora*); monks shave to acquire "interior things" (*interiora*). Monks "plant spiritual things" (*spiritualia seminamus*) and reap; the lay brothers' "carnal things" (*carnalia*), which they provide for the monks. The lay brothers are "outside" (*foris*), exposed to the heat and cold, and need beards and hair for protection, while the monks are "inside" (*intus*), enclosed in claustral discipline, not needing beards and hair. Burchard concludes:

> Observe, finally, that beards are not convenient for the office of the altar, which is ours, but that beards are not inconvenient but well suited for agriculture, which is your office. On entering the holy of holies, we cut away the hairiness of beards, while you, going out to till the fields, show from the state of your beards the kind of work you do. . . . It would be unsuitable for beards to hang over books and chalices; therefore we who are engaged around the altars and chalices are without beards; you, assigned to ploughs and mattocks, have beards.[28]

## Clothing

Walter Daniel, Aelred of Rievaulx's biographer, says in a letter, "I, wretch that I am, wear the habit of a monk, I am tonsured, I

---

[27] I am grateful to Abraham Plunkett-Latimer, who read a paper entitled "Beards and Bodies in Burchard of Bellevaux" at the International Congress on Medieval Studies, Kalamazoo, Michigan, in May 2009.

[28] *Sermo* 2, chap. 6; Burchardus de Bellevaux 1985, 166–67: *Videte denique quod ad officium altaris, quod nostrum est, barbae non conveniunt, sed ad agriculturam. Quae vestri officii est, barbae non disconveniunt sed congruunt. Nos ad sancta sanctorum ingredientes barbaram pilositatem resecamus, vos ad culturam agrorum egredientes ex habitu barbarum ostenditis quod de labore estis. . . . Non deceret super libros aut super calices dependere barbas ideoque sine barbis versamur circa altaria et calices, vos cum barbis deputati estis ad aratra et ligones.*

am cowled."[29] Just as the monk was defined by his cowl and his tonsure, so was the lay brother by his beard and his cloak. According to the *Usages* the clothing of the *conversi* consisted of a cloak or mantle made of coarse common cloth or coarse skins, simple or lined with cloth, four tunics, footwear—either shoes, clogs, or sandals—and a detachable hood that covered his shoulders and chest. The abbot could provide additional clothing for herdsmen, wagoners, and shepherds.[30] Although there is nothing in the *Usages* to say that the mantles were not to be made of new material, this is indicated by a statute from 1159 that stipulates a severe punishment for its contravention: "The lay brothers who have cloaks of new cloth or new skins, which is contrary to our *Usages*, are not to be allowed to go out in them. If they rebel they are not to be allowed to go to Communion, and if they persist they are to be expelled."[31]

The decree that the mantle was to be made of coarse common cloth (*pannus vilis*) and not of wool was not always adhered to. In 1190 the lay brothers of Fontfroide in southern France were accused of persistent disobedience to the command of the Chapter for not dispensing with woolen garments (*cotta floccata*) and were warned that if they continued they would be refused Communion and be barred from entering the oratory and, should they die, they would not be allowed a holy burial place.[32]

Illustrations in art suggest the garb varied from place to place and from period to period. The kneeling lay brother on the left of the Obazine tomb may be seen wearing a tunic, while the lay brother on the right is wearing a mantle with hood over his tunic.[33] A carving in the late-fourteenth-century cloister of Jerpoint in

---

[29] Daniel, Ep M 4; Powicke 1950, 78; CF 57:156. *Habitum ego miser monachi porto, ego tonsus, ego cucullatus.*

[30] UC 16 (Waddell 73–74; 189–90): *Vestitus sit: cappa, pelles grosse, simplices vel cooperate, et grosso et vili panno, tunice, calige, pedules, sotulares, caputium scapulas et pectus tantummodo cooperiens.* For the lay brothers' clothing see Ducourneau 1929, 174–77.

[31] *Statuta* 1159.3 (Canivez 1:70): *Conversi qui mantellos habent de novo panno vel pellibus novis quod est contra usus, nullo modo eis demittantur. Si rebelles sint, interim non communicent et ultimi in ordine constituantur.*

[32] *Statuta* 1190.75 (Canivez 1:132).

[33] See fig. 8.

Ireland shows a figure with a long beard and the distinctive fringe, probably a lay brother who may have been remembered for his part in its construction.[34] He wears a tunic and, unlike the Obazine figures, a longer scapular, a long piece of cloth worn over the head and extending, front and back, to below the knees and fitted with a hood, and he wears a belt. Over these he wears a large cloak. His right hand is raised, and in his left hand he carries a staff and a Pater Noster (an early form of the rosary). He has sometimes been identified as an abbot, the staff considered a crozier. Although the staff does have a crook this is very small and totally without embellishment, and it should therefore be seen as a shepherd's staff, which would be quite normal for a lay brother to carry. He has been described as a monk, as Saint Dominic, and as Saint Bernard, but both hairstyle and habit point to him being a lay brother.

There is no reference to the color of the monastic habit in the Rule or in the early Cistercian texts, and similarly there is no mention of color in the chapter on clothing in the lay brother *Usages* or in any General Chapter statutes.[35] Cistercian monks are known to have adopted white by the 1120s, a choice dictated by the lower cost of undyed wool. Writing in 1135, Orderic Vitalis says of the Cistercian habit that they "dispense with breeches and lambskins . . . and wear no dyed garments."[36] Before entering Rievaulx, Aelred heard tales of "wonderful men, famous adepts in the religious life, white monks by name and white also in vesture. For their name arose from the fact that, as the angels might be, they were clothed in undyed wool spun and woven from the pure fleece of the sheep."[37]

---

[34] Illustrated in France 1998, 134.

[35] For the color of the monastic habit, see France 1998, 78–82. The color of the lay brothers' habit has sometimes been given as black (Cassidy-Welch 2001, 170), based on chapter 16 of the *Usages* where black is mentioned, but only as referring to the blacksmiths' smocks and not to the general lay brother habit.

[36] Orderic Vitalis 1969–1980, 4:325, 311.

[37] Daniel, *Life of Aelred,* 5; CF 57:96–97: *mirabilis quidem et religione insignes, vestitu quoque albos et nomine. Nomen enim ex eo traxerunt quod ovis vellere puro in filum producto et in telam deducto sine fuco cuiuslibet coloris angelice satis tegerentur.*

The use of dyed wool was specifically prohibited by the General Chapter in 1181: "Dyed and modish wools are utterly excluded from our Order."[38] As sheep and wool come in many shades, from a natural white to pale brown or grey to a reddish or darkish brown, so the habit took on a wide spectrum of color from near-white to dark brown, and the Cistercians became known as "white monks" and occasionally also as "grey monks."[39] For at least two centuries the lay brothers' tunics and cloaks were, like the tunics and cowls of the monks, almost certainly also made of undyed wool. The 1181 prohibition was repeated in the 1256 collection of statutes and here the lay brothers are specifically mentioned: "The clothing worn by monks and lay brothers is not to be dyed."[40] The habits of the abbot, the cellarer, and the lay brother depicted in the fourteenth-century Tennenbach property register are all the same shade of grey.[41] It is sometimes said that the color of the lay brothers' habits was originally distinct from that of the monks,[42] made of either grey or brown, but there is no literary evidence to support this. Although in more recent times lay brothers adopted brown for their tunics and mantles, there are no medieval pictorial examples indicating color such as there is in the case of monks, whose cowl was usually white or later sometimes black.

The separateness in hair and clothing which distinguished *conversi* from *monachi*, and which had its external physical expression in the beard and cloak of the one and the tonsure and cowl of the other, was an outward sign of the distinctive spirituality of the two groups: the members of one were largely nurtured by *labor manuum* and those in the other by the *Opus Dei* and *lectio divina*.

---

[38] *Statuta* 1181.11 (Waddell 2002, 96): *panni tincti et curiosi ab ordine nostro penitus excluduntur.*

[39] It occurs, for example, in the *Dialogue between a Cluniac and a Cistercian*, when the Cluniac is accusing the Cistercians: "the grey monks are always on the move" (CF 33:137).

[40] Ducourneau 1929, 176: *Vestes quibus utuntur monachi et conversi non sint tinctae.*

[41] See fig. 11.

[42] Lekai 1977, 336.

# Chapter 5

# Two Monasteries within the Precincts of the Monastery

**M**onks are bound by the Rule of Saint Benedict; lay brothers are not. Monks' lives are regulated by the *Ecclesiastica officia*, lay brothers' by the *Usus Conversorum*. Monks are clerics and are therefore tonsured; lay brothers are not tonsured but are bearded. Monks wear cowls, the distinctive monastic garment; lay brothers wear cloaks. These were some of the distinctive features differentiating the two groups one from the other. Most striking, however, was the demarcation between them in terms of the separate provision made for their spiritual and material needs. To a large extent the Cistercians followed the monastic plan the Benedictines had developed over the centuries, centered on the cloister, but with one major deviation made necessary by the introduction of lay brothers: what emerged was in effect a second monastery for the latter. In the *Dialogue between a Cistercian and a Cluniac* the author Idung, the Cistercian abbot of Prüfening, writing in about 1155, has his monk spelling it out: "We [Cistercians] now have two monasteries within the precincts of the monastery, one of lay brothers and another of clerics" (*Nos modo habemus infra ambitum monasterii, duo monasteria: unum scilicet laicorum fratrum, & aliud clericorum*).[1] When Abbot Charles (1197–1209) moved the abbey of Villers to its final site he is said to have built "two dormitories in stone, one for monks and one for lay brothers" (*duo dormitoria lapidea monachis et conversis*).[2]

---

[1] Idung of Prüfening 3:43; Huygens 1990, 179; CF 33:133.
[2] Coomans 2000, 428.

**DOMUS CONVERSORUM**
**Byland, Yorkshire**

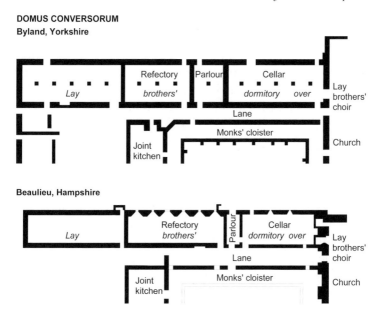

*Fig. 10* Plans of *domus conversorum* at Byland, Yorkshire, and Beaulieu, Hampshire.

The cloister was at the heart of the monastery. It served as the main artery giving the monks access to the buildings that were essential to all aspects of their lives—the church, sacristy, library, chapterhouse, parlor, dormitory, refectory, and kitchen. It provided the monks with all their needs and enabled them to abide by the statute "that a monk ought not to live outside the cloister," quoting the Rule as its authority.[3]

The innermost *claustrum*—a word meaning literally a lock or bolt, a door that shuts up a place—was the exclusive preserve of the monks and therefore was separate from and did not include the west range, which was given over to the lay brothers and to some extent mirrored the accommodation for the monks. With the *claustrum* situated south of the church, as was usually but not always the case, the lay brothers' *domus conversorum* was a long building running south from the church at the west end of the nave,

[3] *Capitula* 16 (Waddell 1999, 410); see RB 4.78 (McCann 1976, 14).

often extending to beyond the south cloister walk (fig. 10). This orientation gave the lay brothers access to their choir in the west end of the church. In a few cases, for example Bordesley and Kirkstall in England, Neath and Tintern in Wales, and Dunbrody and Graiguenamanagh in Ireland, the west range was beyond the west wall of the church, making direct access to the church impossible.[4]

## The Cellarer's Domain

All the buildings west of the cloister, both the lay brothers' range and the utilitarian buildings beyond, have been described as "the cellarer's domain."[5] The cellarer was essential to the administration of the monastery. He was not only responsible for everything to do with the monastic economy but among his duties was also the supervision of the *conversi*. He was also responsible for the hired laborers, for maintaining the monastic buildings and plant, and for the management of the abbey's outlying granges and other property. The well-being of the community depended on his stewardship. The *Ecclesiastica officia* prescribed that the cellarer lead the lay brothers into the chapter room when they asked to be received as novices and also when they made their profession after the year-long novitiate. In some abbeys he may have had the assistance of a sub-cellarer. Not more than two lay brothers at a time might speak to the cellarer.[6] The importance Saint Bernard attaches to the office may be seen by the choice of his own brother, Gerard, as his cellarer at Clairvaux. In Bernard's famous lament on his brother's death he outlined the duties of the cellarer succinctly:

> Did anything ever escape the skilled eye of Gerard in the buildings, in the fields, in gardening, in the water systems, in all the arts and crafts of the people of the countryside? With masterly competence he supervised the masons, the smiths, the farm workers, the gardeners, the shoemakers and the weavers. and yet, he whom all esteemed as supremely wise

[4] Robinson 1998, 72, 132, 149, 188; Stalley 1987, 64.
[5] France 1998b, 1–39.
[6] *EO* 117 (Griesser 1956, 278).

was in his own estimation devoid of wisdom.[7]

A successful term in office as cellarer frequently led to election as abbot.[8] Abbot Johannes Zenlin of Tennenbach in Breisgau, author of the abbey's property register (one of the oldest known records of the possessions of a monastery) had been cellarer before being elected abbot in 1337. The register meticulously records all the abbey's possessions, its granges, houses, meadows, forests, mills, fisheries, and other properties. The opening folio has two magnificent historiated initials in gold with red outline and surrounded by fili-

*Fig. 11* Property Register of Tennenbach with initial containing the seated cellarer Johannes Meiger facing a lay brother and a hired hand.

gree decoration in which are depicted all the figures associated with the Cistercian economy, including a lay brother (fig. 11). Above the initial *O* (*Dee paratum sit opus*) there is an unusual representation of the Trinity with the Holy Spirit in the form of a large one-eyed dove with its wings enveloping the Father and the Son and below it the kneeling figures of Saint Benedict and Saint Bernard. The text gives the date as 1346 and the abbot's prayer—"Although lacking in goodness but faithful to the Order"—that his work may be pleasing to God, invoking the intercession of the two saints. The lower initial *S*(*cripturus igitur possessiones*) has a kneeling abbot identified as the

---

[7] *SC* 26.7 (*SBOp* 1:175; CF 7:66): *Quid, verbi gratia, in aedificiis, in agris, in hortis, aquis, cunctis denique artibus seu operibus rusticorum, quid, inquam, vel in hoc rerum genere Girardi subterfugit peritiam? Caementariis, fabris, agricolis, hortulanis, sutoribus atque textoribus facile magister erat. Cumque omnium iudicio omnibus esset sapientior, solius in sui oculis non erat sapiens.*

[8] Examples from Denmark in France 1992, 508, 511, and 515.

former cellarer by the legend "*Frater Jo(hannes) Zenli(n) Abbas*," and below that a scene unique in Cistercian iconography: a seated monk, tonsured and in a grey habit, writing in an open book—perhaps the manuscript itself—placed on a lectern in front of him. He is identified as "*Frater Jo(hannes) Meig(er)*," probably the abbot's successor as cellarer. In front of him are two standing figures, a bearded lay brother with the distinctive fringe, wearing a grey habit, and behind him a peasant with a stick who has his hand on the lay brother's shoulder. The lay brother may be from one of the workshops or a grange master reporting to the cellarer, who is recording what is being said and perhaps giving him instructions, and the layman accompanying him may be one of the hired laborers.

## The *Domus Conversorum*

In order to establish a distance between the monks' cloister and the lay brothers' quarters, thus reinforcing the segregation of the monks from the *conversi*, there was sometimes a narrow "lane" or *ruelle des convers* between the west wall of the cloister and the *domus conversorum*. It ran the full length of the range from the south aisle at the west end of the church, to which it was connected by a door, parallel to the west cloister alley. It formed the lay brothers' own cloister walk. It was presumably this "lane" the chronicler of Louth Park in Lincolnshire referred to when, in enumerating the buildings constructed during the abbacy of Richard (1227–1246), starting with the east end of the church, he spoke of "the cloister of the *conversi* adjoining the said church."[9]

According to Aubert the lane was once all but universal and it is shown in his plan of an idealized Cistercian monastery.[10] The best-known early example was at Clairvaux, but it also was found in the twelfth century at the other French abbeys of Aiguebelle and Fontfroide and in the thirteenth century at Royaumont. Although almost always without a roof, the "lane" at Fontfroide in southern

[9] *Chronicon Abbatie de Parco Lude*, 1891, 13: *claustrum conversorum eidem ecclesie contiguum.*

[10] Aubert 1947, 2:122 and facing 2:1.

*Fig. 12* The lay brothers' "lane" with thirty-five seats at Byland, Yorkshire.

France was covered by a vault.[11] English examples include Beaulieu, Buildwas, Byland, Rufford, and Sawley. In Wales there was Neath, where the western range, built in the 1170s, is the earliest of the surviving buildings, and in Ireland Mellifont, a daughter house of Clairvaux and the first Irish Cistercian monastery. Most remarkable of those surviving is the "lane" at Byland with its series of thirty-five niche seats reminiscent of the seating sometimes provided for the monks in the north cloister walk, the so-called collation gallery (fig. 12).[12] In some abbeys the "lane" was very much wider and formed what was virtually a second cloister. Examples of this are found at Cîteaux and Clermont in France, at Villers in Belgium, at Eberbach in Germany, and at Kirkstall and Stanley in England.[13] In most abbeys the "lane" has disappeared, often the victim of the enlargement of the cloister in the thirteenth century or later.[14] At

[11] Aubert 1947, 2:122–23 and plans in figs. 23, 29, and 34. Fontfroide is illustrated in fig. 437.

[12] Robinson 1998, plans 68, 80, 82, 168, 170; Robinson 2006, 265; Stalley 1987, plan 36; the Byland "lane" is illustrated in Cassidy-Welch 2001, 174.

[13] Aubert 1947, plans 2:22 and 1:178; Coomans 2001, plan 413 and illus. 424; Robinson 1998, plans 132 and 175.

[14] Aubert 1947, 2:123.

Villers, for example, it was done away with following the rebuilding in the second half of the fifteenth century.[15]

## The Lay Brothers' Choir

The *domus conversorum* was connected to the church by a doorway either at the north end of the "lane" or, where there was no "lane," at the end of the west range itself. The lay brothers' choir in the west end of the nave was separated from the monks' choir by a solid partition or *pulpitum*, sometimes made of stone, and connected to the monks' choir by an opening at the center. It was probably the *pulpitum* Caesarius of Heisterbach was referring to when, in the story of a vision of the Virgin in the monks' choir experienced by the grange master Henry of Himmerod, he said that "the lay brother was not able to see her on account of an obstacle."[16] Examples have survived at Melrose in Scotland and Maulbronn in Germany.[17] Together with the west range, the lay brothers' choir formed what may be termed the "second monastery."

The two choirs were connected by an opening in the middle of the partition. Here the *pax*, which during Mass was passed from one monk to another down through the whole community, would be carried to the senior *conversus*, who presented himself at the screen partition between the two choirs and then passed the *pax* to the rest of the brethren.[18] The lay brothers at the abbey attended Mass on Sundays and on twenty-one other important feast days when they did not work.[19] On a number of solemnities celebrated with two Masses, which are listed in the *Ecclesiastica officia*, the monks were free of work but the *conversi* were not. The more detailed provisions of the later twelfth-century *Breve et memoriale scriptum* applying to Clairvaux include regulations as to how the lay brothers should comport themselves in choir and assign their seating, the

---

[15] Coomans 2001, 399.

[16] *DM* Hilka 1933, 1:85; *sed conversus propter obstaculum videre non potuit.*

[17] Illustrated in Coomans 2004, 244 and 247.

[18] *EO* 57 (Griesser, 226); *BMS* 1 (Waddell, 198).

[19] *UC* 3 (Waddell, 61–62; 172–73).

senior brothers taking the upper stalls nearest the altar.[20] In some redactions of the *Usages* lay brothers received communion only twelve times a year, in others only seven. Although this was a large number for the twelfth century, when non-clerics normally communicated only once a year, it was considerably less than for monks, for whom the norm was once a month in addition to all major feast days.[21] Not all lay brothers were happy with this: Caesarius of Heisterbach heard from the abbot of Dünamünde in Lithuania of a lay brother who had only recently been converted. When he saw the monks receiving communion he longed to communicate himself but realized that this was not possible, at which point "the gracious Lord condescended to come down from the altar and put the sacrament into his mouth without the help of the priest."[22]

The lay brothers' Office began the same way as the monks': all having made the sign of the cross, the senior brother would begin with: *Deus, in adiutorium meum intende*, and all would respond: *Domine, ad adiuvandum me festina*. Then followed a *Pater noster*, *Gloria Patri*, *Kyrie eleison*, and then a series of *Pater noster*s corresponding to the psalms of the monks: ten at the principal Hours of Lauds and Vespers, and five at the lesser Hours.[23]

Caesarius of Heisterbach's *Dialogus miraculorum* has a chapter entitled: "Of a lay brother who saw a demon bring phantasms into the choir."[24] The story goes like this: At one time a devil was seen bringing a herd of swine into the choir. At another time a lay brother saw a devil in the form of the prior with a collar made of a bean stalk around his neck. One of the monks was leading him by the collar as if he were a dog. As the lay brother was watching this strange procession, the prior himself entered the church to arouse any of the lay brothers who might be asleep and the vision immediately vanished.

---

[20] *BMS* 1 (Waddell, 155–56; 197–99).

[21] *UC* 5 (Waddell, 63–64; 175–76).

[22] *DM* 9.37 (Strange 2:193; Scott and Bland 2:139–40): *Et ecce pius Dominus sine sacerdotis ministerio de altari per sacramentum descendere dignatus est in os eius.*

[23] *UC* 1 (Waddell, 57–58; 166–68).

[24] *DM* 5.48 (Strange 1:333; Scott and Bland 1:383): *De conversi, qui vidit daemonem phantasmata minare in chorum.*

It is hardly surprising that the lay brothers, like the monks, fought a constant battle to stay awake, especially at Vigils, and that devils chose to concentrate their attacks at these times when the brothers were at their most vulnerable. Conrad of Eberbach speaks of the "idleness, negligence, and somnolence" (*de inertia et negligentia atque somnolentia*) of the monks during services at Strata Florida in Wales.[25] In his *distinctio* entitled "On Temptation" Caesarius includes nine chapters devoted to *somnolentia* of monks and lay brothers,[26] evidence of a problem that seems to have been endemic in choir but, as we have seen, was equally prevalent when the abbot preached in the chapter house.[27] Lay brothers appear in four of the eight.[28] In one of them we read that "several of the brethren, but chiefly lay brothers, went to sleep."[29] In another the lay brother Conrad reports having seen a serpent creeping over the back of the lay brother William, who fell asleep in choir one day when Lauds were being sung and on many other occasions; another lay brother, Richard, confirmed that he had witnessed the same.[30] Another story tells of a lay brother at Himmerod who noticed a cat sitting on the head of another lay brother who almost always went to sleep. As soon as the cat placed its paws on this brother's eyes the brother began to yawn. When the brother who had fallen asleep was told what had happened he was determined that the devil should no longer mock him, and he arranged his stall in the choir in such a way that if he fell asleep again he would be thrown to the ground, "and thus the demon of somnolence was shaken off by this device, and the lazy brother grew more fervent in the service of God."[31] In

---

[25] *EM* 4.18 (Griesser, 329).

[26] *DM* 4.29, 32, 33, 34, 35, 36, 37, 38, 83.

[27] See p. 61.

[28] *DM* 4.32, 33, 36, 83.

[29] *DM* 4.36 (Strange 1:205; Scott and Bland 1:233): *et plures, maxime de conversis, dormitare.*

[30] *DM* 4.32 (Strange 1:202; Scott and Bland 1:230): *De serpente, quem vidit frater Conradus in dorso conversi dormitantis in choro.*

[31] *DM* 4.33 (Strange 1:203; Scott and Bland 1:230–31): *De converso, cui cattus visus est oculos claudere, cum in choro dormitaret . . . . Quantum daemones illic dormitantes irrideant, ex subiecto cognosces exemplo.*

another chapter Caesarius tells the story he had recently heard from the abbot of Waldsassen in Bavaria who, when he was a novice at Pforta in Thuringia, had known a lay brother called Walter whose idleness had exposed him to the attacks of demons. He was said to "be given to an unusual degree of boredom during the divine praises. He was always going to sleep, always yawning, as soon as possible he went back to his dreams."[32]

### The West Range

The most important survival of a lay brothers' range is that of Clairvaux, built between 1170 and 1180, shortly after the death of Saint Bernard. As was usual, it consisted of two stories, each originally 75 meters long with fourteen bays and divided into three aisles with vaults supported by two rows of pillars.[33] By far the largest range, however, was that at Fountains in Yorkshire. Built during the abbacy of Henry Murdac (1144–1147), it was some 76.2 meters long and provided accommodation on the first floor for 140 lay brothers. Less than a generation later, during the abbacy of Robert of Pipewell (1170–1180), it was replaced by an even larger west range measuring 91.4 meters in length and 13 meters wide (fig. 13). The ground floor consisted of 22 double rib-vaulted bays. That in less than one generation it had become necessary to replace what was already by any other standard a large range with one of enormous proportions provides ample evidence of the colossal influx of lay brothers in the early years.[34] The Fountains *domus conversorum* compares with the ruined west ranges of other English abbeys: Byland, Furness, Jervaulx, and Kirstall, with eighteen, sixteen, thirteen, and eleven bays respectively.[35] Other good examples of monasteries with significant west range remains include Clermont,

---

[32] *DM* Hilka 1937, 3.69: *Vir supra modum in divinis laudibus accidiosus. Semper dormitabat, semper oscitabat, et si quandoque excitaretur, mox cum multa festinatione in sompnum resolvebatur.*

[33] Aubert 1947, 2:130–31, 136–37.

[34] Coppack 2003, 37, 61–62.

[35] Robinson 2006, 158.

*Fig. 13* Lay brothers' range at Fountains, Yorkshire, consisting of twenty-two bays.

Noirlac, Vauclair, Longuay in France, Neath in Wales, Maulbronn and Eberbach in Germany, and Alcobaca in Portugal.[36]

The ground floor of the west range was divided into a number of rooms. It sometimes consisted of only one aisle, as at Le Thoronet and Fontfroide in southern France, but more usually two, as at Noirlac, Pontigny, Vauclair, and Royaumont, or sometimes three, as at Clairvaux, Vaucelles, and Longuay, all of them farther north. On the northern end was the cellar or *cellarium*, used for the storage of provisions that in the earlier Benedictine plan had taken up the whole of the west range.[37] At Fountains, Byland, and Royaumont (Seine-et-Oise), for example, the cellar occupied the first six bays, at Noirlac, Pontigny, and Aiguebelle five. Next, roughly in the center and between the *cellarium* and the refectory, a passage consisting of one or two vaulted bays ran east to west through the middle of the range. A doorway to the west served as the main entrance to

---

[36] Aubert 1947, illustrated on 2:126, 127, 128, 131 (also plan); Robinson 2006, 158; Kinder 1997, 314, 318, 319, and 306 (plan of Alcobaça).

[37] Aubert 1947, 125–32.

the monastery from the outside and another doorway to the east gave access to the cloister and was often aligned with the southern cloister alley. This passageway would also have served as the parlor where the cellarer, who could speak to everyone,[38] would have assigned the lay brothers their tasks and conducted his business with outside visitors. Unusually, the outer parlors at Fountains and Rievaulx were at the junction of the west range and the church.[39]

Beyond the passage the brothers' refectory extended to the end of the range, often well south of the cloister. The size varied enormously and depended on the number of lay brothers for whom it had to cater: Fountains had twelve bays, Byland ten, Vaux-de-Cernay six, Aiguebelle five, and Clermont only four. Unlike the monks, who were read to during meals as laid down in the Rule,[40] the lay brothers took their meals in silence, as they would not have been able to understand the Latin in which books were written at the time. They sat down at table in order of seniority, wearing the cape and hood. The senior brother presided and led the prayers specified in the *Usus conversorum* for before and after the meal, and any errant brother was made to prostrate before him. The brothers' diet was the same as that of the monks and they observed the same fasts, but if the abbot thought fit he could grant some of them what was known as "mixt," consisting of an extra half pound of bread. They were waited on by *servitores*, lay brothers appointed on a weekly basis.[41] Meals were served from the kitchen common to both the monks' and lay brothers' refectories and situated at the western end of the south cloister range between the two refectories. Food was passed to the lay brothers' refectory through a hatch. Lay brothers from other houses were allowed to eat in the refectory only if they had been granted permission from the Chapter at Cîteaux.

According to the *Usus conversorum*, the lay brothers upon hearing the sacristan's bell "immediately enter their own chapter room"

---

[38] *EO* 117 (Griesser 1956, 277–78).
[39] Coppack 1993, 30; Ferguson 1999, 52 (plans).
[40] *RB* 38: "reading will always accompany the meals of the brothers."
[41] *BMS* 4 and *UC* 8 and 15 (Waddell, 156–57; 66–68; 72–73).

(*ingrediantur statim fratres capitulum suum proprium*), suggesting the existence of a separate assembly room in the west range.[42] Although Aubert refers to possible instances at Byland and Kirkstall in England, no separate chapter room has been found and it is thought that their chapter was normally held in the lay brothers' refectory.[43] It took place every Sunday except on certain feast days when the lay brothers were expected to attend the monks' chapter for the abbot's common sermon. The lay brothers' chapter was at the same time as that of the monks and the abbot or his delegate, usually the master of the lay brothers, presided. In the early thirteenth century Abbot Richalm of Schöntal in southern Germany is known to have presided at his lay brothers' chapter. In his own words: "See, yesterday when I was going to speak at the lay brothers' chapter and give them a sermon—often *I am slow and hesitant of speech* (Ex 4:10)—I was inspired and brilliant ideas came to me as to what I had intended to say, so that I began to marvel greatly both then and also afterwards at what had happened."[44]

It may be the lay brothers' chapter that is referred to in the *Life of Waldef* when, as abbot of Melrose in Scotland,

> the saint sat once among the lay brothers dispensing to them spiritual food such as they had not prepared for themselves, speaking of the kingdom of God; and when he had occasion to speak of the beatitude of the saints, he began thus, speaking of himself, but yet as if of another, assuming the third person in his narrative: "A certain monk of our order . . . ."[45]

---

[42] *UC 12* (Waddell, 69–70; 183–85).

[43] Aubert 1947, 139–40.

[44] *LR 33*; Richalm 2009, 22: *Videte, heri ad capitulum conversorum cum loqui deberem et sermocinari— pacior autem sepe in hoc impedimenta lingue—set heri manifeste sensi spiritum loquentem in me et adicientem eciam ad ea, que proposueram dicere, et repetentem et recapitulantem eadem sepius peroptime et currentem ita, ut et tunc et postmodum satis ipse mirarer.*

[45] Jocelin of Furness 1952, 149: *Sedebat Sanctus iste inter laicos fratres dispertiens eis spirituales escas, quas non praeparaverant sibi, loquendo de regno Dei: et cum de beatitudine Sanctorum sermonem faceret, de se ipso, sed tamen quasi de alio, tertiam personam in narrationem assumens, sic exorsus est. Quidam monachus ordinis nostri . . . .*

The whole of the upper floor above the *cellarium*, the parlor, and the refectory served as the lay brothers' dormitory. Even where the lower floor was vaulted, the dormitory above was sometimes timber-framed, as at Le Thoronet, Fontfroide, Noirlac, Vaux-le-Cernay, Clermont in France, and Poblet in Spain.[46] The dormitory at Clairvaux, built between 1170 and 1180, has three aisles with two rows of pillars and, with the floor below, forms the only surviving medieval building at Saint Bernard's abbey. Also having three vaulted aisles, and built in the early thirteenth century, is the dormitory at Longuay (Haute-Marne), while the one at Vauclair (Aisne) consists of two aisles with fourteen bays.[47] The longest lay brothers' dormitory of all was at Fountains, capable of housing four hundred lay brothers.

At Byland there are remains of the day stairs that connected the dormitory to the "lane" below, and in certain churches traces at first-floor level of a doorway in the south aisle indicate the existence of night stairs connecting the dormitory and the church for easy access to the night Office in the same way as the monks' night stairs connected their dormitory in the east range.[48] The lay brothers' latrines were usually at the far south end of the west range, similar in position to the monks' *necessarium* in the east range; both were situated above a common drain.

The lay brothers' bedding was largely in accord with what the Rule prescribed—a mat, a woolen blanket, a light covering, and a pillow—except that instead of the monks' light covering the lay brothers had a coverlet of skins or hides.[49] According to a statute from 1187 the provision was not always observed, but in the same statute an exception was made for *regiones frigidissime*.[50] In 1190 the lay brothers at Fontfroide in southern France were punished for having introduced unauthorized bedding in the form of padded quilts (*cottae floccatae*).[51]

---

[46] Aubert 1947, 134.
[47] Aubert 1947, 135–36.
[48] Kinder 1997, 329; Coomans 2000, 426.
[49] *RB* 58; *UC* 17 (Waddell, 190).
[50] *Statuta* 1187.5 (Waddell 2002, 143).
[51] *Statuta* 1190.56 (Waddell 2002, 210).

The dormitory was, after the choir, the most likely place for the lay brothers to be assailed by demons. When the lay brother Albero from Heisterbach was a novice he was unable to sleep and just before Vigils he left the dormitory, went downstairs, and in the cloister near the *lavatorium* saw what looked like a human shadow that grew larger and larger until it reached the upper story. When the bell rang in the dormitory he went into the bakehouse, where the fire being lighted to bake the bread nearly blinded him. He ran out and was ill both in mind and body for eight days. The explanation given by Caesarius to the novice is that as light and darkness are as contrary to one another as heat and cold, when you pass from the one to the other your sight is troubled and distressed by the sudden change. No wonder that after the sight of the devil human nature is made faint when it sees the light of the world.[52]

The Life of Arnulf, lay brother at Villers in Brabant, includes a story of the time when the brothers used to take a rest after dinner on Sundays and saints' days:

> But the man of God [Arnulf] refused to indulge in outward bodily slumber. He used to seek instead a secluded spot, where he could pour out his prayers more privately to the Lord and relax into an inward sleep of the spirit amid the delights of holy love. However, one of the brothers reproached him for this before the master of the lay brothers, who enjoined him to go and sleep at that time, just as the others did, since, if he kept awake like that, his brothers might be distressed out of pity for his body which was fatigued from his excruciating torments. He obeyed this command of his master, prepared as always to be obedient in everything. When dinner was over, however, and he had entered the dormitory and taken off his shoes to get into bed, there suddenly appeared to him a demon, laughing and making fun of him. It broke out into the words: "Hey, brother, what are you up to?"

Realizing that the demon was out to trick him, Arnulf replied: "'Depart from me, wretched one; depart from me [compare Luke

---

[52] *DM* 5.28 (Strange 1:311; Scott and Bland 1:355–57): *De Alberono conversus, qui diabolum videndo infirmatus est, et quae sit ratio eiusdem defectus.*

4:13]! Whether you like it or not, I'm off to sleep, just to shame and irk you by my repose!' Once he had said this, the ancient foe turned and fled."[53]

Another story in *Dialogus miraculorum* tells of a lay brother who was taking a midday rest in the dormitory when the devil appeared, this time in the guise of a Benedictine nun. She went round the beds of all, passed by most of them, but stopped by his, put her arms around his neck and embraced him. One of the brethren saw the nun vanishing and went over to the lay brother, who was fast asleep but lying in a fashion that was both immodest and exposed. When the bell rang he found himself too ill to get up. He was taken to the infirmary but died a few days later. The story was told by the master of one of the granges who had heard it from the monk who had seen the vision.[54]

The visions experienced by lay brothers resting on their beds at midday did not always involve demons. Walter, the keeper of the wardrobe at Clairvaux, was visited by a venerable girl who ordered him to say Mass and, although illiterate, when he awoke he retained the words in his memory and from then on he remembered every word of it.[55]

---

[53] *VA* 2.24 (*Acta Sanctorum*, 621–22); Cawley 2003, 168–69: *vir Domini quaerebat sibi aliquid diversorium, ubi dum orationes suas secretius ad Dominum funderet, et inter delicias sancti amoris interius in spiritu sua suaviter obdormiret, dormire exterius corpore recusabat. Factum est autem, ut quidam Frater pro hac re reprehenderet eum coram Magistro Conversorum. Qui statim praecepit ei, ut aliis ea hora dormientibus, ipse quoque dormiret; ne si forte vigilaret, Fratres, qui compatiebantur corpori eius, magnis fatigato cruciatibus, id moleste ferrent. Paruit ille precepto Magistri sui, sicut ad omnia paratus et obediens erat. Cum autem post prandium intrasset dormitorium et calceamenta sibi extraheret, ut in lectulo suo se collocare deberet; subito adstitit ei daemon, qui ridendo et irridendo eum, in haec verba prorupit: Frater, eja quid est, quod agis? Recede a me miser; recede a me: modo enim, velis notis, dormiam, ut confundaris et somno meo torquearis. Et cum haec dixisset, antiquus hostis in fugam versus est.*

Although the Rule allowed the monks a period of rest after dinner (*RB* 48), according to Waddell lay brothers were not entitled to this. As compensation they were allowed to sleep until the signal was rung for Lauds (Waddell, 171).

[54] *DM* 5.33 (Strange 1:316; Bond and Scott 1:362–66): *De converso, quem diabolus in specie monialis meridie dormientem complexus, intra triduum exstinxit.*

[55] *LM* 1.32 (PL 185:1304) and *EM* 4.15 (Griesser, 240).

## Infirmary and Guesthouse

Apart from the west range the only other building exclusively devoted to the lay brothers was their infirmary. Just as the monks' infirmary was located adjacent to the east range, the brothers' infirmary was usually close to and west of their range. Although also close to the lay brothers' quarters, the Roche infirmary was south of the west range, close to the drain.[56] At Fountains, a large lay brothers' infirmary with three aisles was built under Abbot Robert Pipewell (1170–1180), following the completion of the west range. It lay west of the latrine block, above the common drain. A large gable wall has survived.[57] Another large lay brothers' infirmary was completed at Waverley to the southwest of their range around 1180.[58] The lay brothers' infirmary at Clairvaux must also have been substantial: the Clairvaux addition to the lay brother regulations refers to the *magister infirmarius*, who had more than one assistant and also his own kitchen.[59] The importance of the infirmary is suggested in the *Life of Waldef* who, as abbot of Melrose, even when he himself was severely ill and had to be held up on the arms of his sons "used every day to visit the infirmaries, not only of the monks and the lay brothers, but of the poor and the guests as well."[60]

Hospitality was an essential feature of monastic life, enjoined on the monks by the Rule, for "all guests that come [are to] be received like Christ, for he will say: *I was a stranger and ye took me in* [Mat 25:35]," and "the guesthouse shall be assigned to a brother whose soul is full of the fear of God."[61] For this reason the guesthouse was one of the essential buildings that had to be provided before a new foundation could function.[62] The guesthouse monk was allowed to speak to all the guests and also to the lay brother who

---

[56] Robinson 1998, 165 (plan).

[57] Illustrated in Coppack 1993, 48.

[58] Robinson 1998, 200 (plan).

[59] *BMS* 5 (Waddell, 157).

[60] Jocelin of Furness 1952, 133: *infirmitoria non solum monachorum et conversorum, sed pauperum et hospitum visitare quotidie consuevit.*

[61] *RB* 53.1, 21 (McCann 1976, 57–59).

[62] *Capitula* 9 and *Instituta* 12 (Waddell 1999, 408, 461).

was his assistant.[63] The guesthouse or *hospicium* was usually situated near the gatehouse west of the cloister and could, like the one at Vaux-le-Cernay in northern France, be of a considerable size and include refectory, dormitory, and infirmary.[64] The Account Book of the English abbey Beaulieu dated 1270 provides us with details of how guests were entertained. Those who arrived on horseback were kept apart from those on foot and were given hospitality according to their station.[65] This distinction no doubt explains the need for two guesthouses, as at Fountains where the east and west guesthouses were built in the 1160s.[66] Gerald of Wales complained that, when he was visiting Strata Florida, the abbot had placed him

> in the public hall among the common guests and the noise of the people. He decreed also, which was more inhuman still, that neither monk nor brother nor even a servant of the house should escort him anywhere from place to place nor show him the way through unknown and lonely places, far from the paths of men, a boon which kind hearts are not wont to deny even to foreign travelers.[67]

Sometimes it would seem that the guestmaster could be a lay brother. John of Ford in his *Life of Wulfric of Haselbury* gives one example, the *conversus hospitalis* William.[68] William was particularly suited to be the abbey's guestmaster. Of noble birth, William was French by culture and language, but being bilingual he would have been able to discharge his duty of hospitality to all and sundry guests, high and low.[69]

Walter, *conversus hospitarius* at Melrose in Scotland, was responsible for "wayfaring strangers appearing at Melrose and seeking the privilege of staying overnight who were respectfully received according to the custom of the Order and especially of this house,

[63] *EO* 119 (Griesser 1956, 278): *monachus hospitalis potest loqui cum hospitali converso.*
[64] Aubert 1947, 2:146–47.
[65] *Beaulieu Abbey* 1975, 33; 277–85.
[66] Illustrated in Coppack 1993, 48.
[67] *Giraldus Cambrensis* 1937, 226.
[68] *VW* 1.14 (John, Abbot of Ford 1933, 28, CF 79:114).
[69] For this see CF 79:24–25.

and being received they were taken into the oratory to pray, in accordance with the Rule of Saint Benedict [RB 53]."[70]

In a fourteenth-century manuscript of Jacques de Vitry in the British Library is a story of a lay brother who had charge of the guests and who was flogged by his miserly abbot for his supposed lavishness.[71] Two lay brothers are known to have served as guest-masters at Eberbach: Herold, referred to as *magister hospitum*, and Burchard, the *provisor in hospitali pauperum*, evidence that there were two separate guesthouses for two classes of guests.[72] The story of another lay brother features in Ralph of Coggeshall's *Chronicle*: Robert, who, during the abbacy of Peter, the fourth abbot of Coggeshall (1176–1194), was in charge of the guesthouse (*qui curam hospitum habebat*). It is a remarkable testimony, like the one from Melrose, to the way the detailed procedure laid down by Saint Benedict in the Rule and fleshed out in the early Cistercian usages was still being enforced in an English monastery toward the end of the twelfth century. Robert is said to have gone into the hall of the guests where

> he found certain persons distinguished both in appearance and attire, wearing the habit of Templars and with skull caps on their heads. There were nine of them or perhaps a little more as the brother had not paid much attention. He greeted them with courtesy. One of them who seemed to be in charge said: "Where can we get something to eat?" He replied: "With the abbot in his chamber," to which they replied: "It is not our custom to eat in private chambers but in the hall with the guests." The brother left the hall to see the abbot, telling him of the guests who had arrived and the abbot immediately ordered him to prepare what was necessary and get the table ready. He promised to have a meal in private with them.

---

[70] Jocelin of Furness 1952, 138–39: *hospites peregrini Melros apparentes et pernoctandi petentes gratiam, devote juxta consuetudinem Ordinis, et maxime domus illius, suscipiebantur; suscepti in oratorium orandi causa, secundum S. Benedicti regulam, deducebantur.*

[71] *Catalogue of Romances* 1910, 3:434; BL MS Harley, 268.

[72] Mossig 1978, 431.

The guests were received very much as prescribed by the Rule and the *Usages*: "let the head be bowed or the whole body prostrated on the ground." The abbot undertook what was expected of him when he broke "his fast for the sake of the guest," and the guestmaster adhered to the *Usages* by feeding the guests, whom he is to serve himself, and by arranging for their bedding.[73]

The story continues:

> When the abbot came to the table he ordered the lay brother to introduce the guests. But, going into the hall, the brother was totally unable to see the guests whom he had seen a short time before. He searched other rooms but was still not able to find them. He knew they must be somewhere and, according to someone, they had been seen going towards the church and had made their way to the brothers' cemetery. He sent a messenger to look for them but he failed to find them. When he asked the door keepers of the guesthouse they asserted that no one had gone in or out. Who these men were, where they had come from, nobody to this day knows. From what we know of the brother's life and the manner of his thinking, and also because he had frequently told us the same things, we had no doubt that he was telling the truth. During his final illness by which he was taken from the light of this world, the community simply related these things. He was a simple teller of these events using just a few words, with no ostentation in what he said or the facts he related.[74]

The meaning of this mysterious story of monastic hospitality and the disappearance of the guests is not at all clear. We have seen the punctilious way in which Robert fulfilled the obligations of his office. We also note the total confidence of his abbot and the community in his word, notwithstanding the strangeness of the episode, and the simplicity with which he recounted this strange tale "using just a few words, with no ostentation in what he said or the facts he related" (*paucis utens verbis, nullam ostentationen in dictis seu in factis*

---

[73] *RB* 53 (McCann 1976, 57–58); *EO* 119 (Griesser, 278).
[74] *Radulphi de Coggeshall* 1875, 134.

*praetendens*), in all ways conforming with the silence enjoined by the *Usus conversorum*.[75] Elizabeth Freeman calls him "a classic personification of exemplary Cistercian qualities,"[76] qualities praised even by Gerald of Wales, one of the severest critics of the white monks, who had to admit that they "incessantly exercise acts of great charity toward the poor and the traveler."[77]

### The Outer Court

Beyond the west range, in addition to the lay brothers' infirmary and the guesthouse, lay a large number of utilitarian buildings— agricultural and industrial—shared by monks and lay brothers. Enclosing these and the main claustral buildings, the monks' infirmary, the abbot's lodgings, and the guesthouse, as well as the common cemetery, gardens, and orchards was a substantial wall that formed a symbolic barrier between the enclosed spiritual world of the community and the secular world beyond as well as a necessary physical demarcation.[78] The precinct wall served the dual purpose of keeping out unwelcome visitors and at the same time marking out the community's space.

The main point of entry and exit was the gatehouse, where the porter was responsible for overseeing the coming and going. The Rule prescribed that he should be a wise old man and that he should be provided with a room at the gate.[79] His duties are described in the *Ecclesiastica officia*. If the visitor were a monk or a lay brother from another abbey the usual rule of silence applied.[80] An external outside chapel or *capella ad portas* for the guests was sometimes adjacent to the gatehouse, as at Écharlis in France, and

---

[75] *UC* 6 (Waddell, 64–66; 177–79).

[76] Freeman 2002, 192.

[77] *Itinerarium Kambriae* 1.3; *Giraldi Cambrensis Opera* 1861–1891, 6:43: *caritate largiflua in pauperes et peregrinos infatigantur exercent.*

[78] For the precinct see Coppack 1990, 100–28, and for ancillary buildings see Aubert 1947, 2:141–59.

[79] *RB* 66.77 (McCann 1976, 74).

[80] *EO* 120 (Griesser 1956, 279–80). For the gatehouse see Williams 1998, 200–2.

sometimes outside the precinct altogether at some distance from the abbey, as at the English abbeys of Hailes and Coggeshall.[81]

The area within the precinct wall formed the wider or true *claustrum*, which contained all the facilities necessary for sustainability, supplemented only by the produce of the outlying granges. This was the enclosure referred to by Saint Benedict when he decreed that "the monastery should, if possible, be so arranged that all necessary things, such as water, mill, garden, and various crafts may be within the enclosure, so that the monks may not be compelled to wander outside it, for that is not expedient for their souls."[82]

The crafts enumerated by Bernard in his eulogy for his brother identify some of those in which monks and lay brothers were jointly engaged in the various workshops. Some of these are enumerated in Arnold of Bonneval's account in the *Vita prima* of the construction of new buildings at Clairvaux in 1135:

> The fullers too, and the bakers and tanners, the carpenters, and other craftsmen all fashioned machinery adapted to their tasks, harnessing the gurgling waters to stream through their buildings, banked up and welling forth from the underground channels wherever it was needed. And those widespread waters, when they had finally completed their special ministry to each workshop, passed on to purge the house of its refuse, afterwards returning to mainstream and restoring to the river the pristine measure of its flow.[83]

At a time when the English abbey of Beaulieu had seventy-three monks and sixty-eight lay brothers (1270)[84] its Account Book lists a large number of departments, some in which monks and lay brothers were jointly engaged with the help of hired workers, and of

---

[81] Aubert 1947, 2:144; Robinson 1998, 124; Knowles and St. Joseph 1952, 133.

[82] *RB* 66 (McCann 1976, 74).

[83] *VP* 2.5.31 (PL 185:285): *Sed et fullones, et pistores ,et coriarii, et fabri, aliique artifices, congruas aptabant suis operibus machinas, ut scatariret et prodiret, ubicunque opportunum esset, in omni domo subterraneis canalibus deductus rivus ultro ebulliens; et demum congruis ministeriis per omnes officinas expletis, purgata domo ad cardinalem alveum reverterentur quae diffusae fuerant aquae, et flumini propriam redderent quantitatem.*

[84] *Beaulieu Abbey* 1975, 17.

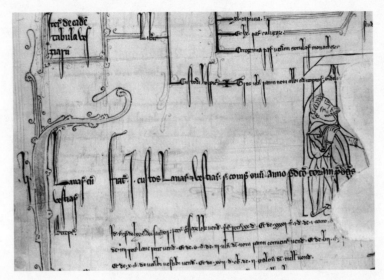

*Fig. 14* Brother J, keeper of the wool-store and wardrobe at Beaulieu, Hampshire.

occupations, some held by monks and others by lay brothers: the pig-gery, the larder, the keeper of salt, the cartilage (kitchen garden), the parchment maker, the forester, the shoemaker, the tanner, the wool-store and the *vestiarius*, the skinner, the cellar, the brew house, the orchard, the stables, the forge, and the bakehouse. This list gives a good idea of the diverse activities and offices involved in the monastic econ-omy. Apart from the lay brothers working in the kitchens, infirmaries, and guesthouses, a number of lay brothers are named in connection with their craft. Among these are Taibald, who was in charge of the forge (*procurator procudii*) at Melrose in Scotland, Gerald the tailor from La Ferté in 1170, Martin the smith from Pilis in Hungary in 1199, Richard the parmenter and William the shepherd from Tintern in 1261, and Adam the carpenter from Combermere in 1307.[85]

One of the offices enumerated in the Beaulieu Account Book, that of *vestiarius*, is illustrated with a drawing in brown ink of a bearded lay brother with the usual fringe (fig. 14).[86] Most of the

[85] Jocelin of Furness 1952, 179; Williams 1976, 118; Williams 1998, 85.

[86] The drawing is in London, British Library, MS add. 48978, fol. 41v; the text surrounding the drawing is in *Beaulieu Abbey* 1975, 219.

seventy-five leaves of the manuscript have large holes where numerous drawings have been cut out. Only six leaves have escaped mutilation, leaving three surviving drawings, two of which have been partly cut away, plus, by another hand, in the lower margin of a folio an inferior drawing of a monk. The figure of the lay brother is complete, but part of the drawing to its right is missing. The post behind the figure and the beam above are similar to those in one of the other drawings, which shows two lay workers in a fulling mill,[87] evidence of the help of hired laborers. As the text next to the figure refers to "Brother J keeper of the wool-store and wardrobe" we may conclude that this is he, and that what he is carrying over his shoulder is either a sack of wool or some cloth. Another scene in the same manuscript shows two men with scissors cutting what is either cloth or parchment.[88] Although the heads have been cut away, the treatment of the tunic of one of them and the fact that he is drawn in brown ink while the other is in orange suggests that this once represented another lay brother.

The only occupations the *Usages* mentions are blacksmiths (who were given permission to have smocks as protection against sparks) and herdsmen, wagoners, and shepherds (who, being exposed to severe weather conditions, could be in need of additional clothing).[89] The *Breve et memoriale scriptum* has more regulations relating to a number of the outer court workshops: weavers are to observe silence except when the master is engaged in teaching; herdsmen are also to keep silence except when hitching up the oxen to their carts or when plowing, unless strangers are passing by; cobblers and skinners and weavers speak only to the abbot or prior, or, if in need of practical advice, to the master; the bakers and the fullers speak to their master; and all the blacksmiths' forges are to be regularly inspected by the *magister conversorum*.[90]

---

[87] MS add. 48978, fol. 39v.
[88] MS add. 48978, fol. 43r.
[89] *UC* 16 (Waddell, 73–74; 189).
[90] *BMS* 6–16 (Waddell, 157–59; 201–9).

## Summary

The "two monasteries" became a distinctive feature of the Cistercian plan, catering to the special needs, spiritual and material, of the two groups making up the Cistercian family: monks and lay brothers. The plan emerged as a practical solution to the separateness of their lives and functions. It had developed from the traditional Benedictine monastic plan and was in due course, following the virtual extinction of the lay brotherhood, to revert to its original form.

# Chapter 6

# "Assigned to Plows and Mattocks"

## Early Grange Formation

The period between 1111 and 1119 saw not only the foundation of the first daughter houses of Cîteaux and the introduction of *conversi* but also the formation of the first granges, the Cistercian system of land utilization *par excellence*, which is intricately associated with lay brothers.

Around the year 1110 Gergueil, with "its lands, meadows, woods, and fisheries," was donated to Cîteaux by Elizabeth de Vergy and her family and was within a few years to become the abbey's first grange.[1] Although the workforce may at first have consisted entirely of hired laborers (*mercenarii*), these were soon joined by lay brothers under the supervision of one of their number, the grange master or *grangiarius*. Before 1117 further lands were acquired that were to become the granges of Brétigny and Gémigny.[2] The years 1116 to 1119 saw the creation of yet more granges at Moisey and Crépey.[3] The establishment of these early granges allows us to conclude that lay brothers were introduced by the Cistercians in the second decade of the twelfth century, more precisely between 1115 and 1119, as suggested by Kassius Hallinger.[4]

---

[1] Cîteaux 1961, 57–58, 141.
[2] Cîteaux 1961, 68–70.
[3] Cîteaux 1961, 76–77, 79–80.
[4] Hallinger 1956, 10.

As we have seen, the grange, sometimes also called *curtis* or *curia*, very early formed the basis of the Cistercian agricultural economy.[5] It has been described as "a farm or, more precisely, the outfarm of the main farm."[6] According to the *Instituta*, "work at granges is to be done by lay brothers and by hired hands,"[7] and the *Exordium parvum* mentions that the monks "had set up farmsteads [*curtes*] for agricultural development in a number of different places, and decreed that the aforesaid lay brothers, and not monks, should be in charge of those dwellings [*domos*], because, according to the Rule, monks should reside in their own cloister."[8]

This early evidence establishes the connection between the introduction of lay brothers and the establishment of granges. As stated above, the concept of the Cistercian lay brother and the concept of the Cistercian grange are inseparably linked. The lay brother/grange link finds expression in an *exemplum* from the Bavarian abbey of Ebrach as follows:

> It had among other possessions a grange called Sulzheim in which the lay brothers lived and worked by the labor of their own hands, by which they and their fathers were able to sustain themselves. Thus was fulfilled the prophecy "You shall eat from the labor of your hands," and "blessed are you so it will be well with you" [Ps 127:2].[9]

An early statute decreed that monks were not to go to the granges to shear sheep or to help with the grape picking or any

---

[5] On the Cistercian grange see Lekai 1977, 295–98; Donkin 1964, 95–144 (in which all known granges in England are listed); Donkin 1978, 51–67; Platt 1969; Williams 1998, 276–95; Rösener 1982; Rösener 2009.

[6] Roehl 1972, 90.

[7] *Instituta* 8 (Waddell 1999, 460): *Per conversos agenda sunt exercitia apud grangias et per mercenarios.*

[8] *EP* 15 (Waddell 1999, 435): *Et cum alicubi curtes ad agriculturas exercendas instituissent, decreverunt ut praedicti conversi domos illas regerent, non monachi; quia habitatio monachorum secundum Regulam debet esse in claustro ipsorum.*

[9] *EC* 7 (Oppel 1972, 21–22): *Habet autem inter ceteras possessiones grangiam unam Sulzehaim nomine, in qua conversi fratres conversantur operantes labore manuum suarum, quo et ipsi et patres eorum valeant sustentari. Ut impleatur illud prophete:* Labores manuum tuorum manducabis, beatus es et bene tibi eris [Ps. 127:2]).

other work.[10] Yet they were allowed to help out with harvesting the crops at the granges, although they were not to stay overnight but had to return to the abbey.[11] At first this stricture was probably generally adhered to, but in 1194 the abbot of Casalvolone was punished for sending some of his monks to stay overnight at a grange.[12]

Modern scholars are agreed that the grange system revolutionized agriculture and contributed to the rapid expansion of the Order. In the words of R. A. Donkin, "without lay brothers the typical Cistercian grange—an island of advanced organization in a sea of peasants' tenements and feudal demesne—would hardly have been possible."[13] Speaking of England, David Knowles says: "It is scarcely too much to say that the perfecting of the converse-and-grange system had revolutionized both arable and pasture farming for the white monks."[14] Louis Lekai claims that "the historical significance of Cistercian lay-brotherhood, however, lies in the fact that it was through the organized labor of unprecedented numbers of *conversi* that, at least for a century, the Order took a leading role in agrarian expansion and facilitated the unparalleled multiplication of Cistercian establishments throughout Europe."[15]

It is no exaggeration to say that without the lay brothers there might not have been any granges or that without the granges there might not have been any lay brothers. Although lay brothers were also engaged alongside the monks as artisans and service workers at the abbeys themselves as well as being agricultural workers on the abbey home farms, the *grangiae juxta abbatiam*, it is in their capacity as the sole managers and labor force at the more distant granges that they, aided by hired laborers or *mercenarii*, had the greatest impact on the monastic economy, and where, almost certainly, the greatest

---

[10] Waddell 2002, 72: *Pro ovibus tondensis, pro vindemiis, vel pro laboribus quibuscumque non licet aliquem conventum monachorum mittere ad grangias nisi pro frugibus colligendis.*

[11] Waddell 2002, 90.

[12] *Statuta* 1194.43 (Waddell 2002, 297).

[13] Donkin 1978, 173.

[14] Knowles 1957, 125.

[15] Lekai 1977, 337.

number were employed. In the words of Donkin, "the *grangia* was the most important single contribution of the new religious orders, and particularly the Cistercians, to the landscape and economy of the 12th and 13th centuries. Throughout Europe it formed the basis of their agrarian operations."[16]

It is in their capacity as managers and the workforce of the granges that we have the most familiar picture of the lay brothers, "those with beards assigned to plows and mattocks," as they were sarcastically described by Burchard, abbot of Bellevaux around 1160.[17] The earliest *conversi* known by name are Petrus and Durannus, who acted as witnesses to a Clairvaux charter dated 1135.[18] As we shall see, many stories of individual lay brothers are sited on the granges.

The grange, the characteristic unit of the agrarian economy of the Cistercians, formed the basic unit of their land planning, and although differences of climate, landscape, and soil dictated a variety of forms of exploitation, from the wine-producing *celliers* of Burgundy, Languedoc, and Hessen to the grain-producing plains of eastern Europe and the sheep stations of Yorkshire, the usual grange was a center of mixed husbandry. The name *grangia* means granary; the French *grange* continues to mean barn, the most important building used for storing grain. *Grangia*, however, refers not just to the barn but also includes all the other buildings, consisting of refectory and dormitory for the lay brothers, accommodation for guests, workshops and ancillary buildings, and usually also a modest oratory, as well as to the complete estate. Its very name reveals the predominance of arable farming, as does the prominence of a number of surviving grange barns, among them some of the finest medieval barns in England. William Morris proclaimed the Great Coxwell barn, belonging to the English abbey of Beaulieu, to be "the finest piece of architecture in England" (fig. 15). Even larger, seventy-four meters long and consisting of seven bays, was another

---

[16] Donkin 1964, 123.

[17] Burchardus, Abbot of Bellevaux. *Apologia de Barbis* 1985, 129: *vos cum barbis deputati estis ad aratra et ligones.*

[18] *Clairvaux* 2004, no. 7.

*Fig. 15* Grange barn at Great Coxwell belonging to Beaulieu, Hampshire.

Beaulieu barn at Saint Leonard's only a few kilometers from the abbey.[19] Large barns belonging to Clairvaux have survived at Cornay, Beaumont, and La Borde. Others include Lissewege, belonging to the Flemish abbey of Ter Doest, and Vaulerent, belonging to Chaalis in northern France.[20] In the same way that these barns gave their name to *grangia*, the *celliers* of the wine-producing regions were named after the cellars in which the wine was stored.

Originally the granges were supposed to be within a day's journey (*non tamen ultra dietam*) of the abbey, a distance variously estimated as fifteen to twenty kilometers and as thirty kilometers (ten, fifteen, and twenty miles).[21] In about 1170 one of the granges belonging to the abbey of Sorø in Denmark, which was only two kilometers (or a little over a mile) from the abbey, is referred to as "suitable for a grange for it was close to the monastery" (*aptam pro grangia eo quod erat monasterio*

[19] Horn and Born 1965, 1 and 36.
[20] Horn and Born 1965, 32; Czmara n.d.; Aubert 1947, 2:168. There are fine monographs on the granges of Vaulerent (Higounet 1965) and Beaumont (Wissenberg 2007).
[21] *Instituta* 5 (Waddell 1999, 459); Williams 1998, 278; McCrank 1976, 142.

*vicina*).[22] At first the regulation regarding the proximity of granges to the abbey was generally adhered to. Thus six of the nineteen Cîteaux granges were within seven kilometers (four miles) of the abbey and the remainder within a radius of forty kilometers (twenty-five miles).[23] Most of Rievaulx's more than twenty granges were within a day's journey, with the exception of one that was forty-five kilometers (thirty miles) away, two over sixty, and one approximately ninety kilometers distant.[24] Of the ten granges belonging to the Danish abbey of Sorø in 1248, seven were within a radius of fourteen kilometers (nine miles) from the abbey.[25] Proximity to the abbey made for more effective control by the cellarer and the *magister conversorum* and also allowed the lay brothers to attend Mass at the abbey on Sundays and major feast days when two Masses were celebrated. Although there is no mention of this requirement in the *Usus conversorum*, it appears in the statute Codification of 1202 and was repeated in 1237 and 1256.[26] The *Collectaneum Clarevallense* refers to a lay brother who on a solemn night stayed behind at a monastery's mill at the command of his superior while the others went to the church "according to the law of the Cistercian Order" (*secundum ordinis legem Cisterciensis*).[27] In an anecdote in the *Exordium magnum* Conrad of Eberbach suggests that it was common practice for the lay brothers to return to the abbey on feast days, saying: "It was the custom, if I remember correctly, that on the most sacred solemnity of the Assumption of the most inviolate and immaculate Virgin Mary, Bearer of God, the brothers at the granges of Clairvaux would hasten to the abbey out of respect for the day."[28]

---

[22] *Diplomatarium Danicum* I, 3: 4.

[23] Barriére 1994, 57.

[24] Burton 1998, 71.

[25] France 1992, 258.

[26] *Distinctio* 14, chap. 21 (Lucet 1964, 166): *De conversis grangiarium. Dominicis et festis diebus ad abbatiam venientibus in dispositione abbatis sit.* The 1237 and 1256 repetitions are in Lucet 1977, 189. See also Ducourneau 1929, 196, n. 4.

[27] *CC* 3.12 (Legendre 2005, 255).

[28] *EM* 4.13 (Griesser, 238); CF 72:344: *Instabat aliquando sacratissima solemnitas Assumptionis, si rite memini, intemeratae et immaculatae virginis Dei genitricis Mariae et fratres grangiarum Claraevallis ob reverentiam tantae diei ad abbatiam festinabant.*

A story in the Ebrach *exemplum* compilation refers to the return of the lay brothers from the grange of Sulzheim to the abbey for Christmas:

> On the Eve of the birthday of the Word, *when the Word was made flesh and dwelt among us* [John 1:14] the lay brothers got together and received from their prelate the obligation to hasten to the monastery as if to the gate of salvation for the great solemnity so that they may be ready for the praises of the mysteries.[29]

Lay brothers were also required to return to the abbey for bloodletting, which was not normally allowed at granges.[30] Although monks were bled four times a year, provision for bleeding the lay brothers was at the discretion of the abbot.[31]

We have a graphic description of how the proximity of a grange to its abbey functioned in practice in Goswin's *Life* of the saintly lay brother Arnulf, of Villers in Brabant.[32] Arnulf lived at the Villers grange of Sart, some thirteen kilometers (eight miles) from the abbey, sufficiently close to make possible a return journey in one day. While at the abbey he was to enlist the help of a domestic to "load harvest grain into sacks and cart it over to the monastery."

> Then, on the return trip, he should bring back in the same sacks enough bread to supply the grange brothers for the next several days of that week. . . . One day he loaded his cart again, came to the monastery, unloaded the cart, emptied the sacks at the front of the mill, and then set out with the cart for some business at the nearby grange of La Neuve Cour

[29] EC 7 (Oppel 1972, 22): *In vigilia Natalis Verbi quod caro factum est et habitavit in nobis* (Jn 1:14), *conversis fratribus consortibus suis sicut a prelato suo acceperant in mandatis ad monasterium tamquam ad portum salutis festinantibus in tanta sollempnitate divinis, ut interessent sacramentorum preconiis.*

[30] *Statuta* 1180.11 (Waddell 2002, 90): *Conversi non in grangiis sed in abbatia minuantur.*

[31] *Statuta* 1184.5 (Waddell 2002, 113–14): *Minuantur conversi quando abbates preceperint. Qui contempserit, perdat minutionem illam.*

[32] For this see McGuire 1981, 37–41, and the Preface by Barbara Newman to Cawley 2003, xxix–xlvii. See also pp. 181–86.

[seven kilometers from Villers]. After completing his business there, he took a pair of pigs and stuffed them into two sacks, for he was intending, with his prelate's permission, to give the pigs to the poor. Tying the openings of the sacks, he laid them on the cart and headed back to the monastery. As he neared the monastery gate, the pigs, ever such unquiet animals, were grunting away so importunately that the man of God feared they would arouse suspicion. And so he addressed those brute animals, just as if they had the use of reason: "Listen, pigs; listen to my words! If it is displeasing in the eyes of the Lord that I dispose of you, as I have been meaning to do, for the benefit of the poor, then permission is yours to grunt away just as you have been doing; but if it is a thing favorable and acceptable to my God that at my hand your flesh should gratify the craving hunger of the poor, then *I command you in the name of Jesus Christ* our God [Acts 16:18; Gregory, *Dial.* 2.8.3] to desist completely from the importunate grunting."

The pigs immediately fell silent. Arnulf went to the bakery to fill his sacks with bread, which he placed on top of the sacks with the pigs, then left and, having gone some distance from the monastery, he gave them permission to grunt again. They then carried on "their insane uproar until the grange was reached," when Arnulf, as he had planned, gave them away to the poor.[33]

---

[33] *VA* 2.4, 5 (*AS* June vol. 5, 617; Cawley 2003, 155–56): *fruges saccis impositas ad monasterium carrucaret; iterumque in eisdem saccis panes, qui fratribus grangiae certis per hebdomadam diebus sufficere possent, reportaret. Contigit autem eum die quadam, cum curris frugibus onerato, ad monasterium de venisse: cumque ante molendinum, saccis a frugibus evacuatis, currum suum exonerasset; cum eodem curru ad proximam grangiam, quae Novacuria dicitur, profectus est. Ubi eum negotium, proque illuc ibat, explesset; etiam duos porcos, quos a Praelato suo licentiatus, dare pauperibus prosuerat, in duobus saccis includens, ora saccorum ligavit, eisque in curru locatis ad monasterium remeavit. Cumque jam portae monasterii propinquaret, idemque porci, tamquam animalia inquieta, importune grunnirent, timens vir Dei, ne forte quisquam huiusmodi occasione in suspicionem laberetur; brutis animalibus, tamquam ratione utentibus, locutus est, dicens: Audite, porci; audite verba mea. Si displicet in oculis Domini, ne, sicut proposui, in usus pauperum vos expendam, licentiam habe tote grunniendi, sicut et facitis; si vero gratum est et acceptabile Deo meo, ut per me de carnibus vestris arida pauperum reficiatur esuries; praecipio vobis in nomine Deo*

This charming story tells us something of the to and fro between a grange and its abbey. However, as with so many of the early regulations that defined ideal circumstances, the Cistercians were not always able to adhere to this rule; especially when they had to rely on donations to increase their landholdings the monks could not always determine the location of enough lands suitable for a grange site, although they often accepted such sites as an asset that might later be exchanged for a more suitable location nearer the abbey. Furthermore, as Constance Berman has pointed out, the observance of many regulations was severely compromised by the numerous houses that joined the Cistercian order by the incorporation of existing monasteries rather than by the traditional way of "apostolic gestation," the model whereby a colony of twelve monks and an abbot would be sent out to establish a new foundation.[34] These houses very often came into the Cistercian Order with an already well-established economy. There might also be positive reasons for wanting distant granges: Obazine had a grange on the island of Oléron on the Atlantic coast some 270 kilometers (180 miles) distant from the abbey from which they obtained salt and, similarly, from their grange of Toaker in the far-away Swedish province of Halland the Danish abbey of Sorø also had access to salt as well as iron ore and valuable building timber.[35] While Grandselve in southern France had twenty-five granges within fifteen to twenty-five kilometers (ten to thirteen miles), another was devoted to the production of salt 180 kilometers (120 miles) distant.[36]

## Depopulation

When monks found it necessary to change the site of the abbey they commonly transformed the old site into a grange. When in 1143 monks settled at Old Byland in Yorkshire the vill was

---

*nostri Jesu Christi, ut penitus ab hoc importuno grunnitu cessatis . . . donec ad grangiam ventum est grunnire et clamoribus insaniae non cessaverunt.*

[34] Berman 1999, 95–97.

[35] *Diplomatarium Danicum* I, 3:223.

[36] Barriére 1994, 60–61.

apparently populated. Four years later they moved to another location on account of the problems caused by their proximity to
Rievaulx and the original site was reduced to a grange.[37] In France,
Pontigny experienced problems over lands adjoining the neighboring abbey of Reigny: between 1146 and 1151 an agreement
was reached between the two to prevent boundary disputes over
sheep grazing; offending lay brothers from either house were to be
banned and sent to other monasteries where they were ordered to
sleep on the ground for three days and only receive one portion of
food per day.[38] In 1151 the abbot of Cîteaux notified all monks of
the Order that a dispute between Pontigny and Vauluisant regarding the pasturage of sheep had been resolved and that lay brothers
who had disobeyed were to fast on bread and water for three days.[39]

Lay brothers frequently became caught up in disputes between
neighboring abbeys. Evidence of one of these comes from Gerald
of Wales (d. 1223), one of the few early observers of the Cistercians outside the Order. As one of the monks' sharpest critics he
is not always trustworthy, but on occasion he was also capable of
praising the Cistercians and, as General Chapter statutes provide
plenty of other evidence of rivalry between abbeys, his testimony
regarding a dispute between two Welsh abbeys he knew well can
be taken seriously.[40] As an example of what he saw as the avaricious
way in which the Cistercians sought to increase the number of
their granges and lands, Gerald of Wales told of two abbeys "situated in the maritime part of South Wales and neighboring in too
close proximity";[41] these were Margam and Neath, approximately
twelve kilometers (eight miles) apart. A new abbot of Margam,
Gilbert (1203–1213), appropriated for his abbey lands belonging
to the poorer Neath. The imbroglio that followed saw an attempt

---

[37] Donkin 1978, 40.

[38] Quantin 1854–1860, 2:416.

[39] Quantin 1854–1860, 2:526.

[40] For Gerald of Wales and the Cistercians see Knowles 1940, 663–72.

[41] Giraldus Cambrensis 1861–1891, 4:129: *in Australis Walliae maritime sitis,
nimiaque vicinitate propinquis.* For this, and the way the Cistercians were portrayed
by Gerald of Wales, see Castora 1997.

by the aggressor *conversi* to destroy the prize stallion belonging to Neath, which daily fought violently with Margam's own champion stallion: "They caused the rear hooves of their stallion to be fitted and armed with strong new pieces of iron and with very long and sharp nails, well formed by the workmanship of a smith, so that he might be able to kick back more powerfully."[42] In spite of their effort, victory went to the champion of the poorer monastery who, according to Gerald, exacted total victory for "he neither stopped kicking nor tearing to pieces until he had left behind a thing lifeless and motionless."[43] Despite this reversal, Margam continued to harass its neighbor, and Neath was obliged to take the case to the General Chapter. Despairing of the outcome, one of the Neath monks, Geoffrey, decided to enlist the help of a group of laymen and lead a raid himself. Gerald recounts how "after as many opponent *conversi* there met with as also Welshmen, similarly assembled from that region to inflict violent injuries, had been wounded and killed and had been there turned back in shameful flight, he, being victorious, carried off all of the booty."[44]

The need to avoid infringing on granges of other monasteries is also evidenced by an agreement reached by Rievaulx with Byland and Fountains and, more generally, by the need for legislation requiring granges belonging to different abbeys to be at least two leagues or approximately eight kilometers (five miles) distant from each other.[45] A dispute occurred over the distance between the granges of the neighboring abbeys of Silvacane and Sénanque in southern France following which the abbots of their respective mother houses of Mazan and Morimond were appointed as

---

[42] Giraldus Cambrensis 1861–1891, 4 :131: *pedes emissarii sui posteriores, quatinus recalcitrare efficaciter posset, ferris fortibus ac novis, clavisque praelongis et acutis ac arte febrili bene calibatis ferri fecerunt et armari.*

[43] Giraldus Cambrensis 1861–1891, 4:131: *nec tundere destitit, nec lacerare, donec exanimatum et penitus inmotum reliquisset.*

[44] Giraldus Cambrensis 1873, 4:132: *tam fratribus adversis ibi repertis, quam etiam Wallensibus, ad violentas irrogandum injurias similiter ex illa parte conductis, vulneratis et confectis, inque fugam turpem ilico conversis, praedam universam victoriosus abduxit.*

[45] Burton 1998, 45–48; *Instituta* 33 (Waddell 1999, 470): *Grangiae autem diversarum abbatiarum distent inter se ad minus duabus leugis.*

arbitrators.[46] Similarly, a dispute in 1190 over a grange between two other southern French houses, Boulbonne and Grandselve, was entrusted to two abbots to resolve.[47] An ongoing dispute between the abbeys of Schönthal and Schönau in Germany over a grange belonging to Schönthal led to the intervention of the General Chapter in 1197, again in 1199, and yet again in 1201 when the abbots of Ebrach and Neubourg were appointed as arbiters.[48] When the regulation regarding the distance between granges was eventually revoked in 1278 the reason given for its original introduction was "to preserve the peace between religious as well as to avoid scandals."[49]

In the case of abbey site changes it was quite common for the old site to be transformed into a grange. When the monks who in 1147 colonized Barnoldswick from Fountains, consisting of an abbot, twelve monks, and ten lay brothers, moved in 1152 to Kirkstall their former site "was reduced to a grange." Included in the original possessions were four vills from which the inhabitants were evicted in order that a grange might be formed, and later the parish church was demolished despite the protests of the parishioners.[50] Similarly in Denmark, when the monks moved to Øm (*Cara insula*) in 1172 they retained the site they had vacated at Veng as a grange.[51] The same happened in Mecklenburg, when the monks who had come from Amelungsborn in 1171 finally moved to Doberan in 1176 from the former site of Althof only a short distance away, and when in 1204 the monks moved from Faringdon in Oxfordshire to settle at Beaulieu in Hampshire, some ninety kilometers (sixty miles) away.[52]

By careful planning the Cistercians amassed under their own direct control extensive areas of land suitable for large-scale farming

---

[46] *Statuta* 1190.24 (Waddell 2002, 200).

[47] *Statuta* 1190.41 (Waddell 2002, 206).

[48] *Statuta* 1197.45 (Waddell 2002, 396); 1199.59 (Waddell 2002, 442); 1201.31 (Waddell 2002, 492).

[49] *Statuta* 1278.1 (Canivez 3:175).

[50] Kirkstall 1895, 173–74.

[51] France 1990, 259.

[52] Knowles 1956, 73.

and used the labor of their own *conversi* and hired hands, *mercenarii*. These estates were formed originally by benefactions and supplemented by purchases, exchanges, and land clearance depending on varying local conditions. The policy of concentrating and consolidating land to enable grange formation led to inevitable clashes with inhabitants who were removed in order to achieve the desired compact demesnes. The Cistercian granges were much larger than the normal tenements, which were widely distributed in strips in open fields, and their formation would not have been possible without the dislocation of the peasant population. As a result, the monks became unpopular. A few years after having evicted the inhabitants of Barnoldswick, Kirkstall acquired the whole of Accrington in Lancashire in exchange for their holding in Cliviger and, during the abbacy of Lambert (1190–1192), having evicted the inhabitants, they transformed it into a grange, whereupon the descendants of the former owners destroyed it and killed three of the lay brothers who were managing the grange, Norman, Humphrey, and Robert.[53] Similar instances of depopulation are found elsewhere: the Fountains granges of Aldburgh and Moreton-on-Moor and the Byland granges of Balk and Thorpe appear to have consisted once of a number of vills that were transformed into compact granges.[54] After acquiring the entire vill of Greenbury, which had until then consisted of characteristic one-bovate tenements, Fountains transformed it into a grange within a few years, and when in 1175 the village of Thorpe Underwood was granted to Fountains it too was converted to a grange after the removal of the inhabitants.[55] When the village of Caiton was acquired by Fountains it was converted into "a very useful grange."[56] The East Bolton grange belonging to Rievaulx was formed in 1173 upon the surrender by five lay tenants of their strips.[57] In Gascony the

[53] Donnelly 1954, 411.

[54] Bishop 1936, 209.

[55] Bishop 1936, 213. For the same development in Germany see Rösener 1982, 144–45.

[56] Donnelly 1954, 410.

[57] Bishop 1936, 213.

attempt by the monks of Berdoues to create a grange was violently resisted by the inhabitants of Cuelas, one of whom killed a lay brother who had attempted to mark out the boundaries of the projected grange.[58] Writing in the late twelfth century, Walter Map drew attention to the reputation the Cistercians had acquired as depopulators: "They proceed to raze villages, they overthrow churches and turn out parishioners, not scrupling to cast down the altars and level everything before the ploughshare."[59] Their success in rapidly increasing their landed possessions seemed to many to be incompatible with their initial ideal of poverty. Writing in the late twelfth century, the English Benedictine satirist and poet Nigel Longchamp (or Wireker), put it like this:

> They lust for land, these plaguy folk, and groan
> If neighbors' fields set limits to their own.
> Enough of milk and wool their beasts provide,
> But with enough they're never satisfied.
> Always encroaching, though their needs are scant,
> Had they the world, they still would be in want.[60]

Criticism was not confined to outsiders. In his *Life* of the anchorite Wulfric of Haselbury, the Cistercian Abbot John of Forde says of his subject that "he clasped all members of the Cistercian Order to him in a close embrace, like sons of his own body, or rather of Jesus Christ's."[61] "This champion and herald" of the Order nevertheless "charged the Cistercians with displeasing God in one thing only: they exploited gifts, that is, properties, in their jurisdiction over-freely, paying more attention to what could be

---

[58] Berman 2000, 174.

[59] Walter Map 1983, 92–93: *eradicant villas, ecclesias parochianos eiciunt evertunt, altaria deicere non abhorrent et ad viam vomeris omnia complanare, ut si videas que videras.*

[60] Wright 1872, 84; trans. Longchamp 1961, 62: *Agrorum cupidi, nunquam metas sibi poni / Vicinis vellent pestis iniqua suis. / Lac et lana greges ovium pecorumque ministrant, / Quod satis est, quamvis nil satis esse putent. / Paucis contenti, non cessant quaerere magna, / Et cum possideant omnia, semper egent.*

[61] *VW* 2.18 (John, Abbot of Ford 1933, 66; CF 79:152): *etiam omnes Cisterciensis religionis professores tanquam viscera sua immo tanquam viscera Jesu Christi sibi artius astringebat.*

than to what should be done, and, in the case of those committed to their patronage, seemed insufficiently mindful of what was due to kindness."[62]

Being in closer contact with the lay population around them than the monks, whether on the home farm, at the granges, traveling on the abbey's business, or at the abbey's town houses, the lay brothers bore the brunt of the outrage of those who saw themselves as the victims of Cistercian avarice. In a dispute in 1270–1271 over pasture rights with Fountains one of the neighboring landowners "wounded and ill-treated Brother Henry Wither, the granger of Kayton, in the common pasture of the said Abbot in the territory of Rippelay, impounding the cattle of the abbot." In a similar case the abbot of Roche instituted a suit in 1253 against one of the abbey's neighbors who had beaten two of his monks and "Brother Thomas le Granger, his lay brother, and did grievously wound and ill-treat them."[63]

An effigy in the cloister of the Catalan abbey of Poblet gives a remarkable testimony to the gratitude of the monks for the exertion of one lay brother on behalf of the abbey. It is an effigy in low relief of Brother William Tost, who died in 1366 and, most unusually, was buried in a prominent position the monks would have passed daily in the east cloister gallery next to the day stairs to the monks' dormitory.[64] On the wall above the grave is a contemporary epitaph in Catalán and Latin that reads: "Here lies Brother William Tost who in asking for justice and in the defense of the forests of Poblet was put to death by the men of Prades. May his soul rest in peace." He is shown with a neat beard and with fringed hair, lying with his hands crossed and wearing the usual *caputium* with hood.

---

[62] *VW* 2.18 (John, Abbot of Ford 1933, 66; CF 79:152): *Unum tantum erat quod hujus ordini fautor et preconator Deo in hac religione displicere causabatur, quod in datis videlicet possessionibus liberius suo jure uterentur, et magis attendentes quod licet quam quod expedit, in causa dominum qui eorum patrinicio commmendati sunt quod satis est pietatis recordari viderentur.*

[63] Donnelly 1954, 416.

[64] Illustrated in France 1998, 127.

## Number of Granges and Number of Lay Brothers

At first, when the usual statutory complement of a new foundation consisted of the abbot and twelve monks, the number of lay brothers would have been quite small.[65] In an exceptional case, that of the foundation of Heisterbach in the Rhineland from Himmerod in 1189, the apostolic dozen was made up of nine monks and three lay brothers.[66] As we have seen, the founding community of Kirkstall from Fountains conformed to the standard number of monks plus ten lay brothers.[67] The account of the foundation of Vitskøl in northern Jutland tells how "twenty-two monks and a larger number of *conversi* with their chalices, books, silver, vestments and cattle" came from Varnhem in Sweden in 1158.[68] Thirty-five named lay brothers appear in the Cîteaux charters as witnesses from the foundation in 1098 to 1182.[69] With the formation of granges, the majority of which had been established by the end of the twelfth century, the number of lay brothers multiplied rapidly; their number has been estimated at between five and fifteen *conversi* per grange.[70] According to Knowles and Hadcock there were altogether 2000 Cistercian monks and 3200 lay brothers in England and Wales in the latter half of the twelfth century, a time when there were approximately seventy houses. In other words, an average of twenty-nine monks and forty-two lay brothers populated each monastery.[71] The recruitment figures for one abbey, Les Dunes in Flanders, record for the period 1259 to 1299 211 monk recruits and 577 lay brother recruits.[72] These figures accord reasonably closely with Lekai's estimate that the lay brothers outnumbered the monks by a ratio of two to one or even three to one.[73] These

---

[65] *Instituta* 12 (Waddell 1999, 461); *Statuta* 1189.3 (Waddell 2002, 155–56).
[66] Toepfer 1983, 115.
[67] Donnelly 1954, 410.
[68] France 1992, 187.
[69] Marilier 1961.
[70] Barrière 1994, 100.
[71] Knowles and Hadcock 1953, 360.
[72] Southern 1970, 266.
[73] Lekai 1977, 337; Williams 1998, 82.

figures may, however, be misleading, for not only is much of the data unreliable but as some of the larger monasteries with their extensive possessions, such as a number of the Yorkshire houses, must have had several hundred lay brothers, the averages mean that others would have had only a very modest number. Walter Daniel tells us that during the abbacy of Aelred (1147–1167) "on feast days you might see the church crowded with the brethren like bees in a hive, unable to move forward because of the multitude, clustered together, rather, and compacted into one angelical body." He goes on to say that there were 140 monks and 500 lay brothers.[74] In his preliminary draft of the *Vita prima* Geoffrey of Auxerre asserts that during the abbacy of Saint Bernard the lay brothers were far more numerous than the monks. He asks:

> Who can number those who through God's goodness had been brought to penitence under his care in one hundred and sixty monasteries? From his monastery alone which in his day had professed the Rule of Saint Benedict in his valley, lists of 888 professions have been found after his death, quite apart from the lay brothers of whom there were a far greater number.[75]

Large numbers are indicated elsewhere as well: the lay brothers' dormitory built at Eberbach at the beginning of the thirteenth century was large enough to house 200 brothers,[76] and the dormitory

---

[74] Daniel, Vita A 30; Powicke 1950, 38; CF 57:119: *Videres festis diebus in oratorio, tamquam in alueolo apes, fratrum turbas constringi et conglomerari, nec pre multitudine usquam progredi valentes, sed consertas adinuicem et collegiatas unum quoddam exprimere corpus angelicum.* The information about the five hundred *laicos fratres* has been wrongly interpreted as meaning *conversi* and laymen and therefore, relating it to data from Waverley, estimated as about 240 *conversi* and 260 laymen. Although the figure of five hundred does seem excessive, *laicos fratres* should nevertheless be translated as just *conversi*.

[75] Bredero 1959, 44: *Aut quis numerat eos qui sub eius cura in centum sexaginta monasterias per Dei benignitatem ad penitenciam sunt adducti? Nam ex his solis qui diebus eius in valle sua beati Benedicti regulam fuere professi, exceptis videliter laicis fratribus, quorum erat longe copiosor numerus, post ipsius decessum simul in uno loco inventi sunt libelli professionum octingenti octo.*

[76] Rösener 2009, 86.

at Fountains, ninety meters (three hundred feet) long, would have been able to accommodate 170 lay brothers.

Other English houses for which figures are known include Waverley with 70 monks and 120 lay brothers in 1187,[77] and Meaux with 60 monks and 90 *conversi* in 1249.[78] The Chronicle of Louth Park records that there were 66 monks and 150 *conversi* during the abbacy of Richard (1227–1246), but of the lay brothers the chronicler adds that "there were frequently rather more than less than this number."[79] Byland had 80 monks and 160 *conversi* in 1231.[80] From the averages cited for England and Wales it is clear that the *conversi* population of many houses would have been much more modest. As we shall see, the numbers declined sharply toward the end of the thirteenth century and even further in the fourteenth century. By 1270, for example, the lay brother population of the English abbey of Beaulieu was virtually the same as that of monks—sixty-eight *conversi* and seventy-three monks.[81] Other abbeys with considerable numbers of lay brothers included Clairvaux with 300 (as against 200 monks), Pontigny, 300 (100 monks), Villers, 300 (100 monks), Eberbach, 200 (100 monks), Himmerod, 200 (60 monks), Salem, 180 (130 monks), Bebenhausen, 130 (60 monks), and Walkenried, 180 (80 monks).[82] While there were nearly 200 lay brothers at Morimondo in Italy in 1237, there were only 50 monks.[83]

As the great majority of lay brothers lived on the granges and only a relatively small number at the monastery itself it is also possible to arrive at an estimate of their numbers by looking at the number and size of the granges. Although the size of granges varied greatly, the range for primarily arable granges was 50 to 400 hectares (125 to 1000 acres), the average being around 150 and 200 hectares

---

[77] *Waverleia, Annales de,* 244.

[78] *Melsa* 1866–1868, 3:37.

[79] *Chronicon Abbatie de Parco Lude* 1891, 15: *sexaginta sex monachorum et centum quinquaginta conversorum extitit pater piissimus, quorum numerus frequentius erat major quam minor.*

[80] Williams 1998, 83.

[81] *Beaulieu Abbey* 1975, 17.

[82] Toepfer 1983, 53–54; Rösener 2009, 85–87.

[83] Comba 1983, 128.

*Fig. 16* Interior of the grange barn at Beaumont belonging to Clairvaux.

(375 and 500 acres).[84] The average size of the fourteen granges belonging to Meaux in Yorkshire has been calculated to have been 186 hectares (465 acres), ranging from 40 and 70 hectares (100 and 175 acres) to two granges that were each over 400 hectares (1000 acres).[85] In southern Germany the average size of the five granges belonging to Tennenbach was 170 hectares (425 acres), the average for Bebenhausen 193 hectares (480 acres), while, on account of more extensive clearing, the four granges belonging to Salem averaged 235 hectares (590 acres).[86] As the primary purpose of the grange barns was the storage of grain, there is a relationship between the surface area of the barns and the acreage of tilled land. There is a remarkable similarity between the known figures for the Chaalis grange of Vaulerent—1650 square meters (17,800 square feet) and 380 hectares (950 acres)—and those of the Clairvaux grange of Beaumont—1200 square meters (1300 square feet) and 275 hectares (690 acres), (fig. 16) or 4.4 square meters (475 square feet) and 4.3

---

[84] Toepfer 1983, 46, 57; for the sizes of granges see also Williams 1998, 279.
[85] Donkin 1978, 63 and Bishop 1936, 209.
[86] Rösener 2009, 74.

square meters (465 square feet) respectively per hectare of land.[87] On the same basis the Ter Doest grange of Lissewege would total 285 hectares (700 acres) and the granges belonging to the English abbey of Beaulieu of Great Coxwell and Saint Leonard's 160 and 330 hectares (400 and 885 acres) respectively.[88]

Granges devoted to sheep herding in barren mountainous regions like Wales could total 2000 to 4000 hectares (5000 to 10,000 acres), and east of the Elbe they could amount to 8000 to 12,000 hectares (20,000 to 30,000 acres).[89] The range in grange size may be seen at Meaux, where one grange was a mere 40 hectares, another 70 hectares, while two others were each over 400 hectares.[90]

Abbeys founded in the first few decades of the twelfth century had set up granges within a few years and the majority had been formed by the end of the twelfth century. Approximately half of the total granges of the abbeys in Burgundy had been created within thirty years of the foundation. There each abbey had ten to twelve granges, the more modest like La Bussière or Lieucroisssant seven to eight, while the larger abbeys like Cîteaux or Cherlieu had nearer twenty.[91] In Germany the range is said to have been between ten and fifteen for smaller abbeys (Loccum, 10; Altenberg, 14) and sixteen to twenty for larger abbeys (Walkenried, 17; Maulbronn, 20; Salem, 20). Eberbach established twelve granges, eight of which were created between 1136 and 1211, and only four more were added in the following two decades.[92] In Lower Saxony, with an average of ten to fourteen, the number of granges was less than in southern Germany.[93] Abbeys with large numbers of granges include Heilsbronn (20), Obazine (20), Grandselve (25), and Poblet in Catalonia (27).[94] The eight Cistercian abbeys in Yorkshire set up

[87] Wissenberg 2007, 71–72.

[88] Horn and Born 1965, 66–67.

[89] Lekai 1977, 275–76, where he also gives 160–200 hectares as an average; Higounet 1983, 169.

[90] Donnelly 1954, 405.

[91] Chauvin 1983, 13–52.

[92] Rösener 1983, 146.

[93] Rösener 2009, 76.

[94] Higounet 1983, 165; Lekai 1977, 296.

a total of ninety-one granges between them, an average of eleven per house, ranging from Fountains with twenty-five granges to Jervaulx with only a single grange. [95] Among the modest houses, Bonnefont in southern France, with five granges by 1165 and a further three by 1263, and Kingswood in southern England with seven granges may be cited. [96]

A closer look at some of this data enables us to estimate the range of the number of lay brothers on the granges: a small house with five granges and an average of five *conversi* for each would have had a lay brother population of twenty-five, whereas a large house like Fountains with twenty-six granges each housing fifteen lay brothers would have had a population of 390 *conversi*. We have detailed information from 1211 of the number of lay brothers on some of the granges belonging to Eberbach, including their names. Fourteen *conversi*, including the grange master and the *submagister* are named at the Gehaborn grange, five at the Dienheim grange including the lay brother in charge of the vineyard (*in ipsa curia tunc erant fratres Guntramus, Cunradus, Ruperthus, Herbordus, Cunradus vinitor*), and altogether eleven at the Berge grange, including the grange master Richard. [97] These figures are, of course, only those of the brothers on the granges, so those residing at the abbeys must be added to this number.

## Grange Chapels

In addition to the usual domestic and agricultural buildings consisting of dormitory, refectory, accommodation for guests, a number of outbuildings, stables, and mills, as well as a substantial barn, which gave its name both to the complex of buildings and to the entire estate, a grange also frequently had an oratory or chapel. [98] Grange chapels were at first intended only for the lay

[95] The granges of Fountains, Meaux, Rievaulx, Byland, Kirkstall, Sallay, Roche, and Jervaulx are all listed in Burton 1999, 274–76.

[96] Lekai 1977, 297; Donnelly 1954, 418.

[97] Mossig 1978, 231, 267, 317.

[98] For grange buildings see Williams 1998, 281–84, and Wiswe 1953, 79–82. Less usual was an infirmary, but in 1253 the General Chapter granted the Italian

brothers' private devotions and not for Mass, for which they were expected to travel to the abbey on Sundays and feast days. An example comes from the grange of Hart belonging to the abbey of Himmerod. Caesarius of Heisterbach tells a story of the saintly lay brother Henry, the master of the grange, who in the chapel after Compline, following the request of one of the lay brothers for his intercession, had a vision of the Virgin.[99] Caesarius's *Dialogus* has several other stories of Henry and other lay brothers from his grange being present in the choir of the lay brothers at the abbey, evidence that the obligation of attending services at the abbey on Sundays and solemnities was still being adhered to.[100] On another occasion Henry was present when a novice was making his profession before the abbot in the abbey's chapter house.[101]

Although altars at granges had at first been forbidden, as the number of distant granges increased and it became necessary for monks to say Mass at the granges, altars, too, increased.[102] A further reason for the introduction of altars in grange chapels was the increasing number of monks helping out at the granges, especially at harvest time. There is, for example, evidence that monks from Cwmhir in Wales were assisting the lay brothers in reaping the corn at their Carnaf and Gabalfa granges.[103] The *Usus conversorum* notes that although, according to the Rule, the monk ought to live in the cloister, he is "permitted to go there [to granges] so often as he is sent, but never to live there for very long."[104] Permission to

---

abbey of Casanova permission to have an infirmary on one of its granges because of the great distance between it and the abbey (*Statuta* 1253.37 [Canivez 1:398]).

[99] *DM* 7.15 (Strange 2:17; Scott and Bland 1:15): *Quod cum promisisset, et die quadam dicto completorio in oratorio grangiae, cuius magister erat, pro ipso preces funderet, apparuerunt oranti tres matronae mirae pulchritudinis.*

[100] For example, *DM* 8.37 (Strange 2:111; Scott and Bland 2:37–38), and *DM* 9.29 (Strange 2:186–87; Scott and Bland 2:131–32).

[101] *DM* 1.3 (Strange 1:9; Scott and Bland 1:9–10).

[102] For the grange chapel see Williams 1998, 286–87.

[103] Williams 1984, 1:158.

[104] *Capitula* 16 (Waddell 1999, 189; 410): *Nam monacho cui ex regula claustrum propria debet esse habitatio, licet quidem quociens illuc mittitur ire, sed nequaquam diutius habitare.*

build chapels at granges had been given by the General Chapter in 1153, although there is no indication that altars were also erected.[105] However, a statute in 1180 forbidding the erection of altars in grange chapels in the future, but stipulating that those already consecrated without the bishop's permission were not to be destroyed, indicates that, in spite of the prohibition, grange chapels with altars were not uncommon.[106] In 1204 the General Chapter ordered the removal of altars and everything needed for celebrating Mass.[107] The rules were gradually relaxed, and in 1236 former Benedictine abbeys that had been incorporated into the Order were allowed to keep their grange chapels.[108] In 1190 the General Chapter also ruled against cemeteries at granges, a measure designed to prevent the Cistercians from encroaching on the rights of the local parish church.[109] Caesarius tells of a grange master who paid an unworthy priest, "a man of perverse and luxurious life," to say Mass at the Hadamar grange belonging to Eberbach.[110] In 1249 Waverley obtained permission from the bishop of Winchester for Mass to be celebrated at its Neatham grange.[111] In 1255 Pope Alexander IV granted the English abbey of Beaulieu permission for Mass to be celebrated in the chapels on the granges, provided there was no prejudice to the local parish church by allowing parishioners to attend. Beaulieu's granges at Great Coxwell, Saint Leonard's, Boverey, Trougham, and perhaps elsewhere all had chapels.[112] There are substantial remains of the late-thirteenth-century chapel at the Saint Leonard's grange (fig. 17).

In 1294 the bishop of Halberstadt gave the abbot of Mariental permission to celebrate Mass at its Habersleben grange.[113] A *Liber*

---

[105] *Statuta* 1153.27 (Canivez 1:49).

[106] *Statuta* 1180.6 (Canivez 1:87): *altaria in grangiis nova non fiant*; Waddell 2002, 88.

[107] *Statuta* 1204.11 (Canivez 1:297–99).

[108] *Statuta* 1236.3 (Canivez 2:153).

[109] *Statuta* 1190.25 (Canivez 1:124).

[110] *DM* 9.54 (Strange 2:208; Scott and Bland 2:158–59).

[111] *Waverleia, Annales de,* 342.

[112] *Beaulieu Cartulary* 1974, 123.

[113] Wiswe 1953, 64.

*Fig. 17* Chapel at the St. Leonard's grange belonging to Beaulieu, Hampshire.

*altarium* from Clairvaux copied in around 1500 from an earlier work identifies the altars at the monastery and their relics and also lists eleven granges belonging to Clairvaux with altars, most of which are said to have had a relic of Saint Bernard's cowl (*de cuculla sancti Bernardi*).[114] Two Clairvaux grange chapels have survived. One is within the main building of the wine-producing *cellier* of Colombé-le-Sec, to this day producing Champagne wine. It consists of the chapel with a large Gothic window, accommodation for the *conversi* and presses above, and a large vaulted *cave* with three bays below with holes through which the juice from the presses was poured. The first master of the *cellier* was named Evrard. Another extant Clairvaux grange chapel is a modest building at Fraville.[115]

[114] Colker 2002, 462–65.
[115] Czmara n.d., 3–5, 14.

## The *Magister Conversorum*

The cellarer was responsible for the supervision of the *conversi*; it was he who received them into the Chapter when they joined and when they made their profession after the year-long novitiate, and it was to him that the grange master was responsible. The cellarer was also responsible for visiting the granges. In the words of the *Exordium magnum*, Saint Bernard's brother, Gerard, who was cellarer at Clairvaux under Bernard, was exemplary in fulfilling his obligation of visiting the granges "as demanded by his office" (*ex debito officii sui*).[116] He was praised for eating the same food as the brothers and for drinking only water, apparently to the surprise of the author.[117] A statute from 1194 rebuking the abbot of Foucarmont for not having visited his granges tells us that the obligation to visit also rested on abbots but, with the number of granges and the obligation also to visit daughter houses, such visits were probably infrequent.[118]

The cellarers in some abbeys had the assistance of a subcellarer as well as of another monk, the Master or *magister conversorum*. When candidates were received for conversion in the Chapter, a Master was assigned to them "capable of training them in good conduct and teaching them the observance,"[119] in other words, a position similar to that of the novice master for monks. According to the later Clairvaux regulations lay brothers coming to the abbey were to observe silence unless they spoke to their Master.[120] One of the Master's duties was to visit the granges. Stephen Lexington confirmed this in one of his instructions following his visitation in the early 1230's: "The Master of the lay brothers should go round all the granges at least every five weeks so that he may carefully enquire concerning the life of the lay brothers and correct any transgressions he may find."[121]

---

[116] *Statuta* 1134.68 (Canivez 1:19).

[117] *EM* 3.2 (Griesser, 278).

[118] *Statuta* 1194.23 (Waddell 2002, 291).

[119] *UC* 12 (Waddell, 70; 185): *Deputetur autem eis magister qui idoneus sit ad mores instruendos et docendum ordinem.*

[120] *BMS* 7 (Waddell, 157; 202).

[121] Griesser 1946, 106: *Item magister conversorum circueat omnes grangias semper infra quinque septimanas, ut diligenter inquirat de moribus conversorum et corrigat excessus.*

Chapter meetings were occasionally held on the granges, depending on the presence of a monk—abbot, prior, cellarer, or *magister conversorum*—who could preside. There is mention of a Master of the lay brothers in one of the local statute collections, which prescribes that the Master first hold a chapter of faults at the abbey at the lay brothers' Sunday Chapter and then, if there is time, deliver a homily until the second signal for Terce.[122] A number of Masters are known by name: Adam appears in around 1210 as a witness in the Cartulary of Byland.[123] In Wales there was J. at Strata Marcella in 1207, G. and Philip at Valle Crucis in 1222 and 1234 respectively, and Madog at Cymer in 1284.[124]

The story of a miracle that took place at the Welsh grange of Trawscoed belonging to Abbey Dore tells us that the customary visitation by the *magister conversorum* was still being carried out in the early thirteenth century and reveals that he ministered not just to the brothers but also to their lay servants and neighbors, an issue that, as we have seen, sometimes led to conflict with the local clergy:

> Easter was approaching, the feast day of Christians, when crowds approach the altar, religious as well as lay people, the old with the young, rich and poor together, in order to receive at the foot of the altar the food of life, the nourishment of the soul, the body of the Lord. The Master of the lay brothers of Dore, as is the custom in that house, went up to the grange to give Communion both to the lay people and the lay brothers. Among them was a certain youth, young in age and handsome in body but inwardly disfigured by the deformity of sin. When he came to receive the body of Christ, behold a miracle! His mouth seemed to be wide open, but was really so closely shut that not the least particle of the sacred Host could enter in. And so the wretched man left the table without having eaten, confused as he had not confessed.[125]

---

[122] Waddell 2002, 630: *Dominica magister conversorum primo loquatur de ordine; postea, si spacium habuerit, exhortatur eos usque ad secundum signum tercie.*

[123] *Byland Abbey* 2004, 371.

[124] Williams 1984, 1:158.

[125] Bannister 1929, 209–11; Hereford, Cathedral Library MS P.I.13, fol. 142r: *approquinquante pascha, die festo Christianorum, die solempni in condensis usque ad*

The importance attached to the office of *magister conversorum* may be judged by the fact that several of its holders, as likewise a number of cellarers, were elected as abbots. Among them was William, who had been Master of the lay brothers at Melrose in Scotland. He was made abbot of the daughter house of Coupar Angus in 1200 and was elected abbot of Melrose in 1202, where he remained until his death in 1207.[126] Others included Cadwgan at Cymer in Wales, who became abbot in 1284, and Peter Pape who, having first served as *magister conversorum* at Øm in Denmark, became prior at Vitskøl and then returned to Øm, where he served as abbot until about 1278.[127]

### The Grange Master

The grange master, *magister grangiae*, or granger, *grangiarius*, also sometimes known as *custos grangiae*[128] and in an example from the German abbey of Amelungsborn as *magister curie*,[129] was the lay brother in charge of the grange. In some larger abbeys he was assisted by a *submagister*: for example, Symon, mentioned in 1209 at the grange of Gehaborn belonging to Eberbach.[130]

The largest number of references to named grange masters are those in which they appear as witnesses to transactions and other

---

*cornu altaris, quo videtis non solum regulares sed eciam seculares, senes cum junioribus: sunt in unum dives et pauperes, pabulum vite, nutrimentum anime, corpus dominicum ad cornu altaris assumentes. Magister conversorum forensium, ut moris est in domo illa, ad communicandum tam seculares quam conversos, ad prefatam grangiam ascendit. Cumque fratribus omnibus communicatis seculares homines communicavit. Affuit inter eos quidam, juvenis quidem etate et elegans corpore, sed interius deformitate deturpatus. Cum vero se sub manu sacerdotis ad suscipiendum corpus Christi applicasset, ecce quid mirabile! Videbatur quidem os suum largo hiatu aperire sed sacerdoti et aliis circumstantibus tam clausum est quod non minima particula sacre hostie poterit [sic] intromitti. Abscedit itaque miser, sacra cena incenata, tam confuses quam inconfessus.*

[126] Jocelin of Furness 1952, 352.

[127] Williams 1984, 1:158; France 1992, 514.

[128] He is, for example, referred to as *custos* in *Registrum Epistolarum—Stephano de Lexington* (Griesser 1952a, 229).

[129] Wiswe 1953, 68.

[130] Mossig 1978, 231.

legal documents, evidence of the trust of their superiors in their probity and powers of judgment. Many of the thirty-five named lay brothers in the early Cîteaux charters were grange masters, the earliest being Walter, who appears in around 1155.[131] The earliest indication of a lay brother serving as grange master at Pontigny is in 1138.[132] At La Ferté, Evrand, a lay brother who had donated land upon entry, later (about 1150) served as grange master.[133] According to the Øm Chronicle, in the thirteenth century another lay brother, Oluf Kviter, had also given property to this Danish abbey upon entry and he was later put in charge of the grange at Tåning: *qui magister erat illius grangie*.[134] The names of a number of grange masters who served on the twenty granges belonging to Villers in Brabant are known: they include William (1228); Bandevin (1234); Walter (1271); and Arnold (1272) from another grange of Schooten, founded in 1161; Francon (1248); Nicolas de Harmont (1281); before these two there was one named Herman from the grange of Sart Risbart, founded before 1177; and four known masters from the Fleppe grange founded before 1190.[135] Welsh grangers are recorded from Margam: John in about 1185 and Richard in 1199, and from Llantarnam, Philip ap Seisil in 1204.[136] Maintaining discipline was not always easy, as may be seen in a reference to Peter, the *grangiarius* of the Kirkstall grange of Barnoldswick who in 1276 cut off the ear of a serving-boy at the grange for stealing two loaves of bread.[137] In 1213 a breach of discipline resulted in a *grangiarius* from Hautefontaine being "removed from office" (*de magisterio amoveatur*).[138]

In the chapter on silence in the *Usus conversorum* lay brothers have permission to speak to the grange master concerning their needs, but they are to do so standing with their hoods on and only

[131] Marilier 1961, 132.
[132] Quantin 1854.
[133] Duby 1953, 109.
[134] France 1992, 153.
[135] Moreau 1909, 194–205.
[136] Williams 1984, 2:256.
[137] Platt 1969, 189.
[138] *Statuta* 1213 (Canivez 1:409).

two at a time. Where necessary, the granger had an assistant who was allowed to speak to the staff and guests concerning necessities.[139] It would not have been necessary for the *grangiarius* to be literate in the sense of being able to read or write Latin, but it was important for him to be numerate and possess some of the technical skills and practical common sense required of someone charged with running what could amount to a sizable business. He was responsible for assigning their various tasks to the lay brothers under him, for employing the *mercenarii*, for submitting accounts, for all purchases and sales, and generally for the satisfactory management of the grange. At times the grange master would also have been responsible for negotiating the purchases or exchanges of land upon which the formation and growth of the granges depended. Three lay brothers of Eberbach, Günther, Berthold, and a Brother Baldemar, are recorded as having been responsible for the purchase of land for their grange of Birkerhof belonging to their abbey.[140] Günther and Berthold were certainly grange masters, and Baldemar probably was also. Another Eberbach grange master, Richard, is said to have been responsible for the exchange of land that led to the formation of the grange of Sandhof.[141]

A successful tenure of office as grange master could be handsomely rewarded. Caesarius of Heisterbach attributes the prophetic powers with which Simon of Aulne was blessed, and of which he mentions a number of examples, to the prudence with which he had managed the grange Colomies belonging to Aulne. He records how Simon "from his boyhood was brought up in Aulne, and kept the flocks of the monastery; then having become a lay brother he showed so much aptitude that he was made master of one of the granges; by the good and faithful administration of outward things, as a good and faithful steward, he won spiritual gifts."[142]

---

[139] *UC* 6 (Waddell, 65; 178).

[140] Mossig 1978, 303.

[141] Mossig 1978, 316: *frater enim Richardus construxit curiam ipsam.*

[142] *DM* 3.33 (Strange 1:155; Scott and Bland 1:173): *Deinde factus conversus, adeo profecit, ut cuiusdam grangiae magister efficeretur. Qui bene ac fideliter administrans exteriora, sicut bonus ac fidelis dispensator, dona meruit interiora.*

On the other hand, failure to live up to what was required of the grange master could have dire consequences, sometimes leading to dismissal. In 1221–1225 the seventh abbot of Meaux, himself a former cellarer, "began to complain of the cunning of the lay brothers and trying to temper their impudence he assigned them to the servants' duties and committed them to keeping pigs and animals and made them plough and forced them to do other tasks of the same kind." He removed a number of lay brothers "in charge of places and granges" (*custodia locorum et grangiarum*)—presumably grange masters—and turned them into stonemasons, carpenters, glaziers, and plumbers.[143]

After becoming abbot of Savigny in 1229 Stephen of Lexington undertook a tour of visitation of the houses of his filiation.[144] As a result of what he found he issued a number of instructions that, among other things, dealt with the administration of the granges and indicate the need for reform. He decreed that "the lay brother master of the grange should three times or twice a week diligently visit all the workshops and other places in his care both outside and inside. . . . Both the cellarer and the master of lay brothers should do the same whenever they come, if they have time, as this pertains to their office."[145]

Stephen also prescribed that the officials, that is the cellarer and master of lay brothers, "should keep an eye on the masters of granges and their servants so that they may be solicitous about the wheat in their care by which the brothers and the guests are kept and also the poor of Christ, in case, which God forbid, the grain should deteriorate or go rotten to the great damage of the house and cost to their souls."[146]

---

[143] *Melsa* 1866–1868, 1:432: *Interim vero, dictus Ricardus abbas noster 7 incepit aliquantulum perpendere versutias conversorum nostrorum, et, ipsorum proterviam temperare satagens, ipsos officiis servientium deputavit, et eos custodies porcorum, animalium, et operibus carucariis tradens, et alia hujusmodi opera subire coegit.*

[144] For Stephen of Lexington see Lekai 1977, 79–82.

[145] Griesser 1952a, 229: *Item conversus magister grangie omnes officinas ipsius et omnia alia intus et foris ad ipsam spectantia diligentissime visitet ter aut bis ad minus in qualibet septimana. . . . Idem faciant ambo cellerarii et magister conversorum, quociensque venerint, si sibi vacaverint, sicut ad ipsorum spectat officium.*

[146] Griesser 1952a, 229: *Item custodes grangii per se et servientes suos ita sollicite bladum cure sue deputatum custodire studeant, ne, quod absit, in grave domus dampnum*

The grange master was the monastery's agent, and like the military sergeant or corporal obeyed orders handed down from above over which he had no say. Many of these orders, like those relating to the depopulation prior to grange formation or to problems in connection with tithe exemption, were often very unpopular with the local lay population who were affected by the abbey's decisions. Being in the front line, closer than anyone, he was the one who bore the brunt of any hostile action. He and his fellow lay brothers on the grange were also the butt for the grievances of neighboring peasants, justifiable or not. Involvement in litigation inevitably entailed having to defend rights that were often open to question. In the early days this involvement in judicial litigations had given the Cistercians an enduring reputation for avarice. The facts of the case are not known, but in the middle of the thirteenth century the lay brothers Adam, *grangiarius* of the Kirkstall grange of Micklethwaite, and Walter, keeper of the plows, were charged with the murder of Adam, the layman forester of Clifford.[147]

The provision of hospitality, especially to visiting abbots or monks from other monasteries, was one of the responsibilities of the *grangiarius* for which he had the assistance of a guestmaster (*hospitalarius grangiae*) who also had permission to speak with the guests.[148] In the *Life of Waldef* of Melrose, Jocelin of Furness names William, described as "upright and God-fearing" (*justus et timeratus*), as *hospitarius* of one of the Melrose granges.[149] Sometimes the number of guests could create a problem. In 1190, for example, fifteen abbots with their secretaries and other staff met at one of the granges belonging to Pontigny.[150] Visits of abbots with their entourages on their way to or from General Chapter at Cîteaux were a frequent burden that was not always welcomed. A lay brother on a grange belonging to Riddagshausen in Brunswick was punished in 1198 for refusing hospitality to the abbot of Lehnin in Brandenburg as he traveled on

---

et anime sue dispendium putrescat vel deterioretur, quo fratres sui et hospites sustentari debent, insimul et pauperes Christi.

[147] *Kirkstall* 1904, 22.

[148] *BMS* 9 (Waddell, 158; 204).

[149] Jocelin of Furness 1952, 178.

[150] *Statuta* 1190.76 (Canivez 1:132–33).

his way to General Chapter.[151] The grange master and guest master of one of the granges belonging to Obazine (Corrèze) were ordered in 1200 to make the journey on foot to Cîteaux to await punishment for having failed to provide straw for the horses of abbots on their way to General Chapter.[152] In another case the grange master of an unidentified grange of an abbey in the Clairvaux filiation was found guilty of inhospitality toward travelers to the General Chapter in 1192 and ordered to be flogged in the lay brothers' chapter and then to spend a year at Clairvaux.[153] In 1213 the grange master of the La Ferté grange of Chaltre was accused of "inhuman conduct in word as well as in deed" (*tam in verbo quam in factum se inhumanum exhibuit*) toward abbots on their way to the General Chapter. He was ordered to go on foot to the motherhouse where he was to eat coarse bread, have no wine, and sleep on the ground for three days.[154]

## Henry, *Grangiarius* of Hart

Henry, the grange master of the Himmerod grange of Hart, is indisputably the most extensively recorded of all lay brothers. He features in no fewer than twelve of the chapters in the *Dialogus miraculorum*, although in some he only receives a cursory mention.[155] Caesarius relied to a large extent on oral sources, the most frequently quoted being Herman, who was elected abbot of Himmerod in 1196 and in 1215 became the first abbot of its daughter house Marienstatt.[156] He is depicted as a forceful abbot of noble birth "whose spirituality and authority are well known," and who is credited with the foundation of Caesarius's own abbey of Heisterbach in 1189.[157] He must have known Henry well and became a

---

[151] *Statuta* 1198.42 (Waddell 2002, 416).

[152] *Statuta* 1200.64 (Waddell 2002, 476).

[153] *Statuta* 1192.20 (Waddell 2002, 243).

[154] *Statuta* 1213.50 (Canivez 1:414).

[155] For example, in *DM* 7.16 (Strange 2:21; Scott and Bland 1:473) and *DM* 8.95 (Strange 2:162; Scott and Bland 2:97–98).

[156] For this see McGuire 1980, 171–82.

[157] *DM* 5.5 (Strange 1:281; Scott and Bland 1:321): *quantae sit vir religiositatis, quantaeve gravitates, bene nosti.*

living witness to his numerous visions, whose authenticity he never doubted and which he communicated to Caesarius, who is himself revealed as the monk in the dialogue with one of his novices.

Henry successfully interceded on behalf of one of the Himmerod monks, and this led to the visions already noted of the Virgin and two female saints and the descent of the Holy Spirit in the form of a dove at the profession of a novice.[158] Henry is described as "a man good and upright, of mature age and virgin in body" who had the gift of seeing demons in different guises. When he mentioned this in confession to Herman, who was not yet abbot, Herman expressed the wish to be granted this favor himself. His prayer was heard when he saw a demon in the form of a thick-set peasant who later transformed himself into a calf's tail.[159] When entering the lay brothers' choir Henry would make a deep reverence before the altar, and then a white dove would leave the cross on the lay brothers' altar and settle on his head. On one occasion the dove flew down from the cross and settled on the head of Abbot Herman who, according to custom, had gone into the lay brothers' choir. When the Gospel was being read the dove flew to the column next to the lectern, listened attentively to the reading, and afterward returned to the cross.[160] Caesarius uses the impeccable reputation and credibility of Henry's testimony to bolster the position of his abbot and at the same time to assert the prestige of the family of all the three Rhineland abbeys of the Clairvaux filiation with which Herman was intimately connected, Himmerod, Marienstatt, and Heisterbach. The good name of the whole Order is invoked in another story. While wandering around the farm one day, Henry came across a white-haired man with a long beard standing under a pear tree. The man inquired as to how Henry liked the Order, adding that "it certainly ought to please you, since there is no manner of life so perfect in the whole Church

---

[158] See p. 43.

[159] *DM* 5.5 (Strange 1:282; Scott and Bland 1:321).

[160] *DM* 8.37 (Strange 2:111; Scott and Bland 2:37–38).

of God," a statement that naturally pleased Henry.[161] This vignette
provides further evidence of the anxiety displayed in other Cistercian sources at the beginning of the thirteenth century, especially
in parts of Germany where the Cistercians were constantly under
attack.[162] In the same story Caesarius has the old man boosting
Herman when he says of him, "I love him because he is a religious
and a lover of discipline and because he prays every day for the
whole Church and the Order."[163]

Caesarius's *Dialogus* contains three more stories in which the
dove appears. Once again Henry saw a snow-white dove, the sign
of the Holy Spirit, descending during the reading of the Gospel
by a visiting monk, and took it as evidence of the excellence of
this monk's life.[164] On another occasion when Herman was celebrating Mass a dove came and settled close to the chalice, indicating the true presence of the body of the Lord.[165] This was perhaps
meant as a sign in defense of the Real Presence at the Eucharist, a
doctrine which at the time was being challenged especially in the
Rhineland. The dove made her appearance again at the deathbed
of a lay brother, this time in response to the prayers of his fellow
lay brothers, and successfully repelled the vicious demonic attack
of two crows that had appeared just before the tablet was struck,[166]
a graphic image of the way demons were thought to congregate at
the deathbed of those who had served the lay brothers.[167]

Caesarius arranged his material into *distinctiones* covering a
number of themes. The stories about Henry are more or less evenly
distributed among these and thus reveal something of lay brother

[161] *DM* 8.96 (Strange 2:162; Scott and Bland 2:98–100): *Quomodo placet tibi ordo tuus frater? Converso respondente, bene; iterum adiecit. Bene tibi placere debet, quia nulla vita tantae perfectionis est in Ecclesia Dei.*

[162] *EM* 1.10 (Griesser, 61).

[163] *DM* 8.96 (Strange 2:162; Scott and Bland 2:99): *Ego, inquit, illum diligo, eo quod religiosus sit et amator disciplinae, et quia quotidie orat pro omni Ecclesia et ordine.*

[164] *DM* 8.38 (Strange 2:111–12; Scott and Bland 2:38–39).

[165] *DM* 9.29 (Strange 2:186–87; Scott and Bland 2:131–32).

[166] *EO* 94 (Griesser 1956, 257).

[167] *DM* 11.16 (Strange 2:284; Scott and Bland 2:251–52).

spirituality: devotion to Mary, to whom three of the stories refer,[168] and a recognition of the value of her special protection; vigilance in the face of the attacks of the devil, especially in choir, which was the center of their life of prayer; reverence for the Eucharist; and an unswerving faith in the power of prayer. We also learn something of the way Henry discharged his duties as a granger: his interest in the successful running of the estate is revealed when we see him "wandering alone round the crops of the farm in the month of May."[169] He presided at the brothers' office in the grange chapel, he made sure that the brothers in his charge fulfilled their obligation of returning to the abbey on Sundays, and he accounted for them to his abbot.[170]

## Other Stories from the Granges

The stories about Henry the grange master at the Himmerod grange of Hart may be the most numerous of all those recorded in *exempla* that occurred at granges, but they are by no means the only ones. An apparently trifling act of disobedience that occurred on one of the Clairvaux granges made so great an impression that it merited being included in three *exemplum* collections. A lay brother went to wash his shoes without first getting permission from his grange master. The *Collectaneum Clarevallense* asserts that "he either forgot himself, or had a disdain for the rules, or perhaps he was just too simple" (*aut sui oblitus, aut contemptor mandati sive nimium simplex*). He heard voices saying to one another, "hit him, push him into the water." One of them replied: "Certainly not!" Although he saw nobody, he felt himself being pushed violently from behind. The pain increased and within a few days he died. The story ends: "the voices he heard were undoubtedly those of demons, which were meant not just for him but also for us so that in that striking

---

[168] See p. 253.

[169] *DM* 8.96 (Strange 2:162; Scott and Bland 2:98): *die quadam Mayo segetes curtis, orationes suas ruminando, solitarius circuiret.*

[170] See references in n. 155.

and the subsequent death we may consider how dangerous it is to those who profess obedience to act in any way disobediently."[171]

The Beaupré compilation has an abridged version of the same story. There is no mention of the grange master, but the dialogue is identical and the moral of the tale is the same, but briefer: "Well now, how dangerous it is for anyone who has professed obedience to act in a disobedient way" (*ecce quam periculosum professit obedientiam quicquam inobedienter agere*).[172] As usual, Conrad of Eberbach gives more detail than the other two accounts. We hear that the lay brother "went out and stood on the bank of the river." After he had heard the voices he was struck with two strong blows, one on the head, the other on his feet. He returned to the grange and he was immediately taken back to the abbey, where he confessed before dying. Unlike the other accounts, Conrad has an introduction to the story saying that as a warning to the lukewarm he would tell a story of "the negligence of a brother and how God punished him for his negligence" (*negligentiam cuiusdam fratris et poenam, quam pro eadem negligentia sua divinitas sustinuit*).[173]

Herbert of Clairvaux tells of a Clairvaux lay brother who was an ox-driver and who, in a dream, saw Christ, holding a goad in one hand and driving the oxen with him from the other side of the wagon. When the lay brother saw this

> he was immediately struck with a violent pain and took to his bed. After six days he finished his labor and pain with death. Blessed Bernard knew the simple, honest conscience of the man and was very pleased when he thought about this vision about which he had been told. The brother being dead now, Bernard revealed that he had confidently told him that he had walked with God. He had even worked with Him and therefore God had taken him up. For it was not possible that

---

[171] *CC* 4.47 (Legendre 2005, 345–46): *Voces istas quas audivit, voces fuisse demonum non dubitamus, quas non sibi sed nobis audivit, ut in illius percussione et subsequuta morte perpenderemus quam periculosum sit professis obedientiam quicquam inobedienter agere.*

[172] *BC* fol. 30v.

[173] *EM* 4.24 (Griesser, 251); CF 72:364.

the Almighty Merciful One, to whom he had been a most worthy companion and collaborator in his labors, should desert his servant in his last agony.[174]

The story is repeated by Conrad of Eberbach who, as was his custom, elaborates on it.[175] He adds that the lay brother "promptly and devoutly did everything enjoined on him by his masters" (*qui omnia, quae sibi a magistris suis fuissent iniuncta, promptus ac devotus*) and he "bore the labors of each day with utmost patience" (*cottidianos labores patientissime tolerebat*). While Herbert has him dying shortly after the vision, Conrad says that "when he awoke and thought about the gentleness, kindness, and sweetness of his very devoted helper, there surged in his heart a vehement desire and he hoped and yearned to see face to face [Gen 32:30] the one whom in his vision he deserved to have as such a compassionate coworker."[176] After this the lay brother became ill and died, but in Conrad's expanded account Saint Bernard was able to visit him to say goodbye before he died.

These stories and the ones about Henry, the granger from Hart, provide us with our best glimpse into the life of the lay brothers: uppermost are the themes of their reliance on the protection of Mary and the importance of the exemplary virtues of obedience and humility. But they also raise the question of why so many of the stories of visions and miracles are located at the granges rather than at the abbey itself. The explanation may simply be that the

---

[174] *LM* 1.15 (PL 185:1291–92): *Quod cum ille vidisset, illico correptus aegritudine, lecto decubuit, et post dies sex laborem et dolorem cum morte finivit. Beatus vero Bernardus qui conscientiam hominis puram ac simplicem noverat, cum visionem hanc ipso referente cogitaret, plurimum inde gratulatus est. Defuncto autem fratre, pronuntiavit de ipso confidenter quoniam cum Deo ambulavit; etiam vere cum ipso operatus est, ideoque transtulit illum Deus. Nec potuit miserator omnipotens servum suum in supremo agone deserere, cui dignantissimus comes et cooperator fuerat in labore.* The story is repeated verbatim in the Fürstenfeld Collection (Kompatcher Gufler 2005, 238).

[175] *EM* 4.18 (Griesser, 243–44).

[176] *EM* 4.18 (Griesser, 244): *Cumque evigilasset et piissimi collaboratoris sui mansuetudinem, benignitatem dulcedinemque mente revolveret, exarsit subito in praecordiis eius ignis vehementis desiderii ipsum suspirantis, ipsum facie ad faciem videre cupientis, quem in beata visione tam socialem collaboratorum habere meruerat.*

total number of lay brothers at the granges was greater than that at the abbey. It may also be that, on the one hand, when they were on their own in a harsher religious environment adherence to the rules was deemed to be specially meritorious, or, on the other hand, that the temptations to contravene the regulations were much greater owing to the brothers' closer contact with the world. There is also evidence that the absence of the daily liturgy caused some lay brothers to consider the grange less attractive than the monastery. Their acceptance of this loss was the subject of praise from Saint Bernard in a chapter sermon to the monks in which he told of the brother who stayed behind at the grange for the feast of the Assumption, having "offered a service of morning worship to our Lady so pleasing, so devoted, so festive, that the contemplation of none of you, however exalted, or your intensive devotion could be preferred to his devotion, which was offered not in the lofty sublimity of contemplation, but in the humble submission of holy simplicity."[177]

---

[177] *EM* 4.13 (Griesser, 239); CF 72:346: *tam iucundum, tam devotum, tam festivum Dominae nostrae matutinarum exsolvisse servitium, ut nullius vestrum quantumcumque suspensa contemplatio seu intensa devotio ipsius devotioni, quam non alta contemplationis sublimitas, sed submissa sanctae simplicitatis effecit humilitas, praeferri potuerit.*

# Chapter 7

# Separate but Equal

## Equal in Life and Death

The physical demarcation between monks and lay brothers that took the form of the "two monasteries" and also expressed itself by the distinctive habit and the lay brothers' beards has been discussed in chapters 4 and 5. Their separate existence and roles are acknowledged in the paragraph of chapter 25 of the *Exordium parvum* announcing the institution of lay brothers: "lay brothers, and not monks, should be in charge of those dwellings [granges], because, according to the Rule, monks should reside in their own cloister."[1] The statement in the same section that monks are "to treat them [lay brothers] as themselves in life and death" (*eosque in vita et morte . . . ut semetipsos tractaturos*) is equally important. In the words of the *Capitula*, "we receive these lay brothers as our family members and helpers under our care, just as we receive monks. We hold them as brothers and, equally with the monks, as sharers in our goods, spiritual as well as temporal."[2] Stephen Harding begins the Prologue to the *Usages* by saying that they "have received from bishops the care of souls of lay brothers equally as of monks" (*cum constet super animas fratrum laicorum aeque ut monachorum curam nos suscepisse ab episcopis*), and he describes the

---

[1] *EP* 15 (Waddell 1999, 435): *decreverunt ut praedicti conversi domos illas regerent, non monachi; quia habitatio monachorum secundum Regulam debet esse in claustro ipsorum.*

[2] *Capitula* 20 (Waddell 1999, 190; 411): *tanquam necessarios et coadiutores nostros sub cura nostra sicut et monachos suscipimus, fratres et participes nostrorum tam spiritualium quam temporalium bonorum aeque ut monachos habemus.*

*Fig. 18* Our Lady of Mercy with four monks on left and four lay brothers on right.

lay brothers as "equals in the grace of redemption" (*pares constat esse in gratia redemptionis*).[3] Their equality is suggested by the ritual at the *Mandatum* on Maundy Thursday when the abbot washed

---

[3] *UC* Prologue (Waddell, 56, 164–65).

the feet of four monks, four novices, and four lay brothers.[4] Saint Aelred asserts the separate but equal roles of monks and lay brothers and their interdependence when he says: "Our lay brothers do not lament that they do not sing psalms or take part in vigils as the monks do. Nor do the monks lament that they do not work as the lay brothers do."[5]

The extent to which the equal status of monks and lay brothers was or had ever been a reality is perhaps the most crucial question in the history of the lay brothers in the twelfth and thirteenth century. Equality is suggested in the depiction of the two groups in one of the oldest versions of Our Lady of Mercy, the so-called *Schutzmantelmadonna*, from the Silesian abbey of Lubiaz (Leubus), dated about 1320 (fig. 18). Within the initial G(*audeamus*) and under a trifoliate arcade, Mary opens her cloak to reveal four tonsured and clean-shaven monks on the left and four bearded lay brothers on the right.

In life the similarity between lay brothers and monks was considerable: according to the *Usus conversorum*,

- "At Vigils as well as at the Day Hours they say their prayers just like the monks" even though, as they were not to have books, the number of prayers was very limited and they were to be learned by heart;[6]

- the term used for their reception into the monastery—*veniens quis ad conversionem*—is the same as that used for monks and is taken from the Rule;[7]

---

[4] *EO* 21 (Griesser 1956, 199): *quattuor monachorum, quattuor novitiorum et quattuor fratrum laicorum pedes lavet.*

[5] *Sermo 7 in natali Sancti Benedicti* (PL 195:249): *Non ergo querantur fratres nostri laici, quod non tantum psallant et vigilant quantum monachi. Non querantur monachi quod non tantum laborant, quantum fratres laici.*

[6] *UC* 1 (Waddell, 57–59; 166–68).

[7] *UC* 12 (Waddell, 70; 185); *RB* 58 (McCann 1976, 62).

- like the monks, lay brothers spent a year as novices and the traditional formula was used for profession, promising obedience *usque ad mortem*;[8]

- at the abbey, lay brothers "ate the same food as the monks, those in health like those [monks] in health, those who have been bled like those who have been bled, those who are infirm like those who are infirm,"[9] and their food was cooked in the same kitchen;

- they observed the same fasts as the monks, although those at the grange fasted only on certain days and were allowed a larger ration of bread;

- they observed the same silence as the monks.[10]

In death the same prayers were used for lay brothers and the same procedures were followed as those for monks. Although no directives are given in the *Usus conversorum*, the *exemplum* literature indicates that the regulations of the *Ecclesiastica officia* were followed and that in death lay brothers were treated as the equals of monks. On the threshold of death the brother was placed on the ground on a blanket lying on a mat or some straw, a tablet or gong was repeatedly struck, the community assembled at the deathbed, and the Litany and the Seven Penitential Psalms were said. When a brother died, the Office of Commendation followed. After being washed, the body was escorted to the church and there was continuous intercession in the form of the recital of psalms until the funeral Mass.[11] After the burial each priest was to say three Masses, each cleric one hundred and fifty psalms, others the same number of recitals of the *Miserere*, and from those who do not know this—in other words, lay brothers—the same number of *Pater nosters*.[12]

---

[8] *UC* 13 (Waddell, 71–72; 186–87).

[9] *UC* 15 (Waddell, 73; 188): *Eisdem cibis vescentur quibus et monachi, sani scilicet ut sani, minuti ut minuti, infirmi ut infirmi.*

[10] *UC* 6 (Waddell, 64–66; 177–79).

[11] *EO* 94–98 (Griesser 1956, 257–62).

[12] *EO* 98 (Griesser 1956, 262).

A story in Herbert of Clairvaux's *Liber miraculorum* has a lay brother from Clairvaux who, knowing that he was about to die, himself ordered the tablet to be struck, saying: "strike the tablets very quickly for it will announce my death."[13] In another story Herbert suggests that lay brothers may have been more equal to monks in death than in life, but that their equality did not extend at all after death, beyond the grave. A monk and a lay brother had died on the same day and had received the same services and been buried in the same tomb, when

> it was shown to a certain holy man in a vision that two most beautiful shrines had been built at Clairvaux, one in the infirmary of the monks, the other in the infirmary of the lay brothers. The first, however, was nobler in length and more graceful. By the construction of the twin shrines . . . the habits of both men are clearly shown to be precious in the sight of God. Yet the differences in the shrines indicate differences of merit, because, however holy the one man, we believe the other to exist with more holiness in God.[14]

Herbert ends by saying that the difference in the two shrines indicated the difference in their merits, but one cannot help wondering whether it may not also have reflected the difference in status between the monk and the lay brother.

Caesarius of Heisterbach gives more detail of the way the regulations to be followed upon the death of a lay brother were

---

[13] *LM* 1:14 (PL 185:1291): "*Pulsate quantocius tabulam, quoniam ipsum praestolantur exitum meum.*" The same story is found in the Fürstenfeld Compilation (Kompatcher Gufler 2005, 237) and in the *Exordium Magnum, EM* 4.23 (Griesser, 250).

[14] *LM* 1.1 (PL 185:1276; Newman 1996, 104): *Et, dum ista fierent, viro cuidam spirituali demonstratum est in visione quod duo pulcherrima templa fabricarentur in Clarevalle; unum in infirmatorio monachorum, alterum in infirmatorio conversorum. Sed primum illud hoc altero longe nobilius erat atque venustius. Constat igitur quia in gemina constructione templorum . . . designata sit evidenter pretiosa in conspectu Domini mors amborum. Templorum autem differentia meritorum distantiam indicat, quia, quamvis utrumque sanctum, tamen alterum altero sanctiorem existere credimus apud Deum.* The difference may of course refer to the difference between the two individuals, but it is more likely to reflect the relative merits of monks and lay brothers in general. Conrad of Eberbach has the same story: *EM* 3.13 (Griesser, 179).

observed. A lay brother who at the end of his life had been placed on the mat saw that

> two crows suddenly flying up circled round him and at last perched on the beam which was over his head. . . . Meantime the board was beaten and the brotherhood hastened there. And when the cross was carried in, a snow-white dove entered the door of the infirmary in front of it and flying above the beam mentioned alighted in the midst of the crows. And fighting with them and beating them this way and that with its wings at last it won the victory and expelled them from the house, settling down in the place of the crows until such time as the lay brother expired, and until washed and put upon the bier he had been restored to that place. And while the brothers were carrying him into the oratory, the dove flew away ahead of the cross and was no more seen.[15]

Another story in the *Dialogus miraculorum* suggests that the detailed regulations contained in the *Ecclesiastica officia* that were to be followed on the death of a monk were also meticulously applied to lay brothers. When the life of the lay brother Obert, who had worked in the infirmary for over thirty years and then himself been in pain for a further twenty years, was coming to an end,

> the board of the dying was beaten for him and rising in haste the brothers came to strengthen their brother in his departure with their prayers. Now he was lying, as was the custom, stretched upon the mat, drawing his last breath. The litany having been said whilst there still seemed some breath

---

[15] *DM* 11.16 (Strange 2:284; Scott and Bland 2:251–52): *duo corvi advolantes inopinate, gyraverunt circa illum, tandem in trabe quae capiti eius imminebat residentes. Quos ut vidit frater Henricus cuius saepe in superioribus mentio facta est, daemones illos esse suspicans, quidnam facturi essent exspectavit. Interim pulsata est tabula, et accurrit conventus. Cumque crux introferretur, columba nivea illam praecedens, ostium infirmitorii prior intravit, et super iam dictam trabam volitans, inter eosdem corvos media resedit. Cumque illis decertaret, hinc inde alis eos verberans, tandem adepta victoria, et de domo eliminatis, ipsa in loco corvorum tamdiu erat residens, donec conversus exspirasset, et donec lotus et feretro impositus, eodem loco restitutus fuisset. Quem cum in oratorium fratres deportarent, columba eadem avolans crucem praecedebat; sicque nusquam comparavit.*

left in him, they began the seven psalms. As they were saying these, he, rousing as if from a light sleep, came to life, turning his eyes all round, and at the bidding of the abbot, he was placed on his bed again and we went away.[16]

When Obert came to himself he told them that he had been soothed by the heavenly music of angels, and that he now wished to return; and so the board was beaten again and he was granted his wish and "will have his portion in the lot of the saints."

Another story from Clairvaux provides further evidence of the way lay brothers were treated in death on a par with monks. We read that when a lay brother died "the brothers assembled for the Office of Commendation, as was the custom."[17] The *Collectaneum clarevallense* has a story entitled "The Value of Community Prayer" about a prior who, in the absence of the abbot, assembled the community in the church to pray for a lay brother whose health was failing but who refused to confess and receive Communion.[18] Evidence of the same equality in death is found in the *Life* of Christian of Aumône in which "after the soul of a certain lay brother had been commended to God, that is, after the obsequies and burial, the community returned from the grave to the church singing the seven psalms as usual. They prostrated and remained like that rendering thanks."[19] The greatest accolade paid to a lay brother upon death was undoubtedly that accorded the pious brother who, according to Conrad of Eberbach, accompanied his abbot from Spain to General Chapter at Cîteaux. The closer he came to the

---

[16] *DM* 11.6 (Strange 2:274–75; Scott and Bland 2:240–41): *pulsata est tabula defunctorum pro eo, et surgentes festinantur, advenerunt fratres, orationibus munientes fratris exitum. Jacebat autem ut moris est positus super mattam, extremum trahens spiritum. Dicta letania cum adhuc aliquid spiramenti superesse videretur, incepti sunt septem Psalmi. Inter dicendum, tanquam de levi somno excitatus, revixit, circumferens oculos, et iubente Abbate repositus est in lectum suum, et reversi sumus.*

[17] *EO* 94 (Griesser 1956, 257–58); *EM* 2.2 (Griesser, 99): *Cumque concurrentibus fratribus commendationis officium ex more fieret.*

[18] *CC* 4.13 (Legendre 2005, 277–78): *Quid valeat conventus oratio.*

[19] Leclercq 1953, 52: *Conversi cuiusdam post obitum commendacione, obsequio sepulturaque iam expleta, conventus a fossa ad oratorium septem psalmos ex more psallendo redierat. Qui prostratus quod inde restabat devote persolvebat.*

much-desired Clairvaux, "the more the brother was seized by a pious longing not only to see such a blessed place but to end his allotted time there in death."[20] He revealed his wish to the community and, as he was near death,

> he was anointed with the sacramental oil and fortified by the body and blood of the Lord, and after a few days, while the abbots were gathering at Clairvaux for the Nativity of Saint Mary before the Cistercian General Chapter, it was there, if I am not mistaken, in the midst of so large and so holy a gathering of abbots, monks and lay brothers, and with the assistance of their brotherly prayers, that he breathed out his spirit, as he had desired. That imposing and venerable assembly celebrated his funeral rites with solemn and devout offices.[21]

Herbert of Clairvaux has a story of Bernard's solicitude for the lay brothers that is repeated verbatim by Conrad of Eberbach and again in the Fürstenfeld Collection.[22] On a visit to a lay brother on his deathbed the abbot told him to have courage, but realizing that the brother's confidence was excessive, he felt bound to chastise him. The brother then told Bernard the secret of his confidence—which he said he had often heard from Bernard: "that the kingdom of God cannot be acquired by nobility of blood or by earthly riches, but solely by the virtue of obedience."[23] Overjoyed at

---

[20] *EM* 6.4 (Griesser, 352): *Quanto magis approximabat desideratae Claraevalli, tanto magis optabat, si fieri posset, non solum eam videre, sed etiam sortis extremae funiculum in ea sortiri.*

[21] *EM* 6.4 (Griesser, 352); *CF* 72:523–24: *Ipse vero sacramentali oleo inunctus et viatico Dominici corporis et sanguinis munitus infra paucos dies abbatibus, qui in Nativitate sanctae Mariae Claramvallem ante capitulum Cisterciense convenerant, ibidem adhuc, ni fallor, demorantibus in medio tantae et tam sanctae multitudinis, abbatum videlicet, monachorum et conversorum, sicut desideraverat, fraternis orationibus protectum spiritum exhalavit. Cuius exsequias magni et reverendi coetus illius frequentia sollemnibus et devotis officiis celebrans terramque terrae adiciens mirabilem Deum in sanctis suis.*

[22] *LM* 1.29 (PL 185:1301–3); *EM* 4.19 (Griesser, 244–45); Kompatscher-Gubler 2005, 244–46.

[23] *LM* 1.29 (PL 185:1302): *regnum Dei non carnis nobilitate, non terrenis divitiis possidetur, sed sola obedientiae virtute acquiritur.*

hearing this, Bernard later preached a sermon to his monks urging them to follow the example of the lay brother.[24]

While Saint Bernard's regard for the lay brothers is well documented in these stories, Bernard's audience was primarily his monks and it is not surprising that lay brothers do not feature prominently in his writings. But when Bernard was away on one of his journeys he wrote back to "his dear brethren at Clairvaux" addressing his letter to "monks, lay brothers, and novices," thus acknowledging the lay brothers as equal and full members of the community by listing them after monks but before novices.[25] Another rare occasion on which Bernard referred to lay brothers comes in his letter to Humbert, first abbot of Igny (1128–1136) in which he chastises Humbert for wanting to lay down his heavy burden for one that was lighter, even though "you have no disobedient monks, nor are your lay brothers slothful in their work."[26] In yet another letter, this time to the abbot of Cuissy, Bernard acknowledges an unusual situation at a grange by pointing out the dangers inherent in men and women living together under one roof when he says: "I refer to that mill where the lay brothers in charge have to submit to the company of women. If I am to be trusted there are only three courses open to you. Either you forbid all access to women or you put the mill in charge of outsiders and not lay brothers or else you give it up completely."[27] Admittedly, Cuissy was Premonstratensian and not Cistercian, but the advice Bernard offered was inevitably based on his experience at Clairvaux and would have been the same if he had been addressing it to a Cistercian monastery.

---

[24] See also pp. 201–3 and fig. 20.

[25] *Ep.* 143 (*SBOp* 7:342; James 1953, 212): *Carissimis fratribus Claraevallis monachis, conversis, novitiis.*

[26] *Ep.* 141 (*SBOp* 7:338; James 1953, 218): *Numquid enim aut monachi tuis erant inoboedientes imperiis, aut conversi segnes in operibus.*

[27] *Ep.* 79 (*SBOp* 7:212; James 1953, 119–20): *De molendino illo dico, quod conversi custodientes feminarum pati coguntur frequentiam. Si mihi creditur, unum e tribus fiet: aut videlicet feminarum accessus omnimodis a molendino prohibebitur; aut molendinum cuicumque extraneo, et non conversis, custodiendum committetur; aut idem omnino molendinum relinquetur.*

## Limitations on Equal Status

In the story of Saint Bernard's visit to a lay brother's deathbed he displays a patronizing manner in his reaction to the brother's overconfidence by referring to him as "a poor miserable sort of fellow who, having nothing or almost nothing in the world, fled to us more out of necessity than out of fear of God."[28] Even though he was happy to praise him in his chapter talk he nevertheless referred to him condescendingly as a "rustic man" or "peasant" (*homine rusticano*). Likewise, in the story of the devotion of a lay brother on the eve of the feast of the Assumption, Bernard praised the piety of "one of the least important and most humble of our lay brothers" (*unum ex minoribus et simplicioribus fratribus nostris conversis*)[29] for staying behind in the fields instead of returning to the abbey. In spite of Bernard's lavish praise for their humility, he nevertheless revealed a certain uneasiness vis-à-vis the lay brothers, perhaps even tinged with remorse at the way he had at times been dismissive of them.

One early thirteenth-century German abbot's low opinion of lay brothers is graphically revealed, together with his other entrenched prejudices, in a short dialogue between Abbot Richalm of Schöntal and the monk-compiler of the *Liber revelationum* known as N:

> *Richalm*: "Perhaps [it signifies] I am a mere *conversus* or just a layman and therefore plain stupid or ignorant. For they often call me a prior of no account, often a Jew, and often a poor man."
>
> *N*: "Why a Jew or a poor man?"
>
> *Richalm*: "A Jew to embarrass me because I look like one, and a poor man just to insult me. To anyone of these speaking to me like that, I reply: 'Oh, you think you are the Lord, and he is very perplexed!'"[30]

---

[28] *EM* 4.19 (Griesser, 244–45); CF 72:354: *collegemus inopem et parem te fecimus in victu atque vestitu ceterisque communitatibus his, qui nobiscum sunt, sapientibus atque nobilibus viris, et factus es quasi unus ex illis.*

[29] *EM* 4.13 (Griesser, 239). For this see also p. 150.

[30] *LR* 54 (Richalm 2009, 67): *Richalmus: "Forte, quod sim conversus vel laicus et inscius et imprudens. Nam et sepe vocant me 'prior nullus,' sepe Iudeum, sepe pauperem." N: "Quare Iudeum vel pauperem?" Richalmus:"Iudeum ad confundendum me, quia fa-*

The ambivalence as to the place of lay brothers in the Cistercian family may be seen in the two words qualifying the claim in the paragraph of the *Exordium parvum* instituting the lay brothers, namely, that they were to be the equals of monks in life and death *excepto monachatu*. These two words are all-important in determining the brothers' inferior status. Chrysogonus Waddell translates the two words as "except that they may not become monks," which, while not a literal rendering, conveys the practical outcome of their meaning.[31] Louis Lekai has "except for [the rights reserved for] choir monks,"[32] and Pauline Matarasso "the status of monk apart."[33] Their inferior status is confirmed in the next line of the institution document, which says that "without the assistance of these [lay brothers and hired hands] they did not understand how they could fully observe the precepts of the Rule day and night."[34] Their *raison d'être* is here established: they are to be auxiliaries or aids to the monks, and they are referred to in the *Capitula* as "helpers under our care" (*coadiutores nostros sub cura nostra*).[35]

Just as a clerk could not enter as a lay brother, a lay brother could never become a monk. Chapter 22 of the *Capitula* entitled "That a Lay Brother May Not Become a Monk" and datable to 1136/7 stipulates that "everyone should remain in the state in which he is called" (1 Cor 7:20), but if a brother has left, "exhorted by the devil" (*suadente diabolo*), and been received as a monk elsewhere, he may never again enter a Cistercian monastery.[36] This differs somewhat from the directive in the chapter in the *Usus*

---

cies aliquatenus talis est; pauperem ad insultandum michi. Quorum alicui sic me vocanti respondi interdum: 'O, tu dominus es? Et inde multum confusus est.'"

[31] *EP* 15 (Waddell 1999, 435).

[32] Lekai 1977, 336.

[33] Matarasso 1997, 7.

[34] *EP* 15 (Waddell 1999, 435): *quia sine adminiculo istorum non intelligebant se plenarie die sive nocte praecepta Regule posse servare.*

[35] *Capitula* 20 (Waddell 1999, 190; 411).

[36] *Capitula* 22 (Waddell 1999, 190; 412): *Ut de converso non fiat monachus. Qua facta, monachus, iam etsi multum petierit, non fiat, sed in ea vocatione qua vocatus est permaneat. Quod si forte alibi suadente diabolo a quolibet vel episcopo vel abbate monachi seu etiam canonici regularis habitum sumpserit, in nulla deinceps nostrarum ecclesiarum suscipiendus erit.*

*conversorum* on "The Profession of Lay Brothers," according to which "from then onwards he is not to become a monk in our Order," but if he leaves and becomes a monk elsewhere, he is nevertheless to be received back as a lay brother after he has put aside the other habit, unless of course he has received holy orders.[37] That the rule was rigorously enforced may be seen from the case of the former *conversus* Lambert from Chaalis, who had entered another abbey as a monk. The General Chapter of 1237 ordered him to remove his monastic habit and return to Chaalis as a lay brother within fifteen days.[38] Exceptions to this injunction were extremely rare and belong to the late Middle Ages. Among the few exceptions was the lay brother Bertrand from Mortemer, whom the General Chapter in 1397 allowed to become a monk on condition that he obtained the consent of his abbot and community.[39] In 1404 the lay brother Bernard from Belleperche was granted permission *ad monachatum ascendere*.[40] More exceptional still was the lay brother Thorkil from the Danish abbey of Øm who not only became a monk but rose to become the abbey's sixth abbot (1199–1216). The reason for this exceptional instance is given in the abbey's Chronicle. He is said to have been "well-acquainted with temporal matters, endured much trouble and made great efforts on behalf of the brothers while he was still a layman and he was always and everywhere engaged in the monastery's business,"[41] attributes shared by many of the most successful cellarers and indeed by many *conversi* who served as grange masters.

---

[37] *UC* 13 (Waddell, 71–72; 186–87).

[38] *Statuta* 1237.32 (Canivez 2:174): *Cum secundum Ordinis instituta nullus conversus monachus fieri debeat a die petitionis ipsius factae in capitulo monachorum, auctoritate Cap. gen. praecipitur, ut frater Lambertus, quondam de Karoliloco conversus, et in monachum nuper receptus, deposito habitu monachi infra dies quindecim emittatur, et si postea digne poenituerit, potest recipi in conversum.*

[39] *Statuta* 1397.48 (Canivez 3:695); Ducourneau, 169.

[40] *Statuta* 1404.39 (Canivez 4:67).

[41] *Scriptores Minores* 1917–1922, 2:193: *in secularibus rebus multum eruditus; qui multos labores et magnas fatigationes in seculari adhuc habitu constitutus sepissime pro fratribus sustinuit et in omnibus negotiis claustri semper et ubique cum omni fidelitate sollicitus fuit.*

Because lay brothers could not become monks they were barred from holding any of the offices in the monastery, including, of course, that of abbot. They always remained subject to the *magister conversorum* and to the cellarer and the highest rank they could aspire to was to serve as master of one of the granges. They attended the monks' chapter only on rare occasions such as when, after a year as a novice, having first given up all possessions, they made their profession.[42] Goswin of Villers records the emotional scene when a lay brother, Baldwin, cured from depression following a vision of the Virgin, finally made his profession:

> Once, too, he unquestionably wept in full view of many. His year of probation was over, and it was the Nativity of the blessed Virgin, and the customary sermon was being given in chapter. Baldwin was seated in view of the abbot, with monks and lay brothers seated around the room. At the opening of his sermon the abbot commended and magnificently extolled the superlative holiness of the Lord's Blessed, and the bashful Baldwin was so touched to the quick *at these words of grace coming from* the abbot's *lips* (Luke 4:22) that he quickly covered his face with his hood, for *the tears were bursting* from his eyes and he could not *hold them back* (Gen 43:30-31). Fittingly did one so given to saluting the mother of salvation now receive from heaven so sustaining a grace![43]

The brothers were also present at the monks' chapter on a limited number of feast days,[44] when they stood in the cloister gallery listening through the doorway between the cloister and the chapter room; they did not have a voice in the business of the monastery. A statute in 1181 prohibited them from participating in abbatial elections.[45] The wording of this suggests that lay brothers may have had a vote prior to 1181. Dom Jean Mabillon reached this conclusion based on a remark made by Saint Bernard in a letter

---

[42] *UC* 13 (Waddell, 71–72; 186–87).

[43] Life of Abundus 19e (Cawley 2003, 242–43).

[44] *UC* 11 (Waddell, 69–70; 183–84).

[45] *Statuta* 1181.2 (Waddell 2002, 92): *Interdicitur generaliter ne conversi intersint electionibus abbatum.*

to Cardinal Hugh, former abbot of Trois-Fontaines, first daughter house of Clairvaux, regarding the disputed election of his successor at Trois-Fontaines.[46] The brethren there refused to accept Hugh's candidate, Nicholas, and Bernard was obliged to accede to their choice, saying: "Not one monk or lay brother, except two or three who were your own countrymen, would consent to having him."[47] This statement suggests that the lay brothers had taken part in the election but, according to Othon Ducourneau, Bernard simply meant to draw attention to the strength of the opposition to Hugh's choice of candidate, among both monks and lay brothers, for the issue was not the election itself but the candidature. It would, Ducourneau claims, in any case have been inconceivable for Bernard to have concurred in this breach of the Cistercian constitution. James Donnelly suggests that the 1181 statute may have been a reaction to problems the lay brothers were beginning to cause not only among the Cistercians but also among the Grandmontines and the Gilbertines, or that it was directed at the mere presence of lay brothers at elections rather than at their active participation.[48] According to a statute from 1243 ten lay brother conspirators from Sobrado in Galicia forced their way into the chapter in an attempt to influence the abbatial election.[49]

## Lives of Humility and Humiliation

In the words of Jean Leclercq, "the lay brothers lived in a humble state, that is, a state of humility, but also one of humiliation."[50] Their humility is copiously documented in the *exemplum* literature. For their humiliation we must examine the ambivalence in much of what is written about them, all of it by definition by monks. It may already be detected in the Prologue to the first version of the *Usus conversorum* written by Stephen Harding at Cîteaux, probably

[46] For this see Ducourneau 1929, 153–55.

[47] *Ep.* 306 (*SBOp* 8:224; James 1953, 443): *ut nec unus quidem monachus sive conversus, praeter duos aut tres, qui vestrates erant, acquieverit assentire.*

[48] Donnelly 1949, 24–26.

[49] *Statuta* 1243.31 (Canivez 2:265).

[50] Leclercq 1965, 241.

in the early 1120s.[51] By the time Stephen wrote this, problems had already arisen: he refers to the fact that some abbots had been too strict while others had not been strict enough, and he asserts that, as it had been necessary to draw up *Usages* for monks in order to enforce unity, he would also make provision for the lay brothers so as to avoid diversity. Using the personal "I" in lieu of the more authoritative "we" used elsewhere, and thereby identifying himself as the author, Stephen bluntly states:

> I am amazed [*miror*] that certain of our abbots devote indeed all due diligence of discipline to the monks, but none or very little to the lay brothers. Some, holding them in contempt because of their innate simplicity, think that material food and clothing are to be provided for them more sparingly than for monks, but that they are nevertheless imperiously to be made to do forced labor.[52]

Others he accuses of exploitation. They are said to give the lay brothers too much food, expecting more work out of them, and he charges that "what they seek from the society of lay brothers is their own interests, not those of Jesus Christ" (*quod de societate conversorum que sua sunt querant, non que ihesu Christi*). In either case he recognizes the vulnerability of the "simpler and uneducated" who are therefore in greater need of the abbot's attention. He was no doubt prompted by Saint Benedict's precept on how the abbot should conduct himself: "Therefore let the abbot show an equal love to all, and let the same discipline be imposed on all in accordance with their deserts."[53]

The inherent dichotomy is voiced here from the very outset. As we have seen, it may already be detected in the qualifying phrase *excepto monachatu* when lay brothers were first introduced. They are described as equal, but at the same time the phrase, added almost as an afterthought, established their place as essentially subordinate and inferior; the apt word *amniculus*, meaning a "prop" such as those

[51] Waddell 2002, 20–21.
[52] *UC* Prologue (Waddell, 56; 164–65).
[53] *RB* 2.22 (McCann 1976, 8).

used to support vines, denotes their role as aids to the monks. As Jacques Dubois has noted, the mystical vine of Cîteaux—that is, the community of monks—was supported by its props, the lay brothers and hired laborers.[54] Although Chrysogonus Waddell is right to caution against imputing modern ideas of social equality when judging twelfth-century conditions,[55] as mentioned above, one cannot help detecting a certain condescending tone in Saint Bernard's rebuke to the overconfident lay brother, saying: "For the sake of God we took you in, destitute, and gave you food and clothing and the common goods, just the same as those men among us who are well educated and nobly born, and made you one of them."[56] We see the same patronizing attitude in the description of a lay brother who "had no less faith and devotion than did the lettered and the learned," almost as if that comes as a surprise.[57] Often, as here, their inferiority was based on the way they were distinguished by their illiteracy as much as by their subsidiary position vis-à-vis the monks in a servant/master relationship. The prohibition of intellectual pursuits has been seen as a means of keeping the lay brothers in an auxiliary position.[58] But the division was perhaps greatest in the superior clerical status given the monks, whose main task was the recitation of the *Opus Dei* as opposed to the subordinate lay status of the brothers, dedicated to their specialized vocation of manual labor, which was considered the lowest occupation in the social hierarchy.[59]

## Martha and Mary

Martha chose a good part, but Mary the better: the rich symbolism of the account of the sisters of Lazarus by Saint Luke (Luke

---

[54] Dubois 1972, 165.

[55] Waddell 2000, 166.

[56] *EM* 4.19 (Griesser, 245); CF 72:354–55: *Nos vero causa Dei collegimus inopem et parem te fecimus in victu atque vestitu ceterisque communitatibus his, qui nobiscum sunt, sapientibus atque nobilibus viris, et factus es quasi unus ex illis.*

[57] *EM* 4.15 (Griesser, 240); CF 72:348: *doctis et litteratis fide et devotione non inferior.*

[58] Lescher 1988, 75.

[59] For this, see Sullivan 1989, 180.

10:38-42) has been used by writers going back to Saint Augustine to affirm the superiority of the contemplative life, exclusively devoted to prayer and represented by Mary, over the active life of Martha, concerned with preaching and the care of souls. In discussing the relationship between contemplation and action, Western mystical writers have also drawn on the contrast made by Saint Paul between *sapientia* and *scientia*, "wisdom" representing contemplation and "knowledge" denoting action. The same symbolism may also be seen in the Old Testament story of the daughters of Laban (Genesis 29 and 30): Leah, dim of sight and unable to grasp the mysteries of God but with many children stands for action, and Rachel the contemplative, although she has few children, has faith without which "it is impossible to please God" (Hebrews 11:6). In a monastic context Martha/Leah usually represented the abbot, cellarer, and other officials, Mary/Rachel were the cloistered monks whose chief occupation was the *Opus Dei*, and the lay brothers had no representative at all in this metaphorical scheme.

Surprisingly, both Saint Bernard and Saint Aelred ignored what might have seemed a more obvious interpretation, assigning the lay brothers to the active role (Martha/Leah) and the monks to the contemplative one (Mary/Rachel).[60] While acknowledging the dilemma of the monk who is "tossed between the fruit of action and the quiet of contemplation,"[61] Bernard linked the officials to an active role like Martha's that was "bound to be stained to some degree with the grime of worldly affairs."[62] In Sermon 57 on the Song of Songs Lazarus represents "the novices now dead to their sins," Martha "the Savior's friend in those who do the daily chores," and Mary is found in those who "have attained to a better and happier state."[63] Bernard

---

[60] Martha Newman draws attention to this anomaly and to the significance of the way lay brothers were ignored by Cistercian writers when describing the diversity of their communities (Newman 1996, 102–3).

[61] *SC* 57.9; *SBOp* 2:125: *Vides virum sanctum inter fructum operis et somnum contemplationis graviter aestuare.*

[62] *SC* 40.3; *SBOp* 2:26: *et non potest terrenorum actuum vel tenui pulvere non respergi.*

[63] *SC* 57.11; *SBOp* 2:126: *novitios utique, qui nuper peccatis mortui; Habemus siquidem Martham, tamquam Salvatoris amicam, in his qui exteriora fideliter administrant; in aliquid melius et laetius proficere potuerunt.*

alludes to Martha and Mary and to Leah and Rachel on a number of occasions, but they are mostly passing references. For Aelred the cloistered monks were the "spiritual militia," distinguished from the active officials.[64] He warns against neglecting Mary in favor of Martha or Martha in favor of Mary: "In this wretched and laborious life, brethren, Martha must of necessity be in our house; that is to say, our soul has to be concerned with bodily actions. As long as we need to eat and drink, we shall need to tame our flesh with watching, fasting, and work. This is Martha's role. But in our souls there ought also to be Mary, that is, spiritual activity."[65]

In describing the rapid growth of the community at Rievaulx during the abbacy of Saint Aelred his biographer, Walter Daniel, rejoiced,

> for our Jacob begat twins by both Leah and Rachel, as he preached fear and justice to the officials and impressed the duties of prayer and love upon the contemplatives in the cloister, saying to the former, "Fear the Lord, ye his saints, for there is no want in them that fear Him," and to the latter, "They that dwell in Thy house, O Lord, shall be always praising Thee" (Ps 83:10).[66]

The Martha/Mary theme was first used in distinguishing between the roles of lay brothers and monks in a letter by Nicholas of Clairvaux. Adding novices as the third group in the threefold order, he defines their roles as follows:

[64] Aelred, *Sermo 17, In natali sanctorum apostolorum Petri et Pauli*, CCCM 2a, 134–38.

[65] Aelred, *Sermo 19, In Assumptione Sanctae Mariae*, CCCM 2a, 151; Squire 1969, 56: *Ideo, fratres, in ista misera et laboriosa vita, necesse est ut Martha sit in domo nostra, id est ut anima nostra studeat corporalibus actionibus. Quamdiu enim necesse habemus manducare et bibere, tamdiu necesse habemus laborare. Quamdiu temptamur carnalibus delectationibus, necesse habemus vigiliis ei ieiuniis et labore corporis carnem domare. Haec est pars Marthae. Debet etiam esse in anima nostra Maria, id est actio spiritualis.*

[66] Daniel, Vita A 20; Powicke 1950, 29; CF 57:111: *quia Jacob noster Liam et Rachelem utramque geminis fecundavit, activis et officialibus timorem et iusticiam predicans, contemplativis et claustralibus oracionem et amorem inculcans, illis videlicet dicens: Timete Dominum omnes sancti eius, quoniam non est inopia timentibus eum; istis indicens: Hi qui habitant in domo tua, Domine, in secula seculorum laudabunt te.*

The novices are those who are tested, the monks those who are approved, and the lay brothers those who work, by whom the poor of Christ, or, rather, Christ in the poor, is nourished. This is the house in which the Savior is diligently received, where Martha serves, Mary remains in prayer, and Lazarus is brought back to life. Understand Martha as the working lay brothers, Mary as the monks contemplating, and Lazarus as the weeping novices who have been brought back from the dead.[67]

Among the saintly lay brothers listed in the Chronicle of the abbey of Villers in Brabant is Herman, who was given to works of charity. He used to repair the old clothes of the monks so that they were as good as new before giving them to the poor. He is likened to the "neglected Martha who sits at the feet of the Lord" (*Martha postposita, sedit ad pedes Domini*).[68]

The superiority of contemplatives over actives had already been the subject of Walter Map, the early critic of the Cistercians, when he contrasted them with the earlier Benedictines in his *Courtiers' Trifles* (*De Nugis Curialium*). In doing so he drew attention to the fact that the most demeaning occupations were the preserve of lay brothers:

> The black monks sit with Mary at the Lord's feet and hear the word, and are not suffered to go out for worldly cares. The white, though they sit at the same feet, go out to work: they practice all manner of tillage with their own hands; inside their precinct they are artisans, outside they are harrowers, herdsmen, merchants, and in each calling most active. They have no shepherd nor swineherd but of their own number. For the basest and most menial cares, or for women's work, such as milking and so on, they employ no one but their own lay brothers.[69]

---

[67] Nicholas of Clairvaux, EP 36 (PL 196:1632): *novitii sunt, qui probantur; monachi qui approbantur; conversi, qui operantur, unde Christi pauperes, imo Christus in pauperibus sustentetur, et haec quidem domus est, in qua Salvator diligenter suscipitur; ubi et Martha ministrat, et Maria vacat, et Lazarus resuscitatur. Martham accipite conversos laborantes; Mariam, monachos contemplantes; Lazarum, novitios plorantes qui nuper sunt a mortuis resuscitati.*

[68] Martene and Durand 1717, 3:1363.

[69] Walter Map 1983, 84–87: *Nigri cum Maria secus pedes Domini verbum audiunt, nec ad sollicitudinem egredi licet; albi cum ad pedes sedeant, ad laborem exeunt, manibus*

To a large extent the subordinate status of lay brothers rested on the perception that their actual role, represented by Martha, was inferior to the monks' "better part," their liturgical function, associated with Mary. According to Orderic Vitalis, those who have renounced the world should not "be compelled to spend their time in servile and unbecoming labors and occupations like lowborn servants in order to earn their bread."[70] In the same way, Peter the Venerable maintained that "it is unbecoming that monks, who are the fine linen of the sanctuary, should be begrimed with dirt and bent down with rustic labors."[71] Hildegard of Bingen made the same point when she said that "by no means would it be proper for a priest to perform the functions of a farmer."[72] We have seen how Burchard of Balerne singled out the *spiritualia* and *interiora* of the monks to the detriment of the *carnalia* and *exteriora* of the lay brothers, claiming that "it would be unsuitable for beards to hang over books and chalices and we without beards therefore are engaged around the altars and chalices; you who have beards are assigned to plows and mattocks."[73]

The same point was made by a canon from Liège in a treatise on the orders and callings of the church dated about 1140 when he said: "I could wish, however, that those who serve the altar every day, and especially those who offer the body of Christ every day during their duties as priests, did not engage in such work, out of reverence for His body, since nothing can be cleaner; but they should leave it to others who are not yet suited for the assumption of such duties in the church."[74]

---

agriculturam omnimodam excercentes propriis, intra septa mecanici, extra runccatores, opiliones negociatores, in singulis officiosissimi; bubulcum non habent vel subulcum nisi ex se, nec ad minimas et viles custodias vel opera feminarum, ut lactis et similium, quempiam preter conversos suos admittunt.

[70] Orderic Vitalis 1969–1980, 4:320–21: *cogantur servilibus et incongruis more vilium mancipiorum studiisseu laboribus occupari pro victo proprio.*

[71] PL 189:112.

[72] PL 197: *Nequaquam autem deceret ut sacerdos officia agricolae.*

[73] Burchardus de Bellevaux 1985, 166–67. See also chap. 4.

[74] Constable and Smith 2003, 60–61: *Vellem tamen eos qui circa altare cotidie ministrant, et maxime illos qui cotidie pro officio sacerdotii corpus Christi tractant ob rev-*

The *monachatus* qualification, the perpetual renunciation of the possibility of advancement as a consequence of making profession, the condescending tone adopted in many of the comments on lay brothers, the "better part" chosen by the monks, the superiority of *spiritualia* over *carnalia*, and the idea that the further removed from the grime of manual labor the higher the social standing: these were among the principal contributing factors to much of the unrest that sullied the reputation of the institution of lay brothers in the second half of the thirteenth and into the fourteenth century.

---

*erentiam ipsius corporis quo nichil mundius esse potest ista non agere, sed aliis qui ad illa officia suscipienda in aecclesia adhuc idonei non sunt, haec agenda relinquere.*

# Chapter 8

# *Vitae* of Lay Brothers
# and Lay Brothers in *Vitae*

There is no doubt that among the multitude of lay brothers there were a large number of saints. Some are remembered from *vitae* dedicated to them; others are mentioned in the *vitae* of others in which they are sometimes portrayed as a kind of catalyst to the deeds of the subject; the vast majority are mostly anonymous lay brothers featured in the extensive *exemplum* literature of the late twelfth and early thirteenth century, so widespread among the Cistercians and especially in the Clairvaux filiation. Among the *exempla* dealing with lay brothers is the following, worth quoting in full:

> Of the Lay Brother Who, Like a Lovely Rose,
> Was Taken up to Heaven with Great Joy.

> A certain lay brother of the Cistercian Order said the Office of Blessed Mary devoutly right through to the end. When he lay on ashes in the open in the middle of winter as the monks were singing Matins in choir one of the monks, after nodding off a bit, saw a ladder reaching from the infirmary up to heaven. Our Lady, the holy Mary, was leaning on the top of the ladder and said to the Angel Gabriel: "Go down quickly and cut down that rose and bring it to me." The monk, who had no idea that the lay brother was sick, saw a very beautiful rose springing up in the infirmary and filling the whole place. When the angel, having come down by descending the ladder, ascended again and gave the rose to

Mary, the tablet was struck. The monk, waking up, ran to the place and looked for the rose, but instead of the rose he found the lay brother dead. The monk told his brethren about this vision and how the soul of the lay brother was taken into heaven like a beautiful rose.[1]

Caesarius of Heisterbach tells an analogous story of a lay brother from Poland from whose heart there grew a small tree with "Ave Maria" written on each of its leaves. His source was Abbot Godfrey of Altenberg in the Rhineland who had heard the story while on a recent visitation of his Polish daughter houses. The lay brother was having problems with praying when the angelic salutation was proposed to him. He is said to have

> learned it quickly, and he used to ruminate on it without ceasing day and night. Eventually he died and was buried. Now behold! A lovely little tree beautifully adorned with branches and leaves sprang out of the grave. Everyone was astonished at this and wondered what it was and what it might portend. . . . Those who knew him well while he was alive were not ignorant of the cause, for in each of the leaves the letters "Ave Maria" could distinctly be seen.[2]

---

[1] *DM* Hilka 1937, 3:195: *De converso, cuius anima ut pulchra rosa in celum cum magna leticia est suscepta. Quidam conversus ordinis Cisterciensis officium beate Marie devote persolvens ad extrema devenit. Et cum iaceret in area acri in hieme super cilicium, monachis in choro matudinas cantantibus, quidam eorum paululum obdormivit et vidit scalam ab infirmario usque ad celum erectam et dominam nostram sanctam Mariam in summo scale innixam, dicentem angelo Gabrieli: "Descende cito et rosam illam abscide et defer ad me." Monachus enim ille, cum nesciret omnino conversum egrotare, vidit in infirmario rosam pulcherrimam crescere et totam planiciem aree replere. Cum ergo predictus angelus prescidisset et cum honore hanc sancte Marie per scalam descendendo et acsendendo deferret, tabula percussa est. Monachus evigilans cucurrit ad locum et rosam querens pro rosa invenit conversum mortuum. Monachus hanc visionem suis fratribus indicavit, quomodo anima conversi quasi pulcherrima rosa in celum esset deducta.*

[2] *DM* Hilka 1937, 3:80: *De converso in Polonia, de cuius corde arbuscula egressa est, in singulis foliis habens "Ave Maria." Citius illam didicit; quam sine cessatione die noctuque ruminavit. Nuper mortuus est homo et sepultus. Et ecce! Arbuscula pulcherrima, ramis et foliis decenter ornata, de illius tumulo egressa est. Mirantibus cunctis, quidnam hoc esset vel quid portenderet. . . . Nec ignorabant causam, qui viventis noverant vitam; nam in singulis foliis distinctis litteris "Ave Maria" apparuit.*

The story appears again in a fourteenth-century versified Marian legend. According to this, shortly after the death of a Polish lay brother who was only able to pray the Ave Maria, a fig tree with "A. M." written on the leaves grew out of his heart: *tumba parit quasi ficum de dulci corde fratris*.[3] The story may, in turn, have given rise to another, included in the *Miracles de Notre Dame* collected by Jean Mielot and written in 1456 for Philip the Good (1396–1467), duke of Burgundy. In this a rich and noble knight renounced the world and became a lay brother. He only knew two words in Latin, *Ave Maria*, but these he said with great devotion. When he was buried the letters AM appeared on his grave and a lily grew up.[4]

These examples of tales from the lives of holy lay brothers, embellished with accounts of visions and miracles representing the surest sign of sainthood, meet two of the main criteria of hagiography: edification and emulation. In most of them the lay brother subject is not identified, but even when he is named, the only thing that matters is the lesson to be drawn from the account, the moral truth being illustrated. There is a contradiction between the basic anonymity of the life of lay brothers, noted as reserved and retiring, and the idea of drawing attention to those whose lives were marked by outstanding virtue. On the one hand the lay brothers were being held up as a shining example while at the same time being kept in the dark. This explains why there are many tales but few *vitae* of lay brothers. The threat to monastic discipline presented by promoting the cult of exceptional members had long been recognized by the Cistercians generally. When, following the death of Saint Bernard, a person seeking a cure prostrated himself before the coffin, Conrad of Eberbach tells us that the abbot of Cîteaux, who had come to assist at the funeral, "was greatly worried that the increase in miracles would attract a large multitude whose unruly behavior might compromise the discipline of the order. . . . He therefore reverently approached the body and forbade it, in the name of obedience, to perform any further miracles . . . and

---

[3] Mussafia 1889, 9.
[4] Warner 1885, 9.

from that day until now he has never been seen to perform any miracles in public."[5]

In the same way, following the death in 1160 of Saint Waldef of Melrose his successor, William, is said to have ordered that the sick who came along should be kept away from the saint's tomb. Although his biographer, Jocelin of Furness, suggests that he may have been prompted by envy, he concludes that "a more likely reason, I think, is the desire that convents of the Cistercian Order avoid the uncontrollable disturbance of crowds flowing in upon them from every side."[6]

The same concern for the adverse effect of miracles on discipline is expressed in a story by Caesarius of Heisterbach. On a visit to Eberbach he had heard of an aged monk there who had the power to heal a variety of diseases by the touch of his hand. Crowds are said to have flocked to the monastery so that "the abbot, seeing the quiet of the brothers disturbed by the crowds and the house not a little burdened by the expense, ordered that brother in future not to lay his hands on any seculars, and immediately the power to work miracles came to an end."[7]

Bernard had himself warned against an exaggerated interest in miracles when he asked:

> Does the word of God then pronounce those blessed who raise the dead, give sight to the blind, cure the sick, cleanse the lepers, heal the paralyzed, cast out demons, foresee the future, shine out with miracles, or is it rather those who are poor in spirit, gentle, sorrowful, hungering and thirsting for righteousness, merciful, pure of heart, peacemakers, persecuted for righteousness' sake? [8]

---

[5] *EM* 2:20 (Griesser, 117).

[6] Jocelin of Furness 1952, 186: *quin potius tamen (ut reor) coenobitae Cisterciensis Ordinis turbarum undique confluentium carerent immoderata frequentia.*

[7] *DM* 10.5 (Strange 2:221: Scott and Bland 2:175–76): *Ex quorum concursu videns Abbas fratrum quietem turbari et domum in expensis non modicum gravavi, eidem converso ne alicui saeculari de cetero manus imponeret praecepit. Et cessavit ex illa hora in eo virtus miraculorum.*

[8] *SBOp* 5:410.

Here Bernard expresses his preference for the somewhat humdrum virtues of the meticulous observance of monastic life over the more spectacular displays of sanctity such as, for example, the miracle tales included by his biographers.

In the same way Saint Aelred of Rievaulx's biographer, Walter Daniel, marveled at Aelred's charity, which "exceeded every novelty of miracle" (*omnem superavit miraculi novitatem*).[9] These examples, and the snide attacks of their detractors, may have been responsible for the reticence of the early Cistercians in promoting the cult of saintly members of the Order, and most especially of the humblest of all, the lay brothers.

## When Silence Stops

Saint Benedict devotes a whole chapter of his Rule to silence (*RB* 6) and in the eleventh degree of humility he directs that when a monk speaks he should "do so gently and without laughter, humbly and seriously, in a few and sensible words, and without clamor."[10] It is hard to reconcile the strictness of the regulations regarding silence with what we know of the interaction of at least some monks and lay brothers with one another and with both lay men and women.[11] Many accounts of friendship, amounting at times to a close spiritual bond, are found in late-twelfth-century *exempla* and *vitae*. The solitary and inward-looking spirituality, informed by silence, that had characterized the lives of monks in earlier centuries had gradually given way to a more open state of dependence based on sharing in the second half of the twelfth century.[12] A close relationship between a lay brother and a monk is recorded in one of the vision stories from the Cistercian monastery of Stratford Langthorne in the *Liber revelationum* compiled by Peter of Cornwall, an Augustinian canon, between 1197 and 1208.[13] It is typical of many other recorded

---

[9] Daniel, *Letter to Maurice* 4; CF 57:156.
[10] *RB* 7.60 (McCann 1976, 21).
[11] For these, see chap. 9.
[12] For this see McGuire 1981, 36–37.
[13] Holdsworth 1962, 197–201; *LP* 7.

Cistercian visions of the period. That the relationship between lay brother and monk expressed itself in extensive verbal exchanges is suggested by the liberal use of direct speech throughout the story. A simple lay brother, Roger, told the author: "When I was only a young man and a novice among the other lay brothers I entered into a friendship with a certain Alexander who was also a novice, a friendship that was greater than any other, and I used to reveal all the secrets of my heart to him and he did the same with me."[14] They "would discuss questions concerning the present life and the death to come,"[15] and they made a pact that whoever should die first would appear to the other and divulge what he had experienced. Alexander, who by then was not only a monk but a priest, was the first to die, and he kept his promise.

Gestures and glances were not enough in the spiritual direction of those who needed comforting when troubled in their vocation or otherwise in distress. Common sense dictated that the rules, although they would have applied in most circumstances, could be set aside when there was something worthwhile to say that might edify the other person. In such cases setting the rules aside was not just allowed but even encouraged. We have here an example of the Cistercian genius for flexibility when a liberal interpretation of rules was deemed to be more important than rigid enforcement.

Wise abbots would have fostered their monks and lay brothers endowed with special gifts. The support of enlightened abbots was essential in releasing gifted brothers from the usual regulations regarding silence. William, abbot of Fountains 1180–1190, a former Augustinian canon of Guisborough who became a Cistercian and subsequently abbot of Newminster before being elected to Fountains, must have been such a man. He is described in Hugh of Kirkstall's *Narratio* as "a respected and holy man who had governed

---

[14] Holdsworth 1962, 197; *Liber revelationum* 7: *"Dum adhuc,"* inquit, *"iuvenis essem et inter quosdam alios conversos ego novitius, quandam pre ceteris cum quodam Alexandro similiter novitio contraxeram societatis familiaritatem, cui omnia secreta cordis mei sicut et ipse mihi communicare solebam."*

[15] Holdsworth 1962, 197; *Liber revelationum* 7: *diversas interserendo questiones de vita presenti et de morte futura.*

his house prudently with pastoral vigilance and with care."[16] It was during his abbacy that there was, as mentioned earlier,[17] a lay brother of unusual holiness of life, Sunnulph, who, "reading the book of experience grew daily in the knowledge of holy things, and also had the spirit of prophecy."[18] It was to him that a knight, Ralph Haget, dissatisfied with the life he had been leading, turned for guidance. Standing before the crucifix, Ralph heard a voice from the cross saying: "And why do you not come? Why do you delay so long?" Falling to the ground, he replied: "Behold, Lord, I come!"[19] Ralph followed Sunnulph's advice "and at the monastery of Fountains you shall put on the habit of religion, and there, when your race is run, you shall end your days."[20] The foretelling of his fate was later repeated by Ralph who, while sick at Clairvaux and not expected to live, declared: "I will not die at Clairvaux; I expect to live out my life at Fountains. For Brother Sunnulph foretold that I should live at Fountains and there should end my life,"[21] which he did.

In view of the importance attached to silence, acknowledged by Ralph when he referred to Sunnulph's "gravity of his silence" (*de gravitate silentii*) even though at the same time admiring "how ready he was to exhort, how helpful his consolation" (*quam alacer in exhortando, quam efficax in consolando*),[22] it is remarkable that Sunnulph was able to establish a close relationship with a lay person and it is safe to conclude that this could only have happened with the consent of his superiors.

---

[16] *Fountains, Memorials* 1863, 115: *virum approbatum et sanctum, et qui curae domum pastorali vigilantia prudenter gubernarat.*

[17] See p. 14.

[18] *Fountains, Memorials* 1863, 118: *et legens in libro experientiae, crescebat cotidie in scientia sanctorum; habens etiam spiritum revelationis.*

[19] *Fountains, Memorials* 1863, 119: *Et ecce, inter orandum, vox de cruce, in haec verba emissa est: "Et quare non venis; quare tam diu tardas?" Ad hanc vocem, corrui pronus in terram, et cum magno cordis affectu, et voce lachrimosa, respondi, "Ecce, Domine; ecce venio!"*

[20] *Fountains, Memorials* 1863, 120: *In monasterio Fontanensi habitum religionis assumes et consummato cursu, diem inibi claudes extremum.*

[21] *Fountains, Memorials* 1863, 123: *Ego apud Claramvallem mori non habeo; apud Fontes depositionis meae diem expecto. Frater enim Sinulphus mihi praedixit quod apud Fontes viverem et ibidem vitam finirem.*

[22] *Fountains, Memorials* 1863, 118.

The gift of prophecy was one of the standard marks of sanctity and one that Simon of Aulne shared with Sunnulph. We have seen how Caesarius recorded Simon's ability to read the thoughts of the novice Conrad, to warn him of the temptations he would encounter, and to foretell that he would one day "be a great personage in our order."[23] In fact, he became abbot of Villers, then of Clairvaux, and finally of Cîteaux before being made a cardinal by the pope. Caesarius gives another example: Evirgeld, a lay brother from Villers whose blood brother, Ulrich, was a monk in the same house, was standing next to Simon in choir one day. Evirgeld thought to himself that Simon was very likely not all that people said of him, and that his sayings did not come from the spirit of prophecy. After the service Simon went to see Evirgeld's brother, Ulrich, and asked him to warn his brother not to make such unwise judgments in future. Evirgeld was naturally perturbed to hear this, realizing that he had by his own experience learned what he had refused to believe from others.[24]

## Villers and Lay Brother Saints

A succession of remarkable abbots of Villers in Brabant played a crucial role in fostering the spiritual well-being of communities of Beguines and Cistercian nuns under their direction. With them they formed bonds of friendship while at the same time devoting themselves to the care of their own monks and lay brothers. Three Villers abbots are featured in the *Dialogus miraculorum*: Charles (1197–1209), formerly prior at Heisterbach, and Walter (1214–21), both of whom Caesarius knew well, and William (1221–36).[25] Under them Villers was unique in the annals of hagiography. The thirteenth-century Villers Chronicle lists a number of saintly lay brothers, honored for their inner lives more than for their achievements.[26] Most of the

---

[23] *DM* 3.33 (Strange 1:152; Scott and Bland 1:170–71): *magna persona erit in ordine.* See pp. 11 and 13.

[24] *DM* 3.33 (Strange 1:153; Scott and Bland 1:171–72).

[25] McGuire 1980, 218–22; McGuire 1981, 34–36; Roisin 1947.

[26] Martene and Durand 1717, 3:1359–74; *Villariensium* 1880, 234–35.

entries contain little information about their subject other than some of the standard hagiographic themes such as austerity of life, dissipation in youth, temptation, and supernatural favors. Other than standard clichés, data that reveals anything of the true character of the subject is scarce. Little of value is revealed of the lay brothers Henry of Brussels, Peter, or the unnamed brother who is said to have suffered from leprosy.

Evrard the Taciturn was strict in obeying the rule of silence.[27] Herman, who like Simon of Aulne and Sunnulph possessed the gift of prophecy, is said to have "altogether avoided important people but to have favored ordinary folk" (*sublimes personas omnino vitavit . . . mediocres vero gratiose tractavit*).[28] Nicolas was a shepherd who was charitable to a large number of people. Arnold, a miller at one of the Villers granges, is said to have healed the spiritual sickness of a "lustful and forward woman" (*mulier lasciva et procax*).[29] Two of the brothers listed came from a military background: John de Wistrezees "was called a soldier by name because his father was a soldier and he wanted to be a soldier himself" (*dictus miles cognomine, eo quod pater ejus miles fuerat, et ipse etiam miles fieri volebat*), and after an illness he promised to take on the "spiritual militia" (*militiam spiritualem*). In the words of the abbey Chronicle, as master of the grange of Chenoit "he acquired much property for us" (*plura bona ibidem nobis acquisivit*).[30] The other former soldier in the list is not named but is said to have been a member of a family by the name of Reve "who left the pomp of the world and changed from the empty militia of the world to the fruitful militia of God" (*qui relicta mundiali pompa, vanam militiam fructuosa militia commutavit*).[31]

The story of another lay brother, also unnamed, told by the seniors of Villers, takes the form of an *exemplum*: when once, on the eve of the Assumption, he was at table with the other brothers at one of the granges, he was overcome with tears followed by

---

[27] See p. 213.
[28] Martene and Durand 1717, 3:1363.
[29] Martene and Durand 1717, 3:1364.
[30] Martene and Durand 1717, 3:1365.
[31] Martene and Durand 1717, 3:1369.

intense laughter. The grange master wanted to know the reason for this, to which the lay brother replied: "When I was assisting at table I saw in the spirit one of our fellow brothers put on a hairshirt at that hour, and then many demons gathered, ejecting him through the stones and tiles of the roof of the refectory."[32] He explained that he had thought when the tablet was struck and the monks had started the Office of the Dead that the brother had died, but then the demons turned in flight and he began to laugh. The master, hesitating, "ordered one of the servants to get on a horse. 'Go to the abbey and enquire about this brother and return and tell me what you hear.' When he entered the monastery he found him dead. He speedily returned to the master and declared to the brothers that he was dead. When they heard this they praised the Lord."[33]

## Life of Arnulf

The section on the saintly lay brother Arnulf in the Villers Chronicle is more exhaustive than that on any of the other lay brothers already mentioned, but it is merely an abbreviated extract from the *Vita* written by the monk and cantor Goswin of Busset (1211–1242), who also wrote the lives of the Villers monk Abundus and of Ida of Nivelles, Cistercian nun of La Ramée.[34] These were not as ambitious as, for example, the *Vita prima* of Saint Bernard: they were not written to advance the cause of their subjects' canonization—at the time the title of saint was in practice only accorded officially by the church to a relatively small number—but to hold their memory in veneration, to edify readers by their lives and draw

---

[32] Martene and Durand 1717, 3:1370: *Cum jam mensae assisterem, vidi in spiritu unum de confratribus nostris imponi cilicio ex hora, pluresque convenisse daemones ad ejus exitum qua erant petrae et tegulae in tecto refectorii.*

[33] Martene and Durand 1717, 3:1370: *unum de servis suis equum ascendere jubet, dicens ei: Vade ad abbatiam, et diligenter inquire de fratre illo, et statim rediens renuntia mihi quid audieris. Qui cum abbatiam intrasset, fratrem illum mortuum invenit, et cito rediens magistro, et fratribus ejus obitum denuntiavit. Quibus auditis Domino benedixerunt.*

[34] *AS* June, 5:606–31; translation in Cawley 2003, 125–50. See also McGuire 1981, 37–40, and McGuire 1993, 241–59.

them to imitation. They were meant for internal use and were not intended to promote a wider cult. Arnulf was born around 1180, entered Villers in 1202, and died in 1228. Goswin was commissioned by Abbot William to write Arnulf's *vita* shortly after Arnulf's death, and he probably finished it before 1236.

The *Vita Arnulphi* consists of two books, the first devoted entirely to a catalogue of Arnulf's severe personal discipline. It contains a most extreme and detailed account of self-mortification, even by the standards of medieval hagiography. Arnulf's bizarre behavior bears witness to a pattern of holiness that a later age finds incomprehensible. The second book not only reveals the intensity of his prayer life, his trust in God's providence, his powers of clairvoyance, and his generosity toward the abbey's poor neighbors, but also throws light on his modest but vital role in the economy of Villers.

Book One begins with a conventional assault on the subject's chastity, reminiscent of a story in the *Vita prima* of Saint Bernard:[35] "Arnulf was once tempted. The instigation was diabolic, but Arnulf proved true. A woman, youthful in age, lewd in behavior, worldly in her living, had seen how handsome a lad he seemed, and, caught in the trap of her own eyes she had blazed into a longing after him."[36]

A little farther on the author once again has recourse to the *Vita prima*: he has Arnulf asking himself "Why have I come to the order?" (*ad quid veni ego ad Ordinem istum?*), a clear reference to the question Bernard posed himself: "Bernard, Bernard, for what have you come?" (*Bernarde, Bernarde, ad quid venisti?*).[37]

Then follows a description of the various ways he inflicted pain on himself. Stripped to the waist, he beat himself with a broom until stripes could be seen on his body, and he did the same with a stick to which he had attached the pelt of a hedgehog. He wore

---

[35] *VP* I, 3.7 (PL 185:230).

[36] *VA* 1.6 (*AS* June, 5:609; Cawley 2003, 130): *Quodam tempore, instinctu diaboli, tentatus est, sed probatus. Cum enim mulier quaedam, aetate adolescentula, lasciva moribus, et seculariter rivens, videret eum adolescentem aspectu decorum; oculorum suorum capta laqueo, exarcit in concupiscentiam eius.*

[37] *VA* 1.8 (*AS* June, 5:610; Cawley 2003, 131); *VP* I, 4.19 (PL 185:238).

a hairshirt of sackcloth and slept in a bed strewn with stones, not straw. In winter, when others wore two or three tunics and a sheepskin as well, Arnulf would only have one tunic, and that the most threadbare. He lived in a hut in the orchard of the grange. He rolled naked in nettles, the same remedy for preserving chastity chosen by the lay brother Gerard from the monastery of Mores near Clairvaux. Herbert of Clairvaux records how Gerard "when struck by a forbidden stirring used to roll on the earth on stinging nettles and as a result his body and limbs became extremely sore. These things strongly repressed the urgings of the unwilling flesh."[38]

Arnulf was warned about the dangers of his extreme self-inflicted penances. His grange master, Sygerus, tried to wean him away from the worst excesses and sometimes the abbot would forbid him to continue, fearing that he might collapse. In the tradition of the desert fathers, Arnulf no doubt sought the suppression of sexual desire, and his discipline may well have helped him in establishing close chaste friendships with women. Among others there was "another devout woman religious, linked to the man of God with so indissoluble a bond of holy love that the pair of them had but *one heart and one soul* [Acts 4:32]."[39] However, by present-day standards it is impossible to understand Arnulf's behavior or to have the slightest sympathy with it.[40] Even Goswin was ambivalent in his attitude to Arnulf's self-inflicted torture and yet overall was positive in his assessment, based on Arnulf's apostolate to his fellow brothers as well as to lay men and women. He makes a special point of the fact that "even as he was whipping himself, he would hold in

---

[38] *LM* 1.18 (PL 185:1293): *ut quando illicitis motibus pulsabatur, super urticas sese in terra volutaret, et ex eis corpus suum ac membra confricaret. Hoc vero saepissime faciens petulantis carnis stimulos fortiter reprimebat, et incentiva libidinum poenali incendio salubriter extinguebat.*

[39] *VA* 2.47 (*AS* June, 5:627; Cawley 2003, 184): *Fuit altera mulier religiosa, indissolubili sanctae dilectionis vinculo viro Dei adstricta, ita ut eis ad invicem esset cor unum et anima una.*

[40] In the words of Brian McGuire (McGuire 1993, 247) "by reference to present-day western definitions of acceptable behaviour, Arnulf was indeed 'out of his head.'"

mind the names of some of his brothers, now some of his friends, and now religious women who were beloved to him in Christ."[41]

In the same way that Caesarius of Heisterbach found Simon of Aulne's contribution to the economy of his abbey as a grange master worthy of mention, Goswin has several stories of Arnulf's toil as wagoner, responsible for transporting goods to and from the various granges and the abbey.[42] And yet Goswin makes it clear that he attached greater importance to his prayer life and his other duties of making himself available to the needs of others than to his labor on behalf of the monastery. There is a rare recognition of this when he was granted dispensation from manual tasks in order to be able to devote himself to what was considered of greater value:

> When, by the Lord's grace, he became engaged in many things quite repugnant to human nature, his masters used to grant him a freedom broad enough to exempt him from virtually all duties and occupations, allowing him to give himself over to whole days of salutary leisure and divine contemplation restful for both mind and body, or else to pursue his devout prayers, or finally to beat and chastise his body.[43]

Apart from Arnulf's extreme acts of mortification, barely equaled in medieval hagiography, he was remarkable in his openness and the way he was able to relate to many persons, including those of knightly rank from the vicinity of the grange who came to him for spiritual counseling. For them he "at times interrupted his colloquies with God for the sake of the guests who flocked

---

[41] *VA* 1.34 (*AS* June, 5:615; Cawley 2003, 147): *Et tunc valide se flagellando, nominatim commemorabat aliquos fratrum suorum, nunc vero aliquos amicorum, nunc vero religiosas mulieres dilectas sibi in Christo.*

[42] For Simon of Aulne see p. 141; for Arnulf, pp. 119–20.

[43] *VA* 1.28 (*AS* June, 5:614–15; Cawley 2003, 143–44): *Mediante Domini gratia multa ageret humanae omnino naturae repugnantia, permissione Magistrorum suorum tanta libertate donatus est, ut ab omnibus fere officiis et occupationibus absolutus, aut salutaribus divinae contemptionis feriis deditus, tam corpore quam mente requiesceret, aut orationibus devotis insisteret, aut etiam verberibus corpus suum castigaret.*

to him."[44] On another occasion a visitor was told by the stable-keeper, Nicholas, that Arnulf was engaged in afflicting his body "in his purgatory." The visitor naturally assumed that he would not be able to see him, but was told: "On the contrary, once informed of your arrival, he will be along without delay."[45]

Arnulf, like several of the other saintly Villers *conversi*, is said to have possessed the gift of prophecy. He correctly predicted that one of two laymen who presented themselves with the wish of becoming lay brothers would make it while the other would not. The one who succeeded, Godfrey, "to this day is one of the blacksmiths, lodging with the brothers of that craft in the smithy adjacent to the monastery."[46] Monks were also among those who looked to him for spiritual guidance. One was a friend who stayed the night together with Arnulf at a grange and with whom he spoke in a way that was "both familiar and intimate as they exchanged remarks on *the good things of the Lord* [Ps 26:13], on the welfare of souls and on their own secrets."[47] When he fell ill he was visited "by monks who were his friends" (*monachis familiaribus suis*).[48] His ministry was not confined to catering to the spiritual needs of those with whom he came into contact, but also encompassed the material well-being of the poor. On one occasion he obtained the abbot's permission to give forty-two loaves to the poor,[49] and we have seen how, on another occasion, he struggled to hide two pigs in sacks in order to give them to the poor.[50] He was instrumental in helping Countess Blanche of Champagne found a house for women at Argensolles

---

[44] *VA* 2.2 (*AS* June, 5:617; Cawley 2003, 154): *Aliquando enim interrumpebat dulcia cum Deo suo colloquia causa hospitum, qui ad se videndum confluebant.*

[45] *VA* 1.13 (*AS* June, 5:621; Cawley 2003, 134): *Imo, ait ille, si vester ei adventus innotuerit, sine mora procedet.*

[46] *VA* 2.55 (*AS* June, 5:629; Cawley 2003, 191): *Ipse est faber ferrarius, qui usque hodie in officina moasterio proxima, cum Fratribus eiusdem artis demoratur.*

[47] *VA* 1.23 (*AS* June, 5:613; Cawley 2003, 140): *quanto familiarius tanto secretius, sermones de bonis Domini, vel de utilitate animarum, sive de secretis suis ad invicem conferebant.*

[48] *VA* 2.61 (*AS* June, 5:630; Cawley 2003, 194).

[49] *VA* 2.8 (*AS* June, 5:618; Cawley 2003, 158).

[50] See pp. 119–20.

after having a vision of a white hen protecting its chicks under its wings, which he understood as representing an abbess with her nuns and indicating God's blessing for the project.[51]

It is possible that Goswin was spurred on to write his *Life* of Arnulf by the reputation of a contemporary lay brother, Simon, from the rival abbey of Aulne. We have in the *Vita Arnulphi*, as in the story of Simon of Aulne, evidence of how, on account of the greater contact of lay brothers with the outside world, it was easier for them than for the cloistered monks to engage in an apostolate to the laity and, most remarkably, one involving closeness to women. This probably explains why the saintly monk Abundus was not known for his affinity with women while the lay brother Arnulf had many devout female friends.[52]

## Lay Brothers in *Vitae*

In the *Life of Abundus*,[53] as in that of Arnulf written by Goswin of Villers, we have a reversal of roles: a monk consoling a lay brother, another instance of a friendship between the two groups within the Cistercian family. According to Goswin, Baldwin, who had been a knight before entering Villers as a lay brother, knew nothing of the "spiritual knighthood" (*militiam spiritualem*), and was having difficulty adjusting to life in the monastery. He "was even thinking of returning to the world, like *a dog going back to its vomit* [Prov 26:11; 2 Pet 2:22]."[54] He was comforted by the saintly Abundus, who prayed for him and equipped him with a shield to protect him against "the ancient foe, who shoots at us with deadly, impassioned arrowheads to make us desert the combat and retreat from the goal."[55] Knowing Abundus's special devotion to the Virgin, Baldwin asked for her to appear to him, recognizing that Mary

---

[51] *VA* 2.30 (*AS* June, 5:622–23; Cawley 2003, 172–74). See also McGuire 1981, 39–40.

[52] For this see McGuire 1981, 43.

[53] Translated in Cawley 2003, 209–46.

[54] *Life of Abundus* 19a (Cawley 2003, 241).

[55] *Life of Abundus* 19b (Cawley 2003, 242).

would grant the favor when requested by Abundus. Here we have one of many examples of lay brothers in their role as witnesses to the sainthood of the subject of a *vita*.

Although Saint Bernard is featured as the mediator between his monks and heaven in numerous episodes in the *Vita prima*, there are no instances of lay brothers being equally favored. Writing much later, Conrad of Eberbach, who called the *Vita prima* "the book of his life" (*liber vitae eius*), introduced his account of Bernard with the statement that, although this book contains much detail of his admirable life and exceptional sanctity, "I nevertheless think it useful to recount, to the memory of so great a man and for the edification of the reader, certain facts which until now have been omitted."[56] Although not specifically mentioned, and almost certainly not particularly in Conrad's mind when he wrote this, one omission from the *Vita prima* was the role lay brothers played in promoting the cult of Bernard. The twenty chapters devoted to Bernard in the second *distinctio* of the *Exordium magnum* do not constitute a *vita*, but, as Conrad himself claimed, they were aimed at edification and they therefore qualify as hagiography.

Among the many inspirational stories Conrad records is one in which Bernard is credited with saving the soul of a lay brother struggling with demons. It is very similar to the story about the assurance given by Christian of Aumône to the lay brother whose soul was attacked by three horrible demons.[57] According to Conrad, when a lay brother died a senior monk heard a throng of devils in the hundreds milling about. The devils prided themselves on having "gotten at least one soul from this lousy valley to share our lot."[58] When the monk told Bernard of the hideous pit into which the lay brother had been tossed, Bernard exhorted the monks assembled in chapter to be more careful, "affirming that the devils' malice is great toward all Christians, but especially toward those

---

[56] *EM* 2.1 (Griesser, 98): *tamen aliqua, quae illic praetermissa sunt, ad memoriam tanti viri simul et ad aedificationem legentium scribere congruum puto.*

[57] See p. 214.

[58] *EM* 2.2 (Griesser, 99): *Saltem modo de hac mala valle unam animam in nostrae sortis partem acquisivimus.*

who profess the monastic way of life."[59] He urged the monks to pray for the poor lay brother consigned to punishment. They did this with great devotion. After a few days the lay brother appeared again to the senior monk. Looking much more cheerful, he took the monk into the church, showed him that at each altar stood a priest celebrating, and said: "Look, here are the weapons of God's grace by which I have been delivered. Here is the might of God's mercy which remains invincible. Here is that unique Victim *who takes away the sin of the whole world* [John 1:29]."[60] The same story had already appeared in the *Collectaneum clarevallense*, where it was introduced by the statement: "Something once happened in Clairvaux in the days of our holy father of blessed memory, Abbot Bernard, which ought not to be relegated to silence."[61] The sequence of events in the two versions is slightly different, and the earlier one ends with: "The Holy Spirit breathes when he wills, and as he wills, and how he wills, and to whom he wills, since his power is invincible, his wisdom beyond reckoning, and his goodness beyond understanding."[62] We have in the two versions an affirmation of the power of prayer coupled with a reminder that it was at the instigation of Bernard that the lay brother was saved.

In another story Bernard is credited with rescuing a convicted robber from being hanged. Conrad's version is identical to the earlier account in Herbert of Clairvaux's *Liber miraculorum* except for the last sentence, in which Herbert asserts that "we both saw and knew him" (*quem nos etiam vidimus, et cognovimus*), a claim Conrad was not able to make. And although they both give his

---

[59] *EM* 2.2 (Griesser, 99): *Multam esse malitiam daemonum erga omnes christianos, tamen praecipue contra monasticae religionis professores affirmans.*

[60] *EM* 2.2 (Griesser, 100): *Ecce, inquit, haec sunt arma gratiae Dei, quibus eruptus sum, haec est virtus misericordiae Dei, quae invicibilis permanent, haec est hostia illa singularis, quae totius mundi peccata tollit.*

[61] *CC* 4.4 (Legendre 2005, 262): *Contigit quondam in Clare Valle, in diebus patris nostri pie memorie sancti B(ernardi) abbatis, unum quid quod sub silencio dignum est non abscondi.*

[62] *CC* 4.4 (Legendre 2005, 263): *Spiritus enim Sanctus quando vult, et prout vult, et quomodo vult, et cui vult spirat, cuius potentia invicibilis, cuius sapiencia innumerabilis, cuius bonitas inestimabilis.*

name, Conrad explains the reason for the choice: "he was called Constantius, expressing by this lovely name the constancy of his intention."[63] When Bernard was reprimanded for wanting to save an undoubted criminal he answered that he was well aware of the man's guilt and did not intend to let him go unpunished: "I will make him suffer daily agony and die a very drawn out death. You would let him die after hanging one or a few days in the gallows; I will nail him to the cross both to live and to hang for many years in punishment."[64] Bernard brought the man back with him to Clairvaux, where he "joined him to the flock of the Lord, making of the wolf a sheep, of the robber a lay brother,"[65] and as a lay brother he remained there until his death some thirty years later.

Two lay brothers are named by Walter Daniel, the biographer of Aelred of Rievaulx, among the witnesses of Aelred's miracles: Argar the shepherd, "who through the merits of the father recovered speech after he had been unable to speak for two days; for he himself testifies to it and *we know that his witness is true* [John 21:24],"[66] and another reliable witness, "Baldric the lay brother, who has been proved in many things."[67]

Two stories in the *Life* of Saint Stephen of Obazine also feature lay brothers promoting the legend of the saint. In one a simple and blameless lay brother is said

> one Sunday to have gotten up for vigils before the others. Passing by the monks' cloister as usual he heard singing voices as if from a procession of monks, in the middle of which was

---

[63] *EM* 2.15 (Griesser, 109); *LM* 2.15 (PL 185:1325): *pulchre nominis sui etimologiam exprimens in constantia propositi sui, Constantius enim vocabatur.*

[64] *LM* 2.15 (PL 185:1325); *EM* 2.15 (Griesser, 109): *Tu furcis appensum per unum aut per plurimos dies mortuum in patibulo manere permitteres, ego cruci affixum per annos plurimos faciam in poena jugiter vivere et pendere.*

[65] *LM* 2.15 (PL 185:1325); *EM* 2.15 (Griesser, 109): *Sociavit eum ovili dominico, de lupo faciens agnum, de latrone conversum.*

[66] Daniel, Ep M; Powicke 1950, 68; CF 57:149: *et conversus opilio noster qui duobus diebus loqui non valens meritis patris loquelam recepit. Nam de se reddit ipse testimonium et scimus quia verum est testimonium eius. Est autem Argarus nomen eius.*

[67] Daniel, Ep M; Powicke 1950, 68; CF 57:149: *Baldricus conversus frater probatus in multis.*

the man of God who seemed as if he was leading the procession and whose voice was clearer and louder than that of the others. As the cloister is shut during the night, he hurried to the church to be able to hear the voices of the singers more clearly and to see, if he could, the man of God standing at his stall. But as he entered, the voices were stilled and he could not hear anything. It is clear, both from the previous as well as this vision, that the man of God never left that place. Even during our sleep, he sings the Divine Office in the church as well as in the cloister.[68]

In another tale from Obazine "a young and strong lay brother who was in charge of a wagon of oxen" suffered a hernia as a result of lifting a heavy load. His condition deteriorated and it was said that "such an affliction could only be cured by an incision, a practice that was formerly forbidden in our Order."[69] He was saddened by contravening the rule more than by the thought of the pain and "deprived of human succor, he turned to the help of God and the holy father, Stephen." In the two stories from Obazine the two lay brothers act as foils to focus attention on the sainthood of Stephen. Apart from the main point of the story, the anecdote regarding the punctiliousness with which the regulations were obeyed, if Stephen's biographer can be trusted, is an indication of the success of the mission of "the eminent masters with which the father of Cîteaux had specially entrusted him [Stephen] to

[68] *Étienne d'Obazine* 1970, 218: *Hic cum ad vigilias, die quadam dominica ante alios surgeret ac juxta claustrum monachorum sicut mos est transiret, audivit voces psallentium veluti processionem agentium monachorum, inter quas viri Dei vox, velut processionem ipsam regentis, clarius ac robustius personabat. Et quia idem claustrum utpote nocturnis horis observatum erat, festinanter ad ecclesiam perrexit ut inde commodius psallentium voces audiret et virum Dei, si fieri posset, in sua sede stantem videret. Sed cum intrasset, voces ille continuerunt et ultra audiri non potuerunt. Unde manifestum est tam ex priore visione quam ex istius certo auditu virum Dei huic loco nunquam deesse et tam in ecclesia quam in claustro nobis licet dormientibus, divine laudis officia decantare.*

[69] *Étienne d'Obazine* 1970, 218: *Quidam frater juvenius ac robustus carrucis boum preerat . . . . Verum quia tale incommodum absque incisione curari non valet que olim in nostro ordine interdicta fuit.* "Incisions" were forbidden by the General Chapter in a succession of statutes: *Statuta* 1157.39 (Canivez 1:64), *Statuta* 1175.45 (Canivez 1:85), *Statuta* 1192.7 (Canivez 1:147), and *Statuta* 1198.15 (Canivez 1:225).

*Fig. 19* Lay brothers on the reverse of the tomb of Saint Stephen of Obazine.

instruct them in the ways of the Order" (*magistros egregios quos illi pater cisterciensis ad docendum ordinem speciale munus concessit*)[70] when Obazine joined the Cistercian Order in 1147.

As we have seen, lay brothers were represented in high relief in the magnificent monument to Saint Stephen of Obazine dated around 1280.[71] Less well known is the other side of the tomb: here the six arcades contain the same groups, but on the day of judgment. Four smiling lay brothers have their hoods over their heads (fig. 19). Three of them are standing while the fourth is sitting on the ground holding a board with the words *Requiescant in pace*. While there are altogether twenty-five members of the Order on the other side, only twenty-three of these are counted out at the gate of heaven—one choir monk and one nun are missing, while all the lay brothers have made it!

It is not surprising to find lay brothers mentioned a number of times in the Cistercian Abbot John of Forde's *Life of Wulfric of Haselbury*, written around 1180. Wulfric was an anchorite and his only contact with the Forde community would have been with members passing by, more likely lay brothers on the monastery's business than monks. Most notable among these was William, the lay brother guest master of Forde, "a man of the highest repute" (*vir clarissimae omnino opinionis*) with whom Wulfric established an intimate friendship. In the words of John of Forde:

> Once he had clasped Brother William closely to his heart and was loved as greatly in return, the man of God held absolutely nothing back from him, clearly deeming him worthy to be let into his chambers and made privy to his hidden treasures. He would discuss with him such matters as the mysteries of God's kingdom and the blessed hope of the saints, how graciously God's mercy had gone before him and how favorably followed after—spiritual things to the spiritual, matching the subject to the man.[72]

---

[70] *Étienne d'Obazine* 1970, 114.

[71] See p. 79, and also fig. 8.

[72] *VW* 1.14 (John, Abbot of Ford 1933, 28–29; CF 79:114–15): *Hunc cum vir Dei magna caritate sibi artius devinxisset et simili ab eo diligenter affectu, nihil erat in*

Brother William is described as one of Wulfric's "closest and most trusted friends," one of those whom the saint sent for when he became gravely ill,[73] and, when he lay dying, "mindful too of keeping truth with Brother William and of the love with which he loved his dear friend to the end, he sent for him as he had promised,"[74] and William hastened over and received his blessing.

This testimonial of a close spiritual friendship is an eloquent literary expression of twelfth-century monastic spirituality, consisting of an exchange of personal experience.[75] It is reminiscent of Goswin's description of the "familiar and intimate" friendship between Arnulf and one of the monks from Villers and of the friendship between the English lay brother Roger and the monk Alexander, both mentioned earlier.

John of Forde uses lay brothers in two other stories to demonstrate two standard features of saints' *vitae*: the ability to foretell events and the power of healing. In one a young boy, later to become a *conversus* at Forde, was suffering from an intestinal complaint and was taken to Wulfric. On the way he threw up and when he arrived Wulfric said: "Why are you bothering this boy when he is already cured?" and he added, "You were healed, son, there where you eased yourself by vomiting."[76] On another occasion the same lay brother, on the way to see Wulfric, "was pestered by dogs

---

*omni facultate sua quod non ostenderet ei, dignum plane aestimans quem introduceret in cellaria sua et arcana secretorum suorum familiariter edoceret. Cum hoc de mysteriis regni Dei et beata expectatione sanctorum, cum hoc Domini de misericordia quam dignanter eum pervenisset, vel quam feliciter esset subsecuta conferre solebat, spirituali utique spiritualia comparans.*

[73] *VW* 3.41 (John, Abbot of Ford 1933, 124; CF 79:208): *in quorum familiaritate maxime requiescebat.* John of Forde mentions William specifically as his source for eight of the chapters of the *Life*: *VW* 1.17, 1.26, 2.2, 2.11, 2.15, 2.16, 3.14, and 3.36.

[74] *VW* 3.42 (John, Abbot of Ford 1933, 127; CF 79:210): *Recordatus quoque veritatis suae fratri Willelmo et caritatis suae qua usque in finem dilexit suum sicut repromiserat vocavit eum.*

[75] For this see McGuire 1988.

[76] *VW* 3.4 (John, Abbot of Ford 1933, 92; CF 79:178): *"Cur," inquit, "vexastis puerum hunc cum jam sanatus sit?" Et respiciens in puerum: "Ibi," ait, "o fili, sanatus es, ubi te in vomitum relaxasti."*

running after him and barking, so he picked up a sharp stone which presented itself, but instead of hurting the dog as he intended, cut his own finger quite badly."[77] When he pretended that it did not hurt, Wulfric said: "'That's not true, because the stone you were trying to hurt the dog near Winsham with, you hurt yourself with instead: but give me your hand and you will be cured.' He then held out his bleeding hand for the holy man's blessing and was healed on the instant."[78]

## Lay Brothers in the *Vita* of Waldef of Melrose

Waldef was an Augustinian canon, head of the priory of Kirkham in Yorkshire, who became a Cistercian, first at Warden then at Rievaulx. In 1148 he was elected abbot of the daughter house of Melrose in Scotland following the deposition of the first abbot, and he remained there as abbot until his death in 1160. Following the discovery in 1206 of the incorrupt body of Waldef, Jocelin, monk of Furness, was commissioned to write his *Life* with a view to canonization.[79] In the traditional way the work was in two parts, consisting first of his youth and life as a monk followed by an account of the posthumous miracles performed by him.

Like Goswin, the biographer of Arnulf, Jocelin was also responsible for two other *Lives* but, unlike Goswin, who wrote the *Vita Arnulfi* shortly after the saint's death, Jocelin made his compilation, which has been dated to somewhere between 1207 and 1214, about half a century after Waldef's death. While Goswin's testimony is therefore based on largely firsthand and personal evidence, Jocelin did not know the person portrayed and was inevitably forced to

---

[77] *VW* 3.5 (John, Abbot of Ford 1933, 92; CF 79:178): *Cumque ambulanti canes et latrando et persequendo molesti essent, lapidem praeacutum qui itineranti se obtulit manu apprehendens dum canem vulnerare intendit digitum suum non modice sauciavit.*

[78] *VW* 3.5 (John, Abbot of Ford 1933, 92; CF 79:178): *"Non ita est," ait, "quia lapide quo canem prope Winesham laedere moliebaris temetipsum laesisti, sed da manum tuam et curaberis." Protulit ergo ille manum cruentam et benedicente viro sancto in omni celeritate sanatus est.*

[79] For this, see Baker 1975, 59–82; Birkett 2010, 201–25.

rely on the pious stories of miracles and visions associated with a nascent cult. Although much of his material was based on hearsay, some was transparently invented, such as the story that "he sorrowed more for the killing of a gadfly than many are accustomed to grieve over their guilt in shedding human blood."[80] Nevertheless, Jocelin also relied on "some accounts which we have received from veracious eyewitnesses, *whose testimony is faithful* [Ps 92:5], and which we accept as based upon truth."[81] He claimed to have sought material from those who had firsthand experience of the saint, and yet he was critical in his selection, saying: "yet we have omitted much of what we heard because, as it seemed to us, it was lacking in sufficiently probable evidence."[82]

One of the outstanding features of the *Vita Waldevi* is the way many lay brothers appear to have been more highly regarded than some monks whose share in the propagation of the saint's legend was generally modest in comparison with that of the lay brothers. Of the one hundred chapters covering the period from Waldef's election as abbot to the end of the *Life*, lay brothers, remarkably, make an appearance in thirty-six, and no fewer than eleven lay brothers are referred to by name. With the help of their testimonials, supplemented with much traditional hagiographical material, Jocelin depicts Waldef as the ideal abbot, possessed of the necessary appreciation of the importance of the office, and contrasts him with his predecessor, Richard, who "made himself intolerable to the convent on account of his ungovernable fits of anger."[83] Jocelin's yardstick is naturally the Rule, which he makes a point of quoting: "Following Saint Benedict's admonition, *he strove more to be loved*

[80] Jocelin of Furness 1952, 124: *sed ille plus doluit pro peremptione oestri, quam plures poenitere solent ob effusionem a se perpetratam sanguinis humani.*

[81] Jocelin of Furness 1952, 164–65: *de quibus aliqua subnectare congruum ducimus, quae a veridicis viris quorum testimonia credibilia facta sunt nimis visa, et veritate subnixa accepimus.*

[82] Jocelin of Furness 1952, 163: *omisimus tamen auribus accepta plura, quia, ut nobis visum est, probabilis testimonii defecit sufficientia.*

[83] Jocelin of Furness 1952, 119–20: *cum se ob impetum irae indomabilem, conventui exhiberet intolerabilem.*

*than feared* [RB 64.15]."[84] The contrast between the two abbots is very much in line with *exemplum* tradition.

Jocelin named his sources for the various stories of Waldef's visions and miracles. Among them are three stories for which Jocelin relied on the testimony of lay brothers. Having reported to Waldef the miracles they had witnessed, they had been enjoined by him to keep the secret until his death, the "key of permission" (*clavi licentiae*)[85] being thereafter in their hands. Chief among Jocelin's sources, and the first of the three Waldef warned against disclosing what they had witnessed, was Walter, the *hospitarius* mentioned earlier as punctiliously fulfilling his duty of hospitality according to the Rule.[86]

Jocelin depicts Walter as the ideal guest master. Whenever the bread basket, which could only hold twelve loaves, was miraculously replenished when empty, to the satisfaction of a large number of guests, Walter was said to rejoice. Told of this, Waldef ordered that "if something like this occurs again, give the glory to God, and *put the finger to your lips* (Judg 18:19),"[87] after which the loaves were used up as they were brought out. Walter is said to have told this story often after Waldef's death, always with tears.

In the previous story three visitors had arrived at Melrose, but when they took their places at the meal there were only two and the third had vanished. Although Walter insisted that there had been three, he was assured that there had only been two. At night he had a dream in which a resplendent figure appeared to Walter and told him that he was the third guest, "the guardian appointed by the Lord for this monastery: hold it certain that your alms and your prayers for the departed ascend before the Lord, and especially the petitions of Waldef your abbot, which pierce the heavens and

---

[84] Jocelin of Furness 1952, 121: *juxta S. Benedicti monita plus amari quam timari studuit.*

[85] Jocelin of Furness 1952, 149.

[86] See pp. 105–6.

[87] Jocelin of Furness 1952, 138: *Si tale quid ulterius evenerit, da gloriam Deo, et pone digitum ori tuo.*

ascend in the sight of the Lord like sweet-smelling smoke."[88] Here the lay brother witnessed both to the power of the saint's prayer and to the privileged position of the Cistercians and the special protection enjoyed by Melrose.

The second to be warned by Waldef not to disclose his secret was Lambert, "a lay brother of laudable life" (*conversus vitae laudabilis*). He once witnessed the saint at prayer in his chapel, which, he reported, had been filled with a gleaming light. Waldef's face was all radiance, indicating "that he burned inwardly with an immense fire of divine illumination,"[89] until he stepped outside, when he resumed his former look. When Lambert had told Waldef what he had witnessed "he was ordered upon his obedience to disclose to no one what he had seen as long as the abbot should breathe upon the earth."[90]

On a third occasion the lay brother Richard, while accompanying Waldef on a journey, had been instrumental in the miraculous healing of a woman who had been laboring for several days in childbirth. When the abbot was asleep Richard took his belt and told the woman to gird herself with it and, without further distress, she gave birth. When told what had happened, Waldef once again "in his usual way strictly enjoined him not to reveal that sign to anyone while he, the abbot, was still alive."[91]

A number of lay brothers were beneficiaries of Waldef's posthumous healing power. There was Gillesperda, who was sent to Melrose, having been expelled from the daughter house of Coupar Angus as a punishment for previous offenses. He was stricken with an incurable form of dropsy but was cured after stretching himself out on Waldef's tomb in the chapter house.[92] Then there was Duramius. Although resorting to a variety of medicines, he was unable to get relief from

[88] Jocelin of Furness 1952, 139: *huius monasterii custos a Domine constitutus: fixum teneas, quod eleemosynae et orationes vestrae in memoriam ascendunt ante Dominum, et praecipue Walthevi abbatis vestri deprecatio.*

[89] Jocelin of Furness 1952, 148: *quod immenso divinae claritatis igne intus ardebat.*

[90] Jocelin of Furness 1952, 149: *illique respondenti et confitenti rei in se veritatem, in virtute obedientiae praecepit, ut nulli, quod viderat, enodaret, quamdiu super terram spirasset.*

[91] Jocelin of Furness 1952, 151: *cuiquam se superstite signum istud divulgaret, more suo districtius indixit.*

[92] Jocelin of Furness 1952, 181–82.

his intestinal pain. Then "one day, standing outside the chapter on the east side near the monks' infirmary, and looking inside through the open window, he caught sight of Saint Waldef's tomb." He rubbed his stomach against the wall, prayed to Waldef, and was instantly cured.[93] A third lay brother, Henry, told Jocelin of his own miraculous cure. All the potions he had tried to heal an ulcerated shin and foot had only made his condition worse. When he laid his bad leg and foot on Waldef's tomb near the foot of the saint he immediately felt some relief, and after a few days he regained the use of his leg.

Most noteworthy in the *Life of Waldef* is the greater role of the lay brothers than of the monks in propagating the saint's legend, and their greater prominence in relation to the more modest appearance of *conversi* in other *vitae*. The reason for this is not clear. It may be an example of how the role of lay brothers was viewed by the monk-authors and how it was constantly evolving to ensure continued relevance. Compared with the minor part they played in earlier *vitae*, their determined propagation of Waldef's cult may reflect Jocelin's need to assert their position in the face of the negative view of the Cistercians that had gradually evolved and for which the lay brothers, with their greater contact with the outside world, bore the brunt of the blame.

---

[93] Jocelin of Furness 1952, 194–95: *Quadam vice foras capitulum stans ad orientalem partem versus infirmitorium monachorum, et per fenestram apertam introspiciens, viso monumento sancti Waltevi.* He was not looking into the chapter house from the cloister, to which lay brothers did not normally have access, but through the window of the eastern outside wall near the usual site of the monks' infirmary.

# Chapter 9

# Virtues and Vices

The Cistercians were at the forefront of what has become known as *exemplum* literature, which had its origin and center at Clairvaux whence it gradually spread first to houses of the Clairvaux filiation and then more widely to other monasteries of the Order. In the final chapter of his *exempla* collection *Exordium magnum*, Conrad of Eberbach, a monk of Clairvaux, asserts the superiority of the Clairvaux family, claiming that "this congregation possesses as its heritage the avoidance of vices and the application of virtues."[1] He urges his readers, "if they find anything that will inspire them with hatred of vice and love of virtue in the pages of this little work, to thank God, the first Author of all good, and to be grateful to our fathers for the industriousness through which these documents have reached us."[2]

Through stories, often vivid and sometimes humorous, the good and evil deeds of the past were put to use to warn against repeating recurrent failings while at the same time providing lessons for future improvement. One *exemplum* compilation, the Beaupré collection dated around 1200, was organized according to various vices and virtues with the titles of the chapters (*Capitula sequentis*

---

[1] *EM* 6.10 (Griesser, 368); CF 72:546: *quia quasi hereditaria successione ad se transmissum tenebat beata illa congregatio vitia declinare et virtutibus operam dare.*

[2] *EM* 6.10 (Griesser, 364); CF 72:541: *hanc a lectore nostro vicissitudinis gratiam postulamus, ut, si aliquid in hoc opusculo invenerit, unde ad amorem virtutum, odium vitiorum sanctaeque devotionis fervorem inflammari se sentiat, Deo, sine quo nihil boni fit, et patribus, quorum industria haec ad nostram notitiam pervenerunt, gratias agat.*

*operis*) listed as pride, humility, envy, and charity (*De superbia, De humilitate, De invidia, De caritate*).[3]

Although the authors of these moralizing tales were monks, they frequently represented lay brothers as the epitome of the main monastic virtues for the edification of their audience, their fellow-monks. In one case, Caesarius of Heisterbach's *Dialogus miraculorum*, the stories, as the title implies, took the form of a dialogue between Caesarius and a novice specifically aimed at the formation of monk-novices even though the subject matter of a large number of the stories was the heroic virtues of lay brothers or their spectacular failure to live up to those virtues.

The lay brothers, not bound by the Rule, did not follow Saint Benedict's directives regarding the celebration of the Divine Office, although their recitations of *Pater nosters* broadly corresponded with the psalms of the monks' Office.[4] Nevertheless, the lay brothers appear in *exempla* as embodying the main virtues acclaimed by Saint Benedict: humility, obedience, and silence, toward which the lay brothers are encouraged to strive. The exhortations are frequently made more dramatic through negative examples, thereby complying with the words of Saint Benedict at the opening of the Prologue to the Rule: "that by the labor of obedience thou mayest return to him from whom thou hast strayed by the sloth of disobedience."[5]

## Humility

Humility, the ability through self-examination to know oneself as one really is, is generally acknowledged as the preeminent monastic virtue. In the spiritual heart of the Rule, chapter 7, Saint Benedict outlines what he calls the twelve-step ladder to humility. The ladder's steps are: fearing God, ignoring desire, submission to a superior in total obedience, holding fast to patience, confessing secret sins, admission of unworthiness, genuine belief in inferior-

[3] Paris, BNF Lat. 15912. For this see McGuire 1983, 211–67.
[4] *UC* 1 (Waddell, 57–59).
[5] *RB* Prologue 2 (McCann 1976, 1).

ity, acceptance of the common rule, silence, a serious disposition, restraint in speech, and constantly pondering the guilt of sin with downcast eyes. Having climbed these, the monk will come to the perfect love of God.[6]

Saint Bernard expresses the formative role of the Rule in his first treatise, *De gradibus humilitatis et superbiae* (The Steps of Humility and Pride), composed probably in 1118/19.[7] The treatise was undertaken at the request of one of his monks who wanted Bernard to develop at greater length the sermons he had given to the community. Bernard interprets Benedict's twelve steps in the light of his own experience, but instead of examining what happens on the way up he chooses to reverse the journey by describing the twelve descending steps of pride. Elsewhere he says that "no one reaches the summit immediately: the top rung of the ladder is grasped by ascending, not by flying."[8] It has been described as a "retro-tour of Saint Benedict's steps of humility, with all the fun that seeing things in reverse can bring."[9] Bernard warns against the least degree of self-exaltation and describes failure in this as "nothing less than the devil's sin and the beginning of every sin, pride."[10] As lay brothers were generally considered the lowliest of all those in the community, paragons of humility and servility, it is not surprising that monastic writers frequently represented them as examples to be emulated.

In a chapter of the *Exordium magnum* entitled "About the great humility of a certain lay brother," Conrad of Eberbach repeats a story already told by Herbert of Clairvaux:[11] when visiting a lay brother on his deathbed, Saint Bernard told him to have courage, but realizing that the brother's confidence was excessive he

---

[6] *RB* 7.67 (see McCann 1976, 16–22).

[7] *De gradibus humilitatis et superbiae*; *SBOp* 3:13–59. For the dating, see Holdsworth 1994, 34–39, 58.

[8] Bernard of Clairvaux, *Sermo 1 in natali Sancti Andreae*; *SBOp* 5:433: *Nemo repente fit summus: ascendendo non volando apprehenditur summitas scalae.*

[9] Kline 1992, 169.

[10] *utique peccatum diaboli et initium omnis peccati, superbia.*

[11] *LM* 1.29 (PL 185:1301–3).

*Fig. 20* Stained glass from cloister of Altenberg depicting Saint Bernard at the deathbed of a lay brother.

felt obliged to chastise him.[12] The lay brother then told him the secret of his confidence, which he said that he had learned from Bernard, that

> the kingdom of heaven is gained not by noble blood or the
> riches of the earth, but only by the virtue of obedience. . . .
> If you wish, ask all my superiors and peers, the brothers
> whom I have obeyed according to your orders, ask them if
> I have ever disobeyed one of them or if I have ever grieved
> any of them by a word, a sign, or, to the best of my ability,
> by any other means.[13]

---

[12] *EM* 4.19 (Griesser, 244–45): *De magna humilitate cuiusdam conversi.* See also p. 23.

[13] *EM* 4.19 (Griesser, 245); *CF* 72:355: *quod scilicet regnum Dei non carnis nobilitate, non terrenis divitiis possidetur, sed sola obedientiae virtute acquiritur.* . . .

Bernard was overjoyed to hear this and preached a sermon urging the community to follow the lay brother's example.

This story is depicted in one of the seventy stained glass panels from the early sixteenth century that formed part of the Bernard cycle formerly in the cloister of Altenberg in the Rhineland (fig. 20). Bernard is seen on the left talking to a monk who marveled at the way the lay brother confronted death without fear and in total peace. To this Bernard answered, as indicated by the scroll: "Why do you marvel? Have you not read 'Blessed are the dead who die in the Lord' [Rev 14:13]?" Nearest to the dying brother are his fellow lay brothers, praying for him and consoling him. It may be noted that a monk, and not a *conversus*, is reading prayers from a book. A fragment of glass showing just the lay brother has been preserved and reveals that a similar panel once existed in the cloister of the Cistercian nuns' house of Saint Apern in Cologne.[14]

The humility of a lay brother was the virtue Saint Bernard is said to have urged his monks to emulate in another story whose impact was so great that it found its way into four *exemplum* collections and, once again, became the subject of a chapter sermon. The Beaupré compilation has an account of a lay brother at a Clairvaux grange who wept because he was not able to be present at the abbey on the eve of a solemnity of the Virgin. In a vision Mary assured him that he could be present: "Certainly you can be there now, for it is just and I want you to be there!" and, when Saint Bernard was told about the vision, the next day he said to the monks in chapter, "Would that we could celebrate the solemn office in church as this happy man celebrated it that night in the field."[15] The story is repeated in an *exemplum* collection now in the

---

*Quaerite, si placet, ab omnibus magistris et sociis, quibus me obsequi ac servire iussistis, si cuiquam illorum aliquando inobediens fui, si de fratribus nostris quempiam verbo aut signo vel quolibet alio modo, quantum in me fuit, contristavi.*

[14] This may be seen on the CD to France 2007 as GL 67.

[15] BC fol. 83v–84r: *Certe iam intereris quia justum est et volo ut intersis. . . . Quod beato Bernardo perspicuum factum innotuit. Unde cum verbum facere in capitulo in die illa inter cetera sic ait. Utinam sic sollempnizaremus in oratorio sicut quidam felix hac nocte sollempnizavit in campo.*

*Bibliothèque nationale* in Paris,[16] and is found again, but in greater detail, in the *Exordium magnum*. We learn that the feast in question was the Assumption, that the grange was close to the abbey, and that the lay brother who had a fervent devotion to Mary was one of those whom the grange master decided should stay behind to look after the sheep. Turning toward the abbey, he recited the prayers lay brothers say in place of Matins (*quae conversis vice matutinarum statutae sunt*), repeatedly saying the *Ave Maria*. Saint Bernard's sermon is then given in greater detail, with the emphasis lying on the humility of the lay brother and his unquestioning acceptance of his place in the community. Although praising the devotion of his monks, Bernard added:

> But I want you to know that one of our humblest and simplest lay brothers, whom obedience forced to celebrate the joys of this great feast tonight out of doors in the mountains and woods, offered a service of morning worship to our Lady so pleasing, so devoted, so festive, that the contemplation of none of you, however exalted, or your intensive devotion could be preferred to his devotion, which was offered not in the lofty sublimity of contemplation, but in the humble submission of holy simplicity.[17]

The story appears again in the Ebrach *exemplum* compilation as one paragraph in a long account of a lay brother to whom the Virgin frequently appeared:

> My most fervent and holy lady was the cause of my sorrow because in such a solemnity of your glorification [Assumption] she did not allow me, a miserable wretch, to be present in the oratory and to take part in your praises with the other

---

[16] Paris, BNF MS lat. 14657, fol. 70r. I am grateful to Stefano Mula, who is editing the collection, for pointing this out to me.

[17] *EM* 4.13 (Griesser, 239); CF 72:346: *Verumtamen scire vos volo unum ex minoribus et simplicioribus fratribus nostris conversis, quem obedientia hac nocte in montibus et silvis istis sub divo tantae festivitatis gaudia celebrare coegerat, tam iucundum, tam devotum, tam festivum Dominae nostrae matutinarum exsolvisse servitium, ut nullius vestrum quantumcumque suspensa contemplatio seu intensa devotio ipsius devotioni, quam non alta contemplationis sublimitas, sed submissa sanctae simplicitatis efficit humilitas, praeferri potuerit.*

brethren or listen to the words of our venerable father Dom Bernard. She said: "Do not be saddened about this, for even though you are not allowed to go to the monastery, you will not miss the solemnity of Matins."[18]

Caesarius of Heisterbach has a similar story about a lay brother from the Westphalian abbey of Marienfeld. Anxious to return to the monastery from a grange for a certain festival he was saddened when he failed to get permission from his grange master. Everything that happened at the abbey was divinely revealed to him and he communicated spiritually even if not sacramentally. When the brethren returned, "he told them first who celebrated the main Mass, next who read the epistle and who the gospel; likewise the monks who sang the responses and what lessons were read, he told them all to their amazement."[19]

Herbert of Clairvaux tells of a Clairvaux lay brother whose humility merited being gloriously revealed in a vision. On the day of his death a monk in a monastery far from Clairvaux told his brethren,

> Today while I was suspended in the spirit above my physical senses, I suddenly found myself entering into a paradise of marvelous delights, into a place so bright that the human senses cannot understand the extent, the beauty, and the charm of it. . . . Charmed by what I saw and heard, I asked the angel who was leading me what the cause of this joy and celebration was. He said, "It is a new celebration for the new saint who is arriving today from the house of Clairvaux and who in this way is solemnly introduced in joy."[20]

---

[18] EC 3 (Oppel 1972, 15): "*Domina mea piissima atque sanctissima, causa mei doloris hec est, quod in tanta sollempnitate glorificacionis vestre michi misero non conceditur oratorium adire vestrisque laudibus cum aliis meis fratribus interesse, sed nec sermonem venerabilis patris nostri domini Bernhardi audire.*" At illa: "*Noli,*" inquit, "*super hoc contristari, quia etsi ad claustrum non ieris, tamen matutinorum sollempniis non carebis.*"

[19] DM 9.45 (Strange 2:200–1; Scott and Bland 2:148–49): *quis missam maiorem celebrasset, quis legisset Epistolam, quis Evangelium; similiter ad vigilias qui monachi quas lectiones vel quae responsoria contassent, cunctis mirantibus exposuit.*

[20] LM 1.7 (PL 185:460–61): *Hodie cum a sensibus corporis in spiritu sublevatus abstraherer, inveni me subito introductum velut in paradiso voluptatis, in loco glorioso atque*

When Saint Bernard was told what had happened, he is reported to have said: "To me it is clearer than day and more certain than the life I live that all who persevere in purity of heart, practicing humility and obedience, will, as soon as they will have shed their flesh, immediately be stripped of all misery and clothed in the glory of immortality."[21]

Conrad of Eberbach repeats the story almost word for word, but after the lay brother has been introduced Conrad speculates about the consequence for those following a different path:

> If the devotion and humility of this blessed man were agreeable to God and pleasing to man, what, I ask, will those who take the opposite path say to the Lord on the terrible day of judgment? Whenever they are accused by someone, they get angry, burst into words of impatience, and do not hide their rancor against those who accuse them, but instead, impelled by resentment and not by any kind of charity, they blame them in turn with all the exaggeration of the fault possible.[22]

The only other difference between the two accounts is that Herbert's ends with Bernard's quotation while Conrad adds a note to the effect that they were greatly encouraged by Bernard's words, not least because "when we hear and read this in the present day, when love has grown cold and lukewarmness and negligence have

---

*praeclaro nimis; cujus aptitudinem, pulchritudinem, atque amoenitatem humani sensus angustia aestimare non sufficit. . . . Ego vero cum nimis obstupuissem, sciscitatus sum ab angelo ductore meo super his quae videbam. Ipse autem respondit: Haec est celebritas nova, novi cujusdam sancti hodie de domo Clarae-Vallensi assumpti, et in gaudia ista modo solemniter introducendi.*

[21] LM 1.7 (PL 185:461): *Mihi siquidem luce clarius, et vita qua vivo certius constat, omnes qui in cordis hujus puritate obedientes et humiles perseveraverint, mox ut carnem exuerint, ab omni miseria protinus exuendos, et immortalitatis gloria vestiendos.*

[22] EM 4.20 (Griesser 246); CF 72:356: *Verumtamen si accepta Deo et grata hominibus erat devotio et humilitas huius beati viri, videant, quaeso, quid responsuri sint Deo in die tremendi examinis eius, qui e contrario nituntur, qui, si forte ab aliquo proclamati fuerint, exasperantur et ad impatientiae verba prorumpunt, rancorum quoque, quem adversus proclamantes se concipiunt, dissimulare nequeunt, seu etiam opportunitatem captant, quo non caritatis, sed rancoris spiritu impulsi eos, qui se clamaverunt, cum quanta possunt exaggeratione culpae reclament.*

begun to infiltrate everything, if only we might be warmed again to imitate the vigor and fervor and devotion of the holy fathers."[23]

## Obedience

Saint Benedict's third degree of humility "is that a man for the love of God subject himself to his superior in all obedience," while the reverse in Saint Bernard's tenth step of pride is defiance or rebellion (*de rebellione*).[24] Many acts of disobedience, conspiracies, rebellions, violence, and even homicide, not only among lay brothers but also among monks, were recorded in the statutes of the General Chapter and other legal sources and will be discussed later.[25] In the *exemplum* literature disobedience is the most frequent lay brother transgression.

The minor act of disobedience of a lay brother who washed his shoes without first seeking permission, which found its way into three *exemplum* collections, has already been mentioned.[26] The moral of the tale is given in the Beaupré version as "how dangerous it is for anyone who has professed obedience to act in a disobedient way."[27]

Another story of a disobedient lay brother is included in the same three collections regarding the humility of a lay brother at a Clairvaux grange. The *Collectaneum clarevallense* version is entitled "How dangerous it is not to obey his abbot." When a lay brother who had been disobedient to his superior was unable to sleep at night he was visited by two demons.[28] When one of them inquired whether he was a lay brother, the other replied: "No, he is a disobedient person.

---

[23] *EM* 4.20 (Griesser, 248); CF 72:359: *Utinam et nos, qui temporibus istis novissimis, quibus refrigente iam caritate tepiditas et negligentia usquequaque subintrare coepit, haec audimus et legimus, recalescamus ad imitandum vigorem fervoris et devotionis sanctorum patrum.*

[24] *RB* 7.34 (McCann 1976, 19); *De gradibus humilitatis et superbiae* 48–49; *SBOp* 3:53.

[25] See chapter 12.

[26] See chapter 6.

[27] BC fol. 30v: *Ecce quam periculosum professit obedientiam quicquam inobedienter agere.*

[28] *CC* 3.13 (Legendre 2005, 256): *Quam periculosum sit abbati suo non obedire.*

Therefore we will accept him."[29] They beat him and dragged him through the dormitory, but fled when some of the other brothers ran to his aid. After he went back to bed the demons returned and snatched and beat him again and, although he cried out loudly, no one came to his help until Mary appeared, saying: "Let him go. It is not your business to avenge sin."[30] A very brief version appears in the Beaupré compilation. There is the same exchange between the demons who beat and dragged the disobedient lay brother through the dormitory. After the demons leave he is then seen prostrate by the other brothers. The story ends: "After he had been horribly manhandled, when he reached the door of the monastery the Blessed Virgin appeared to him and liberated him."[31]

The title of Conrad of Eberbach's rendering is "About the dangers of disobedience."[32] As usual, it is considerably more detailed than the two other accounts. Before beginning the story itself Conrad devotes a whole paragraph to obedience in a general way and he ends by claiming that it is better "to obey with the gentle than to divide the spoils of arrogance and rebellion with the proud [Prov 16:19]." His description of the lay brother and of the two demons is both livelier and more graphic: the brother was "full of rancor and bitterness and unworried about persevering in his obstinacy" and "still satisfying his pride by thinking up wicked plans" before going to sleep, and the evil spirits were "blacker than coal and crueler than dragons."[33] In the dialogue between the demons, instead of the phrase "we will accept him" (*accipiamus*) as in the *Collectaneum clarevallense*, Conrad has "we will drag him to the door"

---

[29] *CC* 3.13 (Legendre 2005, 256): *"Non, sed quidam inobediens," tunc ille: "Ergo accipiamus eum."*

[30] *CC* 3.13 (Legendre 2005, 256): *"Dimittite eum, non est vestrum suum ulcisci peccatum."*

[31] BC fol. 30r: *Quem cum usque ad portam monasterii iam horribiliter pertranxissent, beata virgo affuit et liberavit eum.*

[32] *EM* 5.8 (Griesser, 286–88): *De periculo inobedientiae.*

[33] *EM* 5.8 (Griesser, 287); CF 72:420: *ipse rancoris et amaritudinis felle plenus et in contumacia sua perdurare. . . . sed adhuc dirae superbiae vitio corde machinando malum satisfaceret . . . fuligine taetriores, draconibus crudeliores.*

(*trahamus illam ad portam*).[34] They dragged him out of the dormitory, and outside the monastery "they began to play with him in a horrible way, throwing him from one to the other like men playing ball, throwing and catching him." Unlike the other accounts, this one has the battered lay brother drag himself out of the boggy marsh when he could and sit, filthy and stinking, under a tree.[35] A venerable person, not as in the other accounts identified as the Virgin, although this is implied by the feminine *persona*, comes up to him, saying: "Be of good courage and do not be afraid because of the malicious servants of darkness; the avengers of pride and rebellion will not dare to harm you any more. This has happened to you by the just judgment of God because you were not afraid of being arrogantly rebellious to your superior."[36] When the brothers find him sitting under a tree they call the prior. Asked what has befallen him, the lay brother "bared his teeth like a dog about to bite" (*caninis rictibus morsum*) and reproaches them for not having come to his aid. He is taken to the infirmary and bit by bit learns by reflecting on what he has suffered to be disobedient no longer. The final paragraph is an epilogue in which Conrad rams home the moral of the story in uncompromising language, paraphrasing the teaching of Saint Benedict and Saint Bernard: "Just as rebellion and pride are evils without equal, the proud, the arrogant, and the rebellious will be punished, damned and tortured without parallel. May their sentence be far from all of us who have resolved to love God with humble and sincere charity, and who for his sake obey and submit to his representatives, our superiors."[37]

---

[34] *CC* 3.13 (Legendre 2005, 256); *EM* 5.8 (Griesser, 287).

[35] *EM* 5.8 (Griesser, 287): *coeperunt illudere ei, proh nefas! Ad alterutrum eum iaculantes, sicut solent homines ludentes pilam iacere et capere. . . . Qui se inde, sicut poterat, proripiens subtus quandam arborem consedit totus ex uligine paludis denigratus atque foedatus.*

[36] *EM* 5.8 (Griesser, 287–88); CF 72:421: *Confortare et noli timere, quoniam maligni illi tenebrarum ministri, superbiae et contumaciae ultores, tibi ulterius nocere nequaquam praesument. Haec autem iusto Dei iudicio tibi propterea acciderunt, quia tam superbe inobediens et rebellis esse seniori tuo non timuisti.*

[37] *EM* 5.8 (Griesser, 288); CF 72:422: *Itaque sicut incomparabile malum est superbia et rebellio, ita sine exemplo punientur, damnabuntur et cruciabuntur superbi, arrogantes et*

Disobedience was the subject of another story by Caesarius of Heisterbach. A lay brother from Clairmarais in northern France had suffered from a serious ulcer and repeatedly asked his abbot for permission to visit the tomb of Saint Quirinus in the Rhineland to seek a cure.[38] Although the abbot always refused on the grounds that pilgrimages were forbidden by the Order, the lay brother went without permission and was cured. The abbot could not believe that Quirinus could be a martyr of Christ as he had healed a disobedient lay brother and he refused to have the brother back, but "since the martyr could not bear the threats of the abbot he reinstated the disease in the lay brother." The abbot was now able to accept that Quirinus was a martyr and, after he had prayed with the other brothers, "healing was conceded to the disobedient lay brother in order to declare the greater virtue of obedience just as has been said."[39]

The miraculous saving of a whole crop of peas was the reward for the obedience of a lay brother from Himmerod. Afraid that rain might spoil the crop, the prior ordered all the lay brothers to go out to turn the peas. "At once a lay brother from the infirmary, a simple man in the abounding heat of zeal hurried there before them all. And when he came near the field where the peas lay, they were turning themselves before his eyes." To this Caesarius' novice commented: "I have no doubt now that great is the power of obedience, which is rewarded with such a miracle."[40]

---

*rebelles. Quorum sententia longe sit ab omnibus nobis, qui Deum sincera et humili caritate diligere et vicariis ipsius, praelatis nostris, in omni sollicitudine propter ipsum subdi et obedire decrevimus.*

[38] *DM* Hilka 1937, 3:40–41.

[39] *DM* Hilka 1937, 3:41: *quasi minas abbatis martir portare non posset, ad predicta verba morbum in converso celerius renovavit. . . . Deinde sanitatem converso inobedienti fuisse concessam ad maiorem obediente virtutem, sicut dictum est, declarandam.*

[40] *DM* 10.15 (Strange 2:229; Scott and Bland 2:185): *Mox ex infirmitorio conversorum frater quidam simplex exiens, ex multo fervore obedientiae ante omnes festinabat; et cum agro in quo pisa iacebat propinquasset, illa mirum in modum in oculis eius per diversa loca se vertebat. . . . Iam non ambigo quin magna sit virtus obedientiae, quae tanto miraculo remueratur.*

The Dominican Stephen of Bourbon (1190–1261) tells about a lay brother from Cîteaux whose obedience to his abbot conflicted with the charity his conscience told him he owed to the poor. The brother felt that he had more clothes than he needed. When he came across a poor man who did not have enough, he gave him a tunic in spite of his abbot's prohibition. For this offense he was often and severely rebuked and punished. Pope Alexander III (1159–1181), who was in France between 1162 and 1165, was called in to adjudicate. Realizing that obedience forbade the brother to do what charity dictated, he said: "You, brother, whenever charity dictates, give; you, abbot, whenever the brother disobeys you, punish him."[41]

## Silence

The importance attached to silence was not confined to lay brothers but applied equally to monks. The Rule devotes an entire chapter to silence and elsewhere enjoins that "monks should practice silence at all times, but especially at night."[42] Aelred of Rievaulx acknowledged this in his *Mirror of Charity* when, in his lament for his friend Simon, he says that "the rule of our order forbade us to speak." At the same time he affirmed the non-verbal aspect of their friendship by adding that "his face spoke to me, his bearing spoke to me, his silence talked."[43] The Rule was invoked in a curious General Chapter statute from 1233 according to which a ruling from the previous year

> concerning conversations between abbots and monks should be reformulated in this way: the abbots and monks and equally the lay brothers when they come together in conversation should take care, especially when dealing with anything important and

[41] Etienne de Bourbon 1877: *"Tu, converse, quociens suadebit hoc tibi caritas, semper da; tu, abba, quociens invenietur inobediencia, conversum semper verbera."*

[42] *RB* 6 and 42 (McCann 1976, 15–16; 48).

[43] Aelred, Spec Car 1.107 (CCCM I, 60:1823–26; Squire 1969, 99): *Simul quidem loqui Ordinis nostri prohibebat auctoritas, sed loquebatur mihi aspectus eius, loquebatur mihi incessus eius, loquebatur mihi ipsum silentium eius.*

matters concerning the salvation of their souls, to do so in a
balanced way, avoiding *frivolous and facetious talk.*[44]

The regulation in the *Usages* regarding the observance of silence
by the lay brothers was both strict and clear cut: in the workshops
the same rule applied to them as to the monks:"in their dormitory
and refectory especially are they to observe silence; and in addition to these, in all other places, unless they speak about necessities
at the bidding of the abbot or prior."[45] Likewise, in the granges
silence had to be observed in the dormitory, the refectory, and the
calefactory. Elsewhere the lay brothers might speak to the grange
master concerning necessities.[46]

Caesarius has a story of two lay brothers from one of the
granges belonging to Himmerod in the Rhineland. One day after
Compline one of them, looking up to heaven, had a vision of a
shining cross with the crucified Christ. He wondered whether
the other brother had seen the same, but "because their rule forbade them to speak, he made a sign to his companion as if asking
whether the other saw anything. But the other made signs that he
saw nothing. Then the first signed to him that he should fall on his
knees and pray. And when they had both done this together, the
second rose up after a little while, having become the sharer and
witness of that wonderful vision."[47]

---

[44] *Statuta* 1233.6 (Canivez 2:112): *Definitio anni praeteriti de colloquiis abbatum
et monachorum taliter reformetur: studeant abbates monachi pariter et conversi, ut quando
ad colloquium conveniunt, talia inter se habeant colloquia quae gravitatem redoleant et
salutem respiciant animarum, attendentes quod de omni verbo otioso reddituri sunt aequis-
simo iudici rationem.* The ruling referred to does not appear in the Canivez edition
under 1232 or any of the previous years.

[45] *UC* 6 (Waddell, 65; 177): *In quibuscumque officinis tenent monachi silentium et
ipsi, nec aliquam earum ingrediantur sine licentia. Insuper in suo dormitorio et refectorio
omnino silentium teneant, et preter hec in omnibus locis aliis, nisi forte iussu abbatis vel
prioris de necessariis loquantur.*

[46] *UC* 6 (Waddell, 65; 178): *Similiter qui in grangiis sunt silentium teneant in
dormitorio, in refectorio, et in calefactorio, intra metas ad hoc deputatas. Alibi possunt loqui
cum magistro suo de necessariis.*

[47] *DM* 8.17 (Strange 2:95; Scott and Bland 2:18–19): *Et quia loqui non licebat,
signum fecit alteri, quasi interrogans si aliquid videret. At ille nihil se videre signavit. Tunc*

The way the rule was applied at Clairvaux may be seen from the provisions concerning silence in the *Breve et memoriale scriptum,* which prohibits lay brothers from addressing anyone indirectly, that is, to say to an authorized person something that is in fact directed to another person. Transgressors were to be severely punished.[48] In the granges "they do not speak with those whom they meet; they do not reply to those asking questions, unless it is briefly to give information about the way or about a lost animal. Should someone question them further, they are to say that it is not allowed them to have a conversation with a guest."[49]

The regulation is repeated a little later in the chapter on the shepherds, which states "that they are to observe silence, unless perhaps they point out the right direction to someone, or provide information about a stray animal, or inquire briefly about their own strays."[50] The Villers Chronicle has an account of a taciturn lay brother, Evrard, who refused to be drawn into conversation by a passerby. A knight on horseback rashly boasted that he could make a lay brother talk but, having failed to win his bet, he slapped the brother on the cheek. In true biblical fashion Evrard offered his other cheek, which resulted in the knight repenting, eventually to become a monk at Villers.[51]

A statute from 1200 imposed the penalty of bread and water on lay brothers who got into the habit of talking without restriction at meals when away in towns.[52] This was in contravention of the

---

ipse signum illi fecit, ut genua flecteret et oraret. Quod cum fecissent ambo simul, erectus post pusillum tantae visionis factus est socius et testis.

[48] BMS 7 (Waddell, 157, 202): *Omnibus conversis nostris generaliter est prohibitum, ne per tertiam personam sermonem in aliquem dirigant. Quod si quis transgreditur, graviter inde punitur.*

[49] BMS 7 (Waddell, 157, 202): *Obviantibus non loquuntur, interrogantibus non respondent, nisi pro via, aut bestia perdita breviter indicanda. Si quis amplius eos interrogaverit, dicant, non licere sibi colloqui cum hospite.*

[50] BMS 11 (Waddell, 158, 206): *Euntes et redeuntes silentium tenent ad invicem, et ad omnes, nisi forte viam alicui demonstrent, vel bestiam perditam indicent, vel de suis perditis breviter inquirant.*

[51] Martene and Durand 1717, 3:1367–68.

[52] *Statuta* 1200.12 (Waddell 2002, 457).

*Instituta* prohibition whereby a monk or a lay brother on a journey was not to speak at table unless "he has no one who understands his signs, he may briefly and quietly make his request by uttering single words such as 'water,' 'bread,' and 'wine,' and only other things necessary for the meal."[53]

Jocelin of Furness in his *Life of Waldef* refers to silence as an attribute of a saintly life while at the same time pointing out that the rule regarding its observance was not always adhered to. Waldef was said to be "hooded over and communing within himself with time for God alone" while "the monks and lay brothers whom he had brought with him were intent on their conversation and the swift give-and-take of their clever tongues."[54] Similarly, the saintly Christian of Aumône had a vision of a terrified lay brother in a torn and threadbare habit who, after he had died and been buried, was accused by three horrible demons of not guarding his tongue and of uttering hurtful words, a warning to lay brothers who broke the rule of silence. "When asked whether that soul would gain mercy, Christian replied: 'I think,' he said, 'that he will.'"[55]

Caesarius recounts how a lay brother named Walter from the Flemish abbey of Ter Doest "used to make foolish signs and chattered a lot, and he was lax in his manner of life and frequently broke the rule of silence."[56] God therefore inflicted a serious illness and death on him, but after a few hours he returned to life and was able to describe his experience of purgatory. As he was dying the brothers had noticed that he began to turn black as pitch, then red as fire, then white as snow, and finally he turned into ashes like a cinder. He explained that his body had been dipped into pitch,

[53] *Instituta* 88 (Waddell 1999, 494): *si non habuerit qui signa sua intelligat, singula verba dicendo, ut "aquam," "panem," et "vinum," et caetera comestioni tantum necessaria breviter et silenter requirat.*

[54] Jocelin of Furness 1952, 152: *ipse incaputiatus, ac secum commorans, et soli Deo vacans . . . . monachos atque conversos, quos secum adduxerat, volubili rotatu lubricae linguae mutuaeque intendentes.*

[55] Leclercq 1953, 51–52: *utrum illa habitura esset misericordiam interrogatus respondit: "Estimo, ait, quod habebit."*

[56] *DM* Hilka 1937, 3:115: *de signis otiosis verbisque superfluis modicum curans et, cum levis in moribus esset frequenterque regulas silentii frangeret.*

then thrown into a raging fire, then into frozen water and finally into a cooking vessel filled with boiling water as well as being beaten with iron scourges. He went on to explain that God "out of his exceeding mercy did not want to damn me utterly and so he ordered me to return to my body so that I might announce to those who are living both by word and example the great punishment that is due to sinners."[57] He added that he had seen some monks and lay brothers suffering the same penalties for not making confession for their sins, and "he urged the ones he had seen to go to the abbot secretly one by one and to make a true repentance."[58] Caesarius notes that he owed his information to Walwesan, a lay brother from Himmerod who had the story from Walter himself.

## Greed

Saint Benedict described the possession of private property by monks without the abbot's permission as a vice. The monk was not "to have anything as his own, anything whatever, whether book or tablets or pen or whatever it may be; for monks should not have even their bodies and wills at their own disposal."[59] In an *exemplum* about a disobedient lay brother, Conrad of Eberbach posed the rhetorical question as to how many there are

> who in accordance with the Rule and the Order have renounced all private property, and yet, following the example of Ananias and Sapphira [Acts 1:5-11], with rash presumption do not hesitate to hold property? Even though a single word from the mouth of the apostle Peter punished that pair with a terrible death, no misfortune touches these people; on the contrary, they seem to pass their days happily. May they not suddenly find themselves in hell [see Job 21:13]! In the very Order of Cîteaux, which by the grace of God is pure and free

[57] *DM* Hilka 1937, 3:116: *ex nimia sua misericordia dampnare vellet, ad corpus me redire iussit, ut, quanta pena debeatur peccantibus, tam verbo quam exemplo nuntiem viventibus.*

[58] *DM* Hilka 1937, 3:116: *Quos secrete singillatim ad abbatem ducens eisque que viderat obiciens ad verum adduxit penitentiam.*

[59] *RB* 33.3 (McCann 1976, 40).

from the huge vice of property, there were and, even after that brother received a sentence of death for what seemed a minor fault, there are still some who easily allow themselves exceptions without respect for the holy Order, and then sign or say, "What is wrong?" or "Is it so important?" They take no heed of what and how important it is according to Scripture, where it is written: "he who despises little things, little by little will fall" [Sir 19:1].[60]

A lay brother from Kamp in the Rhineland "secretly caused books to be written for him, that he might possess them, and began to take pleasure in the vice of private ownership," which, Caesarius of Heisterbach asserts, became the means of his undoing.[61] The importance attached to uniformity of observance and strict adherence to the teaching of Saint Benedict by the early Cistercians was articulated in chapter 2 of the *Carta caritatis* and would have encompassed their attitude to monastic proprietorship.[62]

In the *exemplum* tradition, failure to observe the ruling on private ownership sometimes manifested itself in difficulty in receiving the host at communion. The *Liber miraculorum* has a short account of a lay brother from Longpont in northern France who kept one denarius and one heifer without permission, contravening Saint Benedict's injunction. When he was receiving communion at Easter some creature was seen forcing a burning coal into his mouth that, overcome with nausea, he rejected before he could find a pot to

---

[60] *EM* 4.24 (Griesser, 251–52); CF 72:364–65: *qui, cum secundum regulam et ordinem suum proprietati abrenuntiaverint, exemplo tamen Ananiae et Saphirae temeraria nimis praesumptione proprietates habere non verentur, cum illos virtus, quae exivit de ore Petri apostoli, teribili morte multaverit, istos vero nulla plaga tangat, sed a contrario videantur in bonis ducere dies suos, utinam non in puncto ad inferna descensuri! Sed et in ipso Cisterciensi ordine, qui licet per gratiam Dei purus et integer sit a tam enormi vitio proprietatis, nonnulli tamen fuere vel sunt ab illo tempore, quo frater ille pro levi, ut videbatur, culpa tam durae mortis sententiam excepit, qui sine respectu sacri ordinis facile in levibus excedentes solent significare aut verbo dicere: Quid vel quantum est hoc, nec attendunt, quod scriptum est, quoniam, qui minima spernit, paulatim decidit.*

[61] *DM* 5.16 (Strange 1:294–95; Scott and Bland 1:294): *libellos sibi ad hoc idoneos occulte fecit conscribi, coepitque in vitio proprietatis delectari.*

[62] *Carta caritatis* 2 (Waddell 1999, 444).

spit it into. He confessed and "the next day the abbot recounted what had happened to all those present in chapter and, on account of the disrespect for the sacrament, he enjoined a penance on us."[63] The story ends ominously with the brief statement: "Whether he got better afterwards we don't know" (*convaluerit incertum est nobis*).

Caesarius has a similar story of a lay brother from Fontmorigny near Bourges. After hearing the brother's confession the abbot warned him to cleanse his conscience diligently. When the priest gave him the host at Mass he was unable to close his mouth to swallow it and the priest withdrew it and gave it to another man who was able to receive it without any problem. Not long afterward the lay brother died and five shillings were found when his body was washed. Since it "was not lawful for him to have any money"[64] they buried him in the open country and threw the coins on him, saying: "Thy money perish with thee."[65]

In 1190 two recently deceased lay brothers, respectively of Theuley in eastern France and Zwettl in Austria, were found guilty of holding private property, one money and the other a coat. They were both exhumed and neither was to be buried in the abbey cemetery.[66] Similar judgments occur in a number of local statute collections: at Signy and Vauclair in Champagne and at Alcobaça in Portugal monks found to possess "money or other property" (*pecunia vel aliqua proprietas*) were not to be buried in the monks' cemetery.[67] In 1191 the decision regarding the lay brother from Theuley was reversed when further investigation revealed that the money in his possession had been given with the abbot's permission to be used on the abbey's business. A lay brother of Bonneval

---

[63] *LM* 3.27 (PL 185:1373): *In crastinum autem abbas cuncta quae acciderant, in capitulo ad fratrum audientiam retulit, et propter negligentiam sacrae communionis, communem poenitentiam nobis qui adfuimus injunxit.*

[64] See *RB* 33 (McCann 1976, 40).

[65] *DM* 9.64 (Strange 2:214–15; Scott and Bland 2:166–67): *Pecunia tua tecum sit in perditionem.*

[66] *Statuta* 1190.13 (Waddell 2002, 197): *Conversus Theoloci qui pecuniam suam sub lecto absconderat, et conversus de Zuetula qui pro pellicaeo malefacto sibi de cimiterio extumulatus est, ubi sepulti sunt remaneant.*

[67] Waddell 2002, 620, 635, 692.

had been deprived of a church funeral because he had been found upon death to possess three *denarii*. He was said to have been of unsound mind. On condition that three abbots (Bonnevaux, Dalon, and Candiel) who were delegated in 1194 to investigate agreed, he was to be reburied in the community cemetery.[68] In 1228 the General Chapter decided to deny burial in the cemetery of a lay brother who was found to have five *denarii* when he died and had failed to confess and yet had received communion at Christmas.[69]

A statute from 1195 deals with monks or lay brothers who had left their abbeys, taking with them monastery belongings. Although they were allowed to return, they were to wear the clothing of the monastic servants and not the habit of a monk or a lay brother. If they reoffended, the lay brothers were to be expelled while the monks were to be sent off in permanent exile to another monastery.[70]

Gluttony was a vice that troubled some lay brothers. A mid-fifteenth-century manuscript that belonged to the Carthusians in Erfurt contained a number of tales from earlier sources. One of them concerned a lay brother from the Cistercian abbey Oliva in Prussia who is said to have secreted three loaves of bread in time of famine instead of giving them to the poor. The abbot had one of the loaves hung up at the church door as a memorial, inscribed in the local dialect: "When the scheffil [grain measure] was worth forty-eight this stone was made out of one loaf."[71] A late thirteenth-century English collection of three hundred fifteen edifying tales, probably of Dominican origin, contains one about a Cistercian lay brother who, as he was dying, was troubled by the devil until he confessed that he used to eat in secret.[72]

---

[68] *Statuta* 1194.42 (Waddell 2002, 296–97).

[69] *Statuta* 1228.20 (Canivez 2:69): *Conversus qui subito defunctus inventus est habere quinque denarios et non fuit confessus, immo et in sacra solemnitate Nativitatis Dominicae accessit ad sacram communionem non facta confessione, remaneat prout est extra cimeterium tumulatus.*

[70] *Statuta* 1195.23 (Waddell 2002, 321–22).

[71] *Catalogue of Romances* 1910, 703; London, British Library MS Additional 21147, fol. 72v: *Do der scheffil galt acht und firczig dissir steyn von eyme brote wart.*

[72] *Catalogue of Romances* 1910, 496; London, British Library MS Royal 7 D. I, fol. 120v.

The devil did not always find it easy to entrap his victim. Caesarius of Heisterbach records a story of a lay brother he had heard from the brother's own lips. When asleep, "he began to gnaw with his teeth the wood on which he was lying prostrate, the devil making him think that he was chewing meat; and the grinding of his teeth was as the sound of a mouse breaking through the shell of a nut."[73] The cellarer, named Richwin, hearing the noise, inquired what had happened and was told that the devil had brought the lay brother some meat; he was shown the wood that had been gnawed. The moral of the story was that "the enemy tries to deceive in sleep those religious whom he cannot entrap with gluttony when awake."[74]

## Confession

Saint Benedict's fifth degree of humility is that the monk "humbly confess and conceal not from his abbot any evil thoughts that enter his heart, and any secret sins that he has committed."[75] Saint Bernard's reversal of the degrees of humility is the subject of his ninth step of pride, "hypocritical confession" (*de simulata confessione*), in which he asserts that "a false and proud confession is much more perilous than a willful and stubborn defense."[76] Numerous stories in the *exemplum* literature of problems arising from this teaching attest to the importance the early Cistercians attached to adhering to it and, as in those dealing with the chief monastic virtues, they frequently feature lay brothers.

The consequence of making an imperfect confession has already been mentioned in the story of the lay brother from Fontmorigny. At Heisterbach, Caesarius's own monastery, the senior lay brother Henry had "committed a certain sin, which he had never confessed

---

[73] *DM* 4.83 (Strange 1:250; Scott and Bland 1:285): *ex illusione diaboli ipsum super quod prostratus iacebat lignum dentibus rodere coepit, ac si aliquid masticaret. Et erat stridor dentium eius, ut sonus nuris testam nucis dentibus suis perforantis.*

[74] *DM* 4.83 (Strange 1:258; Scott and Bland 1:285): *Sic inimicus viros religiosos quos decipere per gulam non potest vigilando, ad mirus illis illudere conatur dormitando.*

[75] *RB* 7.44 (McCann 1976, 20).

[76] *De gradibus humilitatis et superbiae* 18.46; *SBOp* 3:51: *Multo tamen periculosior est fallax ac superba confessio, quam pervicax et obstinata defensio.*

to abbot, prior, or anyone else."[77] Even though he frequently made his confession, he had never confessed this sin but, as he approached the point of death, he relented. Caesarius warns his novice that this is a very risky business in these words: "Many are ignorant of these things, presuming too much upon a death-bed repentance, unaware that a penitence put off till then is, as we have been saying, so terribly uncertain."[78]

Elsewhere Caesarius records how a lay brother was deceived by counting the call of a cuckoo. He mistakenly interpreted the twenty-two calls as meaning that his life would be prolonged for as many more years and he said to himself: "Why should I mortify myself in the Order all that time? I will go back to the world, give myself up to it, and enjoy all its pleasures for twenty years and then the last two that remain I will spend in penitence."[79] He was caught unawares, and died in apostasy earlier than he had planned.

Herbert of Clairvaux has a story about a lay brother named Stephen who became sick and, wanting to die, would eat scarcely anything.[80] He asked the infirmarian to prepare a meal for him as the cellarer, who had also been sick and in the meantime had died, had ordered him to do. The infirmarian could not understand this as he knew that the cellarer had died, but Stephen replied: "Believe me, brother, that he has come to me and now he is not dead but has evaded death and lives in a better place."[81] When he had eaten, Stephen made his confession and gave up his spirit. The infirmarian, recognizing Stephen's good fortune, asked for his prayers that he might follow him soon. After a few days Stephen appeared to the

---

[77] *DM* 2.14 (Strange 1:82; Scott and Bland 1:91): *peccatum quoddam commiserat, quod nunquam Abbati, neque Priori, neque alicui confessus fuerat.*

[78] *DM* 2.14 (Strange 1:83; Scott and Bland 1:91): *Multi iste ignorant, de finali poenitentia plurimum praesumentes, nescientes poenitentiam, quae in fine agitur, ut supra dictum est, tam incertam esse.*

[79] *DM* 5.17 (Strange 1:295–96; Scott and Bland 1:337–38): *Ut quid tanto mortificem me in ordine? Redibo ad saeculum, et saeculo deditus, viginti annis fruar deliciis eius, duobus annis, qui supersunt, poenitebo.*

[80] *LM* 3.7 (PL 185:1357–58).

[81] *LM* 3.7 (PL 185:1358): "*Crede mihi, frater, quia venit ad me; et jam non est mortuus, sed mortem evasit, et vivit in melius.*"

infirmarian in a vision, begging him to "remember therefore while you are still on the earth that little sin you committed from which you have not yet been absolved in confession. Confess therefore and quickly do penance because if before your death the sin has not been deleted by confession, after your death it will remain unforgiven."[82] When he awoke he remembered the sin he had committed twelve years ago but had completely forgotten. He was quickly liberated by confession and, giving thanks, "he realized that one does not ask for the prayers of the saints in vain, and nor is the sacrament of confession to be lightly regarded without which one remains guilty even of faults one is not aware of."[83]

The same story is found in the *Exordium magnum*.[84] Although Conrad of Eberbach usually expands what has previously been recorded by Herbert, in this case the reverse is true. There is no mention of the intervention of the cellarer, but apart from this the two versions are practically identical.

Conrad tells of an incredibly lucky "lay brother who escaped the sentence of damnation,"[85] the title of the story. His memory for past sins was ostensibly even less acute than that of the infirmarian in the previous story. He was at first unrepentant and then repentant, but he needed two goes at confession before he was finally cleared. Although he had been professed many years earlier at Esrum in Denmark, he had been sent to Clairvaux on account of a serious offense he had committed and for which he had not sought forgiveness. Conrad is careful to point out that "he had not been reared under the very chaste discipline of Clairvaux." When he was

---

[82] *LM* 3.7 (PL 185:1358): *Recordare ergo quia, dum adhuc esses in saecula, illud tale piaculum commisisti, de quo necdum per confessionem absolvi meruisti. Confitere igitur, et poenitentiam age celeriter, quia si ante obitum per confessionem deletum non fuerit, post mortem insolubile permanebit.*

[83] *LM* 3.7 (PL 185:1358): *manifeste cognovit quia non frustra sanctorum suffragia expetuntur, nec parvipendendum est confessionis sacramentum, sine quo etiam tales ignorantiae taliter imputantur.*

[84] *EM* 5.4 (Griesser, 277–78). There is a summary of this story in a later chapter of how a prioress was warned by a revelation to confess (*EM* 6.9; Griesser 363).

[85] *EM* 2.31 (Griesser, 138–41): *De converso, qui per gratiam Dei et orationem venerabilis abbatis Heinrici damnationis sententiam evasit.*

near death he sought a confessor, but he was attacked by a mob of evil spirits worried that they might not be able to trap him as they had hoped. By the intercession of Saint Bernard and the saints of Clairvaux the demons were put to flight and he was rescued. He was now able to confess that he had fathered a son while at Esrum, a sin for which he had not previously done penance. In a vision he had met his son and been greatly disturbed by the son's accusation that he owed his misery to the father's evil deeds. As the abbot gave him absolution, the lay brother said: "Lord, I believe that even if I were to be mired in the depths of hell, your mercy is able to free me from there."[86] Shortly after that the abbot was summoned again as the brother realized that he had not made a full confession and without it he could not be saved. He had forgotten to mention that he had received a tunic from a brother without permission. "By the prayers of the abbot, the soul of the sick man was quieted, and he manifested his improved state by his serene expression. He fell silent again, and after a brief interval he rested in peace."[87] Conrad ends the account with a long paragraph on the boundless mercy of God.

Difficulty in receiving the host at communion as a result of failure to disclose sins in confession, as well as, in the earlier case, of negligence in observing the rule on private property, is a theme found in a number of *exempla*. The story of a layman who was unable to open his mouth when the *magister conversorum* at a grange belonging to Abbey Dore offered him the host has already been mentioned.[88] A second miracle story from the same abbey on the border between England and Wales is found in the same early thirteenth-century manuscript, the origin of which is not known but that may have been written at the Benedictine abbey at Gloucester.[89]

---

[86] *EM* 2.31 (Griesser, 139–40); CF 72:194: *Credo, Domine, quia, si etiam in profundum inferni demersus fuero, inde me potens est misericordia tua liberare.*

[87] *EM* 2.31 (Griesser, 140); CF 72:194: *Qui etiam infirmus orante abbate animaequior factus et ipsa serenatione vultus statum suum melioratum esse significans rursus obmutuit et post modicum intervallum in pace quievit.*

[88] See above, p. 138.

[89] Hereford Cathedral Library MS P.I.13, pp. 71–72: *Referimus quod accidit in monasterio vallis Dore, Cisterciensis aedis, Herefordensis dyocesis.*

In this a lay brother experienced the same difficulty as the layman at the Trawscoed grange. When the sacrament was brought

> and he had received it in his mouth, he could not bite it with his teeth or swallow it, but with his tongue he twisted it about, whole and undiminished, until the priest, who had given it, drawing it out of the wretched one's mouth, swallowed it with wondrous ease. Meanwhile the man was eagerly urged by the wondering brothers who were standing around to search his conscience lest any poison of sin lay hid in his heart to prevent his receiving so salutary a medicine. But he, more oppressed by human shame than by fear of God, professed that there was nothing he was conscious of. At length, on the advice of the elders, he asked to see the abbot. And when, with tears of sorrow, he had confessed his grievous sin, he received and swallowed the sacred body of the Lord with ease.[90]

Another lay brother who experienced a similar difficulty in not being able to receive the host is referred to in a curious *Collectaneum clarevallense* story headed "The lay brother who received communion unworthily."[91] He was guilty of not confessing before going to communion and found that he was unable to swallow the host. Having washed his hands,

> He put a finger into his mouth hoping to take hold of it so that he might either push it down or take it out. When he had done this the holy Body fled from his hand like an enemy.

---

[90] Bannister 1929, 209: *et illud in ore accepisset, penitus nec dentibus illud contigere nec interius potuit deglutire, sed integrum illibatumque lingua sua huc illucque revolvit, donec sacerdos qui illud dederat digitis suis ab ore miseri extrahens et ori proprio imponens mira facilitate deglutivit. Interea homo, a circumstantibus fratribus et mirantibus sollicite rogatus et admonitus ut discuciat conscienciam suam ne quid virus peccati in corde lateret et tantum et tam salubrem medicinam recipere non valeret, ille non plus pudore humano quam timore divino oppressus nichil sibi conscium esse fatetur. Demum seniorum usus consilio abbatem suum petiit arcessiri. Cui cum magnis lacrimis et contricione cordis revelans conscienciam suam et denudans turpitudinem, sacrum sibi presentatum corpus domini tota facilitate sucepit et deglutivit.*

[91] *CC* 4.22 (Legendre 2005, 300–1): *De converso indigne communicato.*

The sacred victim went higher up in his mouth and came to rest near his ears and, going into a narrow passage, escaped from his hands. When he removed his hand the holy Body came down to near his lips.[92]

He tried again to get hold of it, but the holy Body drew back and would not allow him to touch it. He was still not able to receive the host, although he had no problem with eating other food. After a meal he told a prelate and, having confessed, "he immediately swallowed the viaticum" (*statim viaticum glutivit*).[93]

Another story in the *Collectaneum clarevallense* tells of a lay brother from a monastery in the diocese of Rouen in northern France who was almost at death's door but whose depression was such that, although he was urged to receive the sacraments, he "declined to confess, to be anointed, or to receive communion."[94] Since the abbot was away the prior consulted some of the brothers, but none of them had ever experienced a similar situation. They were saddened and worried lest "the proud snatcher and violent destroyer of the Lord's flock should presume to take himself a sheep committed and gathered from the midst of them who had been gained by the Precious Blood of the Lord."[95] They went into the church to pray, after which the prior went into the infirmary where he found the lay brother in a coma with his eyes shut. When the prior touched him the brother opened his eyes and the prior said to him:

> "My brother, do you know me?" and he replied: "Yes, father,
> I ought to know you very well because you and the com-

[92] CC 4.22 (Legendre 2005, 300): *digitos ori apposuit, volens illud apprehendere, ut quoquomodo posset aut inviscerare aut tenere. Quod cum faceret, fugiebat sanctum corpus quasi inimicam manum eius. Illo vero manum suam in ore suo porrigente ut teneret, ascendebat sacra victima superius intra oris angustum domicilium circa partes aurium, huc illucque per fauces persequentis fugitans manum. Cumque ille manum ab ore suo retraheret et corpus sanctum in labiorum vicinia ab alto rediret.*

[93] CC 4.22 (Legendre 2005, 301).

[94] CC 4.13 (Legendre 2005, 277): *confiteri, ungi et communicare renuit.*

[95] CC 4.13 (Legendre 2005, 278): *si raptor superbus et dominici gregis violentus infractor de medio eorum ovem sibi conmissam et aggregatam tollere presumpserit, Domini cruoris precio comparatam.*

munity have today freed me from the hand of the devil by your prayers. Earlier the house had been full of evil spirits who have worn me down and oppressed me to such an extent that I was not able to heed your warnings and I was not even interested in my own salvation. . . . The sacrament of our redemption which I previously rejected, not being of mind, I can now receive."[96]

The *Liber miraculorum* has a somewhat different version of the same story, more concise but at the same time more compelling. Although the lay brother was advised to confess and receive communion, "he was vehemently opposed to this idea and stubbornly set his mind against it."[97] There is no mention of the prior's intervention, but the brothers "implored the Lord with many litanies and psalms, weeping and groaning, that they might rescue from the depths of evil the soul standing on the edge of the cliff."[98] As the recalcitrant brother was nearing death a great crowd of demons besieged him, but the monks and lay brothers gathered together again, attacked the demons, and managed to free the brother. Then "with compunction and penance he received communion with great reverence and piety and immediately he gave up his spirit in a good confession."[99]

Caesarius of Heisterbach relates a story of how a lay brother had seen the blackest coal and not the sacrament put into the mouth of another lay brother, the same theme found in the *Liber*

---

[96] *CC* 4.13 (Legendre 2005, 278): *"Frater mi, nosti me?" Et ille: "Etiam, domine. Ego vos bene nosse debeo, quia vos hodie et conventus per orationes vestras liberastis me de manu Diaboli. Erat autem paulo ante domus ista malignis spiritibus plena, quorum presentia ita spiritum meum deterrebat et opprimebat ut nec salutiferis monitis poteram vestris obedire, nec de salute mea aliquam curam habere . . . sacramenta redemptionis nostre que ante recusaveram non compos mei, pro voto suscipere."*

[97] *LM* 3.26 (PL 185:1372): *quod ille vehementer abhorrans, pertinaci animo recusabat.* The monastery is here named as Bec in Normandy. Although the account clearly states that it was Cistercian, the only monastery by that name was Benedictine.

[98] *LM* 3.26 (PL 185:1373): *multiplicatis litaniis et psalmis in fletu et planctu Dominum exorabant, ut ita periclitantem animam illam de profundo maiorum eriperit.*

[99] *LM* 3.26 (PL 185:1373): *Ipse vero compunctus ac poenitens cum ingenti reverentia et pietate communicavit, et protinus in bona confessione spiritum emisit.*

*miraculorum* account of the illegal possession of private property by the lay brother from Longpont.[100] Caesarius states that those who are guilty are sometimes refused communion and claims that the brother in question, whom he names as Wiricus from Himmerod in the Rhineland, had only marginally amended his life upon entering the Order.[101] Elsewhere Caesarius tells of a priest who was paid to say Mass at the Hadamar[102] grange belonging to Eberbach and who also was seen chewing the blackest of coals at the moment of receiving communion. The grange master commented: "I am obliged to give so much money to the aforesaid priest that he may not neglect the services; for he is a man of perverse and luxurious life, and will often celebrate three Masses in the day."[103] Caesarius explains to the novice that anyone who receives the body of Christ unworthily prepares for himself everlasting flames.

An abbot recounted a story to Caesarius of Heisterbach of a lay brother of Zinna in Brandenburg that he had heard from the brother's own abbot. On the business of the abbey the brother had failed to pay a ferryman the halfpenny he owed for crossing the river Elbe in Saxony. He never mentioned this in confession. When he fell ill, he saw in a vision that the coin "grew to such a size that it seemed bigger than all the world."[104] When he told his vision to the astonishment of all, the abbot immediately sent the ferryman a whole penny. As soon as he received it, the lay brother expired. The lesson was: "The greater the reward men of religion hope to get more than laymen, the more ought they to be careful, that when they die they do not take any of the dust of the world with them."[105]

---

[100] *LM* 3.27 (PL 185:1373).

[101] *DM* 9.63 (Strange 2:213–14; Scott and Bland 2:165–66).

[102] Mossig 1978, 360–61.

[103] *DM* 9.54 (Strange 2:208; Scott and Bland 2:158–59): *Tantum pecuniae oportet me dare praedicto sacerdoti, ne ecclesia divinis careat; est enim homo vitae perversae ac luxuriosus, tres missas frequenter in die celebrans.*

[104] *DM* 11.35 (Strange 2:297; Scott and Bland 2:267): *Qui adeo crevit, ut mundo maior videretur.*

[105] *DM* 11.35 (Strange 2:297; Scott and Bland 2:267): *Unde religiosi quanto saecularibus maius praemium sperant, tanto debent esse solliciti, ne morientes aliquid pulveris secum trabant.*

In the words of Conrad of Eberbach, the purpose of the many *exempla* was to encourage "the love of virtue and the hatred of vice."[106] Written by monks for the edification of monks, these covered not only incidents in the lives of fellow monks but also, as we have seen, frequently those of lay brothers who, because of their lowly status, were thought to possess the main monastic virtues. The stories nearly always have a happy ending, although not one always merited. The *Collectaneum clarevallense* includes a story that nearly had a tragic end: the ill health of a lay brother was so extreme that he considered taking his own life.[107] Unable, however, to find a knife, he returned to bed, repented, and confessed his sins to the abbot and promptly died, fortified by the sacraments. To avert such temptations, the story concludes, the abbot must always be attentive to those near death.[108]

Another example of failure to secure the confession of a lay brother before his death is found in an anonymous *exemplum* collection in which there is a story entitled "The lay brother tradesman (*conversus mercator*) who wanted to confess but could not."[109] The lay brother, who was responsible for his abbey's sales and purchases, had a bad conscience but is said to have been prevented by Satan from confessing. He claimed that whenever he was free to confess it did not suit the abbot, and whenever the abbot was free it was not convenient for him. The abbot replied that he would always make time and said: "You should always have time and put on one side all other business for the sake of confession. Nothing should be preferred to the work of God when it comes to the health of your soul."[110] The *mercator* brother agreed, but his confession was interrupted. Another lay brother who was preparing to accompany the abbot on his

---

[106] *EM* 6.10 (Griesser, 364): *amorem virtutum, otium vitiorum.*

[107] *CC* 4.13 (Legendre 2005, 279–80).

[108] See *RB* 27 on the abbot's pastoral solicitude (McCann 1976, 36).

[109] Paris, BNF MS lat. 14657, fol. 73v and 74r: *De converso mercatore qui volebat confiteri nec poterat.* I am grateful to Stafano Mula for drawing my attention to this exemplum.

[110] Paris, BNF MS lat. 14657, fol. 73v: *vos semper ad hoc tempus habere debetis, et omnia negocia propter confessionem relinquere. Nichil enim huic operi Dei preponendum est in quo precipue salus anime constitit.*

journey on monastery business saw through a window a person with a monstrous red dog whom the *mercator* had mentioned in his confession and who told him not to say any more and the abbot not to listen any more. Before going away the abbot was happy to wait until the *mercator* had finished his confession, saying that "a person who is not willing when he can, is not able when he wills."[111] The *mercator* claimed that he could not recall any other sins. When on their way the other lay brother told the abbot what he had seen, the abbot "spurring his horse on, returned to the house and when he reached it he found that the *mercator* was already dead."[112]

The message of the *exemplum* compilers is clear: in spite of the seriousness of the offenses they describe, divine intervention, the intercession of the saints, and especially the power of the prayers of the community provided the only means of securing the release of the souls of departed brethren. As in the case of the lay brother from Longpont, when no mention was made of any outside mediation Caesarius was compelled to conclude that the outcome was "uncertain."

On rare occasions the outcome could be tragic: a lay brother, who had lived an observant life, and whom Caesarius knew well, nevertheless lost all hope of salvation. As Caesarius did not want to cast a reflection on anyone, he refused to name the brother or his monastery.

> The brother lost all hope of pardon, and when the brethren asked him what it was that he feared, and why he despaired, he would reply: "I cannot say my prayers as I used to, and so I am afraid of hell." Because he was afflicted with this vice of melancholy, accidie laid hold of him, and from the two, despair was born in his heart.[113]

---

[111] Paris, BNF MS lat. 14657, fol. 74r: *Qui quando potest non vult, non poterit quando volet.*

[112] Paris, BNF MS lat. 14657, fol. 74r: *Et urgens equm calcaribus, festinanter remeavit domum. Quo cum pervenisset, invenit mercatorem iam sepultum.*

[113] *DM* 4.41 (Strange 1:210–11; Scott and Bland 1:240): *Cui cum fratres dicerent, quid habetis unde timetis, quare desperatis? Respondit: Non possum dicere, sicut consuevi, orationes meas, et ideo timeo gehennam. Quia tristitiae vitio laborabat, idcirco accidiosus erat, et ex utroque nata est in corde eius desperatio.*

Placed in the infirmary, he went to his master, declaring: "I cannot fight against God any longer." Far from providing the intervention of the community, the master is said to have taken "little heed of his words, so he went away to the fish-pond near the monastery, threw himself in and was drowned."[114]

## Conclusion

The common thread that emerges from the many tales of virtues and vices is of the power of the prayers of the community, both monks and lay brothers, under the leadership of their abbot and, in one case when the abbot was absent, of the prior, to outsmart the temptations invariably placed in the way by demons. The *Collectaneum clarevallense* story from an abbey in Normandy in fact bears the title "The value of community prayer" and ends with "blessed is that community in which charity and love remain and the kindness of true piety and compassion" and "just as every tree shall be known from its fruit, every community from its way of life and discipline."[115] A story in the Goswin collection of a lay brother who had been led astray by demons ends with: "divine grace came to him first from a friend and then a religious monk and he regained his faculties."[116] In the account of Saint Bernard urging the community to pray for a lay brother struggling with demons, the monks celebrating at each of the altars in the church are described as "the weapons of God's grace" (*arma gratiae Dei*).[117]

Many tales testify to the concern of the monks for the welfare of the lay brothers and, as we have seen, the way in which they were

---

[114] *DM* 4.41 (Strange 1:210–11; Scott and Bland 1:240): *Non possum diutius contra Deum pugnare. . . . Illa verba eius minus considerate, ad piscinam monasterio proximam abiit, et in eam se praecipitans suffocatus est.*

[115] *CC* 4.13 (Legendre 2005, 277–79): *Quid valeat conventus oratio . . . benedicta illa congregatio, in qua manet caritas et dilectio, et vere pietatis atque compassionis affectio . . . unaqueque arbor ex suo fructu cognoscitur, sic unaqueque congregatio ex suis moribus vel disciplina.*

[116] Mula 2002, 6: *primum socio post ea religioso monacho mox ei divina gratia subvenit et vires recepit.* For this story in the Gossuin collection see p. 244.

[117] *EM* 2.2 (Griesser, 99).

accorded equality in death with the monks.[118] But, in addition, these tales elicit the question of how they compare with stories concerning the virtues and vices of monks. The source material does not shed a great deal of light, but it may be possible to glean something from Caesarius of Heisterbach, whose books are arranged thematically. It is clear, for example, that the minor matter of falling asleep in choir was common to both monks and lay brothers, although it is possible that, because of their greater manual labor and their inability to understand the liturgy, *conversi* were more prone to nod off. In one area there does seem to have been a difference between monks' virtues and vices and those of lay brothers. Of the sixty-seven chapters of Book 9 of *Dialogus miraculorum*[119]—"Of the Sacrament of the Body and Blood of Christ"—the great majority tell of lay men and women, priests outside the Order, nuns, and to a lesser extent *conversi* (seven altogether), but there are very few concerning monks. Some of those conserved in which lay brothers are featured are quite strange, but so are many others. One refers to a stolen host that was found by oxen in a field; in another bees built a shrine for the Lord's body; in yet another a woman was paralyzed for spreading the Lord's body on her cabbages; and finally mice, when gnawing hosts, did not touch the sacred monogram.[120] Why the monk compilers were less prone to record their fellow monks' experiences with the Eucharist is hard to know unless they felt that their clerical status made it more appropriate for them to describe episodes involving laity. Overall, however, there does not seem to have been a difference between the two. In the other books of the *Dialogus miraculorum* stories of the two groups are more evenly matched, lending support to the suspicion that too much has in the past been made of the lay brother revolts. As we shall see,[121] the *negligentia* that Conrad of Eberbach featured in the last *distinctio* of the *Exordium magnum* afflicted monks and lay brothers equally, and if there were disciplinary problems, they were not confined to the lay brothers.

[118] For this see p. 154.

[119] *DM* 9 (Strange 2:164–217; Scott and Bland 2:105–69).

[120] *DM* 9.7, 8, 9, 11 (Strange 2:172, 172–73, 173–74, 174–75; Scott and Bland 2:113–14, 114–15, 115–16, 117–18).

[121] See chapter 12.

## Chapter 10

# The Onslaught of Demons

In medieval society misfortunes of every sort—natural disasters, failing health, accidents, and all manner of catastrophes—were attributed to the devil, who was thought to be all-pervasive and was universally feared. The more sacred the place, the greater, not less, the risk of attack. When, according to Conrad of Eberbach, Saint Bernard was told of how demons had afflicted a dying lay brother, he said: "The evil directed at all Christians by demons is very great, but greater still is that which they aim at those who have made monastic profession."[1] If we follow Bernard's logic, those presumably at greatest risk were the humblest among the professed, the lay brothers. In the edifying stories that were recorded and circulated about them, the devil's assault on individual lay brothers was frequently presented as an unrelenting tug of war or as a cleverly set trap that the intended prey either avoided or tumbled into.

Conrad refers to how Bernard had exhorted the community to "escape the inexorable lies of the evil spirits."[2] We have already encountered demons afflicting lay brothers in the form of "vultures," accompanied by "horrible men, gigantic and misshapen,"[3] and we read of "the prior wearing on his neck a sort of collar made

---

[1] *EM* 2.2 (Griesser, 99): *multam esse malitiam daemonum erga omnes christianos, tamen praecipue contra monasticae religionis professores affirmans.*

[2] *EM* 5.19 (Griesser, 333); CF 72:492: *ut malignorum spirituum inextricabiles fallacias evadere valeamus.*

[3] *DM* 11.15; see p. 24.

out of a bean stalk" by which he was led as if he were a dog,[4] of a serpent,[5] of a cat that placed its paws on a sleepy brother's eyes,[6] and of something that looked like a human shadow that continually grew larger.[7]

## A Variety of Demons

Cistercian literature abounds in anecdotes of the exploits of demons: Caesarius of Heisterbach, who arranged his material according to what he judged to be the most important topics, devoted the whole of Book 5 of his *Dialogus miraculorum*—a total of fifty-six chapters—to demons.[8] He concludes the first chapter by saying: "That there are demons, that they are many, and that they are wicked, I shall be able to show you by many examples."[9] Numerous examples follow in just one chapter: Henry, the *grangiarius* of the Himmerod grange of Hart, whom we have already met,[10] "used often to see demons under different forms, passing to and fro in the choir at the night offices," where and when they most frequently made an appearance. First he saw "a demon in the form of a thick-set peasant" with "broad breast, pointed shoulders and a short neck; his hair was fashionably dressed in front, and the rest hanging down like drooping ears of grain." At another time the demon "transformed himself into a calf's tail."[11]

In the same chapter other members of Henry's community were confronted with demons in a variety of guises reminiscent of a Bruegel painting: three were levitating above the ground, one

[4] *DM* 5.48; see p. 95.

[5] *DM* 4.32; see p. 96.

[6] *DM* 4.33; see p. 96

[7] *DM* 5.28; see p. 102.

[8] *DM* 5 (Strange 1:274–340; Scott and Bland 1:313–90).

[9] *DM* 5.1 (Strange 1:276; Scott and Bland 1:314): *Daemones esse, multos esse, malos esse, plurimis tibi exemplis potero probare.*

[10] See p. 134.

[11] *DM* 5.5 (Strange 1:282; Scott and Bland 1:321): *unum in forma rustici quadrati inferius iuxta presbyterium intrare. Habebat enim pectus latum, scapulas acutas, collum breve, capillum in fronte satis superbe tonsoratum, crines reliquos sicut haristas dependentes. . . . transformans se daemon in caudam vituli.*

of them a woman wearing a black veil and cloak. There was a demon in the form of a "dragon the length of a spear," others with "shadowy bodies somewhat larger than those of infants and their faces were the color of iron that had first been drawn from the furnace," one "like a white-hot iron," another "like an Ethiopian, of huge size, and as black as if he had that moment been drawn out of hell fire," yet another "in the form of a very bright eye, about the size of a man's fist," and finally, one whose body "was misty and unsubstantial, like a cloud."[12] In another chapter Caesarius records the vision of a lay brother named Ludo from Himmerod who, at the bedside of his fellow brother Gerung, saw "vultures flying up on the bar of his bed, and with them were horrible men, gigantic and misshapen, who came and stood round him."[13]

Demons were even more prominent in the *Liber revelationum* from the Cistercian monastery of Schöntal in southern Germany during the abbacy of Richalm (1216–1219). At first we read a dialogue between Richalm and one of his monks, referred to as *N*, who was also responsible for editing Richalm's notes in the second part, which he called a *tractatus*. The dominant role of demons is indicated by the subtitle of the work: "Concerning the deceit and cunning of demons against men."[14] Richalm saw himself surrounded by demons as numerous as snowflakes in a storm, as grains of sand on the beach, as drops of water in a thundershower.[15] He describes the way a lay brother was attacked when listening to the Rule being expounded in Chapter and the effect it had on him, saying: "I saw a plug being placed in his ear stopping any sound

---

[12] *DM* 5.5 (Strange 1:281–85; Scott and Bland 1:322–25): *femineum vultum, in capite vero velamen nigrum, nigro circumdatus pallio . . . in forma draconis, hastae habentem longitudinem. . . . Reliqui daemones umbrosa habebant corpora, infantibus maiora, quorum facies ferro de igne extracto erant simillimae. . . . in Aethyopis effigie, magnus et nigerrimus . . . in forma lucidissimi oculi, habentis quantitatem pugni . . . forma assumti corporis admodum subtilis, ad instar nubis.*

[13] *DM* 11.15 (Strange 2:283; Scott and Bland 2:251): *vultures advolantes, in pertica lectu eius resederunt, cum quibus homines tetri, magni atque deformes intrantes, eundem circumsteterunt.*

[14] Richalm 2009: *De insidiis et versutiis daemonum adversus homines.*

[15] *LR* 46 and 61; Richalm 2009, 57, 74.

and I understood this to be a demon whose job this was, being one of a number of demons who blocked the ears from hearing the word of God."[16] The lay brother was so disturbed by this that he refused to continue to look after the vines, which was his job, even after the abbot had threatened to punish him. Richalm continues:

> I went to collation and when I got there I sat down and, behold, the spirit which had attacked him and adhered to him came plaintively groaning and growling and making quacking noises like hens, voicing the hen sound *cluck, cluck, cluck, cluck*. When they are enraged they get all mixed up and don't know how to do anything, just as when they are rejoicing they don't know what they are doing.[17]

Seeing how distressed the lay brother was, the spirit ordered him to return and face the "penalty due to him because it is customary for disobedient brethren not only to be driven to the door, but also to be made to fast on bread and water."[18] When Richalm "got up from collation and went toward the cellarer's office, there I saw the brother, responding and obediently going into the vineyard."[19] Richalm's listener, *N*, not surprisingly found it difficult to understand that the spirit had shown such interest in whether the brother should or should not be punished and asked why it was "that he even prefers to induce him to obey rather than be punished?"[20]

---

[16] LR 33; Richalm 2009, 39: *vidi ante aures eius emplastrum obductum et circumpositum: et intellexi hoc esse demonem huiusmodi officii et ex eorum numero, qui obturant aures a verbo Dei audiendo.*

[17] LR 33; Richalm 2009, 39: *Ivi ego ad collacionem; ad quam cum sederem, ecce, spiritus, qui eum inpugnat et adheret ei, venit gemens et miserabiliter fremens et sonos tales inter gemendum proferens, quales proferunt galli, cum vocant gallinas* gloc, gloc, gloc, gloc. *Quando enim irascuntur, nesciunt modum aliquem habere, set omnino confundunt se, sicut et quando gaudent, modum nesciunt.*

[18] LR 33; Richalm 2009, 40: *Ad penam consuetam, quia solet inobedientes non solum ad portam pellere, set eciam in pane et aqua ibidem facit eos ieiunare.*

[19] LR 33; Richalm 2009, 40: *Ego vero surgens a collacione, exivi foras ante cellarium, et, ecce ille frater aderat, spondens se obediturum et in vineam iturum.*

[20] LR 33; Richalm 2009, 41: *ut eciam mallet eum ad obediendum inducere pocius quam puniri?*

## Demons from Pagan Lands

In the twelfth century the Cistercians imagined the dark and distant Nordic lands beyond their experience or knowledge to be peopled by phantasms and demons. A variety of mythical creatures provided the fertile imagination of Norse storytellers and writers with a wealth of material of a high degree of moralizing potential and appeal to their audience. Several tales of old Norse background found their way into Cistercian sources. In his *Chronicle*, Alberic of Trois Fontaines recounts an anecdote redolent of Nordic mythology,[21] concerning an event that occurred in 1134, some years before the Cistercians settled in Scandinavia, when King Magnus of Denmark and five of his bishops were killed in battle, following which their souls took the form of ravens and were heard wailing over Iceland. They were chased by gryphons to the abyss of Mount Hecla, which was considered the mouth of hell. This was witnessed by some shepherds, one of whom later became a Cistercian, probably a lay brother. In the customary way, the story was passed on by abbots from Denmark visiting the General Chapter.

Another story redolent of pagan mythology comes from the Danish abbey of Vitskøl (*Vitae schola*) in northern Jutland and found its way into the *Liber visionem* of the Bavarian abbey of Fürstenfeld.[22] The devil, in the guise of a young servant, had lived at Vitskøl for three years. When "some of the brothers of the monastery were sent to a nearby village on business"[23] they took the young man with them. Because they are referred to as *fratres*, and because they were on the abbey's business, they were most likely *conversi*. While they were all together in a house the young man leaped up and, shaking all over, said in a terrified voice: "Just listen, I hear a great thunderstorm in Greenland" ("*O, o, ecce tonitruum magnum in Granalandia audio*"). After a while he claimed he could hear it in Iceland, then in Norway, and since it was getting ever closer he dared no

---

[21] Alberic of Trois Fontaines, *Chronica,* 829.

[22] Munich, Staatsbibliothek, MS Clm 6914, fol. 33v–34r. Printed in Jørgensen 1912, 17.

[23] Jørgensen 1912, 17: *quidam ex fratribus monasterii pro quodam negotio mitterentur ad proximam vicum.*

longer stay but ran to the water's edge. The brothers followed him, but before they could reach him he had been struck by lightning, which annihilated him. The story ends that "the brothers understood that he was a demon, and later they remembered that they had never seen him go into the church and that they had never detected a sure sign that he was a Christian man."[24]

Herbert of Clairvaux relates a story of a young man who, before he became a lay brother at Fontenay in Burgundy, set out on a journey to a pagan region with a young friend, a count. On their way through a forest

> they found an enormous wooden idol painted with pitch and carved from a straight tree trunk. The inhabitants of the nearby village used to come there to adore it secretly and even to make an offering. They appeared to be frenzied in their devotion to this abominable spirit. These youths, fired up with the zeal of Christian faith, demolished this detestable statue and, having made a fire, reduced it to cinders and ashes. Having done this, they took flight in order to avoid being taken by the fanatical worshipers and punished in a similar way.[25]

The story ends ominously with the lay brother having a dream vision of "a spirit of the night like the burnt idol covered with black pitch who took in his hands the burning cinders, threw them in

---

[24] Jørgensen 1912, 17: *Cognoverunt itaque fratres, quod demonium esset, de quo etiam postmodum recordati sunt omnes, quod numquam viderant ipsum in ecclesiam ingredi, nunquam in eo deprehenderant certum aliquod indicium hominis Christiani.*

[25] *LM* 3.35 (PL 185:1381): *repererunt ibi quoddam simulacrum enorme, intrinsecus ligneum, extrinsecus pice linitum, quod veluti truncus ad stipitem arboris stabat erectum. Illuc ergo secretius adoraturi, aut etiam immolaturi, de villa proxima veniebant ii qui circa nefandi numinis obsequium sese devotiores, imo vero dementiores exhibebant. Succensi itaque fidei zelo christiani juvenes, exsecrabilem statuam in frusta comminuerunt, et protinus igne supposito in favillam et cinerem redegerunt. Quo facto fugam arripuere maturius, ne forte a fanaticis cultoribus deprehensi, poena simili punirentur.* The identical story is found in the Fürstenfeld collection except for the additional information that "in the western part [of the pagan lands] there are still many people living today" (*qui in partibus aquilonis usque hodie plurimi supersunt*) and that the lay brother was a German (Kompatcher Gufler 2005, 254).

*Fig. 21* Choir stall carving at Doberan in Mecklenburg showing lay brother with the devil.

his eyes and said: 'Behold you burned me yesterday, I will burn you today.' When the young man awoke he felt a great agonizing pain in his eyes, which persisted a long time afterward and troubled him greatly.'"[26]

The pagan past of northern and eastern Germany along the coast of the Baltic is evoked in a unique way in the Cistercian abbey of Doberan. The oak choir stalls, dated from around 1295, have a carving in low relief of a small creature with a tail and significantly wearing as headgear the heraldic bull's head associated with Mecklenburg and a symbol of the Wendish pagan past (fig. 21).[27] On the left, facing him, is a much larger figure, unmistakably a bearded lay brother, wearing a cloak with his hood partially over his head but with the distinctive fringe clearly showing. The devil is grabbing the lay brother's cloak with his right hand while with his left he holds a scroll that curls around his head and goes down on the right. It reads: *Quid facis hic frater, vad(e) mecum* (What are you doing here, brother? Follow me) to which the brother, in a longer scroll curling around the top and ending on the right, replies: *Ni(hi)l in me re(per)ies male, c(ru)enta bestia* (You will find nothing evil in me, horrid beast). Above the figures are beautifully carved intertwining maple and oak branches and leaves. Maple stands for Mary, and oak for faithfulness. By turning to Mary the lay brother withstands the devil's temptation and remains true to his vocation. The carving was at the western gable end of the southern side of the lay brothers' stalls, which consisted of two rows of twenty-six stalls on each side. Its position was such that it would have been seen every time the brothers entered their choir from the *domus conversorum*. It served as a reminder of their missionary role in having been sent from Amelungsborn in Lower Saxony to Doberan in 1171 by Berno, the first bishop of Schwerin and himself a Cistercian, a former monk of Amelungsborn, and a warning against a

[26] *LM* 3.35 (PL 185:1381): *spiritus ille noctifer, instar idoli concremati piccus et niger; et projciens in oculis ejus calidos cineres quos manibus praeferebat, dixit ad eum: "Ecce, tu heri combussisti me, et ego comburam te hodie." Evigilans vero juvenis, dolorem magnum et cruciatum in oculis sensit, qui etiam longo postea tempore durans, graviter eum afflixit.*

[27] Schneider 1986, 496–97; Voss 2008, 49–51.

relapse. As a narrative image, aided by text in the form of the scrolls, underscoring a moral lesson, the scene of the lay brother's temptation by the devil may be said to constitute a rare visual *exemplum*, not least in that, unlike the literary examples, it could be readily understood by all lay brothers. Almost certainly it was the work of one of the abbey's *conversi* and an uncommon example of a lay brother acquainted with letters.

## Noisy and Disruptive Demons

The old pagan fear of lightning forms the subject of one of the tales derived from a variety of sources, including the *Dialogus miraculorum* and *Vitae patrum*, in a manuscript from the Cistercian monastery of Waldsassen in Austria. A Cistercian lay brother is said to have had a son who became a monk but got tired of the monastic life, deserted, married, and became a shepherd. To protect his flocks he carried the Host about with him, and when he was struck by lightning and before he died, he ordered his wife to restore the Host to the monastery.[28]

The role of lightning and thunder in disrupting the peaceful monastic atmosphere and breaching the silence essential for recollection and tranquility is expressed in an *exemplum* that found its way into three collections. Conrad of Eberbach has a graphic description of how the devil, described as "the jealous enemy of all good,"[29] failed to make any headway in his onslaught against one of the lay brother shepherds at Clairvaux in spite of his strenuous efforts. One night the brother was "keeping the night watch over his flock [Luke 2:8] and suddenly there was a violent storm, winds howling and rushing, thunder rolling all around in a terrifying manner, with frequent flashes of lightning in the clouds spreading fear and terror in human minds."[30] The brother jumped up, and as he was praying

---

[28] *Catalogue of Romances* 1910, 586; London, British Library MS Additional 15833, fol. 118v.

[29] *EM* 4.31 (Griesser, 264); CF 72:383: *omnium vero bonorum invidus inimicus.*

[30] *EM* 4.31 (Griesser, 264–65); CF 72:383: *vigilans et custodiens vigilias noctis supra gregem suum, ecce subito facta est in aere commotio magna turbinum et compugnantium inter se tempestas valida ventorum. Tonitrua quoque crebra et terribiliter undique*

> he began to hear the clamor and shouting, as it were, of a great
> army coming at a quick march toward him, and the closer they
> came, the more clearly their voices resonated. There was not
> only the din of men and the cry of trumpets, but on top of this
> the roaring of monsters and savage animals and great outcries
> could be heard. This multitude arrived with a deafening hub-
> bub by the sheepfold, as if they were going to tear the sheep
> limb from limb and devour them, but the brother redoubled
> his prayers and repelled the attackers with divine power. The
> band could not break into the enclosure, but the battle lines
> divided and they passed quickly by without causing any harm.[31]

As they failed in their attempt to lead the brother astray in spite of
their best effort, "two enormous giants, blacker than soot" (*statura
enormes et fuligine nigriores*) came toward the brother. One of them
said to the other: "It is truly the devil that leads us on and has
brought us here. Did I not tell you that we would not be able to
cross this good place?"[32] Conrad ends by saying that he had heard
this from the brother himself and that "his way of life was such that
we would think it outrageous to doubt his word."[33]

A somewhat shorter, and very much less vivid version of the
same story is found in the Fürstenfeld *exemplum* collection. It is entitled "Concerning the lay brother who saw demons at the sheepfold but could not be harmed by them."[34] Here the Clairvaux

---

*crepitantia mugiebant, sed et fulgura creberrima caelo erumpentia timorem et horrorem
maximum mentibus hominum incutiebant.*

[31] EM 4.31 (Griesser, 265); CF 72:383–84: *coepit audire strepitum et vocifera-
tionem quasi exercitus ingentis ad partes illas cursu rapido venientis; et quanto amplius
propinquabant, tanto voces eorum clarius resonabant. In quibus non soli hominum clamores
clangoresve tubarum audiebantur, sed insuper diversi generis ferarum monstrorumque rugitus
et voces terribiles inesse deprehendebantur oves usque ad ossa laniaturi et voraturi, fratre
attentius orante divina virtute repulsi sunt et intrare quidem minime potuerunt, sed divisis
agminibus hinc inde celeriter transeuntes nihil eis penitus nocuerunt.*

[32] EM 4.31 (Griesser, 265); CF 72:384: *"Vere diabolus nos deducit et ipse modo
nos huc venire fecit. An non satis dixeram vobis, quia non licet nobis transire per bonum?"*

[33] EM 4.31 (Griesser, 265); CF 72:384: *Cuius nimirum talis erat conversatio, ut
fidem dictis eius non adhibere nefas esse putaremus.*

[34] Kompatscher-Gufler 2005, 248: *De converso, qui vidit ad caulas demones et
nichil nocere poterant.*

shepherd is named as Gerard, but although the description of the storm is less spectacular, other details are identical. The third version, recounted in the *Collectaneum clarevallense*, differs substantially from the other two in several respects although the moral—that good prevails over evil—remains the same. Earlier than the other two, it is somewhat shorter, is set at a mill and not a sheepfold, and has the lay brother guarding the mill on his own while the other brothers had returned to the abbey to attend Vigils. He gave himself to work when "the devil, the enemy of those who are obedient, went up on to the roof of the mill and made a great noise, thereby wishing to put fear into the spirit of the lay brother" but the brother remained unmoved as "a faithful and good athlete of Christ" and "the devil immediately disappeared from the mill and fled to the mountain close to the monastery barking like a dog."[35]

Noise and commotion invariably accompanied demons. When a lay brother of Clairvaux died, one of the monks "heard a throng of devils, milling about in the hundreds, shout with a great noise."[36] The lay brother Walter of Pforta in Saxony, whose idleness had exposed him to demonic attacks, was seen by another brother, Herman, being thrown out of bed twice and at the moment of death "there was such a upheaval in the atmosphere that the building itself seemed to rock."[37] This was also revealed by God to a holy nun at a nearby monastery who reported that

> at the death of this man a great multitude of evil spirits had gathered together and from their concourse the air was thick with trouble and the noise deafening while they were trying to get hold of his soul. They wanted to drag him down to hell, putting on him the vice of laziness, but the Blessed Mother

---

[35] *CC* 3.12 (Legendre 2005, 255–56): *inimicus obedientium Diabolus super tectum ascendit molendini, et faciens ibi magnum et terribilem strepitum, volebat fratris spiritum perterrere . . . sicut fidelis et bonus Christi agonista . . . . Confestim Diabolus a molendino confusus discessit, et per vicinum montem monasterio, latrans ut canis aufugit.*

[36] *EM* 2.2 (Griesser, 99): *Audivit turbas daemonum per centurias suas incedentium cum magni strepitus vociferatione clamare.*

[37] *DM* Hilka 1937, 3:70: *in ipse hora mortis eius tantus motus excitatus est in aere, ut ipsa edificia viderentur ruere.*

of God by her prayers, since she is the Mother of Mercy, had freed him from their power. Although the lay brother was lax in the divine praises and very sleepy, nevertheless up to now he had been disciplined and faithful in his duties.[38]

Lawrence, a lay brother from Clairvaux, was to become a valued member of the community, entrusted with the care of the precious relics of Saint Bernard and Saint Malachy and, as was mentioned earlier, was later sent on a mission to Sicily to negotiate with the king.[39] He had gained his position of responsibility in the community only after making a great effort, for

> at the beginning of his religious life he had been vexed by many temptations and had had daily battles against the poisonous suggestions of malign spirits. One night after [Matins], when he found himself alone in a room, an unclean spirit circled all around him, bellowing and sniveling. He made the sign of the cross on his forehead and asked who he might be. The double-dealing evildoer, to strike fear into the brother's yet inexperienced and tender mind, replied: "I am he who tempted Job and covered him with boils." At these words the brother, who was still new to the religious life, was greatly affrighted and fled the sight of the malignant spirit. He never saw it again.[40]

---

[38] *DM* Hilka 1937, 3:71: *ad obitum illius innumerabilem multitudinem spirituum malignorum confluxisse, ex quorum concursu et aer concitatus est et sonus concussus, cum animam eius extrahere conarentur. Quam cum vellent deducere ad inferos, accidie vitium illi inponentes, precibus beate Dei Genitricis, que mater est misericordie, de manibus illorum liberata est. Licet enim idem conversus in laudibus divinis accidiosus esset et sompnolentus, erat tamen vir admodum disciplinatus et in commissis fidelis.*

[39] *LM* 2.30 (PL 185:1340–42); *EM* 4.34 (Griesser, 268–70). For this, see pp. 6–7.

[40] *EM* 4.34 (Griesser, 268); CF 72:389: *quoniam in primordio conversionis suae multis temptationibus vexabatur et contra malignorum spirituum venenatas suggestiones diuturno certamine exercebatur. Nocte vero quadam, dum finitis matutinis in quodam domicilio solus esset, ecce immundus spiritus mugiens et plangens discursu gyrovago circa eum rotabatur. Ipse vero fronti suae signaculo crucis imposito, quisnam esset, interrogavit. Versipellis autem malignator, ut rudi adhuc et tenerae menti graviorem metum incuteret, respondit: Ego sum ille, qui temptavi et flagellavi Job. Quod audiens frater, quoniam adhuc novus in conversatione sancta erat, timuit vehementer et fugit a facie maligni spiritus et eum ulterius non vidit.*

Unusually, here it is the lay brother who, by fleeing, takes the initiative in removing himself from the possible influence of the evil spirit, whereas it is almost invariably the cowardly demons who vanish, overwhelmed by the sanctity of the monastic milieu.

Sometimes an evil spirit might take hold of a member of the community on account of his unworthiness. A trustworthy witness, a lay brother who was a carpenter at Boulancourt in Champagne, told Herbert of Clairvaux of having seen an evil spirit in the likeness of a monk named Simon leaving the monks' choir after Vigils. Simon dragged a lay brother named Christian out of the church with him. Albert mistakenly concluded that Christian was being led by Simon, but then he saw Simon singing in the choir, and

> he was greatly astonished. When he came to the lay brother's bed he realized that he had fled, taking a great bundle of clothes with him. The next day he asked Simon if he had seen the one who had taken the lay brother from Matins. Simon answered: "I saw no one. I know that for a long time I have been struggling but have now overcome my carnal desires and withdrawn from that filth." . . . That same week he put Satan behind him and did not fear being snatched by him again.[41]

Failure to be deceived by demons disguised in clerical clothes or monastic habits forms the subject of the only two *exempla* featuring lay brothers in the fragmentary collection compiled toward the end of the twelfth century by Goswin, monk of Clairvaux and subsequently of Cheminon and Boulancourt. Unlike the previous story, which refers to a lay brother who had witnessed the distress of another lay brother at the hands of demons, in these two accounts it

---

[41] *LM* 1.27 (PL 185:1301): *admiratus est vehementer. Cumque adhibito lumine venisset ad ejusdem conversi lectum, invenit eum cum magna indumentorum sarcina aufugisse. In crastinum vero cum praedictum Simonem interrogaret utrumne conversum illum de Matutinis extraxisset, ille, ut vere constabat, protestatus est se minime id fecisse. Postea vero consumptis omnibus quae abstulerat, reversus est ad januam ille desertor infamis, et misericordiam ut reciperetur obtinuit. Porro cum frater Albertus sciscitaretur ab eo utrum vidisset eum qui se de oratorio extraxerat, respondit: "Ego quidem neminem vidi; scio tamen quia cum diutius reluctatus essem, tandem a propria concupiscentia abstractus et illectus, zabulo cessi . . . eadem septimana retrorsum post Satanam se trahentem abire non timuit.*

was the lay brother himself who was being tricked and there were no outside witnesses. Like most of Goswin's *exempla*, the first of the two is a short summary, in fact so short that its meaning is unclear:

> A simple lay brother who was a shepherd suffered the assaults of demons. On a certain feast day while he was sitting near the entrance of the church he saw a priest in white carrying a chalice and other ministers carrying a candle, some water, and some wine. He did not, however, see the cross, for the demons were pretending that it was not there. The lay brother prostrated on the ground to ask for forgiveness, while the demons went to the guest house. After a little while he saw them coming back.[42]

In this case clarity seems to be the victim of brevity. Something seems to be missing, but we have the basic message: the lonely shepherd in the field having the vision of demons, the significance to the lay brother of the absence of the cross, the deception and cunning of demons, and the demons' assault on those in the guest house.

Goswin's second story refers to the same lay brother: "At another time when he was looking after the sheep in the field a cunning demon was present clothed in a religious habit."[43] The demon greeted the lay brother and frivolously suggested that he could obtain anything he wanted to which the lay brother replied: "What I want is to be led to heaven so that I may know and see the status of those who live there."[44] The lay brother was then surrounded by a fiery cloud and the demon disappeared. He began to

---

[42] GF (Mula 2002, 6): *Quidam conversus simplex et pastor ovium insidias demonum patiebatur. Qui quadam die festiva dum sederet iuxta introitum ecclesie videt quasi sacerdotem alba indutum et calicem ferentem et alios ministros candelam, aquam et vinum ferentes. Crucem tamen non videt, quoniam demones erant simulantes quod non erant. Conversus ad terram veniam petivit et illi ad hospitale tendebant unde post paululum ut sibi videbatur reversi sunt.* I am grateful to Stefano Mula for drawing my attention to these two *exempla* and for his translation of the above.

[43] GF (Mula 2002, 6): *Alia vice dum idem oves custodiret in campo adest demon quidam callidus religiosis indutus vestibus.*

[44] GF (Mula 2002, 6): *"Volo, ait conversus, usque in celum perduci, ut sciam et videam quis sit inhabitantium status."*

lose his grip on reality until he realized that he had been deceived and that what he had seen were "diabolical illusions" (*diabolicas illusiones*) and he promptly regained his faculties. The lay brother's motive in wanting to ascertain the status of those in heaven may not have been the purest, but as soon as he realized that he had been duped by the devil he repented.

The numerous guises in which demons chose to attack the monastic community were much the same in their pursuit of monks as in their encounters with *conversi*, and their choice of victim was also often the same. Just as, for example, the unworthy carpenter *conversus* from Boulancourt was harassed by demons, the novice monk Charles from Himmerod was frequently followed by the devil "to whom he willingly listened, consented to the gratifications of gluttony and the flesh, and was continually pretending sickness, feigning to limp, and lying long in bed."[45]

In the same way that the Doberan carving served as a warning to the lay brothers to remain vigilant, a similar visual *exemplum* in the form of a capital carved in stone in the monks' choir at the Pomeranian abbey of Kołbacz (Kolbatz) acted as a reminder to the monks to be always alert to demonic onslaughts. Dated to between 1330 and 1340, the capital on one side depicts an altar covered with a cloth upon which is a chalice surmounted by a host. A tonsured monk, his hands clasped in prayer, kneels in adoration. Behind him a monk with his hood over his head is swinging a thurible, while another monk on the other side holds up an open book—a Missal or Gradual. On the other side a large naked devil with long pointed ears holds his tail with his left hand while grabbing hold of the hood of a monk kneeling in prayer before the open book.[46] A similar caution to monks is found in the margin of a thirteenth-century manuscript dated 1220–1230 from Dore abbey in Herefordshire on the border between England and Wales. In the margin a winged devil with long pointed ears is depicted catching hold of a monk's

---

[45] *DM* 5.6 (Strange 1:286; Scott and Bland 1:324): *Hic instinctu diaboli, cuius consilio utebatur, gulae et carnis suae commodis nimis consentiens, infirmitates saepius simulavit; pede claudicavit, lecto decubuit.*

[46] Both sides of the capital are depicted in France 1998, 176, 216.

*Fig. 22* Caesarius of Heisterbach in a miniature from Altenberg; a detail in the upper flourish shows a monster with its legs perched on a lay brother's head.

hood from behind, using a long rod with a hook, a portrayal of the devil as "a fisher of men."[47] Most interesting is the depiction of a demon in an almost imperceptible detail in a fourteenth-century manuscript of the *Dialogus miraculorum*, which contains the only two known portraits of Caesarius of Heisterbach. Within the initial *C(olligite fragmenta)* from the Prologue a tonsured Caesarius in a dark brown habit sits at a desk with an open book in front of him and at his feet a small figure in a white habit, the novice with whom Caesarius is in dialogue.[48] In the other picture, from the beginning of the first chapter, in which he records the foundation of Cîteaux, Caesarius is seen within the initial *C(upiens)* kneeling with his hands folded in prayer and gazing upward to a cross-nimbed and bearded head of Christ looking down at him (fig. 22).[49] In the upper flourish to the right of the initial a tiny bearded head with fringed hair appears within the smaller initial *A(nno)* and a closer look reveals a monster looking at the lay brother, with its hind legs perched on

[47] London, British Library, MS Cotton Cleopatra C XI fol. 25r; illustrated in France, 1998, 217.

[48] Düsseldorf, Universitäts- und Landesbibliothek, MS C 27 fol. 1r; illustrated in France 1998, 87.

[49] Düsseldorf, Universitäts- und Landesbibliothek, MS C 27 fol. 2r.

the brother's head. The monster has a long foliate tail. This vignette recalls a number of *exemplum* stories of the encounters of monks with demons in a variety of guises.

These pictorial examples reflect the preoccupation of the monastic authors and compilers with the onslaught of demons on both monks and lay brothers. Although the themes relating to the two groups are similar, there is a distinct difference in the extent of the coverage of the two respectively as well as the extent to which the activities of demons outside the monastery are dealt with. In the *Exordium magnum* demons occur in twenty-three chapters altogether: twelve of them concern monks, five concern *conversi*, and the remaining six a variety of outsiders, including a woman possessed, a priest, and a knight.[50] The greater emphasis on monks than on lay brothers is understandable; in concentrating their attacks on the most sacred monastic occupations—the Eucharist and the *Opus Dei*—the demons took as their targets the monks officiating and not their auxiliaries, the *conversi*. The same does not apply, however, to the *Dialogus miraculorum*, in which the ratio between monk/demon and *conversi*/demon encounters is reversed; only four chapters in *Dialogus miraculorum* feature monks, while there are eight in which lay brothers are exposed to demonic assaults.[51] It is hard to see why this should be so, but it may be that Caesarius depended more than Conrad on the direct evidence of lay brothers. This is suggested by the fact that Caesarius relied on lay brothers as his source for two of the eight chapters featuring demons: in one a lay brother "does not wish his name to be mentioned."[52] In the other Caesarius asserts that the lay brother Theodoric "told me that when he was a young man, a friend of his promised to make

---

[50] The figures are from the Index of the French edition, *Le Grand Exorde de Cîteaux,* ed. Jacques Berlioz (Turnhout: Brepols, 1998), 533. The five chapters concerning lay brothers are *EM* 2.2, 31; 4.31; 5.8, 10 (Griesser, 99–100, 138–41, 264–65, 286–88, 292–98).

[51] The eight chapters concerning lay brothers are: *DM* 5, 16, 17, 27, 28, 29, 33, and 48 (Strange 1:294–95, 310, 311–12, 312–15, 316–17, 333; Scott and Bland 1:321–25, 336–37, 337–38, 354–55, 355–57, 357–60, 362–64, 383).

[52] *DM* 5.48 (Strange 1:333; Scott and Bland 1:383): *qui nomen suum vult supprimi.*

love to a certain girl in Lübeck on his behalf. He gained the assent of the young woman, but when Theodoric hoped to win her, his friend showed that he had been making a mock of him, and had wooed her for himself."[53]

In addition to this difference between the two collections there is a divergence in the overall treatment of demonic exploits. As we have seen, encounters between demons and the two groups of the monastic community are recorded in twelve of the altogether fifty-six chapters in Book Five of the *Dialogus miraculorum*. This leaves forty-four chapters of Book Five in which demons are described as confronting a variety of outsiders, including priests and lay people but mostly heretics and possessed women. The only explanation for this must be that Caesarius's circle of friends and informants included members of a number of monasteries of the Clairvaux filiation in the Rhineland, some of whom had more frequent contact with women and the outside world, while Conrad of Eberbach's stories, centered on Clairvaux and Eberbach, were more inward-looking and overwhelmingly monastic, coming primarily from Cistercians.

There does not seem to have been any development in the conception of devils and lay brothers from the early days to the thirteenth century. What is worth noting, however, is that devils were as energetic in their pursuit of monks as they were of lay brothers, and that there is no indication either in Conrad's more limited treatment or in Caesarius's more extensive accounts that the less educated and less disciplined lay brothers were more prone to, or deserving of, demonic attacks.

[53] *DM* 5.27 (Strange 1:310; Scott and Bland 1:354–55): *sicut ab eius ore audivi, cum esset iuvenis, puellam quandam in civitate Lubech alter quidam iuvenis ei procabatur, secundum quod illi promiserat. Femina consentiente, cum Theodericus se eius concubitu uti sperasset, socius eius ei illudens, ad illam accessit.*

# Chapter 11

# Visions of the Other World

D eath was an ever-present reality in the Middle Ages and the subject of all-consuming interest. The simple faith of monks and lay brothers about the next world inevitably aroused an insatiable curiosity, and eyewitness accounts of what transpired after death became a favorite subject in *exemplum* literature. Preoccupation with the afterlife among the Cistercians is evidenced by the story of the lay brother Roger and his monk friend Alexander at the monastery of Stratford Langthorne near London, who made a pact whereby whoever should die first would appear to the other and divulge the all-important details of his experience.[1]

The story of the death of an observant lay brother from Clairvaux was recorded both by Herbert of Clairvaux and Conrad of Eberbach.[2] The event was revealed to a monk far from Clairvaux in a vision of heaven, heralding the brother's imminent arrival as "a new saint." The monk found himself

> entering into a paradise of marvelous delights, into a place so glorious and bright that the human senses cannot understand the extent, the beauty, and the charm of it. There appeared a great variety of precious jars in that place, splendid ornaments with all kinds of decorations, placed as if for the reception of some very great emperor or king. Multitudes of saints, shining with tremendous light, were already there and others were coming from every direction, as if hurrying to see a

[1] Holdsworth 1962, 197; *Liber revelationum* 7. See also pp. 176–77.
[2] *LM* 1.7 (PL 185:460–61) and *EM* 4.20 (Griesser, 246–48).

brilliant spectacle and gathering as if for a solemn feast. There
I heard sweet celestial music and echoes of thanksgiving and
the voice of praise.[3]

The source for most of the numerous examples of visions, revelations, and lifelike dreams that have been described was not the
person who experienced them but someone to whom they were
reported, either the writer or compiler of the *exemplum* himself
or someone who transmitted them to the writer either directly
or through a third person. Among the visionary experiences were
a number of stories about the Eucharist. One of them has a lay
brother as the viewer who witnessed a beautiful child being taken
down from the altar and placed in the mouth of a fellow lay brother.[4] In another example Caesarius of Heisterbach's source was the
abbot of Dünamünde in Livonia (Lithuania). A lay brother, who
had only recently embraced the faith, was anxious to communicate
before he was able and had his wish fulfilled when Christ himself
came down from the altar and gave him the sacrament without
the help of a priest.[5] In yet another case Caesarius relied on the
written testimony of a monk from Himmerod for the account of
a lay brother who, when about to make his communion, saw the
blood of Christ appearing to drip into the chalice.[6] Of a different
order were the accounts of visions of the other world, by definition
solitary experiences of journeys in the realm of the dead, often
accompanied by a saint or an angel with vivid descriptions of the
torments of the damned, the pains of those in the process of being

---

[3] *EM* 4.20 (Griesser, 247); CF 72:358: *inveni me subito introductum velut in
paradisum voluptatis, in locum gloriosum atque praeclarum nimis, cuius aptitudinem, pulchritudinem atque amoenitatem humani sensus angustia aestimare non sufficit. Videbatur illic
pretiosorum vasorum aliorumque ornamentorum gloria magna et diversitas multa, infinita
quoque deliciarum praeparatio, quomodo fieri solet in adventu cuiuspiam potentissimi regis
aut imperatoris. Erant etiam illic sancti innumerabiles immensa claritate coruscantes, quorum
alii iam advenerant, alii adhuc de cunctis partibus veniebant quasi ad grande spectaculum
certatim properantes at velut ad diem solemnem undique confluentes. Audiebatur praeterea
ibidem suavitas harmoniae caelestis et resonabat undique gratiarum actio et vox laudis.*

[4] *DM* 9.42 (Strange 2:198–99; Scott and Bland 2:145–47).

[5] *DM* 9.37 (Strange 2:193; Scott and Bland 2:139–40).

[6] *DM* 9.41 (Strange 2:197–98; Scott and Bland 2:144–45).

purged, and the bliss enjoyed by the saved. The flights of imagination employed in these accounts are reminiscent of medieval
church altarpieces or wall paintings. The impact of the stories was
so great and traumatic that the visionaries who had experienced
the visions invariably felt compelled to relate what they had attested
to others, and the impact it had on them was frequently such that
they were never the same again.

The Cistercians are known to have had a predilection for
otherworldly experiences. These accounts were among the most
popular and most widely disseminated accounts of other-world
journeys in the Middle Ages. Among the earliest such accounts
was the vision of the "glory of the blessed and the torments of the
damned" experienced in 1161 by Gunthelm, a Cistercian novice
and former crusader knight. It was also one of the earliest vision
accounts in which the Virgin played a major role, something that
was to become an important ingredient in narratives of visionary
experiences.[7] The account of Gunthelm's vision was also the source
for the 1206 account of Thurkill's vision recorded by the Cistercian
Ralph of Coggeshall.

Even more popular was the story of the journey through Saint
Patrick's Purgatory—the most important pilgrimage site in Ire-
land—of the Irish crusader knight who later became a Cistercian.
The earliest surviving account of it—the *Tractatus de Purgatorio
Sancti Patricii*—was written in about 1180 by the Cistercian Henry
of Sawtry.[8] His source was the Cistercian Gilbert, formerly of Louth
Park and abbot of Basingwerk, who had spent several years in
Ireland helping to found a monastery, probably Baltinglass. Saint
Patrick's Purgatory was later mentioned by Jocelin of Furness,
Gerald of Wales, and John of Cornwall. It appeared in three Middle
English translations and may have eclipsed all other accounts of
otherworldly journeys in popularity on account of the existence of
an actual cave that was believed to give access to the saint's passage
to Purgatory and Paradise. Nevertheless, accounts of otherworldly
visions were relatively few and were easily outnumbered by other

[7] For the Vision of Gunthelm, see Constable 1956.
[8] For Saint Patrick's Purgatory, see Easting 1991.

revelations, visions, and dreams, many of which have already been described. What distinguishes other world stories is the frequency with which three themes occur, sometimes separately but at times also combined: the special devotion of the Cistercians to the Virgin, an exclusively Cistercian Purgatory, and the Cistercians' exalted place in Paradise, evidence of the privileged position of the Cistercian Order.

### Lay Brothers under Our Lady's Cloak

The role that the cult of Mary played in the devotional life of the Cistercians is well known. As an exemplar *par excellence* of humility and acceptance of a subsidiary position, Mary was the perfect role model for monks generally but for lay brothers in particular. Stories of the Marian devotion of lay brothers have already been mentioned, among them the one of the brother whose devout recitation of the Office of Blessed Mary merited his being taken into heaven like a beautiful rose.[9] In the Ebrach compilation Mary is described as "the very special Life, Sweetness, and Hope of the whole Order."[10] The Beaupré collection has an English lay brother who is said to have been "dedicated and devoted to the veneration of the blessed Virgin."[11] Once, when ill in the infirmary, he was

> suddenly rapt in the spirit by two angels leading him toward a shining building of inestimable beauty which they entered as it were with voices of exaltation and praise. In the company of the saints he thought he had been admitted into Paradise, and he said: "O, how happy I would be if the Lord gave me a place here." Meanwhile, one of the angels who had led him brought him secretly to the dwelling place of the blessed and glorious Virgin and introduced him to her. When the pious Virgin heard about this she immediately ordered him to be sent with the glorious choir of virgins congratulating him and giving solemn thanks, asserting that the time for

[9] *DM* Hilka 1937, 3:195. See pp. 172–73.
[10] EC 8 (Oppel 1972, 23): *vita, dulcedo et spes singularis tocius ordinis.*
[11] BC fol. 85r: *In veneratione vero beate virginis sic fuit deditus et devotus.*

retribution had now come, and on account of his labors of obedience she would give him a mansion of eternal quiet at an opportune time.[12]

A fulsome eulogy, based on the account in Revelation, forms the opening of the seventh book of the *Dialogus miraculorum*, which consists of sixty-nine chapters dedicated to the Virgin.[13] Caesarius of Heisterbach deliberately chose to devote Book 7 to stories with a Marian content for, in a typically medieval play on numbers, he points out that seven is the number of virginity since no number below ten can be generated from it.[14] The twelve *Dialogus miraculorum* stories featuring the *grangiarius* Henry who had charge of the Himmerod grange of Hart have already been mentioned.[15] It comes as no surprise that three of these refer to visions of the Virgin. Carrying her Son, she is said to have entered the monks' choir during the Office and then gone to the lay brothers' choir. She stopped at those who were deep in prayer, congratulated and blessed them, but passed by those who were lukewarm or asleep. Henry made a note of the names of those singled out and gave it to Herman who at the time was prior before becoming abbot of Marienstatt.[16] Caesarius has another version of the same story in which the lay brother is not named as Henry but simply as

---

[12] BC fol. 85r–85v: *raptus est statim in spiritu a duobus angelis eum ducentibus versus quoddam edificium inestimante pulchritudinis et fulgoris ubi quasi in voce exultationis et confessionis pariter se ingresisse. In cetu igitur sanctorum se ille quasi in paradiso arbitratus admissum: "o, inquit, quam felix existerem si in hoc loco locum mihi dominus largiretur." Interim unus ex angelis a quibus adductus advenit secretius quoddam habitaculum est ingressus beate et gloriose virgini illum addesse denuntians. Quo audito pia virgo statim illum accersiri precepit cum glorioso virginum choro illi occurens congratulans et gratias officiossissime reddens, quod in eius veneratione tam sollicitus in terra fuerit ac devotus, asserens nunc retributionis tempus adesse, et sibi pro obedientie laboribus mansionem quietis eterne tempore opportune reddendam audisset.* I am grateful to Brian McGuire for providing me with the text and to Fr. Hilary Costello for its transcription and translation. See also p. 74.

[13] *DM* 7 (Strange 2:1–80; Scott and Bland 1:453–546.

[14] *DM* 7 Prologue (Strange 2:1; Scott and Bland 1:453).

[15] See pp. 144–47.

[16] *DM* 7.12 (Strange 2:15; Scott and Bland 1:469–70).

"an old man of mature life and still virgin in his body," and there is no mention of reporting the names to the prior.[17] A parallel story appears in three other *exemplum* collections: the *Exordium magnum*, the Beaupré compilation, and the *Collectaneum clareval-lense*. In these Saint Bernard is said to have had a vision of angels recording the varying degrees of the monks' devotion in choir by writing in gold, silver, ink, or water; for those not singing at all the angels wrote nothing.[18] On another occasion Henry was sitting on his bed in the infirmary when the Virgin appeared. She went in and out among the beds of the sick, blessing them as they slept.[19] A third time, following the request of one of the lay brothers for Henry's intercession, "three matrons of wonderful beauty"—the Virgin, Saint Mary Magdalene, and Saint Elizabeth—appeared in the grange chapel at Hart after Compline.[20]

Herbert of Clairvaux records the vision of heaven experienced by the lay brother Robert of Fontmorigny in the diocese of Bourges, who originally came from Clairvaux, in these words:

> He saw in a vision the Lord Jesus Christ and the most blessed Mother of God with blessed abbot Bernard, standing in a garden of delights. Its vastness and beauty no words can express. He was standing a long way off and asking sincerely for divine mercy. Then the holy Mother said to her son, "Lord and son, what are you going to do for this poor fellow of yours?" The Lord said to her: "What would you like me to do, Mother?" She replied: "I want you to send him to your place of rest." So the Lord said to her: "Let it be as you wish." Then the blessed Virgin replied: "And when is this going to happen?" The Lord said to her: "He will come and be saved in five days."[21]

---

[17] *DM* Hilka 1933, 1:85: *vir senex, moribus maturus et adhuc virgo corpore.*

[18] *EM* 2.3 (Griesser, 1961, 100–1); BC fol. 35r; McGuire 1983, 46; *CC* 4.7 (Legendre 2005, 264–65).

[19] *DM* 7.13 (Strange 2:16; Scott and Bland 1:470–71).

[20] *DM* 7.15 (Strange 2:17; Scott and Bland 1:427–73): *Quod cum promisisset et die quadam dicto completorio in oratorio grangiae, cuius magister erat pro ipso preces funderet, apparuerunt oranti tres matronae mirae pulchritudinis.*

[21] *LM* 2.40 (PL 185:1349–50): *Hic itaque vidit in visione Dominum Jesum Christum, et beatissimam eius Genetricem, cum beato Bernardo abbate stantes in quodam horto*

After the vision, in the usual way, he told the others what he had seen and heard; his sickness grew worse, and on the fifth day, as the Lord had promised, he died.

The story is repeated in a slightly extended form by Conrad of Eberbach. Himself a son of Clairvaux, he could not resist pointing out that, having come from Clairvaux, Robert "never forgot the discipline and observances he had learned there" and that "he especially honored the Virgin Mary, the most blessed Bearer of God." Finally, Conrad concludes the story by stating that the monks "imitated the discipline of Clairvaux that they had seen in him" and that they "devoted themselves with much zeal to the veneration of the holy *Theotokon*, Our Lady, knowing that no work undertaken for her glory is ever lost to them."[22] Conrad of Eberbach's additions show the development and rise in the cult of Mary since the days of Saint Bernard.

Caesarius records how he himself owed his conversion to a story of a vision of Mary he had heard from a Cistercian abbot.[23] He used the age-old expedient of keeping the best story to the end, so he entitles the last chapter of his book of Marian stories "Of a monk who saw in the kingdom of heaven the Cistercian Order beneath Our Lady's cloak." In a vision of heaven a monk saw "the different ranks of the church triumphant, to wit, angels, patriarchs, prophets, apostles, martyrs, confessors, and all of them divided into their particular Orders."[24] Perplexed at not seeing any

---

*deliciarum; cuius amoenitatis et gloriae tanta erat immensitas, ut locutione explicari non valeat. Ipse vero eminus stabat, et respectum divinae miserationis medullitus flagitabat. Tunc piissima mater ait ad filium suum: "Domine fili, quid facturus est de isto paupere tuo?" Et Dominus ad eam: "Quidquid tibi placuerit, mater." At illa respondit: "Volo igitur ut mittas eum in requiem tuam." Dixit autem Dominus ad eam: "Fiat ei sicut vis." Respondit ei beatissima Virgo: "Et quando fiet istud?" Dixit ad eam Dominus: "Quinta die veniat, et salvetur."*

[22] EM 4.32 (Griesser, 265–66); CF 72:384–85: *nequaquam immemor erat, sed virtutis et devotionis exempla fratribus eiusdem loci in omni conversatione sua dabat . . . quod beatissimae Dei genetricis et virginis Mariae servitio devotus insistebat. . . . Claraevallensis quoque disciplinae, quam in eo viderant, aemulatores effecti venerationi sanctae Theotocon, Dominae nostrae, tanto alacrius intendebant, quanto sibi perire non posse sciebant, quidquid eius famulatui impendere potuissent.*

[23] DM 1.17 (Strange 1:24–25; Scott and Bland 1:25–26).

[24] DM 7.69 (Strange 2:79; Scott and Bland 1:546): *ubi dum diversos Ecclesiae triumphantis ordines videret, Angelorum videlicet, Patriarchorum, Prophetarum, Apostolorum, Martyrum, Confessorum, et eosdem certis caracteribus distinctos.*

Cistercians there, he was comforted when Mary opened her cloak and revealed an "innumerable multitude of monks, lay brothers, and nuns."[25] Greatly exulting, and giving heartfelt thanks to her, he then returned to his body and told his abbot what he had seen and heard. Our Lady of Mercy—known in German as the *Schutzmantelmadonna*, Our Lay of the Protecting Mantle—was one of the most popular images in medieval Cistercian iconography.[26] As we have seen, in one of the oldest of these images, dated around 1325 from Leubus in Poland, the standing figure of Mary holding her cloak open reveals four figures on each side, on the right lay brothers identified by their beards and the characteristic fringed hair, on the left monks clearly distinguished by their tonsure.[27] The best known image of Our Lady of Mercy, however, the early-sixteenth-century painting attributed to Jean de Bellegambe, like most other later examples, has monks on one side and nuns on the other but shows no lay brothers.

Literary tributes to the Marian devotion of lay brothers by the *exemplum* writers for the edification and emulation of their fellow monks are matched by visual counterparts in Cistercian art. A prime example is the magnificent small stained glass window dated to around 1280 that would have been seen by the monks passing through the north cloister walk at Wettingen in Switzerland (fig. 23). It is star-shaped with six points, five of them containing palm leaves while the sixth, in the lower left hand, has a kneeling figure with hands clasped in prayer looking up to the large central figures contained within a circular red medallion, madonna and child, each crowned. Mary is shown sideways, her head slightly bowed, looking down in tenderness on both her Son, who is standing on her knee, and the kneeling figure, unmistakably a lay brother. He has variously been described as a monk, an abbot, and even Saint Bernard, but being bearded, having the traditional fringed hair, and wearing a cloak and not a cowl over his tunic, he is clearly

---

[25] *DM* 7.64 (Strange 2:79–80; Scott and Bland 1:546): *innumerabilem multitudinem monachorum, conversorum, sanctimonilium illi ostendit.*

[26] For this see France 1998, 184–86, and France 2002.

[27] See figure 18.

*Fig. 23* Stained glass from the cloister of Wettingen, Switzerland, of lay brother kneeling before the Virgin and Child.

a lay brother. The wrong identification may have been caused by the side of the Virgin's seat being mistaken for a crozier.[28]

## Lay Brothers in the Cistercian Purgatory

The idea of the need for purgation before finally entering heaven goes back to the early Middle Ages, though the word *purgatorium* appeared for the first time only in the 1160s, when it is found in the Cistercian writers.[29] The sense of Purgatory as a place in the geography of the other world is not always articulated, but

[28] He is referred to as a monk in Anderes and Hoegger 1989, 341; as an abbot in van der Meer 1965, 306; and as Saint Bernard in Tobin 1995, 58.

[29] For this see McGuire 1989 and Le Goff 1984.

the idea of the interdependence of the three constituent parts of the communion of saints—the church militant, suffering, and triumphant—is implied in a number of *exemplum* stories. Among them is one recording the successful outcome of the three Masses a lay brother arranged for a cousin who had died young and was "racked with very severe pains,"[30] and another telling of the rescue of a lay brother from "a pit, very wide and hideously deep," as a result of the Masses at a number of altars by priests, "the weapons of God's grace."[31] Although both these stories are included as evidence of the special power of Cistercian prayer, at the same time they evoke the interaction between the living and the dead in the communion of saints and imply the existence of a place of transition in the other world, without naming it as Purgatory, and the belief that the suffering experienced there could be alleviated by the intercession of the living.

The lay brother from Esrum in Denmark who had been sent to Clairvaux for fathering a son realized that, although he "escaped the sentence of damnation" (*damnationis sententiam evasit*), a heavy price still had to be paid. Begging his abbot for mercy, he said:

> I was taken back to the place of punishment, where also it was made known to me that because of the confession I made by God's mercy, and because of the penance I received, by the grace of God I am about to be set free from the pit of eternal damnation, but I am going to atone with suffering in Purgatory for my wickedness and all the sins I have committed even to the last farthing [Matt 5:26].[32]

---

[30] *DM* 12.33 (Strange 2:342–43; Scott and Bland 2:323–24): *et poenis maximis crucior.*

[31] *EM* 2.2 (Griesser, 99–100); CF 72:131, 132: *ad puteum quendam magnae latitudinis et horrendae profunditatis . . . haec sunt arma gratiae Dei.*

[32] *EM* 2.31 (Griesser, 140); CF 72:194: *ad loca poenarum reductus sum, ubi etiam significatum est mihi, quoniam propter confessionem, quam miserante Deo feci, et propter paenitentiam quam accepi, per gratiam Dei liberandus sum ab aeternae damnationis voragine, in purgatoriis tamen suppliciis scelera, quae commisi, et omnia peccata mea usque ad novissimum quadrantem exsoluturus.* See also pp. 221–22.

The Beaupré compilation has an account of an English Cistercian monk's journey in the other world that took him to the "Purgatory of the Cistercian Order" where the Virgin directed those she chose to "the place of coolness and rest," a fate she, although described as "the Mother of Mercy," failed to bestow on a miserable lay brother who had apostatized. Together with his guide, the monk

came to a wall of marvelous height. When they had crossed over it they found a building with four walls resembling a monastery. Approaching the door, they entered, and a woman of great beauty and glory appeared to them. When the monk's guide saw her he genuflected and adored her and the monk did likewise. Then they entered the cloister. In the middle of a small field there was a tree that covered the whole area with extensive branches. Under the tree was a great multitude of boys wailing miserably. From the branches of the tree hung innumerable red-hot metal lamps from which drops fell down, some on their eyes, some on their hands, some on other members of their bodies, afflicting them grievously. In the same cloister a man was bound to a column with ropes of fire. From the bottom of his feet to the top of his head he was totally in flames. When the boys saw the woman passing in front of them they cried out, saying, "Mother of Mercy, have mercy on me." Then calling to those whom she wanted, she handed them to the monk's guide, saying, "Lead them out into the place of coolness and rest." He rejoiced and took them out and spoke consoling words to them. The wretched man who was tied to the column also cried out, but the lady replied: "Hold your tongue! You are not worthy of mercy." Meanwhile a breath of repentant air began to blow and took away the drops falling on the boys and their clamor ceased. When the Mother of Mercy had gone round the cloister seven times, and thus had freed whom she willed, she returned to the door and disappeared. Then his guide said to the monk: "Do you know what you have seen, brother?" And he said: "Not at all, my Lord." And the old man said: "That cloister is the Purgatory of the Cistercian Order. Here are its members who have sinned while alive but are now being tortured. That woman is the Blessed Virgin Mary, and I am the father of the Order, Benedict. The breath of dew and refreshment that took away the drops falling on the boys are the prayers of the Order. But the man whom you saw totally on fire was a certain lay brother in the Order who by his faults was always acting in an irregular way. Finally he rejected the habit of religion, went back to the world, and married a wife. One night when he was sleeping with her, he suddenly died.[33]

This story represents one of the most important expressions of Cistercian self-consciousness. By claiming that Mary has reserved a special place for them—both monks and lay brothers—in Purgatory the Cistercians claimed for themselves a unique status not just in the church but in the communion of saints.

In his *Life of Waldef*, Jocelin of Furness describes in great detail two separate journeys of the lay brother Walter from the Scottish abbey of Melrose to all three areas of the other world following

---

[33] BC fol. 60r–61r: *murum mire altitudinis pervenerunt. Quem transilientes quadratum quoddam edificium in similitudinem claustri repererunt. Cuius ostium cum ingrederentur apparuit eis mulier quedam nimii decoris et glorie. Quam ductor monachi videns flexis genibus adoravit, similiter et monachus sequens eum, et sic claustrum ingressi sunt. Erat autem in medio pratelli arbor quedam que frondium extensione eius superficiem operiebat. Sub arbore illa erat multitudo maxima pueorum miserabili voce eiulantium. Dependebant autem ex ramis arboris illius innumere lampades metallis ferventibus bullientes ex quibus exilebant gutte, et aliis super oculis, aliis super manus, aliis super cetera membra corporis cadentes, eos gravissime affligebant. Erat in eodem claustro homo quidam nexibus igneis cum columpna ligatus, qui a planta pedum usque ad verticem totus ardebat. Pueri vero cum predictam mulierem coram se cernerent transeuntem, clamabant singuli et dicebant: Mater misericordie, miserere mei. Tunc quos voluit advocans ductori monachi tradidit dicens, Duc eos in locum refrigerii et quietis. Qui gaudens suscipiebat eos et verbis consolatoriis demulcebat. Clamabat etiam miser ille cum columpna vinctus, sed ei domina respondebat: Tace, quia non es dignus misericordia. Interea ventus aure repentis leviter aspirans omnes a pueris lampadarum guttas tollebat unde et tunc a clamore cessabant. Cum igitur mater misericordie claustrum septies circuisset et quos volebat sic eripuisset, ad ostium claustri reversa disparuit. Tunc ait monacho doctor suus: Scis frater quid videris? Et ille: Nequaquam, domine mi. Et senex: Claustrum istud purgatorium est cisterciensis ordinis. Porro viverent in peccaverunt in ipsis. Mulier ipsa est beata virgo maria. Ego vero sum pater ordinis benedictus. Ventus autem roris et refrigerii qui guttas tollens longuis cult a pueris, orationes sunt ordinis. Porro homo ille quem totum ardere vidisti, conversus quidam in ordine fuit qui culpis suis exigentibus semper inordinate se habuit. Tandem vero abiecto religionis habitu reversus ad seculum duxit uxorem. Et quadam nocte cum dormiret cum ea, subito expiravit.*

Waldef's death.[34] The cathartic effect the visions had on him was so great that "he became clever and eloquent" and for the rest of his life "he adhered strictly to the rules."[35] In the first vision he was led into "a kind of verdant garden, green, sweet-smelling, flowery, fruitful, altogether lovely, beautiful and spacious"[36] by two shining figures who, on account of his infidelity, threatened him with bitter agonies. When he spotted the saintly abbot, "seated on a bright elevation with a white-clothed throng seated and standing around him,"[37] he made the penitential prostration enjoined by the *Ecclesiastica officia* and asked for pardon.[38] The abbot ordered him to be

> led away to a wheel, of a size and height that were altogether horrible, its top seeming to touch the heavens, its extremity the abyss; and beneath it a fiery flood seemed to flow, so that if the spinning of the wheel were to throw him off, he would be swallowed in the flaming maw. The rim and hub of this wheel and its spokes were toothed all around with long, sharp iron nails. The brother was bent upon it and bound, and creatures with clubs in their hands struck it until it was turning at a dizzy speed, faster than the grindstone of an earthly mill.[39]

After leaving Purgatory, Walter came across a dungeon of great depth, then a barren desert, then a black castle on fire, and finally "a vast valley of infinite length, breadth, and depth, made dreadful

---

[34] See p. 71.

[35] Jocelin of Furness, 176: *Subtilis effectus est et eloquens . . . . Ipse in reliquum vitam suam in magna religione composuit.*

[36] Jocelin of Furness, 171: *hortum viridissimum, vernantem, odiriferum, florigerum, fructiferum, satis amoenum, speciosum, et spatiosum.*

[37] Jocelin of Furness, 171–72: *in eminenti loco et praelucido sedentem, turbamque candidatorum circumstantem et circumsedentem.*

[38] *EO* 70 (Griesser 1956, 235).

[39] Jocelin of Furness, 172: *ductus est et impositus cuidam rotae, cuius statura et altitudo erat horribilis valde, summitas eius caelos tangere putabatur, extremitas abyssum; subtusque eam igneus fluvius decurrere videbatur, ut si quis forte de rotae vertigine caderet, in ignis voragine demergeretur. Erant huius rotae canthi ac modioli radii undique dentati atque densati quasi clavis ferreis acutis et longis. Huic rotae fratre imposito et astricto, quidam in manibus clavas tenentes percutiebant rotam, moxque velociori vertigine versabatur, quam lapis molaris in mundano molendino.*

by roaring flames and full of souls,"[40] some of whom he knew, both lay and religious, even bishops and abbots. Fearing that the flames might catch up with him, he began running as fast as he could, pursued by two black fellows. He was rescued by two white spirits and at this point he awoke. Later the vision of the spirits returned, and he was brought to Waldef, who ordered the spirits to take him "to places of rest and joy" (*ad loca requiei et gaudii*). They took him up

> a very high mountain into a region of light and peace where he saw many mansions, spacious and beautiful, some as of purest gold, some of silver thrice refined, some of ivory polished and shining, some made of the rarest gems. . . . He saw there also a river of sweet-flowing nectar, and many varieties of trees and flowers unknown to earth-dwellers. And as he began to feel an ardent desire to remain, his leaders lifted him up over a high golden wall into another place, far brighter still, by comparison making the light of the former country seem dusk. He listened there to such melody as human ears have not heard, nor has it come into the heart of man to give it words.[41]

Waldef then appeared to Walter again and ordered him to "cease your doubting and believe [John 20:27], and turn your back on evil and do good [Ps 36:27],"[42] and he went on to explain what Walter had experienced:

---

[40] Jocelin of Furness, 173: *Venit ergo ad vallem infinite longitudinis, latitudinis et profunditatis, flammis ferventibus terribilem, animabus plenam.*

[41] Jocelin of Furness, 174–75: *in montem excelsum valde in quadam regionem lucis et pacis latissimam et laetissimam: vidit ibi mansiones multas speciosas et spatiosas, quasdam quasi de auro purissimo, quasdam de argento probatissimo, quasdam de ebore candidissimo, quasdam de lapidibus pretiosis constructas. . . . Perspexit itaque ibi fluvium mellifluum, et nectarreum, plura genera arborum et florum terrigenis ignotorum. Cumque ardentissime desiderasset ibidem demorari, duces ipsius ultra murum quemdam aureum altum nimis transvexerunt illum in aliam regionem lucidissimam, in cuius comparatione prioris patriae lux perexigua censebatur: audivit inibi tale tantumque melos, quale quantumve aures humanae capere vel linguae carnis nequeunt exprimere.*

[42] Jocelin of Furness, 175: *noli amodo esse incredulus sed fidelis; declina a malo et fac bonum.*

The wheel, and the flood, and the solitude, and the valley, which you saw before, are sections of purgatory. Within the keep of the castle you saw is the mouth of hell, and those foul and sulfurous flames are set apart for the faithless and unrepentant. In this second vision, the first section shown to you is assigned to those who are just, but not perfected. And this country next to heaven—no one may enter here unless perfected and innocent, after being completely purged of all stain of sin.[43]

Perhaps the greatest privilege claimed by a lay brother vision-ary is that of the swift passage of Cistercians through Purgatory to Paradise. It is recorded in Peter of Cornwall's *Liber revelationum* as one of the eleven accounts from the Cistercian abbey of Stratford Langthorne. After his death a lay brother appeared to the monk who had looked after him in his sickness in the infirmary. When the monk asked him how he was,

> he replied that he was in pain, but that he would without doubt be freed from his pains after thirty days. He asserted that no one belonging to the Cistercian Order should be in Purgatory more than thirty days unless he had committed a very serious sin. Also, if he died having confessed his serious sin he would not be in Purgatory more than a year, that is, until he had received absolution from the Cistercian General Chapter.[44]

[43] Jocelin of Furness, 175: *Rota, inquit, et fluvius et solitudo ac vallis, quae prius vidisti, loca purgatoria sunt: infra castelli ambitum puteus igneus sulphureus aditus infer-nalis est, infidelibus et criminosis impoenitentibus deputatus. Prima regio in hac visione tibi monstrata iustis, sed imperfectis, est assignata: ista vero patria proxima caelo, quam nullus ingredi poterit nisi perfectus et innocens ab omni naevo peccati penitus purgatus.*

[44] Holdsworth 1962, 196, *LP* 5: *respondit se adhuc in penis esse, sed se liberandum esse a penis post tricesimum diem certissime dicebat. Nullum enim cisterciensis ordinis in purgatorio ultra tricesimum diem esse posse asserebat, nisi quem criminale delictum constrin-geret, talem quoque qui crimine confesso decederet, non ultra annum in purgatorio esse debere dicebat, hoc est donec in communi capitulo et generali cisterciensi anima eius absolveretur.*

### Privileged Position Extends to Lay Brothers

Lay brothers shared with monks the privileged position occupied by the Cistercian Order in the church, a favorite theme in
*exemplum* literature, as we have seen. In Prior John's *Collectaneum clarevallense* a novice is tempted to return to his life as a regular canon
but his novice master persuades him to stay. In a vision one night
he sees that at the Last Judgment the Cistercians are to be given
pride of place in heaven but that when he tries to join them he is
prevented by a branch of a tree in which his feet get entangled.[45]
Another version appears in the Beaupré collection: a novice is again
tempted to leave his community but changes his mind when he
discovers the exalted place of the Cistercians in heaven.[46] Another
Beaupré story tells of a novice who is sent home to try to overcome
his father's opposition to his becoming a monk. When he returns
to the monastery he finds to his horror that it is surrounded by a
swarm of devils. He takes fright and returns home, but when the
abbot explains to him that all the troops were needed to besiege
a powerful fortress he understands and returns to the monastery.[47]
Caesarius of Heisterbach tells of hearing from a Benedictine abbot
that one of the abbot's monks who had died had appeared to two
confrères and told them that in heaven the Cistercians' "reward is
greatest and they shine as the sun in the realm of the sky."[48]

The power of Cistercian prayer in the salvation of the souls
of lay brothers who had strayed, and the special protection the
Virgin accorded monks and lay brothers, are recurrent themes. In
the Ebrach *exemplum* collection the Virgin is credited with con-
firming the white monks' privileged position when, in answer to
a question, she advances the idea of the Cistercians being accorded
a higher place in heaven:

> "Because of your devotion to me and all your prayers I will
> grant you the spiritual grace of seeing the Order that is in

---

[45] *CC* 4.57 (Legendre 2005, 371–72).

[46] BC fol. 61v. See McGuire 1983a, 47.

[47] BC fol. 58r–59v. See McGuire 1983b, 253.

[48] *DM* 12.53 (Strange 2:357; Scott and Bland 2:339): *Praemium illorum maximum est, et lucent sicut sol in regno coelorum.*

my special care. Raise up your eyes and you will see where this Order is." Then in a lightning flash of great brightness I saw the Order suspended without any support and decorated with most sublime glory and with honor beyond all belief.[49]

In accord with the assertion by Polonius in Shakespeare's *Hamlet* that "the apparel oft proclaims the man," another source of the Cistercian sense of superiority was the spiritual power accorded the monastic habit. The theme of the danger of a member of the Order dying without wearing the habit, and the corollary that the habit serves as a passport to heaven, occur in a number of *exemplum* authors. Among them are Herbert of Clairvaux, Conrad of Eberbach who has a chapter entitled "The great danger of a monk dying without his habit, that is without his cowl," and Caesarius of Heisterbach who has an account "of a monk who was not allowed to enter Paradise because he had thrown off his cowl when dying."[50] According to Caesarius, the monk came from Mazières in Burgundy although he had heard the story from the abbot of the German abbey of Riddagshausen. Seriously ill, the monk had a high fever and had been granted the infirmarian's permission to take off his habit and put on a lighter garment. Once dead, he returned to the body and recounted the following vision to his abbot:

> "Lord, I confess to you that I died in such and such a way; but being taken by the angels to Paradise, when I thought I could enter freely, Saint Benedict came to the door and said, 'Who are you?' And when I answered that I was a monk of the Cistercian Order, the saint rejoined: 'Certainly you are not. If you are a monk, where is your habit? This is a place for

---

[49] EC 1 (Oppel 1972, 11): *"Quia tu me sepius oculis tue devotionis obicere consuevisti, proinde tibi faciens gratiam spiritalem dignum tuis precibus, ut hunc ordinem, qui in mea cura est speciali, videas, prebeo consensum. Respice nunc sursum et videbis ubi sit."* Et ecce, in magno claritatis fulgore vidi eum pendere quasi sine medio in sublimis et tanta gloria decoratum et honore, ut vere omnem excederet estimationem.*

[50] *LM* 2.35 (PL 185:1345); *EM* 5.3 (Griesser, 276–77): *Quantum periculum sit monachum sine habitu suo, id est sine cuculla, mori; DM* 11.36 (Strange 2:298–99; Scott and Bland 2:268–69): *De monacho qui propter cucullam quam moriens exuerat prohibitus est intrare paradisum.*

rest, and you are going to enter in your working dress?' After I had gone round the walls of that blessed mansion, through the window I saw some older men of venerable appearance, and one of them looking kinder than the rest I begged him to intercede for me. On this interposition I was allowed to return to the body, that resuming my habit I might attain to the profound state of bliss." After hearing this, the abbot removed the habit in which the man was lying and put on him again that which he had stripped off in his sickness. And so, having received his blessing, he expired again.[51]

The theme occurs again in Peter of Cornwall's *Liber revelationum*, but this time it refers to a lay brother who was at first denied entry into Paradise because he was not wearing his lay brother's habit at the moment of death but was later reprieved following a journey in the other world and appearance before the tribunal of Christ. The lay brother, who had been a shepherd at the abbey of Stratfield Langthorne, apostatized but after living in the world for some years repented and sought permission to return. This was refused, but he was allowed to remain in the monastery wearing only a tunic without a hood and to be a helper in the infirmary. When he died without his hood he was snatched by demons who dragged him to the place in hell that was due to him. Then a throng of good angels came to his help and an argument followed between them and the demons, following which

> they came at last to the judgment of Christ before his tribunal. When Christ asked why the demons had led away

---

[51] *DM* 11.36 (Strange 2:298–99; Scott and Bland 2:268–69): *Domine confiteor vobis quod sic atque sic mortuus est. Ductus vero ab angelis ad paradisum, cum putarem me libere posse intrare, accessit ad ostium sanctus Benedictus, et ait: Quis enim es tu? Respondente me, ego sum monachus ordinis Cisterciensis, subiecit sanctus: Nequaquam. Si monachus es, ubi est habitus tuus? Iste locus est quietis, et tu vis intrare cum habitu laboris? Qui cum circumgyrassem muros eiusdem felicissimae mansionis, et per fenestras seniores quosdam magnae reverentiae illic conspexissem, uni illorum qui ceteris benignior videbatur, ut pro me intercederet supplicavi. Cuius interventu permissus sum ad corpus redire, ut sic habitu a te recepto merear ad promissam beatudinem introire. Quo audito Abbas cucullam in qua iacebat ei extraxit, cucullam quam in infirmitate exuerat ei reinduens. Sicque accepto benedictione rursum expiravit.*

the soul of this brother, the demons replied that he was an apostate and did not deserve to receive the habit because of his own fault. On the other hand, the good angels replied that the brother had led a good life and although he had apostatized he had nevertheless repented perfectly and had asked for mercy and the habit of a lay brother both in life and in death. Therefore he deserved to receive what he had desired to obtain.[52]

Christ ordered the lay brother to tell the abbot that the habit should be given back to him. The lay brother appeared to the abbot, who was away on the continent, presumably attending the General Chapter at Cîteaux. Noticing that his hair was scorched and his clothes full of holes, the abbot asked him what had happened and the brother replied that "burning drops of pitch and sulfur and lead had scorched his head and his hair and flowed down from his hair onto his shoulders where the lay brother's hood was not found and his tunic was burnt and there were holes."[53] The abbot ordered the prior to give a lay brother's habit to the dead brother, whereupon the prior called together the senior brothers and "the body of the dead brother was exhumed from the grave and was clothed with the habit of a lay brother with the hood and again he was buried."[54] When the abbot returned he related to the community all that had happened "so that this was to be admired by

---

[52] Holdsworth 1962, 196, *LP* 6: *ventum est ad iudicium Christi ante tribunal eius. Cumque quereret Christus quare animam fratris illius demones ducerent, responderunt demones quia apostatavit et postea habitum suum culpa propria non accipere meruit. Econtra autem angeli boni responderunt fratrem illum bone conversationis fuisse, et licet postea apostataverit, tamen penituit postea perfecte, et misericordiam et habitum conversi tam in vita quam in morte cum instantia petiit. Et ideo quantum in eo fuit, quod petiit optinere meruit.*

[53] Holdsworth 1962, 197, *LP* 6: *gutte ardentes ex pice et sulphure et plumbo, que capud illius et capillos suos exurebant, et a capillis suis deorsum defluentes super scapulas illius ubi caputium conversi non inveniebatur decidebant, et tunicam illius perforando interius miserrime reliquum illius urebant.*

[54] Holdsworth 1962, 197, *LP* 6: *corpus mortui fratris iam sepultum a sepultura extrahitur, et habitu conversi, hoc est caputio, super alias vestes superinduitur, et sic iterum sepulture traditur.*

them and be given to the glory to the Lord Jesus Christ who wills that all men be saved."[55]

The danger of not wearing the habit at death applied equally to monks and to lay brothers and there is no difference in the way the two groups are perceived in the visions. Accounts of other world visions belong to the late twelfth and early thirteenth century and reveal an awareness of the historical development since the heroic early days. The idealism of former times was still there, but an awareness had arisen of the need for vigilance if the Cistercians were to remain worthy heirs of the spirit of earlier generations. Conrad of Eberbach expressed the danger of *negligentia* when he asked: "what are we to do when negligence, so prone to vice, can, alas, be detected even in the conduct of those under a rule?"[56] As a result of outside challenges a certain sense of insecurity had arisen, especially in Germany, where the black monks will not stop criticizing our sacred Order wherever and to whomever they can."[57] This anxiety manifested itself in expressions of superiority in the Cistercian claim to a special relationship to the Virgin and to preferential treatment in the afterlife, and in their claim to a position as an unrivaled elite made visible by their distinctive habit.

[55] Holdsworth 1962, 197, *LP* 6: et sic factum istud admirandum per illos pervenit ad laudem Domini nostri Iesu Christi, qui vult omnes homines salvos fieri.

[56] *EM* 1.9 (Griesser, 59); CF 72:66: *Quid agimus, quod negligentia, quae, pro dolor! In ipsa quoque religiosorum conversatione deprehenditur, ad vitia tam proclivis est?*

[57] *EM* 1.10 (Griesser, 61); CF 72:69: *ubicumque vel apud quoscumque possunt, sacro ordini nostro derogare non cessant.*

# Chapter 12

# Not *Conversi* but *Perversi*

## Pride Versus Humility

In recent Cistercian historiography it has been assumed that the lay brothers were rebellious from the very beginning, and yet the first recorded such incident involving lay brothers did not occur until around 1182. Conrad of Eberbach devotes the whole of the longest chapter in the *Exordium magnum*, entitled "The Danger of Conspiracies," to the revolt at the Eberbach daughter house of Schönau.[1] He ends this with a quotation from Scripture: "God opposes the proud but accords his favor to the humble" (*Deus superbis resistit, humilibus autem dat gratiam* [1 Pet 5:5]). This perfectly encapsulates the two lay brother stereotypes, the humble whom we meet in many of the *exemplum* stories and in *vitae*, and the recalcitrant who frequently form the subject of General Chapter statutes. The leader of the lay brother conspirators at Schönau should, in the opinion of Conrad, "be called *perversus* rather than *conversus*."[2] Although we meet a great many *perversi* among the lay brothers in the statutes, it becomes clear that there were as many among the monks. The myth that most of the lay brothers were incorrigible agitators is frequently advanced but cannot be substantiated by the facts.

Around the same time as the trouble at the German abbey, Jocelin of Furness in his *Life of Waldef* referred to a lay brother, by name Sinuin, whom he described as "a *conversus* by profession and habit, but *perversus* in act and intent."[3] He was stronger and better

[1] *EM* 5.10 (Griesser, 292–98).

[2] *EM* 5.10 (Griesser, 293).

[3] Jocelin of Furness 1952, 157: *quidam habitu et professione conversus, sed actu perversus ac intentione.*

at manual labor than most, calling others effeminate, but his motive was to show off rather than to please God. He had a vision in his sleep of a knife-wielding giant who cut off Sinuin's limbs one by one but was stopped by an angel who ordered him to restore the brother's limbs. After this the angel turned to Sinuin, "warned the brother to change his attitude, amend his conduct, rectify the balance of his life, and wholly turn himself to God."[4]

The play on the two words *conversus* and *perversus* in the two stories is not connected but is a coincidence based on the somewhat obvious similarity between the two words. Saint Bernard, a great devotee of the play on words, had used it, but referring not to lay brothers but to someone who had broken his vows when he said: "It perverted the converted, and the dog returned to its vomit."[5] Its application to lay brothers was not confined to Conrad of Eberbach and Jocelin of Furness: there were a number of examples in the polemic against the Cistercians by twelfth-century satirists. The *Carmina Burana*, in a parody of prayers from the liturgy, replaced *fratribus conversis* with *fratribus perversis*,[6] and the Benedictine satirist and poet Nigel Longchamp linked the two words in ridiculing the Cistercian lay brothers when he spoke of someone who "spies these *conversi* (nay, from their activities *perversi* would be best)."[7] The source for this pun was a pre-Cistercian late-eleventh-century reference to the old model of Benedictine monk *conversus* and not to Cistercian lay brothers: "What shall I say about the *conversi*, O Lord Christ, who while wanting to be called by their right name ought to be called *perversi*."[8] The play on the two words may appear somewhat trivial on account of the humor it contains, but in a medieval context it was of the utmost gravity,

---

[4] Jocelin of Furness 1952, 158: *ut intentionem mutaret, mores componeret, vitam in reliquum corrigerit, et ad Deum se totum converteret.*

[5] *Ep.* 2 (*SBOp* 7, 18; James 1953, 150): *Subvertit perversus conversum, revertitur canis ad vomitum.*

[6] Batany 1969, 247.

[7] Nigel Longchamp, 1960, 53: *Istos conversos, quos perversos magis esse / Constat, ut ex factis nomina certa trahant.*

[8] Batany 1969, 247: *Quid de conversis, quos recto nomine vero appellare volens perversos dicere debet, Christe, feram?*

as the turning from one to the other implied a conscious, deliberate departure from a solemn vow, the punishment for which was eternal. A German poem from around 1220 repeats the usual two words as well as adding *dispersus* (dispersed) and *diversus*, and it also plays on four other rhyming words, including *maculari* (stained by sin) and *pertubari* (inebriated):

> The general opinion is that the *conversi*
> When gathered together or *dispersi*
> Should not associate with the *perversi*
> Lest they be harmed in the *diversi* [taverns]
> In case they be *maculari*
> So as to become *pertubari*
> And like sinners *imitari*
> And end up in perpetual *damnari*.[9]

## Lay Brother Excesses and Conspiracies

Satirical writers saw the lay brothers as marginal men—neither monks nor peasants, members of the sergeant class, the *Feldwebel*—rather dim, cringing to their superiors, of whom they are afraid, blown up by their own importance, and avenging the arbitrary treatment often meted out to them by tyrannizing those beneath them. As large numbers had joined out of economic necessity and not as a result of a sense of vocation, sooner or later disciplinary problems were bound to arise. A further factor, despite early Cistercian claims to the contrary, was the ambiguity of their second-class status, their inequality and marginalization. A widely different picture both as to the scale of the problem and the extent to which it

---

[9] Karajan 1842, 26: *generaliter conversis,*
*congregatis vel dispersis,*
*suadeatur ne perversis*
*socientur, in diversis*
*quia possunt maculari*
*per eosque pertubari,*
*impios forsan imitari*
*et perpetue damnari.*

contributed to the decline of the lay brotherhood has been painted by different scholars.

Three sets of figures relating to lay brother violence and based almost entirely on General Chapter statutes have been advanced: Jean Leclercq suggests a total of fifty revolts between 1168 and 1300 (twenty between 1168 and 1200 and thirty in the thirteenth century) but he does not list them;[10] Megan Cassidy-Welch lists ninety-three incidents reported to the General Chapter in the period 1200–1300;[11] and James Donnelly lists one hundred twenty-three revolts between 1168 and 1308.[12]

The breaches of discipline were by no means limited to those recorded in the statutes. Apart from the considerable lacunae in the statute collections, it is safe to conclude that on account of the serious obstacles to communication between far-flung abbeys and Cîteaux, leading to irregular attendance at General Chapters, a large number of cases of violence, perhaps even a majority, were not reported to the General Chapter but were dealt with locally. For example, in 1240 an incident is recorded in the Waverley *Annals*: a lay brother who had entered Waverley to disguise his past was arrested by a knight who charged him with murder. He may or may not have been guilty, but in spite of the protests of the abbot and other monks who were responsible for his well-being he was seized and carried off. After much trouble the abbot appealed to the king and the brother was released.[13] Another case of serious indiscipline is recorded in the Kirkstall *Coucher Book*: two lay brothers, the grange master Adam and the keeper of the plows Walter, were charged with the murder of Adam, the forester of Clifford.[14]

In a strife between the Danish abbey of Øm (*Cara insula*) and the bishop of Århus in 1262 a number of named *conversi* were the victims rather than the perpetrators of violent incidents, but when a crisis was reached some of the lay brothers, "encouraged by the

[10] Leclercq 1965, 250.

[11] Cassidy 1997, 48–49.

[12] Donnelly 1949, 71–90.

[13] *Waverleia, Annales de* 1865, 1:325–27.

[14] *Coucher Book, Kirkstall* 1904, 23.

devil, secretly deprived the monastery of its property," absconded, and returned to the world. The abbey's *Chronicle* adds that "there were also many who sold [the abbey's] cattle and horses and corn and all the property of the granges so that, should they be driven out and obliged to flee, they could take something with them."[15] In 1274 *conversi* from the grange of Little Faringdon belonging to the English house of Beaulieu, with the help of a band of more than thirty men, raided a lay manor, killing a horse and damaging the crop.[16] A few years later the abbot of Beaulieu with some of his monks and lay brothers attacked some men while they were peacefully fishing, using "bows and arrows and spears and swords and other arms" (*cum arcubus et sagittis et hachiis et gladiis et aliis diversis armaturus*).[17]

The figures in the three lists of General Chapter statutes are not directly comparable, as the periods covered are somewhat different and, furthermore, while Leclercq includes only "lay brother revolts," Cassidy and Donnelly in their studies list all incidents involving not only lay brothers but also abbots and/or monks. What constitutes an offense sufficiently serious to be included in a list of "revolts" is, of course, open to debate. No two studies would arrive at the same conclusion and the main reason for the wide discrepancy between the numbers is a difference of interpretation.

It seems strange, for example, that a statute from 1213 punishing the *grangiarius* of the grange of Chaltre belonging to La Ferté (Saône-et-Loire) is absent from both lists. The perpetrator in this incident was accused of "inhuman conduct in both word and deed" toward abbots on their way to General Chapter; for this he was made to go on foot to the mother house of Cîteaux where he was to eat coarse bread, have no wine, and lie on the ground for three days.[18] The abbot of Cîteaux had already some years earlier

[15] *Scriptores Minores* 1917–1922, 2:262: *Quidam de conversis, instinctu diabolico furtive subtrahentes boni monasterii, immo patrimonium Jhesu Christi, redierunt retrorsum ad seculum fugientes; multi etiam vendirerunt pecora et iumenta, annonam quoque et alia supellectilia grangiarum pro denariis, ut, si compellerentur fugam inire, secum aspotarent, unde sibimet vite necessaria amministrare potuissent.*

[16] Hockey 1976, 81.

[17] *Beaulieu Cartulary* 1974, 250–51.

[18] *Statuta* 1213.50 (Canivez 1:414): *tam in verbo quam in facto se inhumanum exhibit.*

been ordered to investigate irregularities relating to lay brothers at La Ferté.[19] In 1207 the abbot of Les Pierres was charged with dealing with lay brothers who had "come armed upon receiving abbots on their way to General Chapter."[20] On another occasion, in 1225, a lay brother from Hautecombe in Savoy had been sent away from his own monastery not to return until the following General Chapter for having "inhumanely treated" abbots on their way to the Chapter.[21]

Failure to offer adequate hospitality to abbots on their way to or from Cîteaux or to abbots on visitation, which could be both costly and disruptive to the host abbey, was one of the most frequent offenses punished by the General Chapter.[22] The burden on finances and on discipline is suggested by the apparent complicity of the abbot of Piscaria (San Vito e San Salvo) in Apulia, whose lay brothers in 1275 "laid violent hands on the abbots coming to the Chapter and took away their belongings." The abbot was ordered to restrain the brothers and to compensate the abbots who had been harmed. The following year he was accused of not having reported to the General Chapter, was reminded to satisfy the aggrieved abbots, and was given the punishment of remaining outside his abbatial stall for three days, one of them on bread and water. By 1277 he still had not complied with the ruling. He was instructed to ensure that the lay brothers received their punishment before Easter and was again directed to satisfy the abbots who had been despoiled. He was to remain outside his stall and was not to ride his horse until these things had been fulfilled.[23]

---

[19] *Statuta* 1201.34 (Canivez 1:270).

[20] *Statuta* 1207.61 (Canivez 1:345): *manu armata occurrerunt abbatibus venientibus ad Capitulum.*

[21] *Statuta* 1225.26 (Canivez 2:40): *Conversus de Altacumba qui abbates ad Capitulum generale venientes inhumane tractavit, eo quod abbatem suum in generali Capitulo proclamaverant, emittatur de domo propria, non reversumus usque ad sequens Capitulum.*

[22] Other examples: *Statuta* 1213.50 (Canivez 1:414); 1214.30 (Canivez 1:423); 1214.46, (Canivez 1:426); 1216.32 (Canivez 1:456); 1281.33 (Canivez 3:212).

[23] *Statuta* 1275.22 (Canivez 3:144); 1276.8 (Canivez 3:153); 1277.10 (Canivez 3:165).

In spite of the factors limiting the value of a statistical interpretation of the *statuta*, the disturbances reported to the General
Chapter nevertheless offer a valuable insight into the state of lay
brother discipline and a closer look tells us that the frequency of
recorded incidents increased in the course of the thirteenth century.
In many cases the *statuta* impose a punishment without giving
details of the offense. Apart from the punishment meted out to
the lay brother from La Ferté just mentioned, sentences included,
for example, being on bread and water until Easter,[24] having to eat
and drink outside the refectory and being on bread and water,[25]
not receiving communion or entering the oratory,[26] being sent to
a remote house and not returning without the General Chapter's
permission,[27] expulsion and never returning, or expulsion and only
returning with the General Chapter's permission,[28] occupying
the lowest place for a year,[29] traveling to Cîteaux to be advised of
punishment,[30] being debarred from all offices and forbidden to ride
a horse without the General Chapter's permission,[31] being held in
prison by authority of the General Chapter,[32] or being put into
perpetual prison and, if it should become necessary, invoking the
secular arm,[33] and, worst of all, being put into perpetual prison,
restrained by chains, and sustained on the "bread of tribulation and
the water of distress" for the rest of one's life.[34] This last sentence
was imposed on the lay brother from Heilsbronn who wounded
his abbot with a cudgel and struck him in the head and the arms
with a knife, as a result of which the abbot fainted. The perpetrator

---

[24] *Statuta* 1233.67 (Canivez 2:125).

[25] *Statuta* 1234.4 (Canivez 2:127).

[26] *Statuta* 1190.75 (Canivez 1:132).

[27] *Statuta* 1232.24 (Canivez 2:104).

[28] *Statuta* 1203.50 (Canivez 1:294); 1202.14 (Canivez 1:277); 1209.11 (Canivez
1:359).

[29] *Statuta* 1206.50 (Canivez 1:329).

[30] *Statuta* 1205.14 (Canivez 1:310).

[31] *Statuta* 1277.28 (Canivez 3:168).

[32] *Statuta* 1261.32 (Canivez 2:482).

[33] *Statuta* 1241.19 (Canivez 2:233); 1256.7 (Canivez 2:422).

[34] *Statuta* 1246.31 (Canivez 2:307).

had escaped from a secular prison but was, if at all possible, to be held in the prison of his own monastery.

It is impossible to know what constituted the lay brothers' *transgressio* at Longpont in 1194 or what transpired at the Italian abbey of Arabona when in 1266 the lay brothers ill-treated (*male tractaverint*) their abbot.[35] More serious must have been the offense of the lay brothers of the Hungarian abbey of Szent-Gotthard in 1195 against one of the monks. It was described as "an unheard-of cruelty" (*inaudita crudelitate*), for they were given the sentence of being expelled from their house and from Hungary altogether, and they were ordered never to return.[36]

From what we know of the importance attached to the minutest breach of rules, such as a lay brother washing his shoes without first getting his grange master's permission, a transgression considered important enough to be included in three *exemplum* collections,[37] it is more than likely that sometimes incidents we would regard as trivial in nature found their way into *statuta*. There is, for example, no means of knowing what the *tumultus* caused by the lay brothers of Quincy in 1192 amounted to, although from another statute the same year we learn that it had been instigated by the lay brother Gaufridus Percesac from the neighboring house of Pontigny, who was to go to Clairvaux to receive his punishment.[38] Relatively common was the broad description "*excessus conversorum.*" As with the *tumultus* just mentioned, what constitutes an *excessus* is vague, although at times it apparently involved serious disturbances. Examples include statutes referring to Chaalis in 1204 in which there is merely a mention of *excessus conversorum*, to Bonnecombe in 1232 when the lay brother William Formos was sent to a remote house, to the violence at a grange belonging to Fontenay in 1233, to a lay brother at Eberbach who in 1238 seriously wounded the abbot, to lay brothers at Boschaud who in 1247 attacked the abbot and stole his seal, and to *conversi* at San Martino del Monte in Italy who in

---

[35] *Statuta* 1194.45 (Canivez 1:178); 1266.53 (Canivez 3:46).
[36] *Statuta* 1195.79 (Canivez 1:194).
[37] For this see pp. 147–48.
[38] *Statuta* 1192.19 (Canivez 1:149); 1192.26 (Canivez 1:150).

1271 violently ejected the abbot.[39] An incident at the Italian abbey
of Casanova, of which no detail is given, is described in 1260 as
*excessus gravissimus.*[40] In 1231 the abbot, monks, and lay brothers at
Pilis in Hungary were accused of *excessus intolerabiles et enormes.*[41]
In 1213 the *conversi* at Pilis had already been guilty of one of the
most serious offenses recorded in the *statuta*, burying a lay brother
alive.[42] Others guilty of exceptional crimes were the lay brothers
who at the Austrian abbey of Zwettl in 1275 cut off a monk's
nose,[43] and the lay brother at Heilsbronn in Bavaria who in 1246
killed the abbot and a monk who came to the abbot's defense. He
was arrested by the prior and put in prison. If he escaped he was
to be locked up for good. The abbot of Morimond, head of the
filiation, was sent to Heilsbronn to punish the accomplice *conversi*
and no further *conversi* were to be admitted without his express
consent.[44] Among a number of murders was "the tragic case" of
the lay brother from Tvis (*Tuta vallis*) in Denmark who in 1203
murdered one of the brothers, an incident considered sufficiently
important for the abbot of Cîteaux to be charged with dealing
with it.[45] Some decades later monks and *conversi* from Tvis appear
in the statutes again, accused of injuring their abbot.[46]

The lists, constituting a catalogue of revolt and violence, paint
a picture of unmitigated decadence. Yet one should remember that
the statutes were there to enforce discipline, to correct and punish
infringements of the rules and not to distribute accolades to the
observant. Also, bearing in mind that violence was endemic in the
Middle Ages, we might be surprised that there were only seventy

---

[39] *Statuta* 1204.34 (Canivez 1:303); 1232.24 (Canivez 2:104); 1233.67 (Canivez 2:125); 1238.52 (Canivez 2:195); 1247.20 (Canivez 2:318); 1271.17 (Canivez 3:96).

[40] *Statuta* 1260.25 (Canivez 2:466).

[41] *Statuta* 1233.51 (Canivez 2:121).

[42] *Statuta* 1213.46 (Canivez 1:413): *De conversis de Pelis qui conversum vivum subterraverunt.*

[43] *Statuta* 1275.24 (Canivez 3:145).

[44] *Statuta* 1246.31 (Canivez 2:307).

[45] *Statuta* 1203.50 (Canivez 1:294).

[46] *Statuta* 1268.37 (Canivez 3:64).

cases of homicide committed by monks as well as lay brothers over the whole period in seven hundred Cistercian monasteries.[47] The victims were frequently abbots, the first case being that of Gerard, abbot of Clairvaux from 1170, who was murdered by a monk named Hugh de Basoches in 1175 while on a visitation to Igny.[48]

A closer look at Donnelly's list of revolts further mitigates the part lay brothers played in the disturbances noted by the General Chapters in the last quarter of the twelfth century and throughout the thirteenth. Of the total of 123 incidents listed, Donnelly notes that five referred to nuns' houses, eleven were of unknown origin, and thirteen were what he describes as of "dubious nature." Of the remaining 94 disturbances, 19 were caused by monks, including abbots. A combination of abbots, monks, and *conversi* was responsible for 31 of the remaining 75 incidents and it is safe to conclude that, in the hierarchical world of medieval monasticism, the initiative for the majority of these came from abbots or monks and not lay brothers. That leaves only 44 disturbances out of a total of 123 caused by lay brothers alone. This figure corresponds closely with the figure of 50 given by Leclercq. Although Cassidy-Welch's interpretation of what constitutes a disturbance is more conservative than Donnelly's, only 22 of her 93 cases represent incidents for which lay brothers were not exclusively responsible. What is more surprising is that a large number of the statutes she cites, altogether 42, are not listed by Donnelly, evidence, it would seem, that her examination of the material was more thorough than Donnelly's.

If indeed the lay brothers on average outnumbered monks by two to one and in some cases by three to one as is generally agreed, the conclusion to be drawn from an investigation of the statutes recording lay brother transgressions is that the disciplinary problem was no greater among them, and possibly even less, than within the monastic community as a whole. This view is corroborated by a survey of runaway religious in England in the period 1251 to 1300, according to which of the altogether twenty-four named

---

[47] For this, see Dimier 1972 and Sayers 1990.
[48] King 1954, 254.

apostate Cistercians only seven were lay brothers.[49] If there was a culture of violence it included the monks as well as the *conversi* and simply reflected the general level endemic throughout society.

Further evidence that the standard of discipline among monks was causing concern is found in the grouping together of earlier General Chapter decisions in a more rational way according to subject, called Codifications, beginning in 1202 and amended and brought up to date in 1220, 1237, and 1257.[50] Of the total of fifteen distinctions, the first thirteen were devoted to monks, one, based largely on the *Usus conversorum*, to lay brothers, and finally one to nuns. Conspicuous among the headings of regulations referring to monks are homicides and beatings (*De homicidis et percussoribus*), excommunication for violent manhandling (*De excommunicatis pro violenta manuum iniectione*), which was the punishment for violence against other members of the Order prescribed by statute in 1206,[51] and conspiracies (*De conspiratione in electionibus fugienda*),[52] transgressions frequently associated with lay brothers. In the words of Jean Leclercq, the Codifications "tell us less about the original enthusiasm than about later deviations."[53]

Donnelly discusses other factors that brought about the decline of the lay brotherhood, but because his is the only monograph on lay brothers in English his emphasis on the violations of discipline has undoubtedly resulted in skewing the historiography of the lay brothers in the direction of exaggerating their behavioral problems and making them a symptom of or factor in the decline. His frequently quoted list of the 123 revolts has contributed to this perception and to the view encapsulated in Donnelly's own statement that "the recalcitrance of lay brothers in the monastic

---

[49] Logan 1996, 204–5. The proportion of apostate lay brothers is even smaller in subsequent periods but is not significant as it merely reflects the overall decline.

[50] Lucet 1964; Lucet 1977.

[51] *Statuta* 1206.7 (Canivez 1:321): *Quicumque manum violentam in monachum vel conversum iuiecerit, quia ipso facto excommunicatus est, vitetur ab omnibus, donec a proprio abbate absolvatur.*

[52] Lucet 1977, 123, 124, 144.

[53] Leclercq 1978, 222.

community was more than ordinary."[54] Writing in 1940 before the publication of Donnelly's work, David Knowles, in discussing the restlessness of the *conversi* in Wales, says that although some instructions may have been disregarded, "there is plenty of evidence that the disciplinary system was still in its main lines efficient."[55] Some years later Knowles, citing Donnelly's study, says that the *conversi* in Wales and in England "were drawn from a wilder and more shiftless population" and that in the thirteenth century "gangs of uncouth and often unruly lay brethren were getting out of hand."[56] Commenting on the decline of the institution of lay brothers as reflected in the decrees of the General Chapter in the thirteenth century, Louis Lekai claimed that "instances of revolt among the *conversi* increased steadily. It took the form of intimidation of monks at abbatial elections, violent seizure of monastic property and even plots against the lives of abbots or other superiors. Simultaneously with these riotous incidents the wholesale apostasy of lay brothers became a common phenomenon."[57]

The geographical distribution of revolts by lay brothers on their own, based on Donnelly's list, reveals that the largest number, seventeen altogether, occurred in France, approximately twice as many as in Germany or Italy and three times as many as in the British Isles.[58] Megan Cassidy-Welch has argued that the larger number of incidents reported in France than in England may be due to the greater likelihood that English monasteries would make use of the secular arm to quell revolt rather than taking their cases to the General Chapter.[59] This may be so, but the difference between incidents of revolt in the various countries roughly reflects the relative number of monasteries and suggests there may not be

---

[54] Donnelly 1949, 24. Cassidy-Welch recognizes this when she says: "Historians have tended to rely on the numbers of revolts reported to the General Chapter as evidence of a culture of violence among the lay brotherhood which, as I have argued, is a methodologically problematic enterprise" (Cassidy-Welch 2001, 186).

[55] Knowles 1940, 661.

[56] Knowles 1957, 126.

[57] Lekai 1977, 341.

[58] Donnelly 1949, 24.

[59] Cassidy-Welch 2001, 183–85.

any need to look further. A statute from 1272, although it specifically addresses a serious incident at the abbey of Amelungsborn in the diocese of Hildesheim, refers to the more general malaise in these words: "Frequent and continuously occurring and altogether tedious complaints have come to the ears of the General Council over the transgressions [*excessibus*] committed by the *conversi* in many abbeys of the Order against the abbots and the community."[60] The specific complaint was the threat of the lay brothers to kill or mutilate their abbot and some of the monks, as a result of which the abbot felt obliged to escape by the back door of the infirmary and seek refuge in a neighboring town, and yet it is said that "the folly of the lay brothers did not cease."[61]

An overview of all the material, however, highlights two areas of particular concern: the severe and protracted breaches of discipline at Eberbach and its daughter-house Schönau; and the problems at a number of houses attributed largely to alcohol abuse, notably in Wales but also, to a lesser extent, in England.

## Lay Brother Revolts at Eberbach and Schönau

Eberbach was the first daughter house of Clairvaux in Germany. Its origin may be traced back to Saint Bernard's visit to Mainz in 1135 and his meeting with Archbishop Adalbert, who in the following year replaced the Augustinian canons in Eberbach with monks from Clairvaux.[62] In the decades that followed, a number of daughter houses were established in remarkably rapid succession. In less than a decade Schönau (1142, became Cistercian 1145 as a daughter house of Eberbach, diocese of Worms) was founded, followed by Otterberg (around 1143, diocese of Mainz), Val-Dieu (1180, diocese of Liège, Belgium), and some years later Arnsburg (1197, diocese of Mainz). The regular succession of foundations

---

[60] *Statuta* 1272.5 (Canivez 3:104): *Cum frequens et assidua et omnino taediosa querela ad aures Capituli generalis devenerit super excessibus conversorum in multis abbatiis Ordinis contra abbates et conventus monachorum.*

[61] *Statuta* 1272.5 (Canivez 3:104).

[62] For the history of Eberbach, its granges and the growth of its estates, see Mossig 1978.

indicates the rapid growth and vitality of the community of Eberbach and is eulogized by Conrad of Eberbach, a former monk of Clairvaux and author of the *Exordium magnum*, in these words crediting the vital role of Saint Bernard:

> As a result of the blessing of such an eminent father this house grew in a wonderful way. It had numerous daughter houses and to our day is equal to its illustrious mother in its religious observance, its riches, its renown, the uprightness of its members and authority of its superiors, and the large size of its community, wherefore the church of Eberbach extends the light of its piety and reputation throughout the provinces of Germany.[63]

In 1211 the holdings of Eberbach were recorded in its Property Register, known as *Oculus memorie*, and included twelve granges, to which four more were added later. The abbey had property in eleven towns including important depots in Cologne, Frankfurt, and Mainz used in connection with its extensive wine trade. The abbot of Eberbach had the *cura animarum* of sixteen women's houses. Building began in the middle of the twelfth century and was completed in 1186; it included an enormous *domus conversorum* with a dormitory large enough to house two hundred lay brothers.

Construction had been interrupted in the 1160's, owing to the papal schism in which the Cistercians sided with Alexander III in opposition to Emperor Frederick Barbarossa's candidate, the antipope Victor IV. The crisis had a serious effect on morale at Eberbach and led to the exile of Abbot Eberhard to the abbey of Tre Fontane in Rome. Many of the monks left with him and normality returned only with the election in 1173 of his successor, Gerhard, the former prior of Clairvaux. Conrad of Eberbach refers to the prior, Meffridus or Meffried, who took over the direction of Eberbach in the absence of the abbot, as "an exceedingly devout man as well as one of

---

[63] *EM* 5.17 (Griesser, 326): *Haec itaque domus ad benedictionem tanti patris validissimum incrementum sumens optimeque matrizans religione, divitiis, celebri fama, personarum probitate, praelatorum auctoritate grandique conventus numerositate celsitudinem reverendae matris suae usque hodie aemulatur, ita ut in cunctis Germaniarum provinciis velut speciale religionis et honestatis speculum Everbacensis refulgeat ecclesia.*

considerable stature" (*vir quantum ad Deum religionis eximiae, quantum vero ad saeculum auctoritatis praecipuae*), saying that "in the middle of the terrible storm of the schism, which, in the time of Pope Alexander for long cruelly afflicted the church owing to the activities of the Emperor Frederick, [Meffried] applied himself with remarkable energy and foresight to save his monastery from total destruction."[64]

Conrad also describes how Meffried had to deal with a young monk called Henry, "a negligent brother, running away from work and discipline" (*dissolutus frater laboris et disciplinae fugitans*) who had attracted the attention of his brethren by his sluggishness and inefficiency and who eventually left the Order as an apostate.[65] His concerns, however, were not confined to the monks. News had reached Eberbach that Hildegard of Bingen had voiced her opinion about Cistercian *conversi* and Meffried wrote to her beseeching her "to send us the treatise which we have heard that, inspired by the Holy Spirit, you wrote concerning those secular and unlearned people who have taken up the spiritual way of life, those that we call *conversi*."[66]

Hildegard's reply, dated to around 1169, takes the form of an exegetical treatise in which she interprets the four beasts of Ezekiel in contemporary terms. Of these "the first living creature represents those who have assumed the hood [*cucullatos*], the first ones to withdraw themselves completely from the world like a mighty lion," in other words, monks and nuns, while "the second creature, like a calf, stands for those in clerical habit [*clericali habitu*] who zealously perform the divine sacrifice, that is, those who dig a trench around the vineyard of the Lord of Sabaoth and plow the field of the precepts of God," in other words, priests.[67] Hildegard then continues with her harsh assessment of the lay brothers:

---

[64] *EM* 5.17 (Griesser, 328): *qui etiam domum suam inter horribiles procellas scismatis, quod temporibus Alexandri papae factione Frederici tunc imperatoris ecclesiam Dei diutina evisceratione cruciavit, ne penitus destrueretur, mirabilis industriae providentia conservavit.*

[65] *EM* 5.17 (Griesser, 328).

[66] PL 197:260; trans. Hildegard of Bingen 1994, 182: *Insuper etiam obnixe rogamus, ut litteras quas de saecularibus et idiotis ad spiritualem conversationem conversis, quos nos conversos dicimus, Spiritu sancto vos scripsisse audivimus.*

[67] PL 197:262, 263; trans. Hildegard of Bingen 1994, 185–86: *Animal hoc primum cucullatos homines significat, qui primi in fortitudine leonis, se omnino a saecula*

These two types, symbolized by the lion and the calf, draw another type of person to themselves, whom they call *conversi*. Yet many of these are not truly converted, because they prefer dissension to rectitude, and in their works they resound with rashness, speaking thus about their superiors: Who are these people, and what are they; and what were we, and what are we now? And because they do this, they are like false prophets and they misjudge how God has established His people. You who fear God, therefore, hear what the Spirit of the Lord says to you: Rid yourselves of this wickedness, and cleanse yourselves so that henceforth you exercise more restraint than you have heretofore. Thus purify yourselves before the day of those tribulations when God's enemies, and yours, force you to flee into your proper place of humility and poverty.

Now masters, seize and correct those people I mentioned earlier, the lay brothers in your Order, because day and night the greatest part of them refuses to work, failing to serve perfectly either God or the world. Rouse them out of their ignorance, just as an experienced perfumer eradicates rank weeds from his garden.[68]

Nothing is known of the details or the scale of the problems at Eberbach or the extent to which Meffried was able to "seize and

---

abstrahunt. . . . *Secundum autem animal simile vitulo, in clericali habitu divino sacrificio insistentes ostendit, hos videlicet, qui vineam Domini Sabaoth circumfodiunt, et agrum praeceptorum Dei arando ubique evertunt.*

[68] PL 197:263–64; trans. Hildegard of Bingen 1994, 186–87: *Haec itaque praeclara genera, videlicet hominum illorum, qui per leonem et vitulum designati sunt, aliud quoddam genus hominum ad se trahunt, quos ipsi conversos vocant, quorum plurimi se ad Deum in moribus suis non convertunt, quia contrarietatem potius quam rectitudinem diligunt, et opera sua cum sono temeritatis agunt, de praelatis suis sic dicentes: Qui sunt, et quia sunt isti? Et quid fuimus, aut quid sumus nos? Et quoniam sic agunt, pseudo-prophetis similes sunt, et quia non recte dijudicant, quomodo Deus populum suum constituit. Vos ergo qui Deum timetis, audite Spiritum Domini ad vos dicentem: Haec supradicta mala a vobis auferte, et vosmetipsos ante dies tribulationum illarum purgate, cum inimici Dei et nostri vos fugabunt, et in rectum locum humilitatis et paupertatis vos convertent. . . . Nunc vos magistri supradictos homines, scilicet conversos, in ordine vestro corripite et, corrigite, quia plurima pars eorum nec in die, nec in nocte operatur, quoniam nec Deo, nec saeculo ad perfectum serviunt, et eos ab ignorantia ista excitate, velut bonus pigmentarius hortum suum ab inutilibus herbis purgat.*

correct" or "weed out" any recalcitrant lay brothers, but the chaos was most likely connected with the general unrest and uncertain conditions prevailing during the papal schism.

Conrad of Eberbach, as we have mentioned, gave a lengthy and detailed account of the serious revolt that occurred at Eberbach's neighboring daughter house of Schönau, the earliest recorded lay brother conspiracy.[69] Conrad relied on the eyewitness account of Theobald, who was later abbot of Eberbach, from 1206 to 1221, but who at the time was subcellarer at Schönau and had experienced the revolt.[70] This uprising happened around 1182 when the new abbot, Godfrey, attempted to abolish the old custom of annually issuing new boots to the *conversi* on Christmas Eve at the same time as the monks received theirs.[71] Although there is no evidence of a connection between this and the problems of lay brother discipline Meffried was grappling with at Eberbach at precisely the same time, it is at least possible that the unrest at the mother house was known at the daughter house and acted as an encouragement to the leader of the conspiracy, the one referred to as *non conversus sed perversus*. The abbot was fully entitled to abolish the custom for, in accordance with the *Usus conversorum*,[72] the issuing of new boots to lay brothers was against the practice of the Order, even though a statute from 1195 tells us that it was not always adhered to.[73] The lay brothers' argument was that "they considered their arduous and very demanding work unbearable."[74] Once all the lay brothers had returned from the granges for Christmas, the plan was to invade the monks' dormitory while the monks, wearing night slippers, were at Vigils in the church, remove the boots from all the beds, and cut them to pieces. The abbot was alerted to the plan and succeeded in thwarting it. Before the brothers were able to carry it out, their

[69] *EM* 5.10 (Griesser, 292–98).

[70] *EM* 5.10 (Griesser, 295): *cuius etiam relatione nos ista didicimus.*

[71] It has previously been said to have occurred in 1168 (Donnelly 1949, 34, 72; Newman 1995, 105) but it happened at the beginning of Godfrey's abbacy, which was 1182–1192 (Huffschmid 1892, 97).

[72] *UC* 19 (Waddell, 75; 191–92).

[73] *Statuta* 1195.30 (Waddell 2002, 327).

[74] *EM* 5.10 (Griesser, 293): *ut arduos durissimosque labores . . . intolerabiles iudicarent.*

CONTEMNVNT VETERES CONVERSI SVMERE BOTOS
QVOS ABBS POENA GODEFRIDVS CORRIPIT ACRI.

*Fig. 24* Pen-and-ink drawing of lay brothers at Schönau disobeying their abbot.

leader crashed to the ground and died. The other lay brothers interpreted this as divine retribution and abandoned the plan. At first
the abbot refused to bury the conspirator in consecrated ground,
but he relented after the other lay brothers had repented. In spite of
the severity of his crime, in the end the power of the community's
prayer saved him from the ultimate punishment.

The revolt is depicted in three early-sixteenth-century pen-
and-ink drawings that were intended as sketches for stained glass

windows or wall paintings in the monks' refectory at Schönau but
were never realized. One of them shows the abbot on the left with
the monks on one side and the *conversi* on the other (fig. 24).While
a kneeling monk on the left accepts the boots from the abbot, the
spokesman for the lay brothers on the right refuses them. On the
right of the picture the abbot is seen in the chapter house threat-
ening to punish them, while the devil is sitting on the shoulder of
the lay brother. Below is an inscription:"The *conversi* refuse to wear
the old boots, and for this Abbot Godfrey threatened them with a
severe punishment."Another picture shows the plan being hatched,
the devil presiding.The inscription reads:"The brothers conspire to
harm the monks, but God prevents the plot as the conspirator dies."

At the end of the long account of the Schönau boot revolt we
learn that lay brothers were still causing trouble at the mother house
of Eberbach.[75] In the words of Conrad: "The Lord unquestionably
viewed this house [Schönau] with serene affection. Proof of this
is found in the monastery of Eberbach where, a long time afterwards, the same question of new boots caused an uprising at the
malicious instigation of the devil. It provoked a great scandal and
such calamity that it would be better to cry than to have to put
these things into words."[76] In fact, after the problem at Schönau
had finally resolved itself, the attention of the General Chapter was
drawn in 1202 to a fresh incident when the cellarer Richard and
two lay brothers called Malchoadus and Grandus were accused of
having continuously caused disturbances. The abbot of Eberbach
was charged with notifying them that they were to be sent to
Clairvaux where the abbot was to provide them with lodging.[77]

Evidence that the disturbances continued at Eberbach is also
found at the end of a story by Caesarius of Heisterbach.[78] He writes

---

[75] According to Griesser the rebellion occurred around 1208 or 1210 (Griesser,
297 n. 1).

[76] *EM* 5.10 (Griesser, 297): *certe quam sereno pietatis suae oculo Dominus hanc
domum respexerit, Everbacensis probat ecclesia, in qua, cum longo post tempore novarum
botarum quaestio malignissimo daemonum instinctu mota fuisset, tantorum scandalorum tan-
tarumque calamitatum spinae inde eruperunt, ut eas magis flere libeat quam verbis explicare.*

[77] *Statuta* 1202.46 (Canivez 1:283).

[78] *DM* 5.29 (Strange 1:312–15; Scott and Bland 1:357–60).

that twelve years earlier, in other words probably during the first decade of the thirteenth century, William, the abbot of Eberbach's Belgian daughter house of Val Dieu, was on his way to Eberbach when he decided to visit the possessed sister of one of the Eberbach lay brothers so that he could give news of her when he reached Eberbach. The demon within her divulged to the abbot information about a number of members of the Eberbach community of which she could not possibly have been aware and, speaking privately to the lay brother Adolph, who had accompanied the abbot, the demon also appeared to know that Adolph had given some of the abbey's money without permission. When the demon was asked to show himself in his natural form the woman grew in stature, her eyes flashing and giving out smoke, which caused Adolph and the monk accompanying the abbot to fall down unconscious. The account ends with the demon divulging that the lay brothers at Eberbach have until recently still been causing problems and asking the abbot:

> "Where are you going?" and when the abbot had answered: "To Eberbach," he went on: "I too have been in Sueverbach and fared well enough there," ironically jesting on the name, for that was soon after the time that the lay brothers revolted against the Order. So dreadful and so poisonous is the sight of demons that it not only makes healthy men sick but sometimes even kills them.[79]

One of the many cases of *excessus conversorum* drawn to the attention of the General Chapter in 1238 concerned lay brothers from Eberbach but also brothers from Grandselve in southern France.[80] Again, in 1241 a lay brother of Eberbach who had seriously wounded his abbot was to be imprisoned for life if he could

---

[79] *DM* 5.29 (Strange 1:314–15; Scott and Bland 1:360): *Quo iturus es modo? Respondente Abbate, Eberbachum; subiunxit ille: Ego etiam in Sueverbacho fui, et satis ibi trufavi, yronice nomini alludens. Erat enim post illa tempora, quando conversi se ordini opposuerant. Tam horrendus et tam venenatus est daemonum aspectus, ut non solum sanos infirmet, sed nonnunquam etiam interficiat.*

[80] *Statuta* 1238.52 (Canivez 2:195).

be apprehended, if necessary with the help of the secular arm. Those who had collaborated in this crime were to receive the same sentence.[81]

Nothing more is heard about the Eberbach lay brothers for a couple of decades, but the ferment flared up again in 1261 when "a grave controversy in the house of Eberbach has been reported to the ears of the General Chapter. In these days especially grave offenses have been perpetrated by the lay brothers when one of their number has killed his abbot with sacrilegious hands."[82] The murderer was to be held in prison and no more lay brothers were to be received at Eberbach without the General Chapter's permission. The contribution of the lay brothers was evidently missed, for in 1269 the abbot of Eberbach received the General Chapter's permission to receive up to twenty lay brothers while the lay brother who had murdered his abbot was still in prison. If perchance he had avoided being convicted of homicide, the former sentence was still to remain in force.[83] In 1270 the General Chapter again required an assurance that the lay brother who had murdered his abbot was imprisoned and that no more than twenty lay brothers were to be received without the Chapter's permission.[84] In 1274 the abbot repeated his request to receive lay brothers again and it was decided that the number should be at the discretion of the visitor.[85]

## Alcohol-Induced Revolts at Welsh and English Houses

The word *excessus*, so widely used in the statutes to describe a variety of lay brother disturbances, seems particularly apt when applied to the many instances of alcohol abuse at the granges. As is well known, the production of both wine and beer formed an important

---

[81] *Statuta* 1241.19 (Canivez 2:233).

[82] *Statuta* 1261.32 (Canivez 2:482): *Cum ad aures Capituli generalis gravis querimonia sit delata, quod in domo Everbach per conversos multa sint enormia perpetrata, et maxime his diebus quidam conversus praedictae domus manibus sacrilegis abbatum suum interfecerint.*

[83] *Statuta* 1269.42 (Canivez 3:76).

[84] *Statuta* 1270.25 (Canivez 3:85).

[85] *Statuta* 1274.44 (Canivez 3:135).

part of the Cistercian economy in different parts of Europe. Vineyards formed some of the earliest grants at Cîteaux, but other French abbeys in Burgundy, Languedoc, and many other regions both farther north and farther south of Cîteaux were also substantial wine producers. Many other abbeys like Villers in Brabant, which had vineyards in the Moselle and Rhine valleys, Eberbach in the Rheingau, and, farther afield, Zwettl and houses along the Danube were also important wine producers. Brewhouses may be seen at Villers and Chorin in eastern Germany; remains of the brewery at Fountains in Yorkshire have been excavated; barley and hops are known to have been important crops at many abbeys and used for the brewing of a variety of grades of beer, the best being reserved for guests.[86]

Depending on the region, wine or beer formed part of the daily diet of monks and *conversi*. The increasing number of disturbances toward the end of the twelfth century may in part be attributed to the abuse of alcohol. Although there is no specific mention of drink in the *Usus conversorum*, it was probably included in the stipulation that lay brothers at the abbey follow the same dietary regime as the monks.[87] Lay brothers were forbidden both beer and wine at the granges and a statute from 1180 directed that during the harvest when monks were helping out at the granges they also were to comply with the prohibition.[88] In 1184 the banning of wine and beer at English granges was repeated and extended to Flanders, France, and Normandy, an acknowledgment that its enforcement had not always been possible and that, reluctantly, their consumption still had to be tolerated in other regions.[89] The following year the ban was extended to Aquitaine, then belonging to England.[90] The increasing severity of excessive drinking is indicated by a statute in 1186 ruling that inebriates were to be subject to the same excommunication as conspirators.[91]

---

[86] For Cistercian wine production and brewing, see Williams 1998, 336–42, 206.
[87] *UC* 15 (Waddell, 73, 188–89).
[88] *Statuta* 1180.10 (Waddell 2002, 90).
[89] *Statuta* 1184.15 (Waddel 2002, 118–19).
[90] *Statuta* 1185.9 (Waddell 2002, 124).
[91] *Statuta* 1186.9 (Waddell 2002, 135).

The problems caused by excessive beer-drinking seem to have been particularly acute in England and Wales, but occasionally the General Chapter was obliged to intervene in other countries. In 1199 the *conversi* at an unidentified grange of Fouchères were ordered to abstain from wine "as do lay brothers at other granges."[92] In 1201 the lay brothers of two houses, Le Val and Val-Dieu, were punished for serving wine at their granges.[93] In some cases, such as at Tamié in 1190, Fontmorigny in 1193, and Fontainejean in 1205, the abbots were accused of selling wine on tap at the granges, which was in contravention of the *Instituta*.[94] A further effort to limit the consumption of alcohol, both in the wine-producing *celliers* and in granges, was made in 1195 by allowing only one cooked dish when wine was served instead of the usual two.[95] This can only have been partially successful, for in the following year it was decreed that at granges where two dishes were served there was to be no wine.[96]

General breaches of decrees banning alcohol continued well into the thirteenth century.[97] Incidents attributable to the excessive consumption of wine or beer at English and Welsh houses led to the intervention of the General Chapter.[98] In spite of the earlier prohibition of beer at the granges of English houses in 1192, the General Chapter found it necessary to repeat the ban and to impose more serious penalties for nonobservance as well as to suspend the reception of lay brother novices until the situation had been rectified.[99] In 1190 the General Chapter noted that neither the

---

[92] *Statuta* 1199.38 (Waddell 2002, 434): *In Grangia de Fucheriis conversi a vino abstineant sicut et in aliis.*

[93] *Statuta* 1201.46 (Waddell 2002, 498). Other cases are *Statuta* 1236.4 (Canivez 2:153), and 1238.5, (Canivez 2:186).

[94] *Statuta* 1190.20 (Waddell 2002, 199); 1193.34 (Waddell 2002, 267–68); 1205.21 (Canivez 1:312); *Instituta* 54 (Waddell 1999, 349).

[95] *Statuta* 1195.18 (Waddell 2002, 318): *In Cellariis et Grangiis in quibus vinum bibitur, solummodo unum pulmentum habeatur.*

[96] *Statuta* 1196.51 (Waddell 2002, 369): *De duebus pulmentis non habendis ubi vinum bibitur in grangiis, nil novum statuitur.*

[97] *Statuta* 1236.4 (Canivez 2:153); 1238.5 (Canivez 2:186).

[98] For alcohol-related lay brother disturbances in England and Wales, see Knowles 1940, 656–60 and Cowley 1977, 119–21.

[99] *Statuta* 1192.16 (Waddell 2002, 242).

abbot nor the lay brothers at Margam in Wales had done their penance for allowing beer at the granges. Unless this was rectified the abbot was to have his faculties withdrawn, the sentence to be communicated to him by the abbots of Flaxley and Tintern, abbeys on the border between England and Wales.[100] The following year the General Chapter referred to the failure to comply with its terms as "enormities." The abbot was ordered to vacate his abbatial stall for forty days, to receive the penance of *levis culpa* for six days, one of them on bread and water, while the lay brother ringleaders of the disorders, Jordan the guest master and Ralph, were to report to the mother house of Clairvaux to be advised of the General Chapter's penance.[101] Although no offense is specified, the abbots of Margam and of another Welsh house, Strata Marcella, were summoned to Cîteaux in 1195 to submit themselves to the judgment of the General Chapter (*ad arbitrium Capituli satisfaciant*).[102]

The most serious revolt, however, occurred at Margam in 1206, when the lay brothers conspired against the abbot, threw the cellarer from his horse, armed themselves, and chased the abbot for fifteen miles before barricading themselves in their dormitory and withholding food from the monks. The offending lay brothers were to be punished as conspirators and their ringleaders were to go to Clairvaux on foot, after which they were dispersed throughout houses of the order. Until this was observed no more lay brother novices were to be received at Margam without the General Chapter's consent.[103]

---

[100] *Statuta* 1190.5 (Waddell 2002, 194).

[101] *Statuta* 1191.22 (Waddell 2002, 222).

[102] *Statuta* 1195.73 (Waddell 2002, 343).

[103] *Statuta* 1206.23 (Canivez 1:324): *Conversi de Margan qui conspiratione facta, insurrexerunt in abbatem, et cellerarium de equo eiecerunt, et insequentes armata manu abbatem usque ad XV millaria, qui etiam se in castellaverunt in dormitorio suo, et negato victu monachis, per omnia conspiratorum sententia puniantur, ita quod qui magis culpabiles inventi fuerint, tam de emissis quam de emittendis, ad portam Claraevallis pedites veniant, inde ad nutum abbatis Claraevallis per domos Ordinis dispergendi, hoc observato ne ultra conversi novitii in domo illa de Margan recipiantur, nisi de consensu Capituli generalis.*

Although hardly an objective observer of Cistercian affairs,[104] Gerald of Wales has a very different account of what happened at Margam, whose abbot, Gilbert, was evidently one of those Cistercians of whom he had from time to time fallen foul:

> The said abbot, being equally hated by his neighbors of the same Order through his flagrant injustices against them and by his own house for the internal discord he fomented, strove with all his power to pervert and change for the worse the constitution of his house which had been laid down in the past by religious and holy abbots. Wherefore, when certain monks and lay brothers, zealous for the reputation of the Order, dared to speak out against him, he hired and assembled evil minions of the secular power . . . and did not hesitate to drag them violently from their own house as captives . . . with hands tied behind their backs . . . from the cloisters to the prison cells of the castle.[105]

There is no way of knowing which version of these events is correct, but the fact that it is the last of a long line of offenses allegedly committed by lay brothers at Margam and reported to the General Chapter does suggest that they may have been guilty.

In retaliation for the abbot's attempt to enforce the ban on beer at the granges, the *conversi* at Cwmhir in Wales stole his horses. Like the Margam conspirators, in 1195 they were ordered to go to Clairvaux on foot to receive their sentence.[106] Another statute

---

[104] On Gerald of Wales, see Knowles 1940, 662–74.

[105] *Giraldi Cambrensis Opera* 1873, 4:141–42: *Porro dictus abbas et totiens repetitus, borealis patriae pariter et nutriturae, quoniam ab aquilone mala plerumque pandi solent, mores innatos mutare non praevalens, quoniam "natura expellas furca, etc."; sicut vicinis ordinis ejusdem viris, per apertas injurias, sic et domui propriae per intestinam discordiam molestus existens, statum domus suae, per abbates religiosos et sanctos olim ordinatum, in pejora pervertere et male permutare viribus totis est conatus. Unde et monachos quosdam et fratres zelum honoris et ordinis habentes, ideoque sibi contradicentes, convocatis ad hoc et conductis publicae potestatis ac laicae satellitibus pravis, et ad perpetranda facinorosa paratis, captivos a domo propria violenter abstrahere, cum tamen domus sua tutissimum de jure refugium cui[que offert], et maxime quoque domus sacra, ligatis a tergo manibus, quod horribile quidem est dictu sed longe horribilius fuerat visu, a claustris ad carceres et castra perducere non abhorruit.*

[106] *Statuta* 1195.62 (Waddell 2002, 340).

from the same year underlines the seriousness of the abuse and the difficulty of enforcing its observance. All the abbots of Wales are reminded of the ban and ordered not to receive any further lay brother novices until water was made the only drink available at the granges.[107] The warning was not heeded everywhere: although beer-drinking is not specifically mentioned, in 1196 an *excessus conversorum* is said to have occurred at another Welsh house, Strata Florida, which the abbot of Whitland was ordered to visit in person to correct.[108] In the same year the earlier decision prohibiting beer at the Welsh granges was confirmed and the reception of novices banned until the Chapter's decree was heeded.[109]

Revolts by lay brothers continued at Welsh houses well into the thirteenth century. In 1269 the General Chapter was forced to intervene owing to the "frequent and rash audacity of certain lay brothers of Neath" who had absconded, taking their abbot's horses with them. It is not known whether their crime was alcohol-induced, but they were ordered to return within a month, failing which they would be excommunicated and, when apprehended, thrown into prison.[110]

An unusual case occurred at the English abbey of Croxden in 1202 when the abbot was punished by the General Chapter for having given the lay brothers on the granges permission to drink wine.[111] The matter was not resolved, for seven years later the lay brothers were said to be still drinking wine "to the scandal of the Order and of all neighboring abbeys."[112]

---

[107] *Statuta* 1195.72 (Waddell 2002, 343).

[108] *Statuta* 1196.8 (Waddell 2002, 354).

[109] *Statuta* 1196.9 (Waddell 2002, 355).

[110] *Statuta* 1269.19 (Canivez 3:72): *Contra frequentem et temerariam quorumdam conversorum de Net audaciam.*

[111] *Statuta* 1202.10 (Canivez 1:276). The statute refers to *Vallis S. Mariae* which may be either Croxden or the French abbey Le-Val (Seine-et-Oise) or the German abbey of Marienthal, but as the preceding statute also refers to an English abbey and the following statute in the 1209 reference likewise, both statutes most likely refer to Croxden.

[112] *Statuta* 1209.19 (Canivez 1:360): *in scandalum Ordinis et monasteriorum totius vicinae.*

The most serious case of irregularity concerning beer-drinking occurred at Garendon in Leicestershire, founded in 1133, only five years after its mother house, Waverley, the first Cistercian foundation in England. The Earl of Leicester had donated to the abbey a grange devoted to beer-production, which the General Chapter in 1196 understandably decreed was no longer to be used for the consumption of the *conversi* but sold and the income to be put to other uses or the grange returned to the earl.[113] The resignation of Abbot William recorded in the Waverley *Annals* the previous year may have been occasioned by problems related to the beer-producing grange. He was succeeded by Reginald, who had been abbot of Merevale. He must have made an attempt to enforce the ban, for, according to the entry in the Waverley *Annals* for 1196, one night he was seriously wounded in the infirmary and the General Chapter decreed that all the *conversi* were to be dispersed.[114] The story is repeated in the Margam *Annals*, in which it is said that the perpetrator acted with the consent of other lay brothers and that they were all to be evicted.[115] According to the General Chapter record the matter was more serious: the abbot had been murdered and letters were sent to King Richard I, the archbishop of Canterbury, the bishop of Lincoln in whose diocese Garendon lay, and the earl of Leicester, requesting their help in apprehending and punishing the offenders. The actual murderers, if caught, were to be imprisoned for life while those who had conspired with them were to be exiled to other houses, never to return, and barred from communion except at Easter and when in danger of death.[116]

---

[113] *Statuta* 1196.25 (Waddell 2002, 360): *Grangia quae data est a Comite pro Ceruisia conversis facienda, in eos usus de cetero non expendatur, sed in alias utilitates Monasterii deputabitur aut Comiti reddatur.*

[114] *Annales de Waverleia* 1865, 250: *1196 Reginaldus abbas Geroldoniae graviter vulneratus est in infirmario suo nocte, propter quod jussum est per generale capitulum Cistercii, ut omnes conversi ejusdem loci dispergerentur.*

[115] *Annales de Margam* 1864, 23: *Reginaldo, Gereldoniae abbate, a quodam converso suo graviter in infirmario vulnerato, aliis conversis consentientibus, jussum est in generali capitulo Cistercii omnes conversos ejusdem loci amoveri.*

[116] *Statuta* 1196.24 (Waddell 2002, 359–60).

### *Excessus Conversorum* and the Decline of the Lay Brotherhood

The long catalogue of murders, injuries, plots, uprisings, brawls, and conspiracies committed by lay brothers, as reported to the General Chapter for investigation and punishment, represents the other side of the coin to the picture of the simple and humble, and at times saintly, *conversi* frequently presented in the *exemplum* literature. The level of harmony or discord depended on a number of factors. One was the way the lay brothers were dealt with by their superiors and especially their abbots, in particular the extent to which the abbots heeded the injunction of the Rule that what they had "undertaken is the charge of weakly souls, and not a tyranny over the strong."[117] On the other hand, the ability of the lay brothers, many of whom were not in the monastery by choice, to subject themselves to the discipline expected of them was often tested to the breaking point. Examples abound of the kind of situation Stephen Harding foresaw when he decided to write the *Usus conversorum*.[118] He gave as his reason the likely danger of some abbots holding the lay brothers "in contempt because of their innate simplicity" (*pro ingenita eorum simplicitate contemptui habentes*) while others would give in "to their murmuring more than is expedient" (*murmurationi cedentes, ultra quam expediat animabus*).[119] The abbot of Schönau who refused to give the lay brothers their boots, although perfectly within his rights, may have belonged to the first category, as may the abbot of Margam, guilty of "flagrant injustices" if Gerald of Wales is to be believed, while the abbot of Piscaria who repeatedly failed to reprimand his erring lay brothers and the abbot of Croxden who allowed his *conversi* to drink wine may be said to represent the second category, as may the exiled abbot of Eberbach who, through no fault of his, would have been unable to give his "care and attention" to "those known to be simpler and uneducated."[120]

---

[117] *RB* 27.6 (McCann, 77).

[118] Waddell 2000, 21.

[119] *UC* Prologue (Waddell 56, 164).

[120] *UC* Prologue (Waddell 56, 165): *Nisi quod qui simpliciores et sine litteris esse noscuntur, ipsos magis nostra cura et opera indigere ratio consulta respondet.*

No revolts are recorded in the General Chapter statutes in the first two-thirds of the twelfth century, and the increase in incidents after that is only gradual. This seems to vindicate the importance the early Cistercians attached to trivial breaches of discipline, such as dozing off during services, attachment to small articles of private property, and failing to seek permission for minor tasks like washing shoes, in the belief that such minor transgressions might likely lead to more flagrant neglect. Conrad of Eberbach remarked that in his day there were still those in the Order who were not too concerned about minor faults, a position he forcefully refuted, saying:

> If there are any, God forbid, who think they can commit these little faults without great danger to their souls, and who neglect to remedy their transgressions by the worthy fruits of confession and penance, they can be certain that they cannot stay at this level of negligence, but little by little as they become less careful, the increasing bilge water of negligence will without doubt plunge the ship of their consciences into the depths unless God helps them. Wherefore, let all of us who are professed in this most illustrious Cistercian Order have the zeal to observe faithfully not only the major, but even the least of all its institutes, lest perchance—may it never happen—the fervor of the Order should grow cold and pass away in our times, and we, if we are found guilty before the just Judge of such great sacrilege, shall with the impious receive his strict sentence: not to see the glory of God.[121]

In the introduction to a story on disobedience Conrad repeated his warning against minor transgressions, evidence of the importance he attached to the danger of their escalation, saying: "There

---

[121] *EM* 4.24 (Griesser, 252); CF 72:365: *Ceterum, si qui sunt, quod Deus avertat, qui se haec levia absque gravi periculo animae suae facere posse putant et tales excessus suos condignos confessionis et paenitentiae fructus diluere negligunt, certi sint, quia hoc negligentiae gradu non haerebunt, sed paulatim ipsis minus curantibus sentina negligentiae excrescente navis conscientiae ipsorum sine dubio, nisi Deus succurrat, in profundum demergetur. Quapropter omnes nos, qui praeclarissimo Cisterciensi ordini professionis titulo astricti sumus, studeamus non solum maiora, sed etiam minora eius instituta omni sollicitudine servare, ne forte, quod absit, fervor ordinis intepescat et pereat temporibus nostris et nos, si tanti sacrilegii rei coram iusto iudice inventi fuerimus, districta eius sententia tollamur cum impiis, ne videamus gloriam Dei.*

are some who very carefully and quite properly avoid this kind of flagrant and clearly mortal rebellion, but are less attentive to the little things they are ordered to do, and easily exceed the limits of obedience. Although they attempt to wash away their stains of disobedience by confession and penitence, it is presumption rather than true contrition of heart that makes them do so."[122]

Uniformity in all essentials, even in the observance of minutiae, was indispensable to the maintenance of discipline as well as to strengthening the link between Cistercian monasteries throughout Europe. It was enshrined by Stephen Harding in the *Ecclesiastica officia* and the *Usus conversorum*, regulating the lives of monks and lay brothers respectively. *Negligentia* could and did lead to increasing incidents of breaches of discipline as the enthusiasm of the earlier decades gave way to the changing circumstances of the thirteenth century. In spite of their constant warnings, writers like Conrad of Eberbach were unable to halt this development. Although the disciplinary problem among lay brothers was no greater than that of the monks, the numerous complaints against both that were drawn to the attention of the Chapter at Cîteaux can only be evidence of a general decline and not one confined to lay brothers. Censure of the greed of the Cistercians was not confined to their severest critics outside the Order such as Walter Map and Gerald of Wales. Admitting the decline from earlier fervor, Caesarius of Heisterbach observed that "our own order has often been condemned by the world for avarice."[123] But the severest condemnation comes from the Beaupré compiler, who specifically mentions monks as well as lay brothers as the culprits. He has a remarkable story in which an English hermit has a vision of the Virgin, according to whom "the greatest cause of sorrow was that those who were united with me in

---

[122] *EM* 5.9 (Griesser, 288); CF 72:422: *Sunt vero nonnulli, qui, licet ab hac grossa et quodammodo manifeste peremptoria inobedienta tota sollicitudine, sicut dignum est, declinent, in minoribus tamen praeceptis per obedientiam iniunctis minus cauti limitem obedientiae facile transgrediuntur, sed etsi postea reatum inobedientiae confessione et paenitentia dilure conantur, magis hoc perfunctorie quam vera cordis contritione facere comprobantur.*

[123] *DM* 4.57 (Strange 1:224; Scott and Bland 1:255): *Saepe ordo noster a saecularibus de avaritia iudicatur.*

a very special way, and in whom I used to find rest from the scorn of others, have cruelly withdrawn themselves from my embrace."[124] The esteem in which Mary was held by the Cistercians makes the fierceness of her diatribe the more momentous:

> The monks and lay brothers enter the infirmary without good reason. They grumble about the food. They squabble about the wine. They do not want to go in to sing the psalms or to work unless their stomachs are full and they are belching [Ps 44:2]. They mock the poverty of the Order in food and in dress. All they seek in the Order is bodily pleasure and vanity of heart. They say or do what is not right to say or do and what is inappropriate to think about.[125]

The compiler's harsh words were intended to exhort the monks and lay brothers to return to their *sancto proposito* (holy purpose). As we have seen, the statistics of incidents of transgressions contained in General Chapter statutes point to a general problem of discipline for which the lay brothers were no more, and perhaps even less, responsible than the monks, whom they outnumbered by two to one or even at times three to one. Departure from the founders' ideals is evidence of a general decline, and breaches of lay brother discipline cannot be said to constitute a major contributing factor in the decline of the institution, as has so often been asserted. The decline must therefore be largely attributable to other causes, as we shall see in the next chapter.

---

[124] BC fol. 126r, quoted in McGuire 1983, 249: *Maximam vero mihi luctus prestat materiam paucula gens illa que mihi specialiter adherere colebat et in qua solebam requiescere a fastidio ceterorum et nunc se a meis amplexibus crudeliter avulsit.*

[125] BC fol. 126v, quoted in McGuire 1983, 249: *Monachi et conversi sine causa intrant infirmitorium. Murmurant pro carnibus. Litigant pro vino. Nesciunt vel illi psallere vel isti laborare nisi pleni et ructantes. Paupertatem ordinis in victu et vestitu subsannant. Nil querunt in ordine nisi voluptatem corporis et vanitatem cordis. Dicunt et faciunt quod nec dici vel fieri fas est et quod nefas est cogitari.*

# Chapter 13

# Decline and Near Extinction

In the story of the decline of the Cistercian lay brotherhood there are two crucial dates: 1208, when the General Chapter explicitly sanctioned the departure from the early prescription of direct land cultivation and gave the first tentative permission for the leasing of properties, and 1215, when the Fourth Lateran Council abolished the tithe exemption previously enjoyed by the Cistercians. To these must be added general social and economic changes beyond the control of the monks, and not least the famine, flooding, plagues, and war that further decimated the lay brother population as well as the pool of potential recruits. In some places it led to its virtual extinction.

The emergence and rapid growth of the Cistercian lay brotherhood and, after approximately a hundred years, the beginning of its decline, followed by a century of further reduction, should be seen in the context of the general economic situation. After the early medieval stagnation in western and central Europe caused by waves of invaders, there was a burst of economic activity beginning around the year 1000. In the next three centuries the population of the whole of Europe doubled from approximately thirty-four million to sixty-eight million.[1] The upturn in the economy was particularly rapid from the beginning of the eleventh century. Although the turning point came at different times in different areas, evidence of an expanding economy came early to Burgundy, Flanders, and the Rhineland—precisely the heartland of the early

---

[1] For this and what follows, see Pounds 1974.

Cistercian expansion—while Scandinavia and eastern Europe were among the latest to benefit. The period of growth culminated in the first half of the thirteenth century; after that there remained little uncultivated land in most of western Europe, although there was still room for expansion in eastern Europe. By the fourteenth century the economy had ceased to expand and a period of stagnation and contraction followed.

## From Direct Cultivation to Leasing

Central to the Cistercian reform was the rejection of income from "churches, altars, sepulchers, tithes from the labor or husbandry of another, rural domains, serfs, land rents, revenues from ovens and mills, and other such things contrary to monastic purity."[2] Instead, the monks were to rely on the direct cultivation of the estates under their own control, thereby providing them with ideal conditions by building "monasteries not in cities, nor in walled settlements or villages, but in places removed from populated areas."[3] They were to "draw their subsistence from the work of their hands, from farming, and from animal husbandry" and for this they might have granges "to be supervised and administered by lay brothers."[4]

The rejection of the manorial system previously embraced by the black monks, an essential plank of the Cistercian reform, could no longer be sustained. In 1208 the General Chapter permitted the leasing of "lands that were less useful or too distant for suitable cultivation,"[5] acknowledging that a large number of granges were located more than a day's journey from the abbey, farther than the

[2] *Instituta* 9 (Waddell 1999, 328; 460): *Ecclesias, altaria, sepulturas, decimas alieni laboris vel nutrimenti, villas, villanos, terrarum census, furnorum et molendinorum redditus, et cetera his similia monastice puritati adversantia.*

[3] *EP* 15 (Waddell 1999, 254; 435): *non in civitatibus nec in castellis aut in villis sed in locis a frequentia populi semotis coenobia construxisse.*

[4] *Capitula* 15 (Waddell 1999, 189; 410): *debet provenire victus de labore manuum, de cultu terrarum, de nutrimento pecorum . . . per conversos custodiendas et procurandas.*

[5] *Statuta* 1208:5 (Canivez 1:346): *De terris qui minus utiles fuerint aut sic remotae quod utiliter excoli non possint, sic dispensat Capitulum generale, ut liceat iis qui tales habuerint dare ad medietatem vel aliter prout poterunt competenter.*

statutes allowed.[6] But even before the concession some abbeys had leased land, including Poblet in Catalonia, which leased the entire grange of Cérvoles in 1180, Margam and Strata Florida in Wales, Holy Cross in Ireland, and Fountains in Yorkshire.[7] Sources of income once forbidden (for example, whole villages or individual holdings of developed land owing rents and services, mills and ovens run for profit, as well as churches and other forms of ecclesiastical revenue) had for long been widely accepted. As we have seen, monasteries had already been given lands too far from the abbey for the monks themselves to cultivate them. The Order's development received considerable impetus with the incorporation in 1147 of the thirty houses of the Savigny family as well as the smaller families of Obazine and Cadouin. The economic practices of these new members of the Order varied from those of the Cistercians, and they were not obliged to conform to the Cistercian norm but were allowed to retain their unauthorized possessions after they had joined. It may also be, as Lawrence McCrank has argued,[8] that the farther removed the date of an abbey's foundation was from that of Cîteaux itself, the greater the divergence of its economy from the Cistercian ideal. Furthermore, the greater the distance from Cîteaux, the more likely geographical, cultural, and social factors were to compound this difference from the Burgundian norm. This would have applied to the tracts of land owned by many abbeys in eastern Europe, estates so huge that the monks would not have been able to cultivate them themselves.[9]

The concession granted in 1208 was reversed by the General Chapter in 1214, suggesting that some Cistercians were making a valiant attempt to adhere to direct cultivation as long as possible. The ban against "receiving or acquiring lands, vineyards, ovens, or mills unless they were solemnly given as a free gift" was renewed, only to be reversed again the following year with the qualifying

---

[6] *Instituta* 5 (Waddell 1999, 459).
[7] Williams 1998, 296; Lekai 1977, 307.
[8] McCrank 1976, 164–65.
[9] Donnelly 1949, 41.

clause that newly acquired land was to be the first to be leased.[10] In 1224 the leasing of any land was permitted, subject to the abbot's approval, and, for the first time granges are specifically mentioned.[11] Unrestricted approval of the system of leasing was finally obtained through a bull of December 18, 1302 from Pope Boniface VIII as a reward for the support the Cistercians had given the Pope in his struggle with King Philip IV of France.[12]

## Abolition of Tithe Exemption

Parallel with the widespread changeover to leasing, the gradual extension of the Cistercian freedom from the payment of tithes had the effect of removing the advantage of direct cultivation and thereby making the vast majority of *conversi* superfluous. The closeness of the two key dates of 1208 and 1215 is no coincidence. The founding Cistercians not only renounced the acceptance of tithes but in 1132, in recognition of their support of Innocent II in the schism, they were granted exemption from paying tithes. Previous tithe-privileges had been limited to individual monasteries, but the Cîteaux grant extended the freedom to include "the tithes of the goods which you and the brothers of your entire congregation produce by your own hands and for your own use in order that you may be able to serve God more securely and freely."[13]

The situation that existed when the tithe-privilege was first introduced soon underwent a rapid change. The policy had been designed to help a relatively small number of emergent monasteries,

---

[10] *Statuta* 1214.54 (Canivez 1:427–28): *terras, vineas, furnos vel molendina emere vel acquirere, nisi in puram eleemosynam et solemnem donationem nobis donata fuerint.* *Statuta* 1215.64, 65 (Canivez 1:448).

[11] *Statuta* 1224.10 (Canivez 2:31): *Indulgetur abbatibus Ordinis nostri auctoritate Capituli generalis, qui sibi crediderint expedire, dare saecularibus terras, vineas et etiam grangias, et alias possessiones ad excolendum cum consensu et voluntate conventus sui et patris abbatis, vel visitatoris, facta tamen prius de decimis compositione assensu et auctoritate episcopi diocesani.*

[12] Donnelly 1949, 69.

[13] Innocent II *Ep.* 83 (PL 179:123): *Statuimus ut de laboribus quos vos, et totius vestrae congregationis fratres propriis manibus et sumptibus colitis.* For this see Constable 1964, 240–42.

many of which were located on virgin soil on which no tithes had previously been paid and were badly in need of material support to ensure their survival. The benefit was great and was obtained at a very small cost. The loss to owners of ecclesiastical tithes was at first minimal and the gain of the monks' prayers and prestige within the diocese great. For this reason the privilege originally received widespread support. A serious problem had, however, been created by the phenomenal rate at which the monasteries increased. The growth in the number of holdings through extensive donations, consisting more and more often of lands that had previously been tithed, resulted in a serious loss of revenue to the tithe owners. The first reaction among the dispossessed tithe owners came under Pope Adrian IV (1154–1159), when the privilege was limited by making a distinction between lands previously tithed (*decimae veteres* or *labores*) and new lands (*novalia*).[14] In future tithes the immunity was restricted to the new (noval) lands that had been brought under cultivation by the monks for the first time and for which, therefore, no tithes had ever been exacted. The standard formula for freedom from tithes, which began with the words *sane laborum*, was changed to *sane novalium*.

Under Alexander III (1159–1181) the Cistercians regained their freedom, and grants of tithe-freedom were repeated under his successors Lucius III (1181–1185) and Urban III (1185–1187). Opposition flared up, however, and as the terms of numerous grants were being misinterpreted by tithe owners in an attempt to curtail the monastic freedom, Alexander III intervened, pointing out that if his intention had been to restrict the immunity of the Cistercians to noval tithes he would have referred not to their *labores*, but only to their *novalia*.[15] In 1186 Urban III addressed a bull to the Danish archbishop Absalon of Lund in support of the abbey of Øm (*Cara insula*), whose tithe-privilege had been challenged. The monks fully appreciated the importance of the document and incorporated it into the *Chronicle* of the house. In this the Pope states that

[14] For the crisis of monastic freedom see Constable 1964, 270–306.
[15] Mahn 1951, 108.

in spite of the fact that our Fathers and predecessors have granted the brethren of Øm as well as other brethren of the Cistercian Order that they are not bound to pay tithes to any man on the work of their own hands or at their own cost, and that we have since conceded and confirmed this, yet there are those who, acting against the grant of the apostolic see, presume to claim and coerce them to pay tithes, to distort the contents of the apostolic privileges by a false and incorrect interpretation and to maintain that these refer to *novalia* where in fact it is written *labores*.[16]

The damage done to the reputation of the Cistercians as a result of the exercise of their tithe-freedom and their thereby growing rich at the expense of others was considerable. In 1180 the General Chapter ordered that in future, in spite of their exemption, when lands were acquired on which tithes had previously been paid the monks should continue to pay these, unless the tithes had also been donated to them or an arrangement had been made.[17] A statute in 1199 refers to the prohibition passed forbidding the acquisition of further lands by purchase (*de emptione terrarum*), the purpose of which was to "moderate greed" and thus to remove the cause for complaint.[18] The prohibition was repeated in 1214.[19] The final solution came with the Fourth Lateran Council in 1215.[20] It was decreed that the Cistercians were to pay tithes on all lands acquired in future, whether cultivated by the monks themselves or at their own cost, whereas lands held before the council, but brought into cultivation after it, were to remain free from tithes.

---

[16] *Diplomatarium Danicum* I, 3:122: *Accepimus autem quod cum fratribus Careinsule sicut aliis omnibus Cisterciensis ordinis fratribus a patribus et predecessoribus nostris concessum sit, et a nobis ipsis postmodum indultum et confirmatum, ut de laboribus quos propriis manibus aut sumptibus excolunt nemini decimas solvere teneantur quidam ab eis nichilominus contra indulgentiam sedis apostolice decimas exigere et extorquere presumunt. et prava et sinistra interpretatione apostolicorum privilegiorum capitulum pervertentes. Asserunt de novalibus debere intelligi, ubi noscitur de laboribus esse inscriptum.*

[17] *Statuta* 1180.1 (Waddell, 86).

[18] *Statuta* 1199.71 (Waddell, 446).

[19] *Statuta* 1214.54 (Canivez 1:427–28).

[20] Mahn 1951, 112.

In 1224 Honorius III extended the privilege to lands leased out to tenants. Again various interpretations were put on the terms of the decree by interested parties, and this led to further clarification by successive popes. In practice this tended to have the effect of extending the privilege.

The last important development of the freedom from tithes came in the second half of the thirteenth century as a result of the gradual change in the Cistercian system of land administration. As leasing became increasingly widespread, the privilege, which had until then been confined to lands cultivated by the monks themselves or at their own cost, was extended to include lands farmed out to others for cultivation provided no one had been receiving the tithes of these lands up to that time. The freedom went further than at any time even before the Lateran Council.[21] The papacy, in the matter of monastic tithes, "always showed a dual regard for maintaining the privileges of the Cistercians . . . and preventing the Cistercians from causing trouble in the church by abusing their privileges."[22] The economic decline of the late thirteenth and fourteenth centuries finally made it desirable that the trend toward limitation should be reversed, yet without returning to unlimited freedom. The advantage of direct cultivation and, with the decline in the lay brother population, the incentive to lease lands, including whole granges, to peasant tenants became increasingly tempting.

### Early Decline of Lay Brother Population

The earliest evidence of a shortage of lay brothers comes in a statute from 1237 in which abbeys with no more than eight *conversi* were granted permission to employ lay workers in the kitchens.[23] Hiring seculars to work in the kitchens or infirmaries had previ-

---

[21] Mahn 1951, 114–16.

[22] Mahn 1951, 116: *la papauté fait montre toujours du double souci de maintenir les privilèges des Cisterciens . . . et d'éviter que les Cisterciens ne viennent, en abusant de leurs privilèges, à causer du trouble dans l'Église.*

[23] *Statuta* 1237.3 (Canivez 2:169): *Omnibus abbatibus qui non habent plusquam octo conversos indulgetur a Capitulo generali ut in coquinis suis tam in abbatiis quam alibi faciant, si voluerint, saeculares deservire, servata in omnibus in quantum poterunt honestate.*

ously been forbidden.[24] James Donnelly's characterization of Cistercian *conversi* as "unskilled, uncouth, unlettered, and, especially, undisciplined,"[25] and the impact on the historiography of the lay brothers of his list of 123 revolts, have led some to conclude that the decline in the number of lay brothers resulted from the deliberate policy of the monks rather than a shortage of recruits.[26] The decline, which at first was relatively slow, may be seen in relation to the lessening of the need for lay brothers as workers, as a direct result of the reorganization of the Cistercian agrarian economy. In fact, leasing had already begun at Hauterive in Switzerland by 1217, even though the majority of its eleven granges remained in direct cultivation until the fourteenth century.[27] Other early leases may be traced at the German abbey of Herrenalb in 1220, when its Ottersweiler grange was split up and leased to four tenants, and at the French Aubespierre in 1229.[28] There were, for example, still lay brothers in 1241 on seven granges belonging to the English abbey of Kingswood, probably the total number at that time.[29] Elsewhere granges had not even been established. For example, three of the granges belonging to Meaux in Yorkshire were first established in 1235 and continued to be enlarged until 1279.[30] Among the early leases, on the other hand, were the grange at Bombarral belonging to Alcobaça in Portugal (1248) and the grange of Ceule belonging to the French Vaucelles (1263).[31] Realizing the drawback of leasing entire granges, the General Chapter in 1261 decreed that the traditional privilege of hospitality offered to visiting abbots on granges

---

[24] *Statuta* 1189.27 (Canivez 1:115); 1191.71 (Canivez 1:144); 1195.6 (Canivez 1:183).

[25] Donnelly 1949, 70.

[26] According to David Knowles, "*conversi* were becoming more of a liability than an asset, and it seems certain that in England, as on the Continent, it was desire on the part of the monks to limit their intake rather than a failure in the springs of supply, that led to the gradual decline of the class" (Knowles 1955, 126).

[27] Lekai 1977, 309.

[28] Elm 1982, 153.

[29] Donnelly 1954, 418.

[30] *Melsa Chronica* 1866–1868, 2:56, 59, 115, 153.

[31] Williams 1998, 296.

controlled by the monks themselves was to remain intact even after they had been leased to seculars.[32] In 1274 the General Chapter noted that "at the present time the Order was suffering greatly from a shortage of lay brothers" and therefore granted permission for "reliable and honest" lay workers to serve in the kitchens.[33] In 1267 abbots who had previously been accompanied to the Chapter by lay brothers were in future allowed the use of grooms instead.[34]

The changeover from an economy of direct cultivation to one of rents and leases, at first slow, gathered pace in the last two decades of the thirteenth century. By 1288, for example, a considerable part of the holdings of Kirkstall abbey in Yorkshire had been leased.[35] Yet there were still many granges being farmed by the monks themselves well into the fourteenth century and some even until the second half. Of the total of twenty-three granges belonging to Meaux only five were leased in the period 1286 to 1310 and another five were still under monastic control in 1396.[36] The changeover at Meaux was not always a success. Abbot Roger (1286–1310) reversed the policy of his predecessor. The grange of Skyrene had been let for fifteen years, but after only seven years he bought it back for 320 pounds, incurring a loss of 150 pounds. By the fifteenth century eight of the thirty granges belonging to Fountains were still managed by *custodes*, that is either monks, *conversi*, or laymen.[37]

The gradual change from monastic to peasant cultivation was sometimes accomplished in several stages. With the decline in the lay brother population, hired laborers or *mercenarii* came to play an increasing part, and the last role the *conversi* fulfilled on the granges and in the workshops at the abbey was that of supervising secular

---

[32] *Statuta* 1261.10 (Canivez 2:477).

[33] *Statuta* 1274.12 (Canivez 3:128–29): *Cum praesenti tempore Ordo multam patiatur penuriam conversorum, et ipsos conversos maioribus et honestioribus negotiis deceat occupari, permittitur auctoritate Capituli generalis ut qui voluerint in coquinis per servientes laicos non suspectos, sed bonae famae et conversationis honestae, sibi faciat deservire.*

[34] *Statuta* 1267.8 (Canivez 3:49).

[35] Barnes 1984, 45.

[36] Donnelly 1954, 435.

[37] Bishop 1936, 197.

hands. It is possible that in 1267 Oluf Kviter, who had donated land to Øm (*Cara insula*) in Denmark upon entering as a lay brother, was the lone lay brother *grangiarius* of Tåning, one of only two granges remaining to a house that had previously had sixteen.[38] Here and at other Danish houses, in order to compensate for the shortage of their own labor force, the Cistercians had also acquired villages in the neighborhood of their granges to act as depots for the collection of rents in kind. It was in their capacity as overseers that the lay brothers became regarded as the embodiment of the vice of avarice with which the Cistercians were frequently charged by their critics like Gerald of Wales and Walter Map.[39]

The old granges were transformed in one of two ways. A statute from 1262 makes it clear that granges could be granted to a monk or a lay brother for a fixed rent and that the leaseholder was not entitled to dispose of any surplus except with the abbot's permission.[40] This compromise solution may be seen when in 1310 a Fountains lay brother, Robert of Morton, became the lessee of the important, if remote, grange of Cowton.[41] Other granges were handed over to lay bailiffs to manage. At Esrum in Denmark these were described as secular procurators who were managing the estates (*mansiones*) that "on account of a lack of personnel on your farms at the time, your lay brothers previously managed."[42] Still in Denmark, the monks of Vitskøl (*Vitae Schola*) in 1263 were granted freedom from tithe on all lands "regardless of whether the monks because of shortage of personnel had in the course of time been obliged to place lay bailiffs on those farms their *conversi* used

---

[38] France 1992, 264.

[39] Knowles 1940, 662–78.

[40] *Statuta* 1262.10 (Canivez 3:3): *Item, statuit et ordinat Capitulum generale quod cum aliquis abbas alicui monacho vel converso suo aliquam grangiam suam ad firmam concedit, soluto censu in quo tenetur monachus vel conversus abbatiae, residuum bonorum sibi commissae grangiae non appropriet, nec praeter ordinationem abbatis aliquid inde facere audeat vel praesumat.*

[41] Platt 1969, 96–97.

[42] *Codex Esromensis* 1880–1881, 27: *propter defectum personarum in mansionibus vestris, quas conversi vestri prius regere solebant.*

to manage.”[43] In 1351 Dore on the border of Wales leased its properties in Cantref-selyf for ten years to two of the monks and three laymen for a rent of forty marks a year.[44] An urgent need for ready cash sometimes led to the outright sale of whole granges. In 1269 the General Chapter was reluctantly obliged to permit the practice but, as examples from Theulay in 1269 and Buzay in 1297 show, insisted on the consent of the community and the father abbot.[45]

Many abbeys had been beset with economic problems already in the latter part of the twelfth century, not least as a result of over-ambitious building projects. Statutes were passed in 1182, in 1188, and in 1192 forbidding abbeys with outstanding debts to buy land or erect new buildings.[46] The financial crisis had an adverse effect on recruitment, as evidenced by the statute in 1224 forbidding any house indebted to the amount of one hundred marks or more to receive any person as a monk or a lay brother.[47]

The first generation of lay brothers would have been fit and young. Being without dependents, they would not have had whole families to feed and their standard of living would have been higher than that of hired laborers. Only they had to be fed and housed, thereby reducing labor costs and increasing the yield. This made them a more efficient work force than laborers brought in from outside. In the second and third generation a proportion of the lay brothers would have been old and of less benefit as workers and, as Constance Berman has pointed out, although they provided a life-long permanent labor force they did not replace themselves.[48] The

---

[43] *Diplomatarium Danicum* II, 1:382: *non obstante si iidem monachi processu temporis propter defectum personarum in mansionibus suis, quas conversi eorum prius regere solebant villicos aut procuratores compellantur instituere seculares.*

[44] Williams 1998, 297.

[45] *Statuta* 1269.5 (Canivez 3:69); 1269.29 (Canivez 3:74); 1297.13 (Canivez 3:289–90).

[46] *Statuta* 1182.9 (Waddell, 100–1); 1188.10 (Waddell, 152); 1192.4 (Waddell, 236).

[47] *Statuta* 1224.25 (Canivez 2:34): *Statuitur a Capitulo generale ne aliqua domus Ordinis nostri quamdiu fuerit debito centum marcarum ad pondus Trecense obligata, personam aliquam recipiat in monachum vel conversum, nisi fuerit talis persona quae sine scandalo repelli non possit.*

[48] Berman 1992, 79.

balance in favor of hired laborers is suggested in the curious statute that in 1224 directed that lay brothers were only to be accepted if they could match hired laborers in their work performance.[49]

Evidence of the shortage of lay brothers may also be sought in the architectural provision made for their accommodation. Three examples are known from Denmark alone. At Øm the monks are said to have originally built themselves "huts rather than proper houses" when in 1172 they settled at their final site, after having first made three false starts.[50] The *Chronicle* then records how, having first moved the monks' dormitory, on the eve of All Saints 1257 they "processed with cross, candles, and thurible at the head and, according to custom, took the saints' relics from the old church and brought them ceremoniously to the new church."[51] The plan of the new church—cruciform, with a square-ended presbytery to the east, transepts with two chapels on each side of the crossing, and an aisled nave—conformed to the Cistercian standard with the exception that the nave consisted of only one bay, terminating approximately where the *pulpitum* would have been located and separating the monks' choir from the lay brothers'. The cloister was proportionately of the usual size, which indicates that an extension had originally been planned but, because there was no longer a need to accommodate *conversi* in the western part of the nave, this was never built. The two other Danish abbeys were Vitskøl, where only two bays of the nave, measuring a mere eighteen meters (sixty feet), were completed following a fire of 1287, and Løgum (*Locus Dei*), where a larger nave had been planned but only four bays were built around 1300.[52] Similar truncated naves are found at La Chalade and Villelongue in France, Arbona in Italy, and Eusserthal in Germany, and in England Salley had virtually no nave.[53] The

---

[49] *Statuta* 1224.1 (Canivez 2:30): *Tales de cetero recipiantur in conversos, qui in labore taliter occupentur, quod evidens sit et certum ipsos in officio sibi commisso laborem unius mercenarii compensare, exceptis magistris grangiarum, qui singulis diebus excitent et compellant ad opera mercenarios et conversos.*

[50] *Scriptores Minores* 1917–1922, 2:177: *tuguriis potius quam domibus.*

[51] *Scriptores Minores* 1917–1922, 2:201.

[52] France 1992, 156.

[53] Dimier 1949; Platt 1985, 22.

naves extended only part of the way along the northern cloister walk and were cut off far short of joining up with the western range that housed the lay brothers, making any connection with this and the church impossible. In Ireland the original Cistercian layout was abandoned at Bective in the fifteenth century when the nave was shortened appreciably to the west.[54] Western ranges at the three Danish abbeys were added only in the fifteenth century and were not used for lay brothers. In a number of monasteries what had been the lay brothers' range was later transformed to other uses, as, for example, at Marienfeld in Germany where it became a library in 1403–1404. In other cases, as at Fontenay and Senanque in France and Santes Creus in Spain, the range was demolished.[55]

## Challenge from the Friars

A severe challenge to the recruitment not just of *conversi* but equally of monks was the emergence in the early thirteenth century of the new form of religious life represented by the friars. With their apostolate to the whole world rather than to a landed or literate élite, their popularity was similar to that enjoyed by the Cistercians a century earlier. They presented a new model of simplicity and lowliness with an emphasis on poverty—precisely the qualities that had previously led so many to become lay brothers—which contrasted with the avarice and accumulation of wealth with which the older orders, and particularly the Cistercians, had become associated. The Franciscans or Grey Friars were at first noted for their absolute poverty, their refusal of ecclesiastical privilege, and their renunciation of all human learning, while the Dominicans or Black Friars were particularly associated with preaching against the Albigensian heresy in southern France, an enterprise previously undertaken by the Cistercians with singular lack of success. Both orders of friars received papal approval at the Fourth Lateran Council and within the next half century spread to all parts of Europe. One or the other or often both were represented in most cathedral cites and major

[54] Platt 1985, 23.
[55] Kinder 1997, 330.

towns. In England, for example, within twenty years the Franciscans had settled in two university towns, in fifteen out of nineteen cathedral cities, and in twenty-five other towns. By around 1260 the Dominicans had thirty-six houses. By 1272 this had risen to forty-seven and was ultimately to reach fifty-three, compared to a total of forty-eight of the Franciscans.[56] They attracted many of the ablest and most fervent young men who a century earlier would have joined the white monks, and thereby deprived the Cistercians, both monks and *conversi*, of large numbers of recruits. Although figures are scarce, this switch to the friars was a contributing factor in the decline of the population of choir monks as well as that of lay brothers in the thirteenth century. The friars probably drew off from the monks a number of distinguished individuals, among them the abbot of Walden in England, who joined the Dominicans. The problem of loss is indicated by a statute from 1223 in which the General Chapter declared that monks or *conversi* who crossed to the friars were to be considered *fugitivi*.[57]

Related to the advent of the friars is the impact of the emergence and growth of towns in which they established themselves in response to the spiritual needs of the nascent urban population. Urban growth culminated in the thirteenth century and came to an end in the fourteenth century, after which few new towns were founded.[58] For a rural population the increasing opportunities for employment that towns offered was an attraction that had not previously existed and that must also have had an impact on the ability of the Cistercians to recruit lay brothers, traditionally from rural areas. From the twelfth century onward manufacturing processes gradually shifted from the non-specialized hands of peasants and monastic labor—chiefly *conversi*—to specialist craftspersons who concentrated on manufacture, with merchant middlemen between them and the consumer.[59] The greater efficiency achieved saw the

[56] Knowles 1956, 133, 164.

[57] *Statuta* 1223.12 (Canivez 2:24): *Monachi vel conversi qui ad Ordinem Praedicatorum vel Fratrum Minorum transierint, habeantur pro fugitivis.*

[58] For this see Pounds 1974, 223–58.

[59] For this see Pounds 1974, 283–84.

growth of fairs and markets in which the Cistercians had participated—again chiefly with *conversi*—but in which they were no
longer able to compete.

## A Time of Trials—Famine, War, and Plague

A number of factors contributed to making the fourteenth century one of the lowest points in European history. Chief among these
was the plague known as the Black Death. The most devastating
pandemic ever experienced, it marked a turning point in the history
of the Middle Ages from which it took Europeans a century and a
half to recover.[60] It was not, however, the first or the only trauma; for
a number of decades the economy had been in recession or had at
least ceased to advance. Northwestern Europe was to suffer a cata-
strophic famine in the years 1315 to 1317. A considerable decrease in
the population led to a sharp rise in the cost of labor and a lessening
in the demand for grain. The amount of land required for arable
crops fell sharply, and the result was a wholesale desertion of farms
and of complete villages. The famine had the effect of making the
Cistercians rely almost exclusively on the fixed income they received
from rents, a development that obviated the labor of the lay brothers.
This was the worst famine in European history but only the first of
a succession of recurring outbreaks that were to have a major impact
on the social structure and, in England, would eventually lead to
unrest and breakdown of order in the 1381 Peasants' Revolt. Also
predating the Black Death was the outbreak in 1337 of a sporadic
series of wars known as the Hundred Years' War between the French
royal house of Valois and the English Plantagenets that was only finally resolved in 1453 and put a severe strain on the twin unifying
elements of Cistercian governance, the annual General Chapter at
Cîteaux and the visitation of houses by father abbots.

The Black Death had its origin in China from where it traveled along the old Silk Road to the Middle East. It spread, carried
by merchant ships infested with fleas on black rats, throughout
the Mediterranean, reaching Sicily in October 1347 and Genoa

[60] For the Black Death see Ziegler 1982.

and Venice in 1348. It advanced northward, finally reaching the regions of northern Europe in 1349 and 1350. The toll in lives has been variously estimated to between thirty and sixty percent of the population, with a higher number in southern Europe than farther north. The Cistercians—monks and *conversi* equally—suffered in the same way as everyone else and with the same regional variation. Although evidence is scarce, David Knowles suggests that the religious houses were worse affected than the clergy generally. He estimates that in England the population of monks, friars, and nuns in the early fourteenth century reached 17,500 and that approximately half of these perished in two years, including probably more than half the friars and, because they were in less frequent contact with the general population than the friars, somewhat fewer than half the monks and nuns.[61] The *Chronicle* of the Cistercian abbey of Louth Park in Lincolnshire gives a good idea of the way the plague affected the monks as well as everyone else:

> In the year of Our Lord, 1349, the hand of the only omnipotent God struck the human race with a deadly plague. Beginning in southern regions, it spread to northern, invading all the kingdoms of the world. This plague slew Christians, Jews, and Saracens alike. It annihilated at once the confessor and the penitent. In many places the plague left less than a fifth of the population surviving. It struck terror into the heart of the whole world. Before this time so great a pestilence had never been seen, or heard of, or written about. It is believed that even the waters of the flood in the days of Noah did not carry off so great a multitude. The number of the dead buried before the midday meal was greater than those who were interred after it. In this year many monks of Louth Park perished. Among them Walter of Louth, Lord Abbot, who suffered a great persecution on account of the manor of Cockerington, died on 12 July. He was buried in the front of the high altar by the side of Sir Henry Vavasour, knight.[62]

---

[61] Knowles 1957, 256–57.

[62] *Chronicon de Parco Ludo* 1891, 38–39: *Anno Domini Millesimo CCCxlix manus solius Dei Omnipotentis genus humanum quadam plaga mortifera percussit. Que a regionibus*

## The Twilight Years

In view of its severity, the plague left curiously little evidence of its effect on the Cistercians generally. A rare exception comes from Ebrach in southern Germany. During the abbacy of Abbot Frederick (1306–1327) there were 102 choir monks and seventy-two lay brothers. Under a successor, Otto (1349–1385), this had fallen to forty-six monks and twenty-one *conversi*. In 1280 Kamp in the Rhineland had the same number of monks and lay brothers—seventy-two. Twenty years later there were still seventy-five *conversi*, but by 1355 only twenty-two monks and no *conversi* are recorded.[63] At Bebenhausen there had been sixty monks and 130 lay brothers in the second half of the thirteenth century. By the beginning of the fourteenth century the number of monks had grown to eighty but there were only forty *conversi*, or a third of the previous figure. By the end of the fifteenth century there were still fifty-six monks but only four lay brothers.[64] Bordesley in England had thirty-four monks and ten lay brothers in 1335. By 1380 this had been reduced to fourteen monks and only a single lay brother.[65]

Information regarding the mortality at the Swedish abbey of Alvastra, founded in 1143 from Clairvaux, one of the farthermost Cistercian outposts, described by Conrad of Eberbach as *extremis finibus mundi*[66] and the oldest house in Scandinavia, comes from the

---

*australibus incipiens et ad partes aquilonales pertransiens, omnia regna mundi invasit. Hec plaga Christianos, Judeos, et Saracenos pariter prostravit. Confessorem et confitentem simul extinxit. Hec plaga in multis locis nec quintam partem hominum superstitem reliquit. Hec plaga universum orbem ingenti pavore concussit. Tantaque pestilentia ante hec tempora non est visa nec audita, nec scripture commendata. Creditur enim multitudinem hominum tam copiosam aquis diluvii, quod in diebus Noe evenit, interceptum non fuisse. Major erat numerus defunctorum qui post prandium traditi fuerant sepulture, quam eorum qui ante prandium sepeliebantur. Hoc anno obierunt multi Monachi de Parco Lude. Inter quos obiit Dompnus Walterus de Luda, Abbas, iii Idus Julii, qui maximum sustinuit persecutionem propter manerium de Kokring-ton, et sepultus est ante magnum altare juxta Dominum Henricum le Wavesoure, Militem.*

[63] Lekai 1977, 343.

[64] Toepfer 1983, 54, 57.

[65] Donnelly 1954, 452.

[66] *EM* 4.29 (Griesser, 262).

*Revelations* of Saint Birgitta of Vadstena (ca. 1300–1373). In a vision she had foreseen the death of thirty-three of the Alvastra monks, who are said to have died in the order in which their names had been revealed to Birgitta.[67] The community before the plague is known to have numbered at least forty-one, so that, although the community was not totally destroyed, the losses were nevertheless extremely severe. The abbot, Ragvald, who is mentioned for the last time in 1350, the year the plague reached Sweden, may have been among the victims.[68] The figures from Alvastra correspond closely with what is known of the mortality rate at the English abbey of Meaux in Yorkshire. Before the Black Death there had been forty-three monks and seven lay brothers. The chronicler records the death of the abbot, Hugh de Leven, and five monks on a single day—12 August 1349—and claims that only ten monks and no *conversi* survived.[69] Newenham in southwest England, which only had thirteen monks and four lay brothers at its late (1247) foundation from Beaulieu, had twenty-three monks and three lay brothers before the Black Death but only three monks and no lay brothers after.[70]

A rare case from Alvastra is that of two named lay brothers mentioned in Saint Birgitta's *Revelations*. They are not just numbers but real people imbued with qualities associated with the *exemplum* literature of the early thirteenth century. They bear witness to the quality of life of lay brothers a hundred and fifty years later, the last evidence of their existence in Scandinavia. One was Gerekin, described by Birgitta as "a man of great sanctity"—an almost standard description of so many of the early lay brothers. "For forty years he never went outside the monastery; but day and night, he was absorbed in prayers; and he had this grace: that, during prayer, he almost continually saw the nine choirs of angels; and at the elevation of the Body of Christ, he merited frequently to see Christ in

---

[67] Birgitta, *Revelaciones Extravagantes* 1956, chap. 74.
[68] France 1992, 367.
[69] *Melsa Chronica* 1866–1868, 3:36–37.
[70] Donnelly 1954, 453.

the appearance of a child."[71] Gerekin had also seen Birgitta "raised
from the earth, and, as it were, lightning going forth from her
mouth. And then heard in spirit: 'This is the woman who, coming
from the ends of the earth, shall give countless nations wisdom to
drink. And this will be a sign to you: that she, from the mouth of
God, is going to tell you the end of your life.'"[72]

These stories closely resemble the tales in *exempla* written a
century and a half earlier. The writer is well acquainted with, and
makes a special point of referring to, the rule "that a monk ought
not to live outside the cloister."[73] He also refers to the injunction in
the *Exordium Cistercii* "that women may not even come inside the
monastery gate"[74] when he records that Gerekin was disturbed when
he heard that Birgitta was coming to live "in a monastery of monks,
introducing a new custom against our rule."[75] His fears were allayed
in the beautiful words attributed to Christ: "Do not wonder. This
woman is a friend of God; and she has come in order that at the
foot of this mountain she may gather flowers from which all people,
even overseas and beyond the world's ends, shall receive medicine."[76]

[71] Birgitte, *Acta et Processus Canonizacionis* 1924–1931, 619: *magne sanctitatis et vite, qui xl annis extra monasterium numquam iuit, sed diebus et noctibus vacans oracionibus hanc graciam habuit, quod choros angelorum in oracione quasi continue vidit et in elevatione corporis Christi Christum in specie pueruli cernere merebatur.* Translation in *Birgitta of Sweden: Life and Selected Revelations*, trans. Albert Ryle Kezel, CWS (Mahwah, NJ: Paulist Press, 1990), 79.

[72] Birgitte, *Acta et Processus Canonizacionis* 1924–1931, 545: *elevatum de terra in aere et de ore eius quasi fulmen egrediens, et tunc ipso orante audivit in spiritu vocem dicentem sic: "Hec est mulier, que a finibus terre veniens propinabit innumerabilibus gentibus sapienciam, et hoc erit tibi signum, quod ipsa de ore Dei dictura tibi est finem vite tue."* Translation in *Birgitta of Sweden* (1990), 79–80.

[73] *Capitula* 16 (Waddell 1999, 189): *Quod non debeat monachus extra claustrum habitare.*

[74] *Exordium Cistercii* 18 (Waddell 1999, 189): *Quod nec ingrediuntur portam Monasterii.*

[75] Birgitte, *Acta et processus Canonizacionis* 1924–31, 82: *Cur ista domina sedet hic in monasterio monachorum contra regulam nostram inducens novam consuetudinem.* Translation in *Birgitta of Sweden* (1990), 79.

[76] Birgitte, *Acta et processus Canonizacionis* 1924–1931, 82: *Noli mirari, hec est amica Dei et ad hoc venit, ut sub monte isto flores colligat, de quibus omnes eciam ultra mare et fines mundi recipient medicinam.* Translation in *Birgitta of Sweden* (1990), 79.

The other lay brother was Asgot, who had been ill for over three years. Directed by Christ, Birgitta urged him to confess a grievous sin which he had withheld, a close parallel to a number of stories in the *exemplum* literature, including one of a lay brother who had come to Clairvaux from Esrum in Denmark and who had first confessed a grievous sin on his deathbed and thereby was "set free from the pit of eternal damnation."[77] At first Asgot denied all knowledge of his sin, but after Birgitta had pressed him he dissolved in tears saying:

> I do have something hidden that I never dared to betray because, as often as I repented, my tongue was always, as it were, tied and indeed excessive shame invaded me so that I did not open the matter. Therefore, as often as I made my confession, I invented for myself a new conclusion to my words, saying at the end: "I declare to God and to all God's saints that I am culpable of all the crimes that I have told to you, Father, and of all those that I have not told." I believed that through this conclusion, all was forgiven. But now, if it should please God, I would gladly tell the whole world. And when a confessor had been called, he fully explained everything with tears . . . .[78]

These two lay brothers played an important role in the propagation of Birgitta's legend, very much in the same way as lay brothers had been instrumental in promoting the cult of Saint Waldef in the *Vita* by Jocelin of Furness in the twelfth century.[79]

[77] *EM* 2.31 (Griesser, 140); CF 72:194: *liberandus sum ab aeternae damnationis voragine.* See also pp. 221–22.

[78] Birgitte, *Acta et Processus Canonizationis* 1924–1931, 522: *ex quo tu secreta mea locuta es, dicere volo veritatem, nam quoddam occultum habeo, quod prodere numquam audebam, quia quociens penitui, quasi semper lingua mea erat ligata et nimis eciam pudor invasit me, ne aperirem peccata mea. Ideo quociens confessionem feci, inveni mihi novam conclusionem verborum meorum dicens: "Reddo me culpabilem de omnibus, que dixi vobis, pater, et de aliis, que non dixi, credens per hanc conclusionem omnia peccata mea dimitti, sed nunc, si placeret Deo, libenter dicerem toti mundo."* Vocato igitur confessore plene cum lacrimis omnia peccata sua detexit. Translation in *Birgitta of Sweden* (1990), 90.

[79] For this, see pp. 195–98.

As we have seen, there had already been a sharp decline in the lay brother population largely because of the change from direct cultivation to leasing, the result of which was the demise of the traditional Cistercian grange economy, which made a large number of lay brothers superfluous. They had played a vital part in the tremendous growth of the Cistercian economy in the twelfth century, but their usefulness in material terms was a thing of the past. The serious disturbances of the thirteenth century, for which the lay brothers were not solely responsible, were a manifestation of a general malaise, not the cause of decline. The rapidly expanding urban economy, the growth in the employment opportunities of the rural poor and their gravitation to the rapidly developing towns, and the emergence of other forms of apostolate accelerated a process already underway. The traumas of climate, war, and plague hit choir monks and *conversi* equally in the fourteenth century and their numbers were further decimated.

The drop in numbers, however, was by no means uniform. While the lay brotherhood suffered virtual extinction in many areas, elsewhere the decline appears to have been less severe. In 1322 Obazine had sixty monks and forty lay brothers, but by 1430 only fifteen monks and no *conversi* are recorded.[80] The population at Salem in southern Germany in 1323 was 125 monks and 160 lay brothers. By 1377 there were almost as many monks—one hundred—and, although the number of *conversi* had been halved, there were nevertheless still eighty left. Other houses with few lay brothers were Vaucelles with seventeen, Wettingen in Switzerland with thirteen, and Heisterbach with fifteen.[81] Tennenbach gave up the direct exploitation of eight of its granges between 1310 and 1342, but they still kept three or four for their own cultivation.[82] By 1380 the English houses had only a small number of monks and an even smaller number of *conversi*. Rievaulx, for example, had fifteen monks and three *conversi*, Kirkstall seventeen and six, Byland twelve and three, Jervaulx sixteen and two, Whalley twenty-nine and one,

[80] Barrière 1977, 185, 188.
[81] Toepfer 1983, 56.
[82] Rösener 2009, 92.

while there were still thirty-four monks and ten lay brothers at Fountains.[83] By the time of the great reforming abbot Marmaduke Huby (1495–1526) there were no *conversi* left at Fountains, but they had not been forgotten altogether. In a letter to the equally distinguished Abbot Jean de Cirey of Cîteaux, Huby reports the king, Henry VII of England, as having said that he "was astounded that we have no lay brothers" and that he would offer to get six or eight skilled in some craft, which might attract others.[84] We have no reply to this, and it is unlikely that any further action was taken.

Perhaps the demise of the lay brotherhood was inevitable. It had not been conceived of by the monks who left Molesme to enter into a new form of monastic life, but was introduced as the solution to a pragmatic problem that soon arose as a result of an abundance of donations. The germ of the problem may already be detected in the qualifying phrase *excepto monachatu* used in the document introducing lay brothers. The dichotomy may be seen in the monks' interpretation of the lay brothers' supposed "equality" by, on the one hand, their effusive descriptions of the humility and sanctity of some brothers, and on the other their way of referring to them generally as *homines rusticani*[85] who could never "aspire to the status of a monk."[86] The dilemma had already been recognized by Stephen Harding when drawing up the *Usus conversorum*. In the Prologue he articulated the predicament by saying that while some abbots hold lay brothers "in contempt because of their innate simplicity," others treat them "with greater indulgence as regards food, and greater laxity as regards clothing."[87] Although he ends by stating his purpose in drawing up the document, namely that "in things both temporal and spiritual, diversity may not be found in their [the lay brothers'] way of life,"[88] the problem was never

---

[83] Donnelly 1954, 452–53.

[84] Knowles 1957, 126: *miratur . . . quod conversos non habemus.*

[85] *EM* 4.13 (Griesser, 239).

[86] *Statuta* 1404.39 (Canivez 4:67): *ad monaschatum ascendere.*

[87] *UC* Prologue (Waddell. 56): *pro ingenita eorum simplicitate contemptui habentes . . . eos remissius in cibo et in vestimento dissolucius tractent.*

[88] *UC* Prologue (Waddell, 56; 165): *et in temporalibus et in spiritualibus . . . ne vel in eorum conversatione diversitas inveniatur.*

resolved. Religious, cultural, economic, geographical, and agrarian factors all contributed to the rise and subsequent decline of the institution, but in the end the inescapable flaw of inequality was a signal factor in its demise. The lay brotherhood had been a thriving institution that from its inception had contributed hugely to the spiritual and material development of the Order, but after its heyday in the twelfth and thirteenth centuries it was no longer able to weather the turmoil of a changing age.

# Appendix 1

# Lay Brothers in Miracle Stories

| CC | *Collectaneum exemplorum et visionum clarevallense* | 1165–1181 |
| LM | Herbert of Clairvaux's *Liber miraculorum et visionum* | *circa* 1178 |
| GF | Goswin's *Fragmenta* | *circa* 1195 |
| BC | Beaupré Compilation | *circa* 1200 |
| LP | Peter of Cornwall's *Liber revelationum* | 1197–1206 |
| EM | Conrad of Eberbach's *Exordium magnum cisterciense* | 1206–1221 |
| HM | Himmerod *Liber miraculorum* | after 1213 |
| LR | Richalm of Schöntal's *Liber revelationum* | *circa* 1220 |
| DM | Caesarius of Heisterbach's *Dialogus miraculorum* | 1219–1223 |
| SM | Salem *Liber miraculorum* | after 1223 |
| EC | Ebrach Compilation | 1219–1227 |
| DM Hilka | Caesarius of Heisterbach's *Libri VIII miraculorum* | 1225–1227 |
| FC | Fürstenfeld Collection | |

323

| CC | LM | BC | EM | EC | FC |
|---|---|---|---|---|---|
| IV, 4 | | | II, 2 | | |
| | II, 15 | | II, 15 | | |
| | | | II, 27 | | |
| | | | II, 30 | | |
| | | | II, 31 | | |
| | | | III, 2 | | |
| | I, 1 | | III, 13 | | |
| | | fol. 83v | IV, 13 | 3 | |
| | I, 32 | | IV, 15 | | 68 |
| | I, 17 | | IV, 16 | | 65 |
| | I, 16 | | IV, 17 | | 64 |
| | I, 15 | | IV, 18 | | 63 |
| | I, 29 | | IV, 19 | | 67 |
| | I, 7 | | IV, 20 | | |
| | I, 14 | | IV, 23 | | 62 |
| IV, 47 | | fol. 30v | IV, 24 | | |
| III, 12 | | | IV, 31 | | 69 |
| | II, 40 | | IV, 32 | | |
| | II, 30 | | IV, 34 | | |
| | III, 7 | | V, 4 | | |
| III, 13 | | fol. 30r | V, 8 | | |
| | | | V, 10 | | |
| | | | VI, 4 | | |
| | | | VI, 9 | | |
| | | | VI, 10 | | |
| IV, 57 | | | | | |
| | I, 18 | | | | 66 |
| | I, 27 | | | | 70 |
| IV, 13 | III, 26 | | | | 71 |
| | III, 27 | | | | 72 |
| IV, 22 | | | | | |
| IV, 16 | | | | | |
| | III, 35 | | | | 73 |
| | III, 36 | | | | 74 |
| | III, 37 | | | | 74 |
| | | fol. 85r | | | |
| | | fol. 106r | | | |
| | | | | 7 | |
| | | | | 8 | |

# Index to the Principal Citations of Lay Brothers in *Exempla*

(Numerals to the far right refer to pages of this volume.)

### Collectaneum Clarevallense

3.12     A lay brother stayed behind at a mill by order of his superior. Similar to *EM* 4.31.           118 and 241

3.13     Demons beat a lay brother who was rescued by the Virgin. Repeated in BC fol. 30r and *EM* 5.8.        207–9

4.4      The soul of a lay brother struggling with demons was freed by the prayers of the brothers on the order of Saint Bernard.    188

4.13     A lay brother suffering from depression refused to confess but was saved by the prayers of the community. Repeated in *LM* 3.26.
                                              224–25 and 227

4.16     The Virgin visits the community at harvest to protect them from temptations when away from the cloister.            42

4.22     Lay brother who did not confess before Communion could not swallow the Host.                        223–24

4.47     Lay brother who washed his shoes without permission felt himself being pushed by demons into the water and soon after died. Repeated in BC fol. 30v and *EM* 4.24.        147–48

4.57     Pride of place enjoyed by Cistercians persuades lay brother to stay.
                                                      264

### Herbert of Clairvaux's *Liber Miraculorum*

1.1      The Virgin's visitation of the community at harvest time, and vision of how monks' infirmary was more glorious than lay brothers'. Repeated in *EM* 3.13 and similar to *DM* 1.17.

                                                 42 and 155

1.7   An angel revealed to a monk the cause of celebration: the arrival in heaven of a lay brother from Clairvaux. Repeated in *EM* 4.20.
                                                                      205–6 and 249

1.14   A Clairvaux lay brother rewarded for his life of toil. Repeated in *EM* 4.23.                                          26–27 and 155

1.15   A Clairvaux lay brother saw Christ in a dream driving his oxen. Repeated in *EM* 4.18.                                      148–49

1.16   A lay brother had become eloquent in speaking Latin, which was much admired by the community. Repeated in *EM* 4.17.
                                                                             72–73

1.17   After leaving three times and returning three times a lay brother amended his ways. Repeated in *EM* 4.16.                 67–69

1.18   Lay brother Gerard rolled in stinging nettles to repress the urgings of the flesh.                                            183

1.27   Lay brother saw a demon in the likeness of a monk drag a lay brother out of the church.                                       243

1.29   A lay brother was chastised by Saint Bernard for overconfidence until he said that the kingdom of God could only be acquired by obedience. Repeated in *EM* 4.19.        158–59, 166 and 201–2

1.32   In a dream a venerable girl ordered a Clairvaux lay brother to celebrate Mass. Repeated in *EM* 4.15.                           70

2.15   Convicted robber freed by Saint Bernard and made lay brother at Clairvaux. Repeated in *EM* 2.15.                         188–89

2.30   Lay brother Lawrence's mission to Sicily to get funds to build a new church at Clairvaux and, on the way back, to purchase ten buffalos. Repeated in *EM* 4.34.                          8 and 242

2.40   In a vision a lay brother was freed by the Virgin's plea to Christ. Repeated in *EM* 4.32.                                  254–55

3.7   Lay brother Stephen appeared to the infirmarian in a vision warning him to confess his sins before it was too late. Repeated in *EM* 5.4.                                                        220–21

3.26   Same as *CC* 4.13.                                             225

3.27   A lay brother with private property had a burning coal forced into his mouth when receiving Communion.                         217

3.35   A lay brother had a vision of a pagan idol he had destroyed before becoming a lay brother.                                     236

### Goswin's *Fragmenta*

1    Shepherd lay brother assaulted by demons.    244

2    Same brother tricked by demon in religious habit who offered to reveal the status of those in heaven.    244–45

### BNF ms lat. 15912 ("Beaupré" Collection)

fol. 30r  Same as *CC* 3.13 and repeated in *EM* 5.8.    207–9

fol. 30v  A briefer version of *CC* 4.47 and repeated in *EM* 4.24.
    147–48

fol. 60r  An English monk's vision of the other world, where he witnessed the torment of a lay brother who had apostatized.    259–60

fol. 83v  A lay brother wept because he could not be at the abbey for the Assumption. Repeated in *EM* 4.13 and *EC* 3.    203–5

fol. 85r  Following a vision of Christ, an English lay brother was obliged to learn letters.    74 and 252

fol. 106r A dying lay brother tells of an angel who had appeared to him. Same as BNF MS Lat. 14657, 157.    xxi

### BNF ms lat. 14657

119    Same as BC 83v, *EM* 4.13, and EC 3.    203–5

126    An abbot was unable to save a lay brother who forgot to confess all his sins.    227–28

157    A dying lay brother tells of an angel who had appeared to him. Same as BC fol. 106r.    xxi–xxii

### Peter of Cornwall's *Liber Revelationum*

5    A lay brother claimed that no Cistercian would remain in purgatory for more than thirty days.    263

6    A lay brother who had apostatized repented and after his death was allowed to receive his habit again.    267

7    The friendship between lay brother Roger and monk Alexander.
    176–77 and 249

### Conrad of Eberbach's *Exordium Magnum*

2.2    Same as *CC* 4.4.    187–88, 241 and 258

2.15    Same as *LM* 2.15.                                    188–89

2.20    The abbot of Cîteaux worries at the miracles at Saint Bernard's
        grave.                                                174–75

2.31    A lay brother from Denmark had fathered a child but escaped the
        sentence of damnation.          221–22, 258 and 319

3.13    Same as *LM* 1.1.                               42 and 155

4.13    Same as BC 83v and repeated in EC 3.      150 and 203–5

4.15    The same story as *LM* 1.32, but here the subject is referred to
        as *monachus laicus*.                                     70

4.16    Same as *LM* 1.17.                                    67–69

4.17    A lay brother who, as recorded in *LM* 1.16, had become eloquent
        in Latin "also sang sweet canticles about the mysteries of holy
        Church." Conrad concludes "the fear of God is to be preferred
        to the learning of the schools."                       72–73

4.18    Same as *LM* 1.15, but in greater detail.           148–49

4.19    Same as *LM* 1.29.          158–59, 166 and 201–2

4.20    An extended version of *LM* 1.7.        205–6 and 249

4.23    Same as *LM* 1.14.                       26–27 and 155

4.24    Same as *CC* 4.47 and BC fol. 30v, but adds that the story is a
        warning to the lukewarm.          147–48 and 215–16

4.31    Similar to *CC* 3.12 but at a sheepfold and not a mill.
                                                     118 and 239–40

4.32    Same as *LM* 2.40.                                   254–55

4.34    Same as *LM* 2.30.                              8 and 242

5.4     Same as *LM* 3.7.                                    220–21

5.8     An extended version of *CC* 3.13 and BC 30r.          207–9

5.10    The conspiracy of lay brothers at Schönau.    269 and 285–87

6.4     A lay brother from Spain was granted his wish of dying at
        Clairvaux.                                            157–58

6.10    The final book refers to many examples of models of piety, includ-
        ing lay brothers.                                        199

## Caesarius of Heisterbach's *Dialogus Miraculorum*

1.3     Grange master Henry was present when a novice made his profes-
        sion.                                                     134

1.17   The Virgin's visitation at harvest; she is accompanied by Anne and Mary Magdalene  and not by Mary Magdalene and Elizabeth as in *LM* 1.1 and *EM* 3.13.                    42–43 and 255

1.28   Caesarius claims that many lay brothers were "driven to enter by the furnace of poverty."                    24

1.37   Conversion of the knight Walewan who came to the Order in full armor.                    18

1.39   Caesarius draws attention to the problem of clerks who come to the order and, out of humility, conceal that they are not laymen.                    15 and 59

2.14   Lay brother Henry put off confessing a sin until the point of death.                    219–20

3.33   Simon of Aulne warns his abbot of the temptations that lie ahead for the novice Conrad, who was to become abbot of Villers, then of Clairvaux and of Cîteaux, and finally was made cardinal.                    11–13, 141, and 179

4.4   The lay brother Liffard was tempted by the spirit but was rescued in a vision by seeing the bodies of the dead.                    17–18

4.32   A lay brother saw a serpent on another brother who was asleep.                    96

4.33   A lay brother's eyes were closed by a cat in choir.                    96

4.36   An abbot roused the monks and lay brothers who were asleep by a story of King Arthur.                    61

4.41   A lay brother in despair drowned himself in a fishpond.                    228

4.83   A lay brother who went to sleep at Mass gnawed wood thinking it was flesh.                    219

4.100   On a journey transporting wine a lay brother resisted the advances of a woman.                    7–8

5.5   Grange master Henry saw demons under various forms.                    232–33

5.16   A lay brother was deceived by the promise of a bishopric, and was hanged.                    74 and 216

5.17   A lay brother was deceived by counting the calls of a cuckoo and died in apostasy.                    220

5.27   Lay brother Theodoric was carried by the devil from Lübeck.                    247–48

5.28 Lay brother Albero fell sick at the sight of a demon. 102

5.29 An abbot on his way to Eberbach is warned by a demon of problems with the lay brothers there. 288

5.33 A lay brother asleep during the day was embraced by a demon under the appearance of a nun. 103

5.48 A lay brother saw a demon bring phantasms into the choir. 95

7.12 Grange master Henry gave his abbot list of those singled out by the Virgin. Repeated in *DM* Hilka 1.51. 253

7.15 Grange master Henry had a vision of the Virgin after Compline. 134

7.64 In heaven the Virgin reveals members of the Cistercian Order under her cloak. 255–56

8.17 Two lay brothers had a vision of Christ hanging on the cross. 212

8.37 Lay brother Henry saw a dove above the head of his abbot. 145

8.38 A lay brother saw a dove on the head of a monk reading the gospel. 146

8.96 An old man who had the gift of prophecy appeared to grange master Henry. 145–46

9.29 A lay brother saw Christ in the hands of his abbot saying Mass. 146

9.37 A lay brother from Livonia receives the Host from Christ himself. 95 and 250

9.41 A lay brother saw the blood of Christ drip into the chalice. 250

9.42 A lay brother saw a priest place a beautiful child in the mouth of another lay brother. 250

9.45 A lay brother in his desire to communicate won for himself the spirit of prophecy. 205

9.54 A grange master paid an unworthy priest to say Mass at a grange. 135 and 226

9.63 A lay brother ate coal instead of the sacrament. 226

9.64 A lay brother who had not given up his property was not able to receive the Host at Communion. 217

10.15  Through a lay brother's obedience the peas in the field were turned over. 210

10.54  A tree is felled by the merits of the lay brother Liffard. 17

11.6  Lay brother Obert when dying heard celestial music. 156–57

11.11  The death of Mengoz, a lay brother who returned to life at the bidding of his abbot. 44–45

11.15  As he lay dying lay brother Gerung was attacked by vultures, but they were driven away by a fellow brother. 24

11.16  The death of a lay brother when crows perching on him were driven out by a dove. 156

11.35  A lay brother of Zinna returned to his body because of a halfpenny. 226

12.33  A lay brother arranged Masses for his cousin, who was saved. 17 and 258

### Richalm von Schöntal's *Liber Revelationum*

16  Richalm preaches in the lay brothers' chapter. 100

33  A lay brother is greatly disturbed by attacks by a demon. 233–34

54  Richalm's low opinion of lay brothers. 160

### Salem Miracle Book

9  In a warning against somnolence, a lay brother has a vision of food and a woman being offered, which was refused by all except for two monks and five lay brothers. 60

### Ebrach Compilation

3  Same as BC 83v and *EM* 4.13 203–5

7  A lay brother at a grange heard Matins before the convent. 114

8  A lay brother saw the Blessed Virgin in a vision. 252

### Caesarius of Heisterbach's *Libri Viii Miraculorum*

1.51  Same as *DM* 7.12. 253

3.6  A tree grew with "AM" on the leaves on the grave of a lay brother from Poland. 173

3.18    A disobedient lay brother went on pilgrimage without permission.
210

3.32    A lay brother from Ter Doest, after being raised from the dead, declared what he had seen in purgatory.            214–15

3.41    Idleness exposed a lay brother to the attacks of demons.
97 and 241–42

3.59    Of the lay brother who like a rose was taken up to heaven.
172–73

**Fürstenfeld Collection**

62    Same as *LM* 1.14 and *EM* 4.23.            26–27 and 155

63    Same as *LM* 1.15 and *EM* 4.18.            148–49

64    Same as *LM* 1.16 and *EM* 4.17.            72–73

65    Same as *LM* 1.17 and *EM* 4.16.            67–69

66    Same as *LM* 1.18.            183

67    Same as *LM* 1.29 and *EM* 4.19.    158–59, 166 and 201–2

68    Same as *LM* 1.32 and *EM* 4.15.            70

69    Same as *CC* 3.12 and *EM* 4.31.    118 and 239–41

70    Same as *LM* 1.27.            243

71    Same as *CC* 4.13 and *LM* 3.26.            224–25

72    Same as *LM* 3.27.            217

73    Same as *LM* 3.35.            236

74    Same as *LM* 3.36/37.

# Cistercian Lay Brother *Usages*

H ere is the translation by Fr. Chrysogonus Waddell from his critical edition of the twelfth-century Lay Brother *Usages*.[1] Father Chrysogonus distinguishes three recensions: the first, dated about 1138/1140, consists of a prologue and fifteen chapters and only survives in one manuscript (Trento, Biblioteca comunale, MS 1711); the second, dated around 1147, consists of a prologue and twenty chapters and is represented by twelve manuscripts; the third, from the last quarter of the twelfth century, has a prologue and twenty-three chapters and is attested by seven manuscripts. The translation includes all variations except where there is a small discrepancy in the wording but the meaning is the same, when only one of the versions is given.

## The *Usages of the Cistercian Lay Brothers*

### Here Begins the Prologue

Since it is clear that we have received from bishops the care of souls of lay brothers equally as of monks, I am amazed that certain of our abbots devote indeed all due diligence of discipline to the monks, but none or very little to the lay brothers. Some, holding

---

[1] Chrysogonus Waddell, *Cistercian Lay Brothers, Twelfth-century Usages with related Texts*. Studia et Documenta X (Cîteaux: Commentarii cistercienses, 2000). Reproduced with permission of the editorial board of *Cîteaux, Commentarii cistercienses*.

them in contempt because of their innate simplicity, think that material food and clothing are to be provided for them more sparingly than for monks, but that they are nevertheless imperiously to be made to do forced labor. Others, on the contrary, giving in to their murmuring more than is expedient for souls, indulge bodies the better to get more work if they treat them with greater indulgence as regards food, and greater laxity as regards clothing. And thus in one way or another, they both require work and gloss over faults; and while they studiously expend that care which is of slight avail, and do almost nothing to provide for that which is of the utmost avail, they openly show what they seek from the society of lay brothers is their own interests, not those of Jesus Christ. In a word, if they too have been bought with the same great price, why should they be cared for any differently—those who, it is clear, are equals in the grace of redemption? If we ask reason, reason answers that those known to be simpler and uneducated are the ones most in need of our care and attention. This is why, just as we necessarily indeed had to draw up *Usages* for monks so that unity may everywhere be preserved in our manners, so also we have decided that provision should be made in the following brief document for the lay brothers, in things both temporal and spiritual, so that diversity may not be found in their way of life, either.

## I. The Lay Brothers at the Granges

At Vigils as well as the Day Hours they say their prayers just like the monks. Upon standing up, then, and making the sign of the cross, if there are two or more of them, the senior says: *Deus, in adiutorium meum intende*; and all respond: *Domine, ad adiuvandum me festina.* At Vigils, the senior continues: *Domine, labia mea asperies*; with the rest responding with the same verse. This is done three times. Then, standing upright, they say a silent *Pater noster.* When this has been said, the senior says, as all listen, *Gloria Patri et Filio et Spiritui sancto.* While saying this, he, as well as the others, bow; when it has been said, all stand upright, saying: *Sicut erat in principio et nunc et semper, et in saecula saeculorum, Amen*; and this they do twenty times. Then, after the twentieth *Sicut erat* all continue, with the senior beginning: *Kyrieleison* once, *Christeleison* once, *Kyrieleison* once. Then, as all listen, the senior says the *Pater noster* in its entirety, both at Vigils and at all Hours, adding: *Per Dominum nostrum etc.*; and the others respond: *Amen.* He then adds: *Benedicamus Domino*, which the others complete: *Deo gratias.*

At the Day Hours, after the *Deus in adiutorium*, all bow, and the senior says: *Gloria Patri et Filio et Spiritui sancto.* The others respond: *sicut erat, etc.* The remainder takes place the same way we said above, except that at Lauds and Vespers they say the *Pater noster* with the *Gloria* ten times. Five times at the other Hours. This order of psalmody is observed at all times, except that on twelve-lesson feasts the number of *Pater noster* with *Gloria* is doubled only at the Nocturns: forty in all. When alone or in church, each says the whole of this silently. Note, too, that when they are present at the Hours of the monks, they bow only for those *Glorias* for which the monks bow.

### II. The Time for Rising for Vigils

From September 13 until Holy Thursday the bell is rung when the final psalm of the first Nocturn is just beginning; and then the brethren rise. After the collect at the end of the Nocturns has been said, they go to work. But on feast days when we work the signal is rung at the beginning of the second Nocturn, and then they rise; and after the collect at the end of the *Te Deum laudamus* has been said, they leave.

But from Easter until 13 September, because they have no siesta, they sleep until Lauds; and when the signal has been rung they rise for church. After the prayers of Vigils, Lauds, and even Prime have been made, they leave. But they do not go to church for the other Day Hours; instead they make their prayers wherever they happen to be working, unless it is a day without work.

On Sundays, however, and on other days when they do not work, in winter as well as in summer, they rise for Vigils when the monks do. But those who have come from the granges or from a journey on that day, leave to go back to sleep after the fourth responsory, if they so wish; the others, however, do not leave, but

listen to the entire service, unless some obedience calls them elsewhere. But on summer season feasts on which they work, they rise
when the signal is rung at the Canticles.

From 13 September until Easter the lay brothers at the abbey go
to church for Compline daily; but for the rest of the time only on
Sundays and feasts when they do not work—for both Complines.
On ferial days, however, and on feasts when we work, they devote
themselves to their tasks as long as they can work by daylight. And
then the lay brother appointed for this sounds the tablet for the
end of their work. When the tablet has been sounded, they leave
their tasks and sing Compline.

But the brethren who are working at the grange keep watch
from 1 November until the Chair of Peter at least one fourth of
the night; and from the Chair until Easter, and from 13 September
until 1 November they rise so as to finish the prayers of Vigils and
Lauds before light. When these have been finished they work at
whatever is necessary. But from Easter until the aforesaid 13 September they rise at daybreak.

### III. Solemnities When They Do Not Work

The lay brothers do not work on these solemnities: The day
of the Lord's Birth, and the three following days; On the Cir-
cumcision; On Epiphany; On Good Friday; On Easter and Easter
Monday; On the Ascension; On Pentecost and Pentecost Monday;
On the solemnities of Saint Mary; Of Philip and James; Of the
Birth of St. John the Baptist; Of the apostles Peter and Paul; Of St.
James, apostle; Of St. Lawrence; Of Bartholomew; Of Matthew;
Of Michael; Of Simon and Jude; Of All Saints; Of Martin, bishop;
Of Andrew, apostle; Of Thomas, apostle; And on the Dedication
of the church, for those staying at the monastery. And even on
these feasts, if anything seems necessary, let them do what they are
ordered to do.

But on those solemnities when the lay brothers work and the
monks are free from work, the lay brothers at the abbey are able to
hear only the first Mass; and then they leave for work. And know
that during winter, in the interval after Nocturns, they prepare the

farm produce. On transposed feasts the monks do not work, but the lay brothers do.

## IV. Days When They Have Mass

On whichever days two Masses are sung, and on the major fasts, or when the body of a deceased is present—monk, novice, or lay brother—and on the solemn Commemoratives of All the Departed, they are present for the celebration of Mass, unless obedience prescribes otherwise.

In church, however, for their standing upright and their bows and their other observances, they act in the same way as the monks except that all are seated for one psalm, and all stand together for the next psalm. But for the holy water, they come forward according as the layout of each oratory so allows.

## V. About Communion

Only twelve times a year will they receive Communion,[2] except someone whom the abbot, for a particular reason, judges may go to Communion more often or more rarely: that is, on the Birth of the Lord, the Purification of Saint Mary, Holy Thursday, Easter, Pentecost, the Birth of Mary, the solemnity of All Saints.

Whoever is unable to receive Communion on the above mentioned feasts will receive Communion on the day he can fittingly do so.

Lay brothers at a considerable distance from their abbeys are permitted to go to Communion outside their abbeys, and also to receive blessed ashes in houses of religious, should the abbot so see fit. Lay brothers who receive Communion on Holy Thursday use only lenten fare until they have received their Easter Communion.

---

[2] This is according to Recension I, Trento, Ms 1711; all other manuscripts have seven times a year.

## VI. Places Where They Keep Silence

In whichever workshops the monks keep silence, so do they; nor may they enter any of them without permission. Moreover, in their own dormitory and refectory especially are they to observe silence; and, besides these, in all other places, unless they speak about necessities at the bidding of the abbot or prior, or even of cellarer—provided, however, that this authority has been given the cellarer.

Cobblers are everywhere to keep silence with each other and with all others, unless the abbot has perchance designated some place outside the work area for them, where they may speak among themselves briefly, and only about the necessities of their trade, and this only standing. So also for all the monastery craftsmen: millers, namely, weavers, skinners, and so on. Only in the case of the blacksmiths can a place within their workshop be designated where they may speak in the aforesaid manner concerning necessities, since they can hardly keep silence while at their task without detriment to their work. The masters of the masons, of the cobblers, and of craftsmen of this sort are not to speak with those under them on non-work days or in the evening after they have left their tasks.

Likewise, those at the granges are to observe silence in the dormitory, in the refectory, and in the calefactory, within the bounds designated for this. Elsewhere they can speak with their master concerning (their) necessities, and this standing, and only two at a time; and know that they are allowed to speak without their hoods. The grange master has an assistant where necessary. He is, namely, to be in charge of the house after him (the grange master). He is allowed to speak with the staff and guests concerning necessities. However, in the absence of the master, he may speak with everyone wherever speaking is allowed. Apart from this, they may not speak without permission either inside or outside, either with each other or with others. Shepherds, however, and herdsmen can speak with their juniors, and the juniors with them, at their work, and about necessities. When greeted, they return the greeting. If a traveler asks for directions, they give him the information verbally, but briefly. If he should speak about some other matter, he (the brother) is to reply that he is not allowed to speak further. He is to reply in this way to anyone disturbing him and trying to get him to speak.

## VII. That No Woman May Enter the Grange Court

No woman is to enter the grange court except at the command of abbot or prior; nor may anyone speak alone with a woman.

## VIII. About Mealtime Prayers

Upon being called to a meal by some sign, the brothers all say in unison: *Benedicite. Kyrieleison. Christeleison. Kyrieleison. Pater noster.* Then the senior of them, standing erect, says: *Et ne nos inducas in tentationem*; and the others respond: *Sed libera nos a malo.* Then the senior, tracing the sign of the cross with his hand, says: *In nomine Patris et Filii et Spiritus sancti*; the others respond: *AMEN.* And they thus sit down at table in order of seniority, and eat. And note that they are not allowed to eat in their refectories or elsewhere without cape and hood, if they are able to have them. And if anyone perchance misses the verse three times, his portion of wine is removed, and he eats last in rank.

When the meal is over, the senior stands and begins: *Miserere mei, Deus*; and he says the entire verse; and all say the next verse; and thus they say the other verses alternately, adding: *Gloria Patri. Sicut erat. Kyrieleison. Christeleison. Kyrieleison. Pater noster.* Then the senior says: *Et ne nos inducas in temptationem*; and the others respond: *Sed libera nos a malo.* When he (the senior) adds: *Benedicamus Domino*, the others respond: *Deo gratias.* And thus, having entered the church, they say the *Pater noster* there in silence; and making the sign of the cross, they retire.

However, the servants complete their verse in the refectory, and do not say that *Pater noster.* At the granges, too, that *Pater noster* is not said; but after the meal, they begin the *Miserere mei, Deus*, and enter the oratory. Lay brothers of a different Order are not to eat with ours in our refectory, except lay brothers of those houses to which this has been granted at the Chapter at Cîteaux.

## IX. What They Have to Learn

No one is to have a book or learn anything except the *Pater noster*, the *Credo in Deum*, the *Miserere mei, Deus*, and the other things which it has been decreed that they should learn—and this not from a written text, but only by heart.

## X. About the Discipline

From the Octave of Pentecost until the Birth of the Lord, and from the Octave of the Theophany until Easter, they receive the discipline every Friday, unless some feast occurs when they do not work. But if one is impeded because of some negligence, it is to be made good on the first available day.

## XI. About the Chapter

On all Sundays other than those on which a sermon for everyone takes place in the chapter room of the monks—only on those days do the brothers enter the monks' chapter room—on those days, I say, when the sacristan rings the bell to call the monks to chapter, the brothers immediately enter their own chapter room, so that while the chapter of the monks is being held, their chapter may also be held, either by the abbot or by one appointed for this. Upon coming in and before being seated, while all the others are standing turned towards the east, he says: *Pretiosa in conspectu Domini mors sanctorum eius*, and the rest that follows, in the manner of monks sent on a journey, and with the brethren making the suitable responses. He then sits down and says: *Benedicite.* After the response: *Dominus*, he gives the sermon. At its end, after all have added their *Amen*, the one presiding over the chapter says: *Loquamur de ordine nostro.* When this has been said, if a novice is to be received, the brother appointed for this says: *Recipiendus est nouitius.* The one presiding at chapter says to the brethren: *Frater quidam receptus est in capitulo monachorum. Veniat, et mittemus eum in ordine suo*; and at his bidding the aforesaid brother leads him in. He prostrates; and then, as he stands before him, he (the one presiding) explains to him how rough and mean the way of life is. Then he prays for his perseverance; and, after the *Amen* has been said by all, he bids him take his place according to his rank. Then they (the brothers) prostrate and make their proclamations; and everything takes place as in the monks' chapter. When everything has been finished, and the *Adiutorium nostrum in nomine Domini* has been said, and the brethren have responded: *Qui fecit caelum et terram*, they make a bow and withdraw.

## XII. How Brothers Are Received

Brothers coming for conversion are received in the chapter of the monks, nor are they to be joined to the community of the brothers before being received in their chapter. For this reason (their chapter) can be assembled on any day. But let a master be assigned them, one capable of training them in good conduct and teaching them the observance.

If a novice lay brother buys clothes for himself, let him buy such as we have; but the cloak he is not to buy.

## XIII. About Profession

At the end of a year, the novice comes into the chapter of the monks, where, having first given up all possessions, he makes profession in this way. First of all, he prostrates and asks for mercy. Then he rises at the abbot's command, and, kneeling before the abbot, he joins his hands, and placing them between the hands of the abbot, he promises him obedience in good until death. And the abbot responds: *Et Dominus det tibi perserverantiam usque in finem*, with everyone responding: *AMEN*. Then, after kissing the abbot, he withdraws. And be it known that from that day on which he makes his petition in the chapter of the monks, and is thus received in the novitiate of the lay brothers he is not to become a monk in our Order. But if, at the instigation of the devil, he leaves the Order and receives the habit of monk or canon regular from anyone whomsoever, he is to be received as a lay brother after he has put aside the habit, unless perchance—which God forbid—he has received Holy Orders. If he has received them, he is not from then on to be received.

## XIV. About Brethren Sent on a Journey

A brother on a journey is to keep silence in all churches and at his meals and after Compline; and he is to behave in everything like a monk sent on a journey, except that he is not obliged to fast other than in a manner in which the brothers fast at the granges. When he comes to a monastery or a grange of our Order, he follows the exercises in all respects, like the brothers of that place. However, he will be able to speak about necessities with the brother in charge of the stable, such as shoeing the horses, or when he gives them their allowance of fodder and hay; and this he does standing. It is granted to have a brother who is in charge of the stable, who may speak with the brethren of our Order as with the other guests when the multitude of guests so requires. But if he (a lay brother) travels with a monk, he conforms to his orders.

## XV. About Food

They eat the same food as the monks, those in health like those in health, those who have been bled like those who have been bled, those who are infirm like those who are infirm. Those in the monastery receive the same amount (as the monks) and at the same time. But if the abbot judges it fitting that some should take mixt, let them take mixt. This, however, is the measure of mixt: a half-pound of their bread, or a larger amount of coarse bread, and water. Those at the granges, however, will not fast except on the major fasts and in Advent and on Fridays from 13 September until Lent; and each will have a pound of bread, and, over and above this, as much coarse bread as necessary.

## XVI. About Clothing

The clothing consists of: a cloak, tunics, footwear, sandals, shoes, a hood covering shoulders and chest only. For herdsmen, wagoners, and shepherds the abbot will be able to provide more amply. Also coarse, simple skins. But should any abbot think that some of those coarse skins, since they are already old, ought to be lined (with cloth), this should be done only with cloth that is old and common. Should any abbot discover that an unauthorized cloak is being worn by some lay brother who is passing through, he should retain it. Lay brothers are permitted to have four tunics, if this seems good to the abbot. But only blacksmiths have permission to have smocks—which have to be black and rounded.

## XVII. About Bedding

They have beds like monks have, apart from the woolen blanket, instead of which they use skins.

## XVIII. About the Punishment for the Disobedience of Lay Brothers

A lay brother who is disobedient to any whomsoever master assigned him, for his penance takes his meals for three days seated on the floor before the brothers in the refectory, and without a napkin. He also receives the discipline in chapter.

## XIX. About Boots

Lay brothers at the granges do not have boots, but not even at the abbey, unless perhaps, because of Vigils, the abbot gives them to someone in the abbey; and they should be second-hand. The same abbot may give some of these second-hand boots, if a supply is on hand, to one of the brothers, to make them available, when necessary, to those coming from the granges.

## XX. About Bells

Lay brothers at the granges do not have bells other than the small handbells in the refectory to call the brothers to the meal. These may be had by whoever wants them.

## XXI. That No One Washes Another's Head

One lay brother is not to wash the head of another lay brother. In the case of a lay brother unable to wash himself because of illness, let the one whom the senior so bids wash him. Whoever does otherwise is, without further discussion, to be flogged in the chapter of the lay brothers.

## XXII. Which Skins They Do Not Wear

Our brethren do not wear skins of woodland animals: no cat skins, no rabbit skins, no squirrel skins or miniver or others of this sort, even if on one or another occasion they are to be had; for their purchase is absolutely forbidden.

## XXIII. That They Are Not to Take Oaths upon the Gospels

Our lay brothers are not allowed to take oaths upon the Gospels.

There are two alternatives to Chapter XXIII:

1. Our lay brothers are not allowed to take oaths except for an affair of their own, and for absolutely no other necessity whatsoever.
2. Concerning fugitives at the point of death at abbeys, this lies within the discretion of the abbot; and let the decision of times past be observed.

# Bibliography

## Contemporary Sources

*Account-Book of Beaulieu Abbey, The.* Edited by Stanley Frederick Hockey. London: Royal Historical Society, 1975.

Alberic of Trois Fontaines. *Chronica.* ["Chronica Albrici Monachi Trium Fontium"]. Edited by Paulus Scheffer-Boichorst, 631–950. *Monumenta Germaniae Historica: Scriptorum* 23. Hannover, 1874; repr. Leipzig: Hiersemann, 1925.

*Autobiography of Giraldus Cambrensis, The.* Edited and translated by Harold Edgeworth Butler. London: J. Cape, 1937; repr. Rochester, NY: Boydell Press, 2005.

*Beaulieu Cartulary, The.* Edited by Stanley Frederick Hockey. Southampton: University Press, 1974.

Bernard, Saint. *Sancti Bernardi Opera.* Edited by Jean Leclercq, Henri M. Rochais, and C. H. Talbot. 8 vols. Rome: Editiones Cistercienses, 1957–1977.

Birgitte, Saint. *Acta et Processus canonizacionis beate Birgitte, efter col. A14 Holm., cod Ottob. Lat. 90 o. cod. Harl. 612.* Edited by Isak Gustaf Alfred Collijn. Uppsala: Almquist and Wiksell, 1924–1931.

——. *Den Helige Birgittas Revelaciones Extravagantes.* Edited by Lennart Hollman. Uppsala: Almquist and Wiksell, 1956.

Burchardus, Abbot of Bellevaux. *Apologia de Barbis.* Edited by E. P. Goldschmidt. Cambridge: Univesity Press, 1935.

——. *Apologia de Barbis.* In *Apologiae Duae.* Edited by Robert B. C. Huygens. Introduction by Giles Constable. Corpus Christianorum, Continuatio Mediaevalis 62. Turnhout: Brepols, 1985.

Caesarius of Heisterbach. *Caesarii Heisterbacensis monachi Ordinis Cisterciensis Dialogus miraculorum.* Edited by Joseph Strange. 2 vols. Cologne: J. M. Heberle (H. Lempertz), 1851.

——. *The Dialogue on Miracles.* Edited and translated by Henry von Essen Scott and Charles Cooke Swinton Bland. 2 vols. New York: Harcourt, Brace, 1929.

——. *Die Wundergeschichten des Caesarius von Heisterbach.* Vol. 1. Edited by Alfons Hilka. Bonn: Hanstein, 1933.

——. *Die Wundergeschichten des Caesarius von Heisterbach.* Vol. 3, *Die beiden ersten Bücher der Libri VIII miraculorum.* Edited by Alfons Hilka. Bonn: Hanstein, 1937.

345

*Cartulary of Byland Abbey, The.* Edited by Janet Burton. Publications of the Surtees Society 208. Woodbridge, Suffolk: Boydell Press; Rochester, NY: Boydell & Brewer, 2004.

*Catalogue of Romances in the Department of Manuscripts in the British Museum.* Edited by John Alexander Herbert. Vol. 3. London: British Museum, 1910.

*Chartes et Documents concernant l'Abbaye de Cîteaux: 1098–1182.* Edited by Jean Marilier. Rome: Editiones cisterciensis, 1961.

*Chronicon Abbatie de Parco Lude = The Chronicle of Louth Park Abbey, With Appendix of Documents.* Edited by Edmund Venables. Translated by Arthur Roland Maddison. Horncastle: Lincolnshire Record Society, 1891.

Clark, E. K. "The Foundation of Kirkstall Abbey," 169–208. In *Miscellanea. Publications of the Thoresby Society* 4 (Leeds, 1895).

*Codex Esromensis.* Edited by Oluf August Nielsen. Copenhagen: Rudolph Klein, 1880–1881.

*Collectaneum exemplorum et visionum Clarevallense e codice Trecensi 946.* Edited by Olivier Legendre. Turnhout: Brepols, 2005.

Conrad of Eberbach. *Exordium Magnum Cisterciense sive Narratio de Initio Cisterciensis Ordinis.* Edited by Bruno Griesser. Rome: Editiones Cistercienses, 1961. English: *The Great Beginning of Cîteaux.* Translated by Benedicta Ward and Paul Savage. Edited by E. Rozanne Elder. CS 72. Collegeville, MN: Cistercian Publications, 2012.

*Coucher Book of the Cistercian Abbey of Kirkstall: in the West Riding of the County of York, The.* Edited by William Thomas Lancaster and William Paley Baildon. Leeds: Thoresby Society, 1904.

Daniel, Walter. *Vita Ailredi cum Epistola ad Mauricium; The Life of Ailred with the Letter to Maurice.* Translation with an Introduction and Notes by F. M. Powicke. London: Nelson, 1950. *The Life of Aelred and the Letter to Maurice.* Translated by F. M. Powicke. Introduction by Marsha Dutton. CF 57. Kalamazoo and Spencer: Cistercian, 1994.

*Diplomatarium Danicum.* Series I–IV. Copenhagen: Reitzel, 1938– .

Etienne de Bourbon. *Anecdotes Historiques, Légendes et Apologues: tirés du receuil inédit d'Etienne de Bourbon, Dominicain du XIII. siècle.* Edited by Albert Lecoy de La Marche. Paris: Librarie Renouard, 1877.

*Étienne d'Obazine, Vie de.* Edited and translated by Michel Aubrun. Clermond-Ferrand: Institut d'Études du Massif Central, 1970. English: *Robert of La Chaise-Dieu and Stephen of Obazine.* Translation and introduction by Hugh Feiss, Maureen M. O'Brien, and Ronald E. Pepin. Lives of Monastic Reformers 1. CS 222. Collegeville, MN: Cistercian Publications, 2010.

Geoffredo di Auxerre. *Super Apocalypsim.* Edited by Ferruccio Gastaldelli. Rome: Edizioni di storia e letteratura, 1970. English: *Geoffrey of Auxerre on the Apocalypse.* Translated by Joseph Gibbons. CF 42. Kalamazoo, MI: Cistercian Publications, 2000.

*Giraldi Cambrensis Opera.* Edited by J. S. Brewer, James F. Dimock, and Sir George F. Warner. 8 vols. London: Longmans, Green, 1861–1891.

Hildegard of Bingen. *Letters*. Translated by Joseph L. Baird and Radd K. Ehrman. Oxford and New York: Oxford University Press, 1994–2004.

Humbert de Romanis. "Sermo XXX ad Conversos Cistercienses," 430. In Marguerin de la Bigne, *Maxima Biblioteca Veterum Patrum* 25. Lyon: Jean et Jacques Anisson, 1677.

Idung of Prüfening. *Le moine et ses deux ouvrages: argumentum sur quatuor questionibus et Dialogus duorum monachorum*. Edited by Robert B. C. Huygens. Spoleto: Centro Italiano di Studi sull'Alto Medioevo, 1972.

———. *Cistercians and Cluniacs: The Case for Cîteaux*. Translated by J. F. O'Sullivan. CF 33. Kalamazoo, MI: Cistercian Publications, 1977.

Jacobus de Voragine. *The Golden Legend: Selections*. Translated by Christopher Stace. Harmondsworth: Penguin, 1998.

Jocelin of Furness. *The Life of Waldef, Abbot of Melrose*. Edited and translated by George Joseph McFadden. Dissertation Columbia University, 1952. Ann Arbor: UMI, 1991.

John, Abbot of Ford. *Wulfric of Haselbury*. Edited by Maurice Bell. Somerset Record Society 47. Frome: Printed by Butler & Tanner, 1933.

John of Ford. *Sermons on the Final Verses of the Song of Songs*. Translated by Wendy Mary Beckett. 7 vols. CF 29, 39, 43–47. Kalamazoo, MI: Cistercian Publications, 1977–1984.

John of Forde. *The Life of Wulfric of Haselbury, Anchorite*. Translated by Pauline Maud Matarasso. CF 79. Trappist, KY: Cistercian Publications; Collegeville, MN: Liturgical Press, 2011.

Longchamps, Nigel. *Speculum Stultorum*. Edited by John H. Mozley and Robert R. Raymo. Berkeley and Los Angeles: University of California Press, 1960.

———. *A Mirror for Fools; or, the Book of Burnal the Ass*. Translated by John H. Mozley. Oxford: Blackwell, 1961.

Map, Walter. *De Nugis Curialium = Courtiers' Trifles*. Edited and translated by M. R. James, et al. Oxford: Clarendon Press, 1914; new ed. 1983.

"Margam, Annales." In *Annales Monastici*. Vol. 1. Edited by Henry Richard Luard. London: Longmans, Green, 1864.

*Memorials of the Abbey of St. Mary of Fountains*. Vol. 1. Edited by John Richard Walbran. Publications of the Surtees Society 42. Durham: Andrews, 1863.

*Monasterii de Melsa, Chronica: a fundatione usque ad annum 1396, auctore Thoma de Burton, abbate: accedit continuatio ad annum 1406 a monacho quodam ipsius domus*. Edited by Edward A. Bond. 3 vols. London: Longmans, Green, 1866–1868.

Orderic Vitalis. *Ecclesiastical History*. 6 vols. Edited and translated by Marjorie Chibnall. Oxford: Clarendon Press, 1969–1980.

Ralph of Coggeshall. *Radulphi de Coggeshall Chronicon Anglicanum*. Edited by Joseph Stevenson. London: Longmans, Green, 1875.

*Recueil des Chartes de l'Abbaye de Clairvaux*. Edited by Jean Waquet, Jean-Marc Roger, and Laurent Veyssière. Collection des documents inédits sur l'histoire de France, Série in-8o, 32. Paris: C. T. H. S., 2004.

*Recueil des Pancartes de l'Abbaye de la Ferté-sur-Grosne, 1113–1178.* Edited by Georges Duby. Aix-en-Provence: Editions Ophrys, 1953.

Reimbaldus. *Libellus de diversis ordinibus et professionibus qui sunt in Aecclesia.* Giles Constable and Bernard S. Smith, editors and translators. Oxford: Clarendon Press, 2003.

Richalm von Schöntal. *Liber revelationum.* Edited by Paul Gerhard Schmidt. Monumenta Germaniae Historica 24. Hannover: Hahnsche Buchhandlung, 2009.

*Scriptores Minores Historiae Danicae: Medii Aevi.* 2 vols. Edited by Martin C. Gertz. Copenhagen: Gad, 1917–1922.

"Villariensium, Gesta Sanctorum," in *Monumenta Germaniae Historica, Scriptores* 25. Edited by Georg Waitz. Berlin: Weidmann, 1880.

*Waverleia, Annales Monasterii de.* In *Annales Monastici* 2. Edited by Henry Richards Luard, 127–411. London: Longmans, Green, 1865.

*William of Malmesbury's Chronicle of the Kings of England: From the Earliest Period to the Reign of King Stephen.* With notes and illustrations by J. A. Giles. London: George Bell and Sons, 1904; repr. New York: A. M. S. Press, 1968.

Wright, Thomas. *The Anglo-Latin Satirical Poets and Epigrammists of the Twelfth Century.* London: Longman, 1872.

## Modern Works

Abeele, Baudouin van den. "Trente et un nouveaux manuscrits de l'Aviarium: regards sur la diffusion de l'oeuvre d'Hugues de Fouilloy." *Scriptorium* 57 (2003): 253–71.

Anderes, Bernhard, and Peter Hoegge. *Die Glasgemälde in Kloster Wettingen.* Baden: Baden-Verlag, 1989.

Aubert, Marcel. *L'Architecture Cistercienne en France.* 2 vols. Paris: Vanoest, 1947.

Baker, Derek. "Heresy and Learning in Early Cistercianism." In *Schism, Heresy and Religious Protest.* Edited by Derek Baker, 93–107. Cambridge: Cambridge University Press, 1972.

———. "Legend and Reality: the case of Waldef of Melrose." In *Church, Society and Politics: Papers Read at the 13th Summer Meeting & the 14th Winter Meeting of the Ecclesiastical History Society.* Edited by Derek Baker, 59–82. Studies in Church History 12. Oxford: Blackwell, 1975.

Bannister, A. T. "Miraculous happenings at Dore." *Transactions of the Woolhope Naturalists' Field Club,* 209–11. Hereford, 1929.

Barnes, Guy D. *Kirkstall Abbey 1147–1539: an Historical Study.* Leeds: The Thoresby Society, 1984.

Barrière, Bernadette. *L'Abbaye Cistercienne d'Obazine en Bas-Limousin: Les origines, le patrimoine.* Tulle: n. p., 1977.

———. "L'économie Cistercienne du Sud-Ouest de la France." In *L'économie cistercienne. Geographic Mutations du moyen age aux temps modernes.* Edited by Charles Higounet. *Flaran* 3: 75–99. Auch: Commission d'histoire de Flaran, 1983.

———. "Les patrimonies cisterciens en France," 45–69. In *L'espace cistercien.* Edited by Léon Pressouyre. Paris: Comité des travaux historiques et scientifiques, 1994.

Batany, Jean. "Les Convers chez quelques moralistes des XIIe et XIIIe siècles." *Cîteaux* 20 (1969): 241–59.

Berlioz, Jacques. *Saints et Damnés—la Bourgogne du Moyen Age dans les récits de Étienne de Bourbon, inquisiteur (1190–1261).* Dijon: Édition du Bien public, 1989.

Berman, Constance H. *Medieval Agriculture, the Southern French Countryside, and the Early Cistercians: A Study of Forty-Three Monasteries.* Transactions of the American Philosophical Society 76. Philadelphia: American Philosophical Society, 1986.

———. *The Cistercian Evolution: The Invention of a Religious Order in Twelfth-Century Europe.* Philadelphia: University of Pennsylvania Press, 2000.

———. "Conversae and Conversi." In *Women and Gender in Medieval Europe.* Edited by Margaret Schaus, 169–70. Routledge Encyclopedias of the Middle Ages 14. New York and London: Routledge, 2006.

Białoskórska, Krystyna. "Polish Cistercian Architecture and Its Contacts with Italy." *Gesta* 5 (1966): 14–22.

Birkett, Helen. *The Saints' Lives of Jocelin of Furness.* York: Woodbridge, 2010.

Bishop, T. A. M. "Monastic Granges in Yorkshire." *English Historical Review* 51 (1936): 193–214.

Bouchard, Constance Brittain. *Holy Entrepreneurs.* Cornell: Cornell University Press, 1991.

Bredero, Adriaan H. "Un brouillon du XIIe siècle: l'autograph de Geoffroy d'Auxerre." *Scriptorium* 13 (1959): 27–60.

———. *Bernard of Clairvaux: between Cult and History.* Grand Rapids: Eerdmans; Edinburgh: T & T Clark, 1996.

Burton, Janet. "The Estates and Economy of Rievaulx Abbey in Yorkshire." *Cîteaux* 49 (1998): 29–94.

———. *The Monastic Order in Yorkshire 1069–1215.* Cambridge: Cambridge University Press, 1999.

———. *The Foundation History of the Abbeys of Byland and Jervaulx.* York: Borthwick Institute, 2006.

Canivez, Joseph-Marie. *Statuta Capitulorum Generalium Ordinis Cisterciensis ab anno 1116 ad 1786.* 8 vols. Louvain: Bureaux de la Revue, 1933–1941.

Casey, Michael. "Herbert of Clairvaux's *Book of Wonderful Happenings.*" *CS* 25 (1990): 37–64.

———. "Reading Saint Bernard: the Man, the Medium, the Message." In *A Companion to Bernard of Clairvaux.* Edited by Brian Patrick McGuire, 62–107. Leiden: Brill, 2011.

Cassidy-Welch, Megan. "*Non Conversi sed Perversi*: The Use and Marginalisation of the Cistercian Lay Brother." In *Deviance and Textual Control: New Perspectives in Medieval Studies*. Edited by Megan Cassidy-Welch, Helen Hickey, and Meagan Street, 34–55. Parkville, Victoria: Department of History, University of Melbourne, 1997.

———. *Monastic Spaces and their Meanings: Thirteenth-Century English Cistercian Monasteries*. Turnhout: Brepols, 2001.

Castora, Joseph C. "The Cistercian Order as Portrayed in the *Speculum Ecclesiae* of Gerald of Wales." *AC* 53 (1997): 73–97.

Cawley, Martinus. *Send Me God: The Lives of Ida of Nivelles, Arnulf of Villers and Abundus of Villers*. Turnhout: Brepols, 2003.

Chauvin, B. "Réalités et Évolution de l'Économie Cistercienne dans les Duché et Comté de Bourgogne en Moyen Âge." Edited by Charles Higounet, *Flaran* 3: 13–52. Auch: Commission d'histoire de Flaran, 1983.

———. "Un disciple méconnu de Saint Bernard, Burchard, abbé de Balerne puis de Bellevaux." *Cîteaux* 40 (1989): 5–68.

Choisselet, D. & Vernet, P. *Les* Ecclesiastica Officia *du XIIème Siècle*. Reiningue: Documentation cistercienne, 1989.

Clark, Willene B. *The Medieval Book of Birds: Hugh of Fouilloy's Aviarium*. Binghamton, NY: Medieval and Renaissance Texts and Studies, 1992.

Colker, Marvin L. "The *Liber Altarium* and *Liber Sepulchorum* of Clairvaux." *Sacris Erudiri* 41 (2002): 391–466.

Comba, Rainalda. "Aspects Économiques de la vie des Abbayes Cisterciennes de l'Italie du Nord-Ouest." Edited by Charles Higounet, *Flaran* 3: 119–33. Auch: Commission d'histoire de Flaran, 1983.

Constable, Giles. "The Vision of Gunthelm and other visionaries attributed to Peter the Venerable." *Revue Bénédictine* 66 (1956): 92–114.

———. *Monastic Tithes From Their Origin to the Twelfth Century*. Cambridge: Cambridge University Press, 1964.

———. "*Famuli* and *Conversi* at Cluny." *Revue Bénédictine* 83 (1973): 326–50.

———. "The Lay Brothers and Lay Sisters of the Order of Sempringham." In *Medieval Studies in Honour of Avrom Saltman*, 83–96. Ramat-Gan: Bar-Ilan University Press, 1995.

Constable, Giles & Smith, Bernard. *Libellus de diversis ordinibus et professionibus qui sunt in aecclesia*. Oxford: Clarendon Press, 2003.

Coomans, Thomas. *L'abbaye de Villers-en-Brabant: Construction, Configuration et Signification d'une Abbaye Cistercienne Gothique*. Commentarii cistercienses. Brussels: Racine; Brecht: Cîteaux, 2000.

———. "From Flanders to Scotland: the Choir Stalls of Melrose Abbey in the Fifteenth Century." *Perspectives for an Architecture of Solitude*. Edited by Terryl N. Kinder, 235–50. Turnhout: Brepols, 2004.

Coppack, Glyn. "According to the Form of the Order—the Earliest Cistercian Buildings in England and their Context." In *Perspectives for an Architecture of Solitude*. Edited by Terryl N. Kinder, 35–45. Turnhout: Brepols, 2004.

Cowley, Frederick George. *The Monastic Order in South Wales 1066–1349*. Cardiff: University of Wales Press, 1977.

Czmara, Jean-Claude. *Sur les traces de Saint-Bernard*. Bar-sur-Aube, n.d.

Debuisson, Marc. "La provenance des premiers cisterciens d'après les lettres et les *vitae* de Bernard de Clairvaux." *Cîteaux* 43 (1992): 5–118.

Dijk, Clemens van. "L'Instruction et la culture des frères convers dans les premiers siècles de l'ordre de Cîteaux." *Collectanea Ordinis Cisterciensium Reformatorum* 24 (1962): 243–58.

Dimier, Marie-Anselme. "Une découverte concernant le bienheureux Simon d'Aulne." *Cîteaux* 21 (1970): 302–5.

———. *Recueil de Plans d'Églises Cisterciennes*. 2 vols. Grignan: Abbaye Notre-Dame d'Aiguebelle; Paris: Librairie d'art ancien et moderne, 1949.

———. "Violences, Rixes et Homicides chez les Cisterciens." *Revue des Sciences Religieuses* 46 (1972): 38–57.

Donkin, Robin A. "The Cistercian Grange in England in the 12th and 13th Centuries, with Special Reference to Yorkshire." *Studia Monastica* 6 (1964): 95–144.

———. *The Cistercians: Studies in the Geography of Medieval England and Wales*. Toronto: Pontifical Institute of Mediaeval Studies, 1978.

Donnelly, James S. *The Decline of the Medieval Cistercian Laybrotherhood*. Fordham University Studies: History Series 3. New York: Fordham University Press, 1949.

———. "Changes in the Grange Economy of the English and Welsh Cistercian Abbeys 1300–1541." *Traditio* 10 (1954): 399–457.

Dubois, Jacques. "The Laybrothers' Life in the Twelfth Century." *CS* 7 (1972): 161–213.

[Ducourneau], Othon. "De l'institution et des Us des convers dans l'ordre de Cîteaux." In *Saint Bernard et Son Temps*, 2: 139–201. Dijon: Association Bourguignonne des Sociétés Savantes, 1929.

Easting, Robert. *St Patrick's Purgatory: Two Versions of Owayne Miles and the Vision of William of Stranton together with the long text of the Tractatus de purgatorio Sancti Patricii*. Oxford and New York: Published for the Early English Text Society by the Oxford University Press, 1991.

Farmer, Hugh. "A Letter of St Waldef of Melrose concerning a recent vision." *Studia Anselmiana* 43. *Analecta Monastica* 5th Series (1958): 91–101.

Ferguson, Peter. "The First Architecture of the Cistercians in England and the work of Abbot Adam of Meaux." *Journal of the British Archaeological Association* 176 (1983): 74–86.

France, James. *The Cistercians in Scandinavia*. CSS 131. Kalamazoo, MI: Cistercian Publications, 1992.

———. *The Cistercians in Medieval Art*. CSS 170. Kalamazoo, MI: Cistercian Publications, 1998a.

———. "The Cellarer's Domain—Evidence from Denmark." *Studies in Cistercian Art and Architecture*. Vol. 5. Edited by Meredith Parsons Lillich. CSS 167, 1–39. Kalamazoo, MI: Cistercian Publications, 1998b.

————. "Cistercians under Our Lady's Mantle." *CSQ* 37 (2002): 393–414.

Freedman, Paul H. *Images of the Medieval Peasant*. Stanford, CA: Stanford University Press, 1999.

Freeman, Elizabeth. *Narratives of a New Order: Cistercian Historical Writing in England, 1150–1220*. Turnhout: Brepols, 2002a.

————. "Models for Cistercian Life in Jocelin of Furness's *Vita Waldevi*." *CSQ* 37 (2002): 107–21.

Gottschalk, Joseph. "Die älteste Bilderhandschrift mit den Quellen zum Leben der hl. Hedwig." *Aachener Kunstblätter* 34 (1967): 61–161.

Graves, Coburn V. "The Economic Activities of the Cistercians in Medieval England." *ASOC* 13 (1957): 3–60.

Greenia, Conrad. "The Laybrother Vocation in the Eleventh and Twelfth Centuries." *CS* 16 (1981): 38–45.

Griesser, Bruno. "Registrum Epistolarum Stephano de Lexington abbatis de Stanlegia et de Savigniano." *ASOC* 2 (1946): 1–118; *ASOC* 8 (1952a): 191–378.

————. "Ein Himmeroder Liber Miraculorum und seine Beziehungen zu Caesarius von Heisterbach." *Archiv für Kirchengeschichte* 4 (1952b): 257–74.

————. "Die *Ecclesiastica Officia Cisterciensis Ordinis*." *ASOC* 12 (1956): 153–288.

Hall, Jackie. "East of the Cloister: Infirmaries, Abbots' Lodgings, and other Chambers." In *Perspectives for an Architecture of Solitude*. Edited by Terryl N. Kinder, 199–211. Turnhout: Brepols, 2004.

Hallinger, Kassius. "Woher kommen die Laienbrüder?" *ASOC* 12 (1956): 1–104.

Harrison, Stuart A. *Byland Abbey, North Yorkshire*. London: English Heritage, 1999.

Higounet, Charles. *La Grange de Vaulerent: Structure et Exploitation d'un Terroir Cistercien de la Plaine de France, XIIe–Xve siècle*. Paris: S. E. V. P. E. N., 1965.

————, ed. *Flaran 3. L'Économie Cistercienne*. Auch: Commission d'histoire de Flaran, 1983.

————. "Essai sur les Granges Cisterciennes." In *Flaran 3*, 157–80. Auch: Commission d'histoire de Flaran, 1983.

Hinnebusch, John Frederick. *The Historia Occidentalis of Jacques de Vitry*. Fribourg: University Press, 1972.

Hoffmann, Eberhard. *Das Konverseninstitut des Cistercienserordens in seinem Ursprung und seiner Organisation*. Études historiques de Fribourg 1. Fribourg: Gschwend, 1905.

Hockey, Frederick. *Beaulieu—King John's Abbey*. Beaulieu: Pioneer Publications, 1976.

Holdsworth, Christopher John. "Eleven Visions connected with the Cistercian Monastery of Stratford Langthorne." *Cîteaux* 13 (1962): 185–204.

————. "The Blessings of Work: the Cistercian View." In *Sanctity and Secularity: the Church and the World*. Edited by Derek Baker, 57–76. Oxford: Basil Blackwell, 1973.

Horn, Walter William, and Ernest Born. *The Barns of the Abbey of Beaulieu at its Granges of Great Coxwell and Beaulieu St Leonards.* Berkeley: University of California Press, 1965.

Huffschmid, Maximilian. "Beiträge zur Geschichte der Cisterzienserabtei Schönau bei Heidelberg." *Zeitschrift für die Geschichte des Oberrheins* 45 (1892): 69–103.

Jacobs, John C. *The Fables of Odo of Cheriton.* Syracuse: Syracuse University Press, 1985.

Jamroziak, Emilia. *Rievaulx Abbey and its Social Context 1132–1300.* Turnhout: Brepols, 2005.

Jørgensen, Ellen. "Djævelen I Vitskøl Kloster." In *Danske Studier,* edited by Marius Kristensen and Axel Olrik, 15–17. Copenhagen: Gyldendalske Boghandel; Nordisk, 1912.

Karajan, Theodor G. von. "Sermones nulli parentes." *Zeitschrift für deutsches Altherthum* 2 (1842): 25–26.

Kienzle, Beverly Mayne. "The Conversion of Pons of Léras and the True Account of the Beginning of the Monastery at Silvanès." *CSQ* 30 (1995): 219–43.

Kinder, Terryl N. *L'Europe Cistercienne.* La Pierre-qui-Vire: Zodiaque, 1997.

———. *Perspectives for an Architecture of Solitude.* Turnhout: Brepols, 2004.

King, Archdale A. *Cîteaux and her Elder Daughters.* London: Burns & Oates, 1954.

Knight, Gillian R. *The Correspondence between Peter the Venerable and Bernard of Clairvaux.* Aldershot: Ashgate, 2002.

Knowles, David. "The Revolt of the Lay Brothers of Sempringham." *English Historical Review* 50 (1935): 465–87.

———. *The Monastic Order in England.* Cambridge: Cambridge University Press, 1940.

———. *The Religious Orders in England.* 2 vols. Cambridge: Cambridge University Press, 1956–1957.

———. *The Historian and Character.* Cambridge: Cambridge University Press, 1963.

———, and John Kenneth Sinclair Saint Joseph. *Monastic Sites from the Air.* Cambridge: Cambridge University Press, 1952.

———, and R Neville Hancock. *Medieval Religious Houses: England and Wales.* London, New York, and Toronto: Longmans, Green, 1953.

Kompatscher-Gufler, Gabriela. *Herbert von Clairvaux und sein Liber miraculorum: die Kurzversion eines anonymen bayerischen Redaktors.* Bern: Peter Lang, 2005.

Lawrence, C. H. "Stephen of Lexington and Cistercian University Studies in the Thirteenth Century." *Journal of Ecclesiastical History* 11 (1960): 164–78.

Leclercq, Jean. "De la vie de Christian d'Aumône." *Analecta Bollandiana* 71 (1953): 21–52.

———. "Comment vivaient les Fréres Convers?" *AC* 21 (1965): 239–58.

———. "Aspects de la vie Cistercienne au XIIIe S." *Studia Monastica* 20 (1978): 221–26.

Lefèvre, J. A. "Les traditions des *Usus conversorum* de Cîteaux." *Collectanea ordinis cisterciensium Reformatorum* 17 (1955): 11–39.

———. "L'Evolution des *Usus conversorum* de Cîteaux." *Collectanea ordinis cisterciensium Reformatorum* 17 (1955): 65–97.

Le Goff, Jacques. *The Birth of Purgatory.* Translated by Arthur Goldhammer. Chicago: Univesity of Chicago Press; London: Scolar Press, 1984.

Lekai, Louis J. *The Cistercians: Ideals and Reality.* Kent, OH: Kent State University Press, 1977.

Lescher, Bruce. "Laybrothers: Questions Then, Questions Now." *CS* 23 (1988): 63–85.

Liebers, Andrea. "Rigor Ordinis—Gratia Amoris." *Cîteaux* 43 (1992): 161–220; *Cîteaux* 44 (1993): 36–151.

Lieftinck, Gerhard I. *De librijen en scriptoria der Westflaamse Cistercienser-abdijen Ter Duinen en Ter Doest.* Brussels: Paleis der Akademien, 1953.

Logan, F. Donald. *Runaway Religious in Medieval England c. 1240–1540.* Cambridge: Cambridge University Press, 1996.

Lucet, Bernard. *La Codification Cistercienne de 1202 et son évolution ultérieure.* Rome: Editiones Cistercienses, 1964.

———. *Les Codifications Cisterciennes de 1237 et de 1257.* Paris: Éditions du Centre national de la recherche scientifique, 1977.

Luddy, Ailbe J. *Life and Teaching of St Bernard.* Dublin: Gill and Sons, 1950.

Mahn, Jean-Berthold. *L'Ordre Cistercien et son Gouvernement des Origines au Milieu du XIIIe Siècle.* Paris: De Boccard, 1945, 1951.

Mantour, Moreau de. "Description Historique des Principaux Monuments de l'Abbaye de Cisteaux." *Histoire de l'Académie Royale des Inscriptions et Belles Lettres* 9 (1736): 193–232.

Martene, Edmond, and Ursin Durand. *Thesaurus novus anecdotorum,* 5 vols. Paris: Lutetiae Parisiorum: Sumptibus F. Delaulne [etc.], 1717; repr. New York: B. Franklin, 1968.

Matarasso, Pauline. *The Cistercian World.* London: Penguin, 1993.

Mayr-Harting, Henry. *Religion, Politics and Society in Britain 1066–1272.* Harlow: Longman, 2011.

McCrank, Lawrence J. "The Economic Administration of a Monastic Domain by the Cistercians of Poblet, 1150–1276." In *Studies in Medieval Cistercian History 2.* Edited by J. R. Sommerfeldt. CSS 24, 135–65. Kalamazoo, MI: Cistercian Publications, 1976.

McGuire, Brian Patrick. "Structure and Consciousness in the *Exordium Magnum Cisterciense*: The Clairvaux Cistercians after Bernard." In *Cahiers de l'Institut du Moyen Âge Grec et Latin* XXX–XXXI, 33–90. Copenhagen: University of Copenhagen, 1979a.

———. "Written Sources and Cistercian Inspiration in Caesarius of Heisterbach." *AC* 35 (1979b): 227–82.

————. "Friends and Tales in the Cloister: Oral Sources in Caesarius of Heister-bach." *AC* 36 (1980): 167–247.

————. "The Cistercians and the Transformation of Monastic Friendships." *AC* 37 (1981): 1–63.

————. *The Cistercians in Denmark*. CSS 35. Kalamazoo, MI: Cistercian Publications, 1982.

————. "A Lost Clairvaux Exemplum Collection Found: The *Liber Visionum et Miraculorum* compiled under Prior John of Clairvaux." *AC* 39 (1983): 26–62.

————. "The Cistercians and the Rise of the Exemplum in Thirteenth-Century France: a Reevaluation of Paris *BN MS lat. 15912.*" *Classica et Mediaevalia: Revue Danoise de Philologie et d'Histoire* 34 (1983): 211–67.

————. *Friendship and Community: The Monastic Experience 350–1250*. CSS 95. Kalamazoo, MI: Cistercian Publications, 1988.

————. "Purgatory, The Communion of Saints, and Medieval Change." *Viator* 20 (1989): 61–84.

————. "Self-Denial and Self-Assertion in Arnulf of Villers." *CSQ* 28 (1993): 241–59.

————. *Friendship and Faith: Cistercian Men, Women, and their Stories, 1100–1250*. Aldershot: Ashgate, 2002.

Meer, Frederic van der. *Atlas de l'Ordre Cistercien*. Amsterdam and Brussels: Elsevier, 1965.

Mielot, Jean. *Miracles de Notre Dame*. London, 1885. Repr. edited by George F. Warner. Melbourne: State Library of Victoria, 1982.

Mikkers, Edmund. "L'Idéal Religieux des Frères Convers dans l'Ordre de Cîteaux au 12e et 13e siècles." *Collectaneum Ordinis Cisterciensium Reformatorum* 24 (1962): 113–29.

Milis, Ludo J. R. *Angelic Monks and Earthly Men*. Woodbridge: Boydell Press, 1992.

Moreau, Edouard de. *L'Abbaye de Villers-en-Brabant*. Brussels: Albert Dewit, 1909.

Morlot, François. "Troisième abbé de Mores." *Herbertus* III (2002): 39–51.

Mossig, Christian. *Grundbesitz und Güterbewirtschaftung des Klosters Eberbach im Rheingau 1136–1250*. Darmstadt and Marburg: Historische Kommission für Hessen, 1978.

Mula, Stefano. "I frammenti di Gossuinus, Edizione dal ms. Firenze, Laurenziana, Ashburnham 1906." *Herbertus* III (2002): 7–16.

————. "Twelfth- and Thirteenth-Century Cistercian Exempla Collections: Role, Diffusion, and Evolution." *History Compass* 8/8 (2010): 903–12.

————. "Geography and the Early Cistercian *Exempla* Collections." *CSQ* 46 (2011): 27–43.

Mussafia, Adolfo. *Studien zu den mittelalterlichen Marienlegende III*. Sitzungsberichte der Kaiserlichen Akademie der Wissenschaften, Philosophisch-historische Klasse 119. Vienna: K. Gerold, 1889.

Mynors, Roger A. B., and Rodney M. Thomson. *Catalogue of the Manuscripts of the Hereford Cathedral Library*. Cambridge: D. S. Brewer, 1993.

Newman, Martha G. *The Boundaries of Charity: Cistercian Culture and Ecclesiastical Reform 1098–1180*. Stanford, CA: Stanford University Press, 1996.

———. "Crucified by the Virtues: Monks, Lay Brothers, and Women in Thirteenth-Century Cistercian Saints' Lives." In *Gender and Difference in the Middle Ages*. Edited by Sharon Farmer and Carol Braun Pasternack, 182–209. Minneapolis: University of Minnesota Press, 2003.

Noell, Brian. "Expectation and Unrest among Cistercian Lay Brothers in the Twelfth and Thirteenth Centuries." *Journal of Medieval History* 32 (2006): 253–74.

Oppel, Hans D. "Eine kleine Sammlung cisterciensischer Mirakel aus dem 13. Jahrhundert." *Würzburger Diözesan-Geschichtsblätter* 34 (1972): 5–28.

*Ordensstudien 1: Beiträge zur Geschichte der Konversen im Mittelalter*. Edited by Kaspar Elm. Berlin: Duncker & Humblot, 1980.

Osheim, Duane. "Conversion, *converse*, and the Christian Life in Late Medieval Tuscany." *Speculum* 58 (1983): 368–90.

Paffrath, Arno. *Bernhard von Clairvaux*. Vol. 1, *Leben und Wirken, dargestellt in den Bilderzyklen von Altenberg bis Zwettl*. Bergisch Gladbach: Altenberger Dom-Verein; Cologne: Dumont, 1984.

Platt, Colin. *The Monastic Grange in Medieval England*. London, Melbourne, and Toronto: Macmillan, 1969.

———. "Relaxation of the Rule." *History Today* 34 (July 1985): 21–26.

Poncelet, Albert. "Miraculorum B.V. Mariae quae saec. VI–XV latine conscripta sunt—Index postea perficiendus." *Analecta Bollandiana* 22 (1902): 241–360.

Pounds, Norman J. G. *An Economic History of Medieval Europe*. London and New York: Longman, 1974.

Quantin, Maximilien. *Cartulaire Général de l'Yonne*. 2 vols. Auxerre: Perriquet et Rouillé for Société des Sciences Historiques et Naturelles de L'Yonne, 1854.

Robinson, David M. *The Cistercian Abbeys of Britain*. London: Batsford, 1998.

———. *The Cistercians in Wales*. London: The Society of Antiquaries, 2006.

Roehl, Richard. "Plan and Reality in a Medieval Monastic Economy: The Cistercians." In *Studies in Medieval and Renaissance History* 9, 83–113. Lincoln, NE: University of Nebraska Press, 1972.

Rösener, Werner. "Grangienwirtschaft und Grundbesitzorganisation südwestdeutscher Zisterzienserklöster vom 12. bis 14. Jahrhundert." In *Die Zisterzienser. Ergänzungsband*. Edited by Kaspar Elm, 137–64. Cologne: Rheinland-Verlag, 1982.

———. "L'Économie Cistercienne de l'Allemagne Occidentalle." In *Flaran 3*. Edited by Charles Higounet, 135–56. Auch: Commission d'histoire de Flaran, 1983.

———. "Die Konversen der Zisterzienser. Ihr Beitrag zum wirtschaftlichen Erfolg am Beispiel von Eberbach und anderen Zisterzienserklöstern." *Nassauische Annalen* 111 (2000): 13–27.

———. "Die Agrarwirtschaft der Zisterzienser: Innovation und Anpassassung." In *Norm und Realität*. Edited by Franz J. Felten and Werner Rösener, 67-95. Berlin: LitVerlag, 2009.

Roisin, Simone. *L'Hagiographie Cistercienne dans le Diocèse de Liège*. Louvain and Brussels: Bibliothèque de l'Université, 1947.

Rudolph, Conrad. *Violence and Daily Life: Reading, Art and Polemics in the Cîteaux Moralia in Job*. Princeton: Princeton University Press, 1997.

Sayers, Jane. "Violence in the Medieval Cloister." *Journal of Ecclesiastical History* 41 (1990): 533–42.

Schneider, Ambrosius. *Die Cistercienser—Geschichte, Geist, Kunst*. Cologne: Wienand Verlag, 1986.

Seiner, Wilhelm. *Brevis Notitia Monasterii B. V.M. Ebracensis Sac. Ordinis Cisterciensis in Franconia*. Rome, 1738.

Sledmore, Edwin. *Abbey Dore, Herefordshire, Its Building and Restoration*. Hereford: Jakeman and Carver, 1914.

Southern, Richard W. *Western Society and the Church in the Middle Ages*. Harmondsworth: Penguin, 1970.

Squire, Aelred. *Ailred of Rievaulx*. London: SPCK, 1969.

Stalley, Roger. *The Cistercian Monasteries of Ireland*. London and New Haven: Yale University Press, 1987.

Stercal, Claudio. *Stephen Harding: A Biographical Sketch and Texts*. CSS 226. Collegeville, MN: Cistercian Publications, 2008.

Sullivan, Lisa M. "Workers, Policy-Makers and Labor Ideals in Cistercian Legislation 1134–1237." *Cîteaux* 40 (1989): 175–98.

Thiele, Augustinus. "Laienbrüder—Mönchspriester, eine Entwicklung." *Studien und Mitteilungen zur Geschichte des Benediktiner-Ordens* 89 (1978): 577–96.

Tobin, Stephen. *The Cistercians*. London: The Herbert Press, 1995.

Toepfer, Michael. *Die Konversen der Zisterzienser*. Berlin: Duncker & Humblot, 1983.

Voss, Johannes. *Das Münster zu Bad Doberan*. Munich and Berlin: Deutscher Kunstverlag, 2008.

Vacandard, Elphège. *Vie de St Bernard*. 2 vols. Paris: Librairie Victor Lecoffre, 1927.

Waddell, Chrysogonus. *Narrative and Legislative Texts from Early Cîteaux*. Cîteaux: Commentarii cistercienses, 1999.

———. *Cistercian Lay Brothers: Twelfth-Century Usages with Related Texts*. Cîteaux: Commentarii cistercienses, 2000.

———. *Twelfth-Century Statutes from the Cistercian General Chapter*. Cîteaux: Commentarii cistercienses, 2002.

Wardrop, Joan. *Fountains Abbey and its Benefactors 1132–1300*. CSS 91. Kalamazoo, MI: Cistercian Publications, 1987.

Werner, Ernst. "Bemerkungen zu einer neuen These über die Herkunft der Laienbrüder." *Zeitschrift für Geschichtswissenschaft* 6 (1958): 353–61.

Wiener, Wolfgang. "Die Ebracher Klosteranlage vor dem barocken Neubau." In *Festschrift 700 Jahre Abteikirche Ebrach 1285 1985*. Edited by Wolfgang Wiener and Gerd Zimmermann, 263–353. Ebrach: Forschungskreis Ebrach, 1985.

Williams, David H. *The White Monks in Gwent and the Border*. Pontypool: The Griffin Press, 1976.

———. *The Welsh Cistercians*. 2 vols. Caldey Island: Cyhoeddiadau Sistersiaidd, 1984.

———. *The Cistercians in the Early Middle Ages*. Leominster: Gracewing, 1998.

———. "Cistercian Grange Chapels." In *Perspectives for an Architecture of Solitude*. Edited by Terryl N. Kinder, 213–21. Turnhout: Brepols, 2004.

Wissenberg, Christophe. *Beaumont, ancienne grange de l'abbaye cistercienne de Clairvaux*. Paris: Picard, 2007.

Wiswe, Hans. "Grangien niedersächsischer Zisterzienserklöster." *Braunschweigisches Jahrbuch* 34 (1953): 5–134.

Zaluska, Yolanta. *L'Enluminure et le Scriptorium de Cîteaux au XIIe Siècle*. Cîteaux: Commentarii cistercienses, 1989.

Ziegler, Philip. *The Black Death*. Harmonds-worth: Penguin, 1982.

*Zisterzienser, Die*. Exhibition Catalogue. Edited by Kaspar Elm. Cologne: Rheinland-Verlag, 1981.

# Index

Absalon, archbishop of Lund, 304
Abundus, monk of Villers, 181, 186–87
Adalbert, archbishop of Cologne, 281
Adam, *conversus* of Combermere, 110
Adam, *magister conversorum* of Byland,
   138
Adam, granger of Kirkstall, 142, 272
Adam, monk of Clairvaux, 49
Admont, Benedictine abbey, 32
Adolph, *conversus* of Eberbach, 288
Adolph, *conversus* of Val-Dieu, 9
Adrian IV, pope, 304
Aduard, abbey, 51–53
Aelred, Saint, of Rievaulx, 43, 84, 86,
   129, 167–68, 175, 189, 211
Aiguebelle, abbey, 92, 98, 99
Alan, *conversus* of Buildwas, 51
Alan of Lille, *conversus* of Cîteaux,
   14–15
Alberic, abbot of Cîteaux, 15
Alberic of Trois Fontaines, 235
Albero, *conversus* of Heisterbach, 102
Alcobaça, abbey, 98, 217, 307
   grange: Bombarral, 307
Aldburgh, grange of Fountains, 125
Alexander III, pope, 211, 282, 304
Alexander IV, pope, 135
Alexander, abbot of Kirkstall, 49
Alexander, prince of Scotland,
   *conversus* of Foigny, 11

Altenberg, abbey, xxv, 10, 132, 203
   abbot: Godfrey, 172
Alvastra, abbey, 316–18
   *conversi*: Gerekin, 317–18, Asgot,
      319
Amelungsborn, abbey, 124, 139, 238,
   281
Andrew, brother of Saint Bernard, 2
Andrew II, king of Hungary, 10
Arabona, abbey, 276, 311
Argar, *conversus* of Rievaulx, 189
Arnold, *conversus* of Villers, 180
Arnold, *magister grangia* of Villers, 140
Arnold of Bonneval, Benedictine
   abbot, 109
Arnold von Bramshorn, *conversus* of
   Himmerod, 18
Arnsburg, abbey, 281
Arnulf, *conversus* of Villers, xvii,
   102–3, 119–21, 181–86
Asgot, *conversus* of Alvastra, 319
Aubert, Marcel, 40, 92, 100
Aubespierre, abbey, 307
Aulne, abbey, 11, 62
   granger: Simon, 11–13, 141, 179,
      180, 184, 186
   grange: Colomies, 13, 141
Aumône, abbey, xxv
   *conversus*: Christian, xxv, 157, 187,
      214

Baldemar, granger of Eberbach, 141

Baldric, *conversus* of Rievaulx, 189

Baldwin, *conversus* of Villers, 163, 186–87

Balk, grange of Byland, 125

Baltinglass, abbey, 251

Bandevin, granger of Villers, 140

Barnoldswick, first site of Kirkstall, 50, 124, 125; later grange, 140

Basingwerk, abbey, 251
    abbot: Gilbert, 251

Beaulieu, abbey, 79, 93, 105, 109, 110, 124
    *conversus*: Brother J, 111
    granges: Great Coxwell, 116, 132, 135; Saint Leonard's, 117, 132, 135; Boverey, 135; Trougham, 135; Little Faringdon, 273

Beaumont, grange of Clairvaux, 117

Beaupré Collection, 26, 148, 199–200, 203, 207–8, 252–53, 254, 259–60, 264, 298–99

Bebenhausen, abbey, 53, 130, 131, 316

Bective, abbey, 312

Belleperche, abbey, 162
    *conversus*: Bernard, 162

Bellevaux, abbey, 65
    abbot: Burchard, 65, 83–84, 116, 170

Berdoues, abbey, 21, 126

Berge, grange of Eberbach, 133

Berman, Constance, xvi, 121

Bernard, *conversus* of Belleperche, 162

Bernard, Saint, xxiv, 1, 6, 9, 23, 25, 27, 33, 43–44, 47, 49, 50, 65–66, 68, 69, 90–91, 97, 109, 129, 136, 149, 150, 158–60, 163–64, 167, 175–76, 182, 187–89, 201–4, 206, 209, 231, 242, 254, 281

Bernard Sicard, *conversus* of Valmagne, 19

Berno, bishop of Schwerin, 238

Berthold, granger of Eberbach, 141

Berthold, *conversus* of Maulbronn, 53

Birgitta, Saint, of Vadstena, 317–19

Bishop, T.A.M., xvi

Bjørn, monk of Øm, 7

Black Death, 314–17

Blanche, countess of Champagne, 185–86

Bolton, grange of Rievaulx, 125

Bombarral, grange of Alcobaça, 307

Boniface VIII, pope, 303

Bonnecombe, abbey, 276
    *conversus*: William Formos, 276

Bonnefont, abbey, 133

Bonneval, abbey, 217

Bordesley, abbey, 90, 316

Boschaud, abbey, 276

Boulancourt, abbey, 242, 245

Boulbonne, abbey, 21, 124

Boverey, grange of Beaulieu, 135

Bredero, Adriaan, xix, 33

Brétigny, grange of Cîteaux, 113

*Breve et memoriale scriptum*, xvii, 94, 111, 213

Buildwas, abbey, 93
    *conversus*: Alan, 51

Burchard, abbot of Bellevaux, 65, 83–84, 116, 170

Burchard, *conversus* of Eberbach, 106

Buzay, abbey, 310

Byland, abbey, 22, 51, 93, 97, 98, 99, 100, 101, 123, 130, 320
    *magister conversorum*: Adam, 138
    *conversus*: Serlo, 22
    granges: Balk, Thorpe, 125

Cadouin, abbey, 302

Cadwgan, abbot of Cymer, former *magister conversorum*, 139

Caesarius of Heisterbach, xxii, 3, 13,

15, 17, 18, 20–21, 24, 42–44, 61,
74, 94, 95, 96–97, 102, 134, 135,
141, 144–47, 155–56, 172–73,
175, 179, 184, 200, 205, 210, 212,
214–17, 219–20, 225–26, 228,
230, 232–33, 246–47, 250, 264,
265–66, 287–88, 298
Caiton, grange of Fountains, 125
Callistus II, pope, 35
Canivez, Joseph-Marie, xvii
Carnaf, grange of Cwmhir, 134
Casalvilone, abbey, 115
Casanova, abbey, 277
Casey, Michael, 61
Cassidy-Welch, Megan, xvii, 33, 40,
272, 273, 278, 280
Cawley, Martinus, xvii
cellarer, 90–91, 137
Cérvoles, grange of Poblet, 302
Ceule, grange of Vaucelles, 307
Chaalis, 117, 131, 162, 276
*conversus*: Lambert, 162
grange: Vaulerent, 117, 131
Chaltre, grange of La Ferté, 144
Charles, abbot of Villers, 179
Charles, monk of Himmerod, 245
Cheminon, abbey, 243
Cheniot, grange of Villers, 180
Cherlieu, abbey, 132
Chorin, abbey, 290
Christian of Aumône, *conversus*, xxv,
157, 187, 214
Christian, monk of Himmerod, 4
Cîteaux, abbey, xiv, xxiii, 8, 33, 34, 38,
48, 76, 93, 94, 113, 122, 128, 132,
144, 166, 174, 190, 211, 273–75,
277, 292, 302–3
abbots: Robert, 32, 36, 38;
Stephen Harding, 9, 15, 27, 33,
34, 35, 41, 45, 47; Alberic, 15,
33; Conrad, 13, 179; Jean de

Cirey, 15, 321; Guy, 27;
Raynard de Bar, 27
*magister conversorum*: Walter, 140
*conversi*: Milo, 11; Alan of Lille,
14–15
granges: Brétigny, Gémigny,
Moisey, Crépey, 113
Clairmarais, abbey, 62, 210
Clairvaux, abbey, xx, 1, 5, 6–7, 9, 17,
25, 33, 48–49, 50, 57, 62, 92, 93,
97, 98, 101, 104, 118, 130, 136,
144, 147, 157, 159, 178, 199, 213,
221–22, 238, 241, 249, 276, 281,
287, 292, 293, 316, 319
abbots: Geoffrey of Auxerre,
xx–xxiii, 129; Stephen
Lexington, xxvi, 137, 142;
Gerard, 9, 278; Conrad, 13, 179
prior: Philip, 6
monks: Rainald, 42; Geoffrey
d'Ainai, 49; Adam, 49; Nicholas,
65, 168; Gerard, Bernard's
brother, 2, 90–91, 137; Andrew,
Bernard's brother, 2; Goswin,
243; Hugh de Basoches, 278
*conversi*: Yves (Vivian) xx;
Lawrence, 6–7, 242; Tescelin
Smack, 26; Humbert, 69; Walter,
70, 103, Petrus, Durandus, 116;
Evrard, 136; Constantius, 189
Stephen, 220–21; Gerard, 241
granges: Cornay, 117; Beaumont,
117, 131; La Borde, 117;
Colombé-le-Sec (*cellier*), 136;
Fraville, 136
Clermont, abbey, 93, 97, 99, 101
Cluny, Benedictine abbey, 31, 32, 37
Coggeshall, abbey
abbots: Ralph, 106, 251; Peter,
106–8, 109
*conversus*: Robert

*Collectaneum exemplorum et visionum Clarevalense,* xxii, 42, 118, 147–48, 157, 188, 207–8, 223–25, 227, 229, 241, 254, 264

Colombé-le-Sec, *cellier* of Clairvaux, 136

Colomies, grange of Aulne, 13, 141

Combermere, abbey, 110

*conversus:* Adam, 110

Conrad, *conversus* of Heisterbach, 96

Conrad, abbot of Villers, Clairvaux and Cîteaux, then cardinal, 13, 179

Conrad of Eberbach, xxii, xxiv, xxv, 3, 5, 6, 23, 26, 44, 58, 73, 81, 96, 118, 148, 149, 158–59, 174, 187–88, 199, 201, 206, 208–9, 215–16, 221–22, 227, 230, 231, 238–39, 247–50, 255, 265, 268, 269–70, 282–83, 285, 287, 297–98, 316

Constable, Giles, xv

Constantius, *conversus* of Clairvaux, 189

*conversi*
and literacy, 4
and social background, 4, 11–21
names of, 16
motivation, 21–26
origin, 27–29, 32–35
and beards, 27, 76–84
"old style" and "new style," 29–32
as builders, 48–56
and literacy, 57–75
clothing, 84–87
death and burial, 154–58
and guests, 104–8
and crafts, 109–11
number of, 128–30, 133
unequal status, 164–66, 171
and demons, 231–48
and cult of Mary, 252–57
and purgatory, 257–63
privileged position, 264–68

and revolts, 271–99
decline, 306–15, 320

Cornay, grange of Clairvaux, 117

Cowton, grange of Fountains, 309

Coyroux, women's abbey, xxvi, 79

Crépey, grange of Cîteaux, 113

Croxden, abbey, 294, 296

Cuissy, Premonstratensian abbey, 159

Cunradus, *conversus* of Eberbach, 133

Cunradus *vinitor, conversus* of Eberbach, 133

Cwmhir, abbey, 134, 293
granges: Carnaf, Gabalfa, 134

Cymer, abbey, 138
abbot: Cadwgan, former *magister conversorum,* 139

Cymer, *magister conversorum* of Valle Crucis, 138

*Dialogus miraculorum,* 20, 95, 103, 144–47, 156–57, 179, 200, 230, 232, 239, 246–48, 253

Dienheim, grange of Eberbach, 133

Doberan, abbey, 79, 124, 238–39, 245

Dominicans, 312–13

*domus conversorum,* 92–103

Donkin, R.A., xvi, 115–16

Donnelly, James S., xv, xvi, xvii, xviii, 32, 39, 164, 272, 273, 278–80, 307

Dore, abbey, 138, 222–23, 245–46, 310
grange: Trawscoed, 138, 223

Dubois, Jacques, 20, 28, 34, 166

Ducourneau, Othon, xvii, 1, 20, 32, 164

Dünamünde, abbey, 95, 250

Dunbrody, abbey, 51, 90

Duramius, *conversus* of Melrose, 197

Durandus, *conversus* of Clairvaux, 116

Eberbach, abbey, xxii, 93, 98, 129, 130, 132, 133, 175, 269, 276, 290, 296

abbots: Conrad, xxii; Eberhard, 282; Gerhard, 282
cellarer: Richard, 287
prior: Meffried, 57, 282–85
grangers: Symon, 139, Günther, Berthold, Baldemar, Richard, 141
*conversi*: Wolfram, Siegfried, Ortwin, 22; Herold, 106; Burchard, 106; Guntramus, Cunradus, Ruperthus, Herbordus, Cunradus *vinitor*, 133; Richard, 133; Malchoadus, Grandus, 287; Adolph, 288
granges: Leeheim, 16; Hadamar, 21, 135, 226; Gehaborn, 22, 133 139; Dienheim, 133; Berge, 133; Birkerhof, 141; Sandhof, 141
lay brother revolt: 281–85, 287–89
Eberhard, abbot of Eberbach, 282
Ebrach, abbey, xxiii, 114, 119, 124, 204–5, 252, 264–65, 316
abbots: Frederick, Otto, 316
*conversus*: Konrad Zeuffel, 11
grange: Sulzheim, 114, 119
*Ecclesiastica officia*, 34–35, 41, 58, 81, 90, 94, 108, 154, 156, 298
Elizabeth de Vergy, 113
Engelbert, archbishop of Cologne, 19
Esrum, abbey, 8, 221–22, 258, 309, 319
Eusserthal, abbey, 311
Evergeld, *conversus* of Villers, 4, 11, 179, 213
Evrard, *conversus* of Clairvaux, 136
Evrard, *magister conversorum* of La Ferté, 140
Evrard the Tacitun, *conversus* of Villers, 180, 213
*Exordium Cistercii*, 48, 318
*Exordium magnum*, xvii, xxii, 42, 68, 73, 81, 118, 137, 187, 199, 201–2, 204, 221–22, 230, 254, 269

*Exordium parvum*, xiii, 1, 27, 32, 33, 41, 48, 76, 114, 151, 161

Faringdon, former site of Beaulieu, 124
Flaran, abbey, 53
Flaxley, abbey, 292
Fleppe, grange of Villers, 140
Foigny, abbey, 11
*conversus*: Alexander, 11
Fontainejean, abbey, 291
Fontenay, abbey, 276, 312
Fontfroide, abbey, 85, 92, 98, 101
Fontmorigny, abbey, 217, 291
*conversus*: Robert, 254–55
Forde, abbey, 4
abbot: John, 4, 16–17, 41, 105, 126, 192–98
*conversus*: William, 17, 105, 192–93
Fossanova, abbey, xxi
abbot: Geoffrey of Auxerre, xxi
Foucarmont, abbey, 137
Fouchères, abbey, 291
Fountains, abbey, 49, 50, 59, 97, 98, 99, 101, 104, 105, 123, 124, 128, 130, 133, 290, 302, 308, 321
abbots: Ralph Haget, 14, 178; Henry Murdac, 97; Robert of Pipewell, 97, 104; William, 177; Marmaduke Huby, 321
*conversi*: Sunnulph, 14, 59, 178–79 180; Gilbert, 22; Henry Wither, 126, Robert of Morton, 309
granges: Aldburgh, Moreton-on-Moor, Greenbury, Thorpe Underwood, Caiton, 125–26; Cowton, 309
Franciscans, 312–13
Francis de Lachem, *conversus* of Villers, 18
Francon, granger of Villers, 140
Fraville, grange of Clairvaux, 136

Frederick, abbot of Ebrach, 316
Frederick Barbarossa, emperor, 282
Freeman, Elizabeth, 108
Fürstenfeld, abbey, xxiii, 158, 240
Furness, abbey, 7, 97

G., *magister conversorum* of Valle Crucis,
    138
Gabalfa, grange of Cwmhir, 134
Garendon, abbey, 295
Gaufridus Percesac, *conversus* of
    Pontigny, 276
Gautier de Coincy, 82
Gehaborn, grange of Eberbach, 22,
    133, 139
Gémigny, grange of Cîteaux, 113
General Chapter at Cîteaux, 10, 15,
    20, 51, 77, 87, 99, 122–24, 135,
    143, 144, 157, 207, 211–12, 218,
    235, 267, 272, 273–76, 287–92,
    300–303, 305–10, 313–14
Geoffrey d'Ainai, monk of Clairvaux,
    49
Geoffrey of Auxerre, abbot of
    Igny, Clairvaux, Fossanova,
    Hautecombe, xx–xxiii, 129
Gerald of Wales, xxiv, 105, 108, 122–
    23, 251, 293, 296, 298, 309
Gerard, *conversus* of Clairvaux, 241
Gerald, *conversus* of La Ferté, 110
Gerard, *conversus* of Mores, 183
Gerard, brother of Saint Bernard, 2,
    90–91, 137
Gerekin, *conversus* of Alvastra, 317–18
Gerhard, abbot of Eberbach, 282
Gerlach von Rheimbachweiler,
    *conversus* of Himmerod, 18
Gerung, *conversus* of Himmerod, 24
Gilbert, abbot of Basingwerk, 251
Gilbert, abbot of Margam, 122, 293
Gilbert, *conversus* of Fountains, 22
Gille of Seis, *conversus* of Margam, 22

Gillesperda, *conversus* of Melrose, 197
Gimont, abbey, 21
Godfrey, abbot of Altenberg, 173
Godfrey, abbot of Schönau, 77
Goswin, monk of Clairvaux, 242–45
Goswin, monk of Villers, 163, 181–
    86, 194
Goswin's *Liber miraculorum*, xxiii, 229,
    242–45
Graiguenamanagh, abbey, 90
granges, 113–21, 130–36
    formation, 113–16, 125
    location, 117–21
    size of, 130–32
    number of, 132–33
    grange chapels, 133–36
Grandselve, abbey, 16, 19, 121, 124,
    132, 288
Grandus, *conversus* of Eberbach, 287
grange master, *see* granger
granger, 43, 116, 127, 133, 135,
    139–43
*grangiarius, see* granger
Graves, Coburn V., xvi
Great Coxwell, grange of Beaulieu,
    116, 135
Greenbury, grange of Fountains, 125
Greenia, Conrad, xv
Gregory the Great, pope, 34, 45, 65
Günther, *conversus* of Eberbach, 141
Guntramus, granger of Eberbach, 133
Guy, abbot of Cîteaux, 27

Habersleben, grange of Mariental,
    135
Hadamar, grange of Eberbach, 21,
    135, 226
Hailes, abbey, 109
Haina, abbey, 19
Hallinger, Kassius, xv, xviii, 31, 34,
    113
Hart, grange of Himmerod, 43

Hautecombe, abbey, xxi, 274
  abbot: Geoffrey of Auxerre,
  xx–xxiii, 129
Hart, grange of Himmerod, 43, 134,
  144–47, 149, 232, 253–54
Hautefontaine, abbey, 140
Hauterive, abbey, 307
Hedwig, Saint, duchess of Silesia,
  70–71
Heiligenkreuz, abbey, 62, 64
  *conversus:* Salamon, 11
Heilsbronn, abbey, 132, 275–76, 277
Heinrich von Dudenhofen, *conversus*
  of Himmerod, 18
Heisterbach, abbey, xxii, 128, 145, 320
  monk: Richwin, 219
  *conversi:* Conrad, William, Richard,
  96; Albero, 102; Henry, 219
Henrik, *conversus* of Øm, 7
Henry, *conversus* of Heisterbach, 219
Henry, *conversus* of Ter Doest, 67, 79
Henry, *conversus* of Villers, 4
Henry, granger of Himmerod, 43, 94,
  134, 144–47, 149, 232, 253–54
Henry, monk of Sawtry, 251
Henry de Lacy, 50
Henry de Marcy, abbot of Clairvaux,
  44
Henry de Weiss, *conversus* of Villers, 18
Henry of Brussels, *conversus* of Villers,
  180
Henry Wither, *conversus* of Fountains,
  126
Henry Murdac, abbot of Fountains,
  97
Henry II, king of England, xxi
Henry VII, king of England, 321
Herbert of Clairvaux, xxii, 3, 6, 26,
  67–68, 70, 72, 73, 82, 148–49, 155,
  158, 183, 188, 201–2, 205–6, 220–
  21, 236–38, 242, 249, 254–55, 265
Herbordus, *conversus* of Eberbach, 133

Herman, abbot of Himmerod, then
  Marienstatt, 144–45, 253
Herman, *conversus* of Øm, 7
Herman, *conversus* of Pforta, 241–42
Herman, *conversus* of Villers, 180
Herman, granger of Villers, 140, 169
Hermann von Virneburg, *conversus* of
  Himmerod, 18
Herold, *conversus* of Eberbach, 106
Herrenalb, abbey, 307
Herrevad, abbey, 4, 8
Hervé de Montmorency, 51
Higounet, Charles, xvi
Hildegard of Bingen, 24, 57–58, 170,
  283–84
Himmerod, abbey, 4, 96, 128, 130,
  134, 144–45, 210, 212, 250
  abbot: Herman, 144–45, 253
  monks: Christian, 4; John, 4;
  Isenbard, 45; Charles, 245
  granger: Henry, 43, 94, 134,
  144–47, 149, 232, 253–54
  *conversi:* Liffard, 17–18; Arnold
  von Bramshorn, Hermann von
  Virneburg, Paynus von Gilsdorf,
  Gerlach von Rheimbachweiler,
  Heinrich von Dudenhofen,
  18; Walewan, 18, 215; Gerung,
  24; Ludo, 24, 233; Henry, 43, 94,
  134; Mengoz, 44; Obert,
  156–57; Wiricus, 226
  grange: Hart, 43, 134, 144–47,
  149, 232, 253–54
Hirsau, Benedictine abbey, 31
Hoffmann, Eberhard, xv, 32
Holdsworth, Christopher, xix
Holy Cross, abbey, 302
Honorius III, pope, 305
Hugh, abbot of Trois-Fontaines, later
  cardinal, 164
Hugh de Basoches, 278, monk of
  Clairvaux, 278

Hugh of Fouilloy, 61–65
Hugh of Kirkstall, Ralph Haget's biographer, 14, 177–78
Humbert, abbot of Igny, 159
Humbert, *conversus* of Clairvaux, 69
Humbert of Romans, 23
Humphrey, *conversus* of Kirkstall, 125

Ida of Nivelles, nun of La Ramée, 181
Idung of Prüfening, 76–77, 88
Igny, abbey, xxi, 159, 278
    abbots: Geoffrey of Auxerre, xxi; Humbert, 159
Innocent II, pope, 9, 303
Innocent III, pope, 13
*Instituta*, 41, 114
Isenbard, sacristan of Himmerod, 44

J., *magister conversorum* of Strata Marcella, 138
J., brother, *conversus* of Beaulieu, 79
Jacques de Vitry, 106
James de Glym, *conversus* of Villers, 18
James of Voragine, 1
Jean de Bellegambe, 256
Jean de Cirey, abbot of Cîteaux, 15, 321
Jerpoint, abbey, 85–86
Jervaulx, abbey, 22, 97, 133, 320
Jocelin's *Life of Waldef*, 3, 8, 71–72, 143, 194–98, 214, 260–63, 269–70, 319
Johannes Meiger, cellarer of Tennenbach, 92
Johannes Zenlin, abbot of Tennenbach, 91–92
John, abbot of Forde, 4, 16–17, 41, 105, 126, 192–98
John, granger of Margam, 140
John, monk of Himmerod, 4
John de Roist, *conversus* of Vilers, 18
John de Salinth, *conversus* of Villers, 18

John de Wistrezees, *conversus* of Villers, 180
John of Ailburton, *conversus* of Tintern, 16
John of Cornwall, 251
John Gualbert, abbot of Vallombrosa, 31
John the Hermit, 25
Jordan, *conversus* of Margam, 292

Kamp, abbey, 10, 74, 216, 316
    *conversus*: Odacar (Gerard), 19
Kinder, Terryl, 33
Kingswood, abbey, 133, 307
Kirkstall, abbey, 49, 50, 90, 93, 97, 100, 124, 125, 128, 272, 308, 320
    abbots: Alexander, 49; Lambert, 125
    grangers: Peter, 140, Adam, 142, 272
    *conversi*: Norman, Humphrey, Robert, 125, Walter, 142, 272
    grange: Barnoldswick, 140
Kirkstead, abbey, 49
Knowles, David, 26, 115, 280, 315
Kolbacz (Kolbatz), abbey, 245
Konrad Zeuffel, *conversus* of Ebrach, 11

La Bussière, abbey, 132
La Chalade, abbey, 311
La Ferté, abbey, xxiii, 7, 33, 274–75
    *magister conversorum*: Evrard, 140
    *conversus*: Gerald, 110
    grange: Chaltre, 144, 273
Lambert, abbot of Kirkstall, 125
Lambert, *conversus* of Chaalis, 162
Lambert, *conversus* of Melrose, 197
lane, lay brothers', 92–94, 101
Lateran Council, Fourth, 305–6, 312
Lawrence, *conversus* of Clairvaux, 6–7, 242
lay brothers, *see conversi*

Leclercq, Jean, xviii, 164, 272, 273, 278–79
Leeheim, grange of Eberbach, 16
Legendre, Olivier, xxii
Lehnin, abbey, 143
Lekai, Louis, xviii, 115, 128, 161, 280
Les Pierres, abbey, 274
Le Thoronet, abbey, 98, 101
Le Val, abbey, 291
*Liber visionum et miraculorum*
   *Clarevallense*, xxii, xxiii, 42, 70, 73, 81, 155, 188, 216–17, 225–26
Liffard, *conversus* of Himmerod, 17–18
Lissewege, grange of Ter Doest, 117, 132
Little Faringdon, grange of Beaulieu, 273
Llantarnam, abbey, 140
   granger: Philip ap Seisil, 140
Loccum, abbey, 132
Løgum, abbey, 4, 66, 311
   *conversus*: Tue, 66
Longpont, abbey, 216, 226, 228, 276
Longuay, abbey, 98, 101
Lorsch, Benedictine abbey, 32
Louth Park, abbey, 92, 130, 315
   abbot: Richard, 92, 134
Lubiaz (Leubus), abbey, 70, 153
Lucius III, pope, 304
Ludo, *conversus* of Himmerod, 24, 233

Mabillon, Jean, 163
Madog, *magister conversorum* of Valle Crucis, 138
*magister conversorum*, 59–60, 137–39, 163, 222
*magister grangiae, see* granger
Malachy, Saint, 242
Malchoadus, *conversus* of Eberbach, 287
manual labor, 36–44
Margam, abbey, 122–23, 296, 302
   lay brother revolt, 291–94

abbot: Gilbert, 122, 293
grangers: John, Richard, 140
*conversi*: Anian, Cnaithur, Caradog, Ketthereth, Richard Cnicht, Rhiryd, 16; Gille of Seis, 22; Jordan, Ralph, 292
Marienfeld, abbey, 205, 312
Marienstatt, abbey, 19
   abbot: Herman, 144
Mariental, abbey, 135
   grange: Habersleben, 135
Marmaduke Huby, abbot of Fountains, 321
Martha and Mary, 166–70
Martin, *conversus* of Pilis, 110
Matarasso, Pauline, xvii, 161
Mazan, abbey, 123
Mazières, abbey, 7, 265
Maulbronn, abbey, 53, 93, 98, 132
   *conversus*: Berthold, 53
Mayr-Harting, Henry, 5
McCrank, Lawrence, 302
McGuire, Brian, xix
Meaux, abbey, 50, 130, 131, 132, 142, 307, 308
   abbot: Roger, 308
   grange: Skyrene, 308
Meffried, prior of Eberbach, 57, 282–85
Mellifont, abbey, 93
Melrose, abbey, 8, 71, 93, 106
   abbots: Waldef, 8, 71, 100, 104, 194–98, 214, 261–63, 319; William, former *magister conversorum,* 138, 175; Richard, 195
   *conversi*: Walter, 71, 105; Taibald, 110; William, 143; Lambert, Richard, Gillesperda, Duramius, 197; Henry, 198; Sinuin, 269–70
Mengoz, *conversus* of Himmerod, 44–45

Merevale, abbey, 295

Michaelsberg, Benedictine abbey, 32

Mielot, Jean, 174

Mikkers, Edmond, xviii

Milis, Ludo, 40

Milo, uncle of Saint Bernard, 11

Moisey, grange of Cîteaux, 113

Molesme, abbey, 36–38, 321

Mores, abbey, xxii
    abbot: Herbert of Clairvaux, 3,
        26, 67–68, 70, 72, 148, 155, 158,
        183, 188, 201, 205, 220, 236,
        243, 249–50, 254, 265
    *conversus*: Gerard, 183

Moreton-on-Moor, grange of
    Fountains, 125

Morimond, abbey, xxiii, 7, 33, 123,
    277

Morimondo, abbey, 130

Morris, William, 116

Mortemer, abbey, 162
    *conversus*: Bertrand, 162

Mula, Stefano, xix, xxii, xxii


Neath, abbey, 90, 93, 98, 122–23, 294

Neatham, grange of Waverley, 135

Neubourg, abbey, 124

Newman, Martha G., xviii, xix, 66

Newminster, abbey, 49
    abbot: Robert, 49

Nicholas, monk of Clairvaux, 65, 168

Nicholas, *conversus* of Villers, 185

Nicolas, *conversus* of Villers, 180

Nicolas de Harmont, granger of
    Villers, 140

Nigel Longchamp, 126, 270

Noell, Brian, xviii

Noirlac, abbey, 98, 98, 101

Norman, *conversus* of Kirkstall, 125


Obazine, abbey, 10, 85, 121, 132, 144,
    189–92, 302, 320

abbot: Stephen, xxvi, 3, 79, 189–92

Obert, *conversus* of Himmerod,
    156–57

Odacar (Gerard), *conversus* of Kamp,
    19

Odo, duke of Burgundy, 48

Odo of Crediton, 82

Øm (*cara insula*), abbey, 7, 8, 43, 50,
    124, 272–73, 304–5, 308, 311
    abbots: Ture, 7; Thorkil, 16,
        162; Peter Pape, former *magister*
        *conversorum,* 139
    monk: Bjørn, 7
    granger: Oluf Kviter, 22, 140
    *conversi*: Herman, 7; Henrik, 7
    granges: Veng 124, Tåning, 309

Old Byland, former site of Byland,
    121

Oliva, abbey, 218

Oluf Kviter, granger of Øm, 22, 308

Orderic Vitalis, xiii, 1, 36–37, 46, 48,
    86, 170

Otterberg, abbey, 281

Otto, abbot of Ebrach, 316

Ottobeuren, Benedictine abbey, 32


Paynus von Gilsdorf, *conversus* of
    Himmerod, 18

Peter, abbot of Coggeshall, 106

Peter, *conversus* of Villers, 180

Peter, granger of Kirkstall, 140

Peter Damian, abbot of Fonte
    Avellana, 31

Peter de Roya, 42

Peter Pape, abbot of Øm, former
    *magister conversorum*, 138

Peter the Venerable, abbot of Cluny,
    31, 37, 170

Peter of Cornwall, Augustinian canon,
    175, 263, 266–67

Petrus, *conversus* of Clairvaux, 116

Pforta, abbey, 28, 53, 97, 241

*conversi:* Walter, 241; Herman, 241–42

Philip, *magister conversorum* of Valle Crucis, 138

Philip, prior of Clairvaux, 6

Philip ap Seisil, granger of Llantarnam, 140

Philip the Good, 174

Philip of Harvengt, xiv, 38

Philip IV, king of France, 303

Pilis, abbey, 110, 277
　*conversus:* Martin, 110

Piscaria, abbey, 274, 296

Platt, Colin, xvi

Poblet, abbey, 101, 127, 132, 302
　*conversus:* William Tost, 127
　grange: Cérvoles, 302

Pontigny, abbey, xxiii, 33, 98, 122, 130, 140, 143, 276
　abbot: Guichard, 9
　*conversus:* Gaufridus Percesac, 276

Purgatory, 257–63

Quincy, abbey, 276

Ralph, abbot of Coggeshall, 106, 251

Ralph, *conversus* of Margam, 292

Ralph Haget, abbot of Fountains, 14, 178

Rainald, monk of Clairvaux, 42

Rainier, Augustinian *conversus*, 62–64

Raynard de Bar, abbot of Cîteaux, 27

Reginald, abbot of Waverley, 295

Reigny, abbey, 122

Reinhold, archbishop of Cologne, 10

Richalm of Schöntal, xxiii, 100, 160, 233–34

Richard, abbot of Louth Park, 92, 130

Richard, granger of Eberbach, 133

Richard, cellarer of Eberbach, 287

Richard, *conversus* of Heisterbach, 96

Richard, *conversus* of Melrose, 197

Richard, granger of Margam, 140

Richard the Parmenter, *conversus* of Tintern, 16, 110

Richard I, king of England, 10, 295

Richwin, cellarer of Heisterbach, 219

Riddagshausen, abbey, 142, 265

Rievaulx, abbey, 50, 99, 118, 122, 123, 320
　abbot: Aelred, Saint, 43, 84, 86, 129, 167–68, 175, 189, 211
　monk: Walter Daniel, 84–85, 129, 168; Simon, 211
　*conversi:* Argar, Baldric, 189
　grange: Bolton, 125

Robert, abbot of Newminster, 49

Robert, *conversus* of Coggeshall, 106–8

Robert, *conversus* of Fontmorigny, 254–55

Robert, *conversus* of Kirkstall, 125

Robert of Pipewell, abbot of Fountains, 97, 104

Roche, abbey, 104, 127
　*conversus:* Thomas, 127

Roehl, Richard, xvi, 3, 26

Roermond, women's abbey, 8

Roger, abbot of Meaux, 308

Roger, king of Sicily, 6

Roger of Kingswood, *conversus* of Tintern, 16

Romuald, abbot of Camaldoli, 31

Rösener, Werner, xvi

Royaumont, abbey, xxv, 92, 98

Rufford, abbey, 93

Rule of Saint Benedict, xiii–xiv, 28, 30, 36, 38, 88, 89, 99, 101, 106, 108, 114, 134, 161, 165, 176, 195–96, 200–201, 207, 209, 211–12, 215, 219

Ruperthus, *conversus* of Eberbach, 133

Saint Apern, Cologne, nuns' abbey, 203

Saint Leonard's, grange of Beaulieu, 117, 135

Saint Mary's, Dublin, abbey, 51

Saint Mary's, York, Benedictine abbey, 38, 49

Salamon, *conversus* of Heiligenkreuz, 11

Salem, abbey, xxiii, 19, 53, 60, 81, 130, 131, 320

San Martino del Monte, abbey, 276–77

Santes Creus, abbey, 312

Sart Risbart, grange of Villers, 140

Savigny, abbey, 302

Sawley, abbey, 93

Sawtry, abbey, 251
    monk: Henry, 251

Schönau, abbey, 54–56, 124, 269, 296
    lay brother revolt: 281, 285–87
    abbot: Gottfried, 54, 77, 285–87

Schöntal, abbey, 124, 233–34
    abbot: Richalm, xxiii, 100, 160, 233–34

Schooten, grange of Villers, 140

Sénanque, abbey, 123, 312

Serlo, *conversus* of Byland, 22

Signy, abbey, 77, 217

Silvacane, abbey, 123

Silvanès, abbey, 10
    *conversus*: Pons, 11

Simon, *conversus* from Tuscany, 54

Simon, monk of Rievaulx, 211

Simon of Aulne, lay brother, 4, 11–13, 141, 179, 180, 184, 186

Sinuin, *conversus* of Melrose, 269–70

Skyrene, grange of Meaux, 308

Sobrado, abbey, 164

Sorø, abbey, 21, 117–18
    grange: Toaker, 121

Southern, R.W., 1, 3

Stanley, abbey, 93

Stephen, *conversus* of Clairvaux, 220–21

Stephen Harding, Saint, abbot of Cîteaux, 9, 15, 27, 33, 34, 35, 41, 45, 47, 151, 164–65, 296, 298, 321

Stephen Lexington, abbot of Cîteaux, xxvi, 137, 142

Stephen of Bourbon, 211

Stephen of Obazine, Saint, xxvi, 3, 79

Stocking, former site of Byland, 51

Strata Florida, abbey, 96, 105, 294, 302

Strata Marcella, abbey, 138, 292
    *magister conversorum*: J., 138

Stratford Langthorne, abbey, 176–77, 263, 266–67
    monk: Alexander, 177, 248
    *conversus*: Roger, 177, 248

Sulejów, abbey, 53–54

Sullivan, L.M., 46

Sulzheim, grange of Ebrach, 114

Sunnulph, *conversus* of Fountains, 14, 59, 178–79, 180

Sven, bishop of Århus, Denmark, 43

Sygerus, granger of Villers, 183

Symon, granger of Eberbach, 139

Szent-Gotthard, abbey, 276

Taibald, *conversus* of Melrose, 110

Tamié, abbey, 291

Tåning, grange of Øm, 309

Tennenbach, abbey, 81, 87, 131, 320
    abbot: Johannes Zenlin, 91–92
    cellarer: Johannes Meiger, 92

Ter Doest, abbey, 67
    *conversi*: Henry, 67, 79; Walter, 214–15
    grange: Lissewege, 117, 132

Ter Duinen (Les Dunes), abbey, 62, 128

Tescelin Smack, *conversus* of Clairvaux, 25–26

Theobald, Count of Champagne, 2

Theuley, abbey, 217, 310

Thomas Becket, archbishop of
   Canterbury, xxi
Thorkil, *conversus* and later abbot of
   Øm, 16
Thorpe, grange of Byland, 125
Thorpe Underwood, grange of
   Fountains, 125
Tintern, abbey, 90, 292
   *conversi*: John of Ailburton,
      William of the Marsh, Roger
      of Kingswood, Will Penreche,
      16; Richard the Parmenter, 16,
      110; William, 110
Toaker, grange of Sorø, 121
Toepfer, Michael, xv, xvi, 3, 39
Trawscoed, grange of Dore, 138, 223
Tre Fontane, abbey, 282
Trois-Fontaines, 164
   abbot: Hugh, later cardinal, 164
Trougham, grange of Beaulieu, 135
Tue, *conversus* of Løgum, 65
Ture, abbot of Øm, 7
Tvis (*tuta vallis*), abbey, 8, 277

Ulrich, monk of Villers, 4, 179
Urban III, pope, 304
*Usus conversorum*, xvi, xvii, xxiii, 35,
   57, 77, 81, 85, 88, 95, 99, 107, 111,
   134, 151–54, 161–62, 164–65,
   212, 279, 285, 290, 296, 298, 321

Vacandard, Elphège, 2
Val-Dieu, abbey, 9, 281, 291
   abbot: William, 288
   *conversus*: Adolph, 8
Valle Crucis, abbey, 138
   *magister conversorum*: G., Philip,
      Madog, Cymer, 138
Valmagne, abbey, 47
   *conversus*: Bernard Sicard, 19
Varnhem, abbey, 128
Vaucelles, abbey, 98, 307, 320
   grange: Ceule, 307

Vauclair, abbey, 77, 98, 101, 217
Vaudey, abbey, 49
Vaulerent, grange of Chaalis, 117, 131
Vauluisant, abbey, 122
Vaux-le-Cernay, abbey, 99, 101, 105
Veng, grange of Øm, 124
Victor IV, anti-pope, 282
Villelongue, abbey, 311
Villers, abbey, 4, 88, 93–94, 130, 179–
   81, 213, 290
   abbots: Conrad, 13–14; Walter,
      13–14, 179; Charles, 88, 179;
      William, 179
   monk: Ulrich, 4, 179; Goswin,
      163, 181–86, 194; Abundus,
      181, 186–87
   grangers: William, Bandevin,
      Walter, Arnold, Francon, Nicolas
      de Harmont, Herman, 140, 169,
      John de Wistrezees, 180;
      Sygerus, 183
   *conversi*: Evergeld, 4, 11, 179;
      Henry, 4; Henry de Weiss, John
      de Salinth, John de Roist,
      Walter de Riklam, Francis
      de Lachem, James de Glym, 18;
      Arnulph, 102–3, 119–21,
      181–86; Baldwin, 163, 186–87;
      Henry of Brussels, 180; Peter,
      180; Evrard the Taciturn, 180,
      213; Herman, 180; Nicolas, 180;
      Nicholas, 185; Arnold, 180;
   granges: Schooten, Sart Risbart,
      Fleppe, 140; Cheniot, 180
*Vita prima*, xix, xxi, 1, 43, 48–49, 109,
   129, 187
*Vita quarta*, 69
Vitskøl, abbey, 128, 235, 309, 311

Wachock, abbey, 54
Waddell, Chrysogonus, xvii, xxiii, 20,
   161, 166

Waldef, abbot of Melrose, 8, 71, 100, 104, 194–98, 214, 261–63, 319

Walden, abbey, 313

Waldsassen, abbey, 97, 239

Walewan, *conversus* of Himmerod, 18, 215

Walkenried, abbey, 55, 130, 132

Walter, abbot of Villers, 13–14, 179

Walter, *conversus* of Clairvaux, 70, 103

Walter, *conversus* of Kirkstall, 142, 272

Walter, *conversus* of Melrose, 71, 105

Walter, *conversus* of Pforta, 241

Walter, *conversus* of Ter Doest, 214–15

Walter, *magister conversorum* of Cîteaux, 140

Walter, granger of Villers, 140

Walter Daniel, monk of Rievaulx, 84–85, 129, 168, 175, 189

Walter de Riklam, *conversus* of Villers, 18

Walter Map, xxiv, 48, 126, 169, 298, 309

Waverley, abbey, 104, 130, 135, 272, 295

   abbots: William, Reginald, 295

   grange: Neatham, 135

Werner, Ernst, xviii

Wettingen, abbey, 256–57, 320

Whalley, abbey, 320

Whitland, abbey, 294

Will Penreche, conversus of Tintern, 16

William, abbot of Fountains, former abbot of Newminster, 177

William, abbot of Melrose, former *magister conversorum*, 138, 175

William, abbot of Villers, 179

William, abbot of Waverley, 295

William, *conversus* of Forde, 17, 105, 192–93

William, *conversus* of Heisterbach, 96

William, *conversus* of Melrose, 143

William, *conversus* of Tintern, 110

William, *magister grangia* of Villers, 140

William of the Marsh, *conversus* of Tintern, 16

William, Count, founder of Meaux, 50

William Formos, *conversus* of Bonnecombe, 276

William of Malmesbury, xiii, xix

Winandy, Jacques, 40

Wiricus, *conversus* of Himmerod, 226

Wiswe, Hans, 40

Woburn, abbey, 49

*Wulfric of Haselbury, Life of*, xvii, 4, 126, 192–98

Zinna, abbey, 226

Zwettl, abbey, 62, 217, 277, 290